SWAMI RAM CHARRAN'S

LifeCode #7

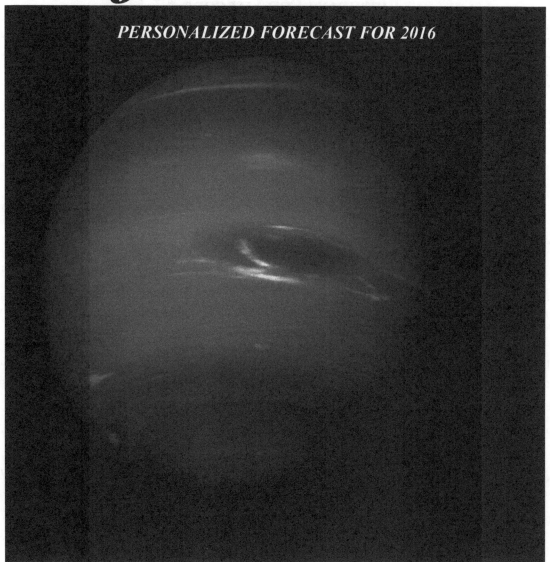

PERSONALIZED FORECAST FOR 2016

*Chakra Square Healing Center * 12922 sw 133rd Court * Miami, FL 33186*

*(305) 253 – 5410 * www.swamiram.com * www.shop.swamiram.com*

LifeCode Series™

PRESENTS

2016 LifeCode #7

The Consciousness Of Time & Spirituality

BIRTHDAYS FOR LIFECODE #7					
06-January	22-March	20-May	27-July	15-October	31-December
15-January	31- March	29-May	08-August	24-October	
24-January	03-Apr	01-June	17-August	05-November	
05-February	12-Apr	10-June	26-August	14-November	
14-February	21-Apr	19-June	07-September	23-November	
23-February	30-Apr	28-June	16- September	04-December	
04-March	02-May	09-July	25-September	13-December	
13-March	11-May	18-July	06-October	22-December	

We use the Sun as a measurement that makes the day, the Moon as a measurement that makes the Month, the year is created by the movement of the Earth around the Sun in the solar system.

Using Vedic Mathematical methods of calculation the day of the Month plus the Month of the Year can be used as real number in the above equation. Let's say the baby was born on February 12, 1956 then the equation for birth will be: SUN + MOON = 12 (day) + 2 (Month) = Moment of Birth = 14 = 1 + 4 = 5

In this case the numbers above 9 are repetitions of the real numbers so in Vedic mathematics the higher numbers are reduced to real numbers so in this case 14 is really 5. This final number from the above equation is then referred to as your **LifeCode**.

Please Note: For Eastern countries, it is important that you check the book also with the day after the above day shown in the table if the Birth was in the evening in the Eastern Time zones of the world. The reason why is because the forecasts measurements in this book were calculated based on North American and South American time zones and dates. For places such as those located in Africa, Europe, Asia and the Far East, and the birth occurred in the evening local time, then the LifeCode number after the above one should be consulted also.

Swami Ram Charran

COPYRIGHT INFORMATION

KNOWLEDGE SHOULD NEVER BE COPYRIGHTED. AS WE, ALL KNOW IF KNOWLEDGE IS SUPPRESSED THEN THE WORLD DOES NOT PROGRESS, AND LIFE REMAINS STAGNANT. HAD THE SAGES OF HINDUISM COPYRIGHTED THEIR KNOWLEDGE, THEN THE AMERICANS, EUROPEANS AND OTHER CULTURES WOULD NOT HAVE BEEN ABLE TO PROGRESS USING THE KNOWLEDGE AND EXPERIENCE OF THE ANCIENT SAGES.

In old days, the knowledge was freely given to all those who seek it. At that time, all knowledge was used to make the world a better place. There was no abuse of knowledge. Teachers were highly regarded and respected, and everyone who freely received knowledge transferred it freely to other people.

After the European invasion of the Eastern countries and the seizing of the countries by corrupted rulers, everybody started to distrust each other and such Knowledge was used as a weapon. After Hitler, and Several World Wars, the motivation for power called for the person with the most knowledge thus, the people with more knowledge had positions that are more powerful. Eventually those in power (like the Catholic Pope of the Old World) suppressed the knowledge from the common people. In the 1700's and 1800's people became so ignorant that if anyone had more knowledge than others did, it was considered WITCHCRAFT. Hence, many people were killed unnecessarily by their own people for ignorant reasons. While the Westerners in America were suppressing Knowledge and burning witches, the people in India were creating more and more knowledge. Therefore, India became a country with an abundance of Knowledge.

Today, many Westerners are copying the knowledge of the East and placing copyrights of ownerships on it, even though they are not the originators of this knowledge. Swami Ram Charran does not believe that knowledge should be copyrighted. If someone copies his book and uses it for good purposes then he is permitted to do so. However if a person copies Swamiji's book and sells it for monetary gain, WITHOUT THE PERMISSION OF THE SWAMI OR THE ASHRAM, then he or she will be subjected to the laws of karma. BY KARMA, HE WILL NOT BE ABLE TO GAIN ANY PROSPERITY FROM HIS ACTIONS, and instead will suffer later because of his illegal actions.

Swami Ram Charran gives specific instructions to all about the COPYRIGHT OF THIS BOOK: He says, "NO *ONE IS AUTHORIZED TO COPY THIS BOOK AND SELL IT WITHOUT PERMISSION FROM THE AUTHOR. THIS BOOK CAN BE ONLY FOR PERSONAL USE, TEACHING OR RELIGIOUS PURPOSES.*"

For general information on our other products and services, please contact Chakra Square Healing Center at (305) 253-5410.

Swami Ram Charran's LifeCode #7 Yearly Forecast for 2016

Author Credits:

Editor in Chief:	LUERESA RAMCHARRAN
Designed by:	SWAMI RAM CHARRAN
Cover Design by:	LUANA RAMCHARRAN
Printed by:	CHAKRA SQUARE HEALING CENTER

Table of Contents

Preface

The Purpose and Benefits of The LifeCode

1   To provide ALL PEOPLE with accurate predictions of his or her life so that steps can be taken to avoid negative experiences.

2   To help ALL PEOPLE determine when is a good time to:

a)	Get married	e)	Filing a lawsuit
b)	Move into a new home	f)	Investing in the stock market
c)	Undergo medical operations	g)	Travel
d)	Open a business	h)	and more....

3   To provide ALL PEOPLE person with monthly, yearly, and daily forecast of his or her life based on their LifeCode

4   To assist ALL PEOPLE, to take control or change his destiny and avoid negative experiences in his life through the help of Vedic Science, used in this book.

5   To assist ALL PEOPLE by bringing back the use of ancient formulas that were used by the great Rishis and Sages for creating a successful life style so that we can properly use it for the elimination of bad marriages, unhealthy babies, financial disasters, and so on. To bring back the old science of the ALL PEOPLE, a science greater than the science of today, thereby creating a better world for our future generation.

6   If you wish to perform yearly forecast predictions on your own life then you need to know these very details as shown above based on your actual date of birth. Since this book only covers the present year to get your birth information you may need to get a "100 YEAR LIFECODE BOOK" that we publish and personalize according to you.

7   In this book you can find out who your ISHTA DEVTA or Karmic Ruler is and the same for anyone in your family. Using this you will be able to predict most of the experiences that you will have in this year or the coming year. You will also be able to predict your monthly and your daily experiences, determine if your marriage is compatible and whether your home is a good location for you....and many more.

8   Suggestions for timing certain events in your life such as when to move, when to travel, when to borrow money, when to file a court case, and so on, can be found on the section called Daily Forecast for 2016 in the latter half of this book. It is well known that the time or day that you start something will determine its success or failure.

PLEASE NOTE:
ANY QUESTIONS ABOUT THIS BOOK OR ABOUT LEARNING THE SCIENCE CAN BE ANSWERED BY CALLING THE CHAKRA SQUARE HEALING CENTER AT (305) 253-5410.

Section 1

LIFECODE # 7 – VEDIC DEITY SHIVA

A General Look at Your Whole Life Karmas

- ❖ Your mind is running at a thousand miles an hour.
- ❖ You are constantly thinking and analyzing everything.
- ❖ Sometimes you keep most of your thoughts to yourself.
- ❖ You do not tell your plans very easily to others.
- ❖ You feel you are right in everything 33% of the time.
- ❖ Sometimes you think everyone is against you.
- ❖ You are very beautiful, or handsome in the case of males.
- ❖ You attract the opposite sex very easily.
- ❖ Your need for love and romance is very high.
- ❖ You experience many difficulties in your marriage.
- ❖ A sure key to happiness for you is meditation and music.
- ❖ You are very kind hearted and are sometimes deceived easily by your lovers.
- ❖ You should avoid the color black...wear light colors.

Seven is the most significant and magical of the numbers. It has long been held sacred, as is shown by the extraordinary frequency of seven in mythology, the Bible, and classifications of all kinds: there are seven notes in the musical scale, seven phases of the Moon, seven seas, seven heavenly bodies in the old Ptolemaic system, seven wonders of the world, seven hills of Rome, seven virtues, seven deadly sins, seven days of creation, seven plagues of Egypt, seven sentences in the Lord's Prayer, seven trumpets in the Apocalypse, and many more. The seventh son of a seventh son is believed to possess great magical powers. People who are Sevens are sometimes great thinkers and may have an occult or psychic side. They may be researchers, investigators, or inventors. They have an affinity with the sea and often travel widely. But they must use their powers wisely, avoiding pride and cynicism, and accepting that their talents will never make them materially rich.

You have a secretive and sometimes very private personality. You hardly speak about what you are thinking but your mind is running at 100 miles per hour. However, when you do speak your words are like fire ready to destroy the person you are directing it at. People around you see you as an egg shell ready to break with the slightest intimidation so your partner or lover feels like he or she is always walking on eggshells because he or she never knows when you are going to find something wrong with him or her. Your criticism of others can be very high and may prevent others from getting very close to you. You tend to hold back a lot of your personal feelings about others. Even your beloved one will ask you when you are going to say "I love you." It is very important that you do not analyze others too much for there are no such persons who are perfect in everything. The first lesson you must learn in life is that no one can be perfect. Once you have learnt this your love life and your marriage life will be much happier. You possess a very high temper and may sometimes speak very harshly to others. If this is a quality that is carried into your marriage it may surely end in divorce. Out of all others in this astrological analysis you possess the highest ego there is. You will never admit when you are wrong. You will never admit when you feel weak inside and you will always put up an outward appearance much different from the one that is inner. Your true feelings never seem to come out, even though your true feelings given to the other person will solve all the problems. If you are an extremely negative individual you may be addicted to drugs, alcohol or smoking. You may also be constantly complaining over petty or unnecessary matters. A small matter may worry you a great deal. You are constantly studying or reading if you are not sleeping or relaxing watching TV. You are very slow in your movements and may experience many delays in your life as a result of this. You may get married very late in life. If you do get married early there may be a possibility of separation. Late marriages are usually more successful. Your interests may lie in the field of medicine and if you study medical sciences you will be successful in a career associated with it. If you are a positive individual you may become a priest, a yogi or saint. If you are religious you may experience inner encounters with God and other divine manifestations of the universal deities. If you happen to find yourself a GURU you may experience a divine connection through that personality. If this path is followed most of your wishes will be fulfilled in life and your desires may become a reality. You may encounter many religious individuals in your life. You are advised to pay much attention to what they say for their advice may be very beneficial to you. Respect must be given to all holy people or elders in the family. Christians are advised to say the Lord's Prayer 11 times every day.

POSSIBLE HEALTH PROBLEMS

- ❖ Heart problems, addiction to drugs and alcohol
- ❖ Insanity, possession by spirits and physical disabilities
- ❖ Children may be born retarded or disabled.
- ❖ Can be given false medicine by doctors

MEDITATION RECOMMENDATIONS

- ❖ Your primary meditation focus is love and godly things.
- ❖ I recommend that you meditate for at least 30 minutes, to slow your thoughts.
- ❖ While meditating you should always be in the lotus position of sitting with folded feet, with your thumb and forefinger touching.
- ❖ You should always close your eyes during meditation, as you are always looking at your inner self.
- ❖ A holy location, temple, mountain or place of worship is your best place for meditation

LifeCode #7 Predictions for the Year 2016

Forecasts by the Vedic Deity Lord Shiva

The key word is **rest**. Learning, studying, spirituality, religion, worries and mental afflictions are the influences of this year. This will be a good year for just loafing around if the bankroll permits. This is a fine year for study, self-improvement. A good year to give some thought as your mission in life, what you wish to accomplish. It is a bad year for investments or speculations of any sort or if you are considering a new business. You are advised to spend some time alone, attend meditation classes or groups and get your thoughts in order for the next two years after this year is ended. Last year was a hectic year for you and you might have had a few disagreements with those around you or with a close family member. If it was a very negative year last year, it is most important that you accept the invitations of religious individuals or priests that you will meet in this year. You may find yourself reading astrology books or meeting with astrologers or psychics. This year is bad for everything connected with material affairs but good for any mental improvement or educational course. Do not look for perfection in anything whatsoever and avoid criticizing others when they have made mistakes or errors. Curb any feelings of jealousy and do not hold any grudges against anyone. The self will be alone a lot during the year. The energy of this year will affect your emotions badly sometimes. This is the time for introspection. Use this time to prepare for the money that will come your way next year. It is also time to prepare for the possible negative experiences that will come to you in two years. It is not the time to brood over past errors. It is the time for positive thinking. You should look over at the past six years in a positive manner during this time. Use it correcting mistakes, realizing within the self the errors you have made. It is a good time to make a religious journey or to take a health vacation for relaxation. Avoid any pleasure trip. During this year, you need to think about what your goals are in life. For those who have been positive, spiritual activities, study, teaching, writing, will all meet with success. There will be inner harmony, love, deep sexual satisfaction and romance for those partners who have remained sincere to each other over the past two years.

For those who have been negative and critical of others or quarrelsome, it is now the time to correct your behavior and attitude or else, all ventures into the material world will fail. You must learn now to live the best way possible or this will be a period of misery, poverty, and loneliness. Brooding or crying about it is only going to make it worse. It is most important that you see an astrologer or priest. A religious pilgrimage or occult course of study will result in many benefits and enlightenment at this time. Attendance to religious functions will be gainful and rewarding. Any conflict with the government will result in losses. Positive association with the government will result in financial rewards, next year. If you are bored, read or meditate, as this will help you survive your troubles at this time.

Avoid any strenuous work as this could affect your health. It is important that you avoid any excessive use of drugs, alcohol and confrontation with others. If you are troubled this year you must do a SHIVA POOJA, see a GURU and Christians should meditate on Christ as the Teacher.

Although the main influences of the year 2016 are described above, there are different influences that affect you according to your version of Bramha. The influences that affect you for this year depending on your Version are detailed below.

LifeCode #7 Money, Health, Love, Career and Other Predictions in 2016

Your Life Will Be Affected By: Neptune Known As Varuna in Vedic Science

MONEY THIS YEAR

Income will be slow this year, but there will be enough to support all your expenses. Spiritual people asking for charity will approach you; do not hesitate to give. Any short-term investments will not be good at this time. However, if proper research is done, long term investment for more than one year will be profitable. Do not over spend this year. Try to equalize income and expenses. Give thanks to God for your money. You will be thinking about seeing an astrologer for guidance.

HEALTH THIS YEAR

Your energy will be up and down this year. However, you will need to sleep a great deal this year. You will feel much spiritual energy within your body. You will spend a lot of time thinking about the existence of God, your reason for living and so on. Drugs given to you either by doctors or otherwise will be dangerous to your health. Alcohol will be attractive to you but could affect your health, so do not drink. Your mind will generate most of your health problems this year. It is a good time to visit a doctor to get a checkup.

LOVE THIS YEAR

Depending on your marriage partner or lover, this year should be a very peaceful year in regards to love life. If you separated from your lover last year, then you will be spending a lot of time thinking about your life this year. If you remained with your partner from last year and overcame the disagreements, then both of you will be seeing each other's real feelings during the year and you will enjoy a better love life. Both of you should listen to astrologers and priests. Their suggestions might seem somewhat scary but you must take their advice. Go to the temple and pray together.

CAREER THIS YEAR

Nobody will bother you at your workplace this year. Co-workers and employers will stay out of you way. You will be able to work alone and peacefully. Your thoughtfulness will prevent you from wanting too much communication. However, be careful, your reputation could surface in gossip conversation. Avoid gossiping with co-workers. Do a great deal of reading and learning about your job. This will help you in the end. Let people know what you are thinking, as you tend to keep your thoughts to yourself. It is not a good time for a raise.

LEGAL, GOVERNMENT AND COURTS IN THIS YEAR

After all the problems with government last year, it will be a relief to see them ease up this year. Court problems will create less pressure on you. If your problems have resulted in any kind of confinement, then you will be thinking a lot about your life this year. Since you will be able to spend some time alone, you should take advantage of the situation and start a meditation discipline. You may be connected with priests, spiritual teachers or astrologers.

ROBBERY BURGLARY AND LOSSES IN THIS YEAR

You may have felt someone has not been honest with you in financial affairs last year. Your losses could have come from strangers, friends or relatives. You may have a hard time recovering any loans you made last year. It is better to be patient and wait until next year rather than making any demands. You may very well get your money back that way. If attacked by thieves or criminals, you may not be able to recover from your losses last year. This is a Divine test, it is recommended that you attend church and give donations to the temple. No robbery is forecasted for the year.

ACCIDENTS, CONFRONTATIONS AND CONFLICTS IN THIS YEAR

No accidents this year are foreseen. The only conflict I see you may have is between you, God and spiritual leaders. You are advised to support the temple or religious activities, make donations and be helpful in holy places. All this will benefit you next year and will make up for the bad year you had last year. Meditation and mantra chanting are recommended.

FAMILY, FRIENDS AND RELATIVES IN THIS YEAR

After the quarrels, disagreements and frustrations of last year, you may now find this year to be very peaceful, quiet and relaxing. Try to lower your ego and spend some time loving and paying attention your family members.

CHILDREN IN THIS YEAR

Avoid criticizing the children, they may have lots of questions that need answers and you may be the only source that can provide them. Try to pray with them and teach them Divine Principles. You may be worried at this time that a child may be using drugs or alcohol. Try to work with the child.

SEXUALITY AND ENERGY IN THIS YEAR

Your sexuality is high and your inner energy is low. You may feel rejected by lovers and decide to become addicted to alcohol or drugs. Try to avoid taking this destructive path as next year promises a much better love life. Watch movies and enjoy spending time alone

PRAYERS, MEDITATION AND YOGA THIS YEAR

This is an excellent year for prayers, meditation and yoga. Seek the company of priests, astrologers, Divine teachers and nature lovers. Make sure your diet consists of more vegetables than meats and seek advice from astrologers and spiritual guides. Any health problems will be mental in nature. Drink lots of water and liquids.

TRAVEL, MOVING AND MAJOR CAREER CHANGES THIS YEAR

This is a good year for you to travel, move or make a change in your job. You may get a new career opportunity towards September when the changes to the next year start to take place. All travels or moves will be profitable at this time. Even though you are worried about your goals and objectives, it will all come to a positive conclusion by the end of September of this year.

OPENING A BUSINESS, PROFITS, NEW PRODUCTS, MARKETING, AGREEMENTS AND CONTRACTS THIS YEAR

This is a good year for opening a business. Your investments will pay off well next year and profits will remain. If you opened the business last year chances are your business will experience some downfall this year. You may have to close and reopen the business because of this. Any new marketing efforts, new products, new businesses will pay off handsomely next year. Make sure you check the Location Code, Business Opening Day Code and the Business Name Code before opening the business. All agreements and contacts signed this year will be profitable in the coming years

REAL ESTATE BUYING AND SELLING IN THIS YEAR

This is an excellent year to buy a home or a building for a business. If you are selling is best to wait until the end of the year until September when you may make a bigger profit. Make sure and check your Location Code and Home Code before buying a home, since some places may be negative for you.

GAMBLING IN THIS YEAR

Gambling is not a bad idea this year; however, it should not be at a Casino. You could buy lottery tickets or have fun at the race track. Your winnings will be very little but after September you may get lucky and make more money. My advice is to try to avoid gambling as much as possible until after September. If you want to receive good winnings next year use your money in spiritual work instead of gambling.

How to Avoid Negative Effects from the Planets This Year

1. Do charity works, go to the Ashram or Temple regularly, and welcome holy people to your home, Talk to Astrologers, Priests and Psychics. It is a good time for you to find a Guru or Spiritual Teacher to guide you.

2. If you are thinking about your life a lot, seek the help of someone spiritual, who can advise you properly. Perform Shiva or Ganga Puja with a competent Brahmin Priest.

3. Take a pilgrimage trip to a holy place. Bathe in the Ocean waters, avoid the colors red and black, and do not drink milk at night. Bathe with milk once every month.

4. Write books, learn to sing, join a band or singing group, do not criticize others, and spend a lot of time meditating, fast on Tuesdays for this year.

Section 2
Health, Illness and Surgery

There is nothing more important to any human being than their health. When we are healthy many times we take it for granted and we abuse it by improper eating and drinking or by wearing black clothes that block our light and health, or by sleeping in an incorrect manner or not exercising, but when our health is not there, we try to look for solutions everywhere. If you have wealth and no health, you cannot enjoy it.

Your brain, heart and fluid system are the weakest parts of your body. Individuals born under this life code usually have an addiction to drugs and/or alcohol or smoking - this can lead to heart problems, insanity or physical disabilities. Common afflictions in this Life Code are mental retardation, heart diseases, diabetes, insanity or depression. Due to your high mental and brain activity, it is highly recommended for you to meditate one or two times per day for 10 to 15 minutes. Rest and relaxation will help to ease the stresses and headaches of your extremely active mind. The less meat and fish you eat the better your health will be. Your body becomes divine when you are vegetarian and you will not get sick easily. If you eat meat and drink alcohol or take drugs in your body you will be afflicted with terminal diseases. You must also avoid excesses in all things such as too much of any one type of food will be considered an excess. If not religious and calm in your temperament you can destroy yourself as well as all around you. Avoid being critical of others, the karma could distress you later on. Certainly #7 individuals are very strong headed and egotistical. You suffer from doubt and will not believe anything or anybody until you see it. It is this quality that makes you enter into arguments and disbelief. If brought up with divine qualities you will become a powerful leader and will be helpful to the world. Your diet should consist of a variety of different foods, not a concentration of any specific food. Some white meat as well as fish should accompany your meals often in small amounts as your body needs the Omega 3, 6 and 9 protein nutrients. Fruits and vegetables of all types especially Vitamin C should constantly be part of your diet.

WHEN SHOULD I GO SEE MY DOCTOR OR SCHEDULE A SURGERY?

If you ever wonder when you should visit the doctor, when is best to schedule a surgery and wish you could consult with someone, this year your LifeCode Book comes with the answer to those questions. *DO NOT have any medical procedures, particularly surgical during FULL MOON. NEW MOON is best for surgeries. A mother that gives birth during FULL MOON gets high blood pressure.

	MEDICAL SERVICES CODE								
YOUR LIFECODE	**DAY OF THE MONTH YOU ARE SCHEDULING MEDICAL SERVICES**								
	1 *10* *19* *28*	*2* *11* *20* *29*	*3* *12* *21* *30*	*4* *13* *22* *31*	*5* *14* *23*	*6* *15* *24*	*7* *16* *25*	*8* *17* *26*	*9* *18* *27*
7	8	9	1	2	3	4	5	6	7

Medical Services Code 1:

Positive Day for all types of medical services and surgery except if you feel depressed, postpone the appointment.

Medical Services Code 2:

Excellent Day for medical services, surgery and prescriptions.

Medical Services Code 3:

Positive Day to acquire knowledge about your medical conditions, to consider natural, herbal, Ayurvedic and allopathic methods.

Medical Services Code 4:

Neutral Day. It is a stressful day, but at the same time is a good day to visit the doctor, have surgery or any medical treatments. Surgery will not have to be repeated.

Medical Services Code 5:

Negative Day. There is the possibility of receiving false medical information, it is not recommended for surgical procedures, and problems may arise the next day.

Medical Services Code 6:

Negative Day. Any diagnosis will be wrong, you will experience a great deal of pain, and the surgery will have to be repeated.

Medical Services Code 7:

Excellent Day. It is a good day for medical procedures, there is no pain and usually results are good.

Medical Services Code 8:

Excellent Day for medical services and procedures, but it will usually be expensive.

Medical Services Code 9:

Negative Day. Definitely not a good day to visit the doctor, today the doctor will find all kinds of diseases, all diagnoses will be negative and surgery will have to be repeated or could have very negative results.

Section 3

The Vedic Hourly Code

To Set Appointments, Take Naps, Avoid Stress, Make Business Deals, or Call A Lover at A Specific Time of the Day to Create Success and Happiness for You

WHAT IS THE BEST TIME (HOUR) TO ASK FOR A RAISE OR TALK TO MY SPOUSE?

There are certain hours that you will feel very sleepy and there are certain hours that you will feel very frustrated. It is advisable to take the hours that are "Sleepy" or "Stressful" as a point in time where you need to relax, meditate, and pray. During your sleepy hour, you should try to take a nap so that your body can reenergize during the day. In the hour of "Business", "Enjoyments," or "Creative," you need to use that time to do interviews, make deals, or involve yourself in creative projects (i.e. listening music or watching a video). After some trial and error, because of the EST (Eastern Standard Time) you will be able to successfully determine all the hours of the day that will be successful for you, when to sleep, and so on.

HOURLY CODE		Table 3.1 - YOUR LIFECODE NUMBER HOURLY
HOURS	EFFECT:	
12:00 AM	Creative	Good for Appointments, beg projects, Meditation, Work Alone, Don't be bossy.
1:00 AM	Financial	Good for investments, Avoid overspending or credit, Business, Promotions etc.
2:00 AM	Destructive	Tension, Accidents, Ego conflicts, Police or Govt., Fear of enemies/ spirits.
3:00 AM	Creative	Good for Appointments, beg projects, Meditation, Work Alone, Don't be bossy.

Time	Type	Description
4:00 AM	Romantic	A time for love, musical moments, contact with opposite sex, A good Phone call,
5:00 AM	Energetic	Expression, letter writing, Telephone calls, reading, children etc.Pain in the hip area,
6:00 AM	Tiredness	Work, Concentration, Career interviews, Repairs, Real Estate, Job problems,
7:00 AM	In Motion	Short trips, sexuality, BE CAREFUL of deception, false news, Gossip,Car Problems,
8:00 AM	Frustrating	Avoid personal contacts, Keep Temper down, handle all responsibility,
9:00 AM	Sleepy	Active Mind, Prayers, Worry about Love, Astrology, Criticism, Spiritual...
10:00 AM	Financial	Good for investments, Avoid overspending or credit, Business, Promotions etc.
11:00 AM	Destructive	Tension, Accidents, Ego conflicts, Police or Govt., Fear of enemies/ spirits.
12:00 PM	Creative	Good for Appointments, beg projects, Meditation, Work Alone, Don't be bossy.
1:00 PM	Financial	Good for investments, Avoid overspending or credit, Business, Promotions etc.
2:00 PM	Destructive	Tension, Accidents, Ego conflicts, Police or Govt., Fear of enemies/ spirits.
3:00 PM	Creative	Good for Appointments, beg projects, Meditation, Work Alone, Don't be bossy.
4:00 PM	Romantic	A time for love, musical moments, contact with opposite sex, A good Phone call,
5:00 PM	Energetic	Expression, letter writing, Telephone calls, reading, children etc.Pain in the hip area,
6:00 PM	Tiredness	Work, Concentration, Career interviews, Repairs, Real Estate, Job problems,
7:00 PM	In Motion	Short trips, sexuality, BE CAREFUL of deception, false news, Gossip,Car Problems,
8:00 PM	Frustrating	Avoid personal contacts, Keep Temper down, handle all responsibility,
9:00 PM	Sleepy	Active Mind, Prayers, Worry about Love, Astrology, Criticism, Spiritual...
10:00 PM	Financial	Good for investments, Avoid overspending or credit, Business, Promotions etc.
11:00 PM	Destructive	Tension, Accidents, Ego conflicts, Police or Govt., Fear of enemies/ spirits.
12:00 AM	Creative	Good for Appointments, beg projects, Meditation, Work Alone, Don't be bossy.

PLEASE NOTE THAT TIMES MAY VARY BECAUSE OF DAYLIGHT SAVING TIME

Section 4

How does Location affect you?

What Does The Place Where You Live Have To Do With Anything?

Most people do not realize that the energy of the place where they live affects them in different aspects of their lives, affects them differently every year and additionally, these influences are felt differently in specific areas of their home. I have designed this chapter to help you determine what Vedic number is the energy of your house and how that affects you personally. Additionally, I will let you know the energy that your house will have for this current year. Finally, how the energy is distributed within your home to help you use spaces for your own benefit.

If you already know your home's Vedic Code, proceed to the section of the Vedic Location Code; otherwise, follow the instructions below to determine the Location Code for your home.

What Is My Location Code? Add up the digits of the apartment number, building or home number to get a single digit as the Vedic Building or Location Code. For example, if your house address is 3149 Maccabee Drive, add the 3+1+4+9 and then reduce the results (17) to a single digit to get the Vedic Building Code, i.e. 1+7=8. The #8 is the Vedic Building Code for this address.

LOCATION CODE COMPATIBILITY

How a particular location affects each individual depends on the Location Code of the place in combination with the LifeCode of the individual. The table below will give you the effect of your home combined with your LifeCode Number.

YOUR LIFECODE	LOCATION NUMBER								
	1	2	3	4	5	6	7	8	9
7	8	9	1	2	3	4	5	6	7

Location Code 1: Loneliness, separation rejection and worry, promotions and progress, don't be too bossy or dominating, you may get into trouble, good for starting projects or businesses.

Location Code 2: Weddings, marriages, romance may take place at this location, lots of visitors and guests at this location, enjoy good food, lots of shopping and a rewarding love life, clean, decorate, repair, remodel and enjoy,

Location Code 3: Children visit, pregnancy, news of birth, menstrual cycle or uterus problems, studies, writing and reading books, too much TV and computer, childishness, immaturity, irresponsibility, social events, children's problems.

Location Code 4: Possible job problems, hard work, overtime, low pay, tension, high-blood pressure, high temper, gossip will create arguments, and home may experience construction and repairs that will improve its value.

Location Code 5: Travel, vacations, unauthentic visitors, long distance calls and relationships, possibility of illicit affairs or some fraudulent transactions, conscious of physical appearance. Common ailments are feet or sexual organs.

Location Code 6: Conflicts, disagreements, power struggles, frustration and responsibility, be careful of visits from family, possible police, court, or collection agencies, divorce, separation, accidents, surgeries, in-law problems.

Location Code 7: Inhabitants feel tired, sleepy, worry about life path, goals, objectives, and future, feel the need to meet with astrologers, psychics, Hindu priests and Swamis, are very secretive, house will be visited by lots of snakes.

Location Code 8: Inhabitants receive or spend a lot of money, changes to expensive furniture or fixtures, renovations, starting profitable business, people in this house are beautiful and presentable, expensive parties or purchases.

Location Code 9: Possible sewer, flooding, boiler, water problems, death, sickness, operations, government problems, accidents, money spent unexpectedly, spouses sleep separate, failed businesses, delays selling house, job frustrations

Section 5

How Will My Home Be in 2016?

Every year your home goes through a cycle of influence that harmonizes with the universe. The position of the sun, moon, planets and the gravitational effects of other bodies in the universe can create the vibration that can make your location positive or negative. The number or Vedic Location Code can be used to identify this vibration. In the following table the years are indicated in the rows above, which will cross the Vedic Location code as it matches with your Vedic Building Code. This Vedic Location Code for the year in question will describe the influences for the location that year.

YOUR LIFECODE	LOCATION YEAR CODE FOR 2016								
	1	2	3	4	5	6	7	8	9
7	8	9	1	2	3	4	5	6	7

Location Year Code # 1:
During this year in this house people will experience loneliness, separation and worry, promotions and progress may affect the inhabitants, some people could experience rejection from others while living here at this time, avoid being too bossy or dominating, you may get into trouble. It is a good time to start new projects or business at this home or location

Location Year Code # 2:
During this year in this house people will experience weddings, marriages or romance; there will be many visitors and guests; people in this house will be enjoying good food, lots of shopping and a rewarding love life during this year. It is a good time to clean, decorate, repair, remodel and to enjoy this home. Lots of dressing up, new clothes and eating of sweets will be some of the activities in this house now.

Location Year Code # 3:

During this year in this house many children will visit; possible pregnancy or news of birth; menstrual cycle or uterus problems; lots of studies, writing and reading of books; too much watching of television and computer activities; childishness, immaturity, and irresponsibility at this time. There will be many social parties and engagements this year. The year will bring problems of children, schools, or abortions to this home if the inhabitants are negative and also problem with telephone equipment and billing.

Location Year Code # 4:

During this year in this house people will experience possible job problems, hard work, overtime, low pay and general career problems will affect the people in this home at this time. Tension, high-blood pressure, and high temper will affect the people in the home. Gossip will create lots of arguments and negative feelings. This home may experience construction and repairs which will improve the value of your house.

Location Year Code # 5:

During this year in this house people will experience travel or vacations. There will be many visitors to this home; some of them may not be genuine. Long distance calls and long-distance relationships may be popular during this time. It is possible, that some inhabitants will have illicit affairs or some fraudulent deals or transactions. People in this house will be more conscious of their physical appearance and most of the women living or visiting here will appear beautiful. Common ailments in this house will affect the feet or sexual organs at this time.

Location Year Code # 6:

During this year in this house people will experience conflicts, disagreements, power struggles, frustration and responsibility. Be careful of disturbing visits from family members who will have an attitude towards the inhabitants. There is the possibility of influences from police, court, or collection agencies communicating with the people living here. There may be suggestions of divorce or separation among the couples. One or more of the people living in this house may experience accidents or surgical operations. Check the forecast on Medical Services Code to make better choices for your health care. There may be possible problems from in-laws

Location Year Code # 7:

During this year in this house people will experience tiredness and sleepiness. Inhabitants will worry at this time about their life path, their goals, their objectives, and their future. They will feel that they need to meet with astrologers, psychics, Hindu priests and swamis.

People in this house will become very secretive at this time. This house may be visited by snakes this year

Location Year Code # 8:

During this year in this house people will be receiving or spending a lot of money. This house may experience a change in furniture or fixtures, which may be very expensive. It is a good time to do reconstruction or renovations in this house. Starting a business will become very profitable in this house. People in this house will look more beautiful and presentable this year. Expensive parties or purchases may affect inhabitants of this house.

Location Year Code # 9:

During this year in this house people will experience possible sewer, flooding, boiler, or water problems; possible death or news of death sickness or operations. There may be government, city, or state problems, accidents where only the vehicle is damaged; money spent unexpectedly. Husbands and wives will find themselves sleeping separately and any business started at this time will fail; attempts to sell this house will be delayed. There will be frustrations with your job; do not do any construction or rebuilding at this time

Section 6

Best Places to Sleep in the House

The Effect of the Vedic Location in Your Home

Sleeping in the right location within the home can make a whole lot of difference in your life, your prosperity, your love life , your health and your happiness....make sure you set #1 on the eastern side of the house to calculate

TABLE 6.1

POSITIVE/ NEGATIVE SECTIONS OF THE HOME /BUSINESS LOCATION		
NORTH		
#4- NEUTRAL *BEST LOCATION FOR:* KITCHEN DINING ROOM WORK/ REPAIRS GARAGE	**#3 – POSITIVE** *BEST LOCATION FOR:* BEDROOMS TELEVISION SOFAS PLAY ROOM LIBRARY	**#8 – POSITIVE** *BEST LOCATION FOR:* BUSINESS MONEY BUSINESS COMPUTERS DESK SLEEPING
#9- NEGATIVE *BEST LOCATION FOR:* BATHROOM SEWER POOL STORAGE EMPTY SPACE	**#5- POSITIVE** *BEST LOCATION FOR:* MEETINGS EXERCISE KITCHEN ROMANCE SITTING ROOM	**#1- NEUTRAL** *BEST LOCATION FOR:* MEDITATION PRAYER ALTARS RELIGIOUS BOOKS
#2- POSITIVE *BEST LOCATION FOR:* DRESSING ROOM GUEST ROOM KITCHEN SITTING ROOM DINING/ DEN	**#7- NEUTRAL** *BEST LOCATION FOR:* BEDROOMS READING LIVING ROOM MEDITATION GUEST ROOM	**#6- NEGATIVE** *BEST LOCATION FOR:* STORAGE POLITICS FOUNTAIN
SOUTH		

WEST (left side) — *EAST* (right side)

As you can see the center parts of any location is always energetic, active and positive. The South East corner is the worse part of the space for resting or peace. The Mid Western part is where the most tension or quarrels are experienced. The best part of house for resting and good sleep is the mid north or South West. Money should be kept in the North East corner, and businesses should be conducted there. In the table you can follow the numbers as follows:

1. Fairly good energy for meetings and being alone
2. Excellent energy for all things & visitors
3. Excellent for children, study and social events
4. Good for cooking, and performing work like a garage
5. Excellent for lovemaking, exercise, planning, phones
6. Negative area – possible bad news, losses, frustration
7. Peaceful area for sleeping, relaxing, thinking, reading.
8. Money, dresser, jewelry, conducting business, investing
9. Negative space, news of death, bad dreams, losses, expenses

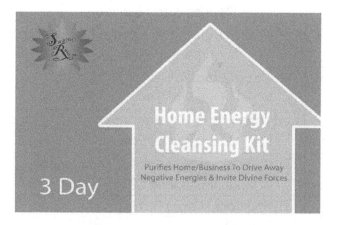

Section 7

YOUR CAREER IN 2016

Are You Compatible with Your Job / Career?

IT'S A **POSITIVE** YEAR TO START A NEW JOB OR CHANGE YOUR CURRENT JOB

Account/ Tax Services	A good career, loved by your co-workers, Good bosses for you	POSITIVE
Advertising Agency	Active career, Avoid being playful, Many Opportunities for you	POSITIVE
Amusement / Recreation	Lots of work, Promotions, Leadership and favor with Superiors	NEUTRAL
Antique Store	Slow and easy jobs, Not many promotions, avoid gossip, Envy...	NEUTRAL
Architectural Firm	A good career, loved by your co-workers, Good bosses for you	POSITIVE
Artist / Designer	Hard work, Low pay in this career, slow advancement, Stress....	NEUTRAL
Auto / Car Body Repair Shop	Active career, Avoid being playful, Many Opportunities for you	POSITIVE
Auto / Car Dealership	Active career, Avoid being playful, Many Opportunities for you	POSITIVE
Bakery / Pastry Shop	Uncomfortable with this job, Stressful, loss of promotions, Conflicts.	NEGATIVE
Barber / Hair Stylist	Much Responsibility in this job, Co-worker conflicts & Jealousy...	NEGATIVE
Beauty & Nails Salon	Much Responsibility in this job, Co-worker conflicts & Jealousy...	NEGATIVE

Bed & Breakfast	Uncomfortable with this job, Stressful, loss of promotions, Conflicts.	NEGATIVE
Bicycle Shop	Active career, Avoid being playful, Many Opportunities for you	POSITIVE
Bookstore	Lots of work, Promotions, Leadership and favor with Superiors	NEUTRAL
Building / Contractor	A good career, loved by your co-workers, Good bosses for you	POSITIVE
Café / Bar	Slow and easy jobs, Not many promotions, avoid gossip, Envy...	NEUTRAL
Carpentry	A good career, loved by your co-workers, Good bosses for you	POSITIVE
Casual Dinning	Uncomfortable with this job, Stressful, loss of promotions, Conflicts.	NEGATIVE
Catering Services	Uncomfortable with this job, Stressful, loss of promotions, Conflicts.	NEGATIVE
Children / Nursery	Lots of work, Promotions, Leadership and favor with Superiors	NEUTRAL
Chiropractor	A good career, loved by your co-workers, Good bosses for you	POSITIVE
Civil Engineering	A good career, loved by your co-workers, Good bosses for you	POSITIVE
Cleaning Services	Slow and easy jobs, Not many promotions, avoid gossip, Envy...	NEUTRAL
Clubs / Associations	Good Career, Good Pay, Many opportunities, Liked by Bosses....	POSITIVE
Computer Store	A very active job, will involve travel, changes, avoid love affairs	POSITIVE
Consulting services	Good Career, Good Pay, Many opportunities, Liked by Bosses....	POSITIVE
Contractor / Home Repairs	A good career, loved by your co-workers, Good bosses for you	POSITIVE
Cosmetics / Beauty Supplies	Much Responsibility in this job, Co-worker conflicts & Jealousy...	NEGATIVE
Courier Services	Active career, Avoid being playful, Many Opportunities for you	POSITIVE
Dentist	Uncomfortable with this job, Stressful, loss of promotions, Conflicts.	NEGATIVE

Developer / Construction Company	A good career, loved by your co-workers, Good bosses for you	POSITIVE
Doctor	Hard work, Low pay in this career, slow advancement, Stress....	NEUTRAL
Driving School	Active career, Avoid being playful, Many Opportunities for you	POSITIVE
Educational Services	Lots of work, Promotions, Leadership and favor with Superiors	NEUTRAL
Electrical Service	Hard work, Low pay in this career, slow advancement, Stress....	NEUTRAL
Electronic / Electrical Appliances	Hard work, Low pay in this career, slow advancement, Stress....	NEUTRAL
Engineering Consultants	A good career, loved by your co-workers, Good bosses for you	POSITIVE
Event Panning	Lots of work, Promotions, Leadership and favor with Superiors	NEUTRAL
Faith-based Organization	A very active job, will involve travel, changes, avoid love affairs	POSITIVE
Fashion / Clothing	Much Responsibility in this job, Co-worker conflicts & Jealousy...	NEGATIVE
Florist / Flower Shop	Much Responsibility in this job, Co-worker conflicts & Jealousy...	NEGATIVE
Funeral services	Slow and easy jobs, Not many promotions, avoid gossip, Envy...	NEUTRAL
Furniture store	A good career, loved by your co-workers, Good bosses for you	POSITIVE
Gardening / Landscaping	A good career, loved by your co-workers, Good bosses for you	POSITIVE
General Manufacturing	A good career, loved by your co-workers, Good bosses for you	POSITIVE
Glass and Glazing	A good career, loved by your co-workers, Good bosses for you	POSITIVE
Goods Transporting & Hauling	Active career, Avoid being playful, Many Opportunities for you	POSITIVE
Gym / Fitness / Recreation Sports	A good career, loved by your co-workers, Good bosses for you	POSITIVE

Hardware Store	Uncomfortable with this job, Stressful, loss of promotions, Conflicts.	NEGATIVE
Heating, Ventilation & air Conditioning (HVAC) Services	A good career, loved by your co-workers, Good bosses for you	POSITIVE
Home Decor / Accessories	Slow and easy jobs, Not many promotions, avoid gossip, Envy...	NEUTRAL
Home Improvement	A good career, loved by your co-workers, Good bosses for you	POSITIVE
Hotel	A good career, loved by your co-workers, Good bosses for you	POSITIVE
Insurance services	A good career, loved by your co-workers, Good bosses for you	POSITIVE
Interior Design	Active career, Avoid being playful, Many Opportunities for you	POSITIVE
Investment Adviser	A good career, loved by your co-workers, Good bosses for you	POSITIVE
IT-Consulting / Services	Much Responsibility in this job, Co-worker conflicts & Jealousy...	NEGATIVE
Jeweler / Jewelry	Much Responsibility in this job, Co-worker conflicts & Jealousy...	NEGATIVE
Laundry / Dry Cleaning Services	Much Responsibility in this job, Co-worker conflicts & Jealousy...	NEGATIVE
Law office / Notary	Slow and easy jobs, Not many promotions, avoid gossip, Envy...	NEUTRAL
Locksmith	Hard work, Low pay in this career, slow advancement, Stress....	NEUTRAL
Motorcycle Shop	A very active job, will involve travel, changes, avoid love affairs	POSITIVE
Moving Services	Active career, Avoid being playful, Many Opportunities for you	POSITIVE
Nightclub	Active career, Avoid being playful, Many Opportunities for you	POSITIVE
Non-profit Organization	Lots of work, Promotions, Leadership and favor with Superiors	NEUTRAL
Optician	A very active job, will involve travel, changes, avoid love affairs	POSITIVE

Painter / Paperhanger	Much Responsibility in this job, Co-worker conflicts & Jealousy...	NEGATIVE
Personal services	A very active job, will involve travel, changes, avoid love affairs	POSITIVE
Pet Care	Good Career, Good Pay, Many opportunities, Liked by Bosses....	POSITIVE
Pharmacy	Slow and easy jobs, Not many promotions, avoid gossip, Envy...	NEUTRAL
Photography Studio	A very active job, will involve travel, changes, avoid love affairs	POSITIVE
Physiotherapy / Massage	Much Responsibility in this job, Co-worker conflicts & Jealousy...	NEGATIVE
Plumber/ Plumbing Contractors	Uncomfortable with this job, Stressful, loss of promotions, Conflicts.	NEGATIVE
Printing / Duplication Services	Slow and easy jobs, Not many promotions, avoid gossip, Envy...	NEUTRAL
PR/ Marketing Services	Active career, Avoid being playful, Many Opportunities for you	POSITIVE
Real Estate	Much Responsibility in this job, Co-worker conflicts & Jealousy...	NEGATIVE
Restaurant	A good career, loved by your co-workers, Good bosses for you	POSITIVE
Retail / Shops	Uncomfortable with this job, Stressful, loss of promotions, Conflicts.	NEGATIVE
Retirement Homes	Much Responsibility in this job, Co-worker conflicts & Jealousy...	NEGATIVE
Roofing	Slow and easy jobs, Not many promotions, avoid gossip, Envy...	NEUTRAL
School	Slow and easy jobs, Not many promotions, avoid gossip, Envy...	NEUTRAL
Shoe Store	Lots of work, Promotions, Leadership and favor with Superiors	NEUTRAL
Spa / Beauty Salon	Slow and easy jobs, Not many promotions, avoid gossip, Envy...	NEUTRAL
Sports Clubs / Associations	Slow and easy jobs, Not many promotions, avoid gossip, Envy...	NEUTRAL
Sports / Outdoor Equipment	Good Career, Good Pay, Many opportunities, Liked by Bosses....	POSITIVE

Stationery / Office Supply	Good Career, Good Pay, Many opportunities, Liked by Bosses....	POSITIVE
Tailoring / alteration Services	Good Career, Good Pay, Many opportunities, Liked by Bosses....	POSITIVE
Taxi services	A good career, loved by your co-workers, Good bosses for you	POSITIVE
Tiling Services	Active career, Avoid being playful, Many Opportunities for you	POSITIVE
Toy Store	A good career, loved by your co-workers, Good bosses for you	POSITIVE
Transportation	Lots of work, Promotions, Leadership and favor with Superiors	NEUTRAL
Travel agency	Active career, Avoid being playful, Many Opportunities for you	POSITIVE
Vacation Rentals	Active career, Avoid being playful, Many Opportunities for you	POSITIVE
Veterinarians	Active career, Avoid being playful, Many Opportunities for you	POSITIVE

Section 8

Love & Marriage LifeCode Compatibility

The compatibility of a marriage or love union can determine the level of happiness and understanding the couple will enjoy throughout their lives together. It can also alert the couple of what are the most likely issues or tests they will have to confront together and there are some suggestions about what tendencies come with a particular energy and how to avoid them to have a better and happier marriage.

There are three equations to determine perfect marriage time for a couple. Add your Life code of each partner to the year of the Marriage and this equation will determine whether it is a good year for marriage or not. Add the LifeCode of each partner, and that equation will determine if it is a good Month for the marriage. In the third equation the Life code number of each partner is added to the Day to determine the right day for the marriage. For example using February 12 and March 13 as the birthdates of two people. Let's say the date for their marriage is April 19, 1987. The six equations are as follows:

HUSBAND to be (Feb 12) = Life code # 5
$$5 + 1987 \text{ (year)} = 21 = 3$$
$$5 + 4 \text{ (month)} = 9 = 9$$
$$5 + 19 \text{ (day)} = 15 = 6$$

WIFE to be (Mar 13) = Life Code #7
$$7 + 1987 \text{ (year)} = 32 = 5$$
$$7 + 4 \text{ (April)} = 11 = 2$$
$$7 + 19 \text{ (Day)} = 17 = 8$$

As we can see from above numbers the year numbers are good for both Husband and wife, but the month and day is bad for the husband. Marriage is still possible, because of the good year, but there will be delays on the bridegroom side that day since both his month and day for marriage is negative. The Bride side of the wedding should go perfect. The following table will apply to the year month or day results for the chosen day.

1. Fair
2. Excellent
3. Excellent
4. Fair
5. Good
6. Very Bad
7. Good
8. Excellent
9. Very bad

Now I hope that people will plan their marriage successfully by choosing the right date and time for marriage.

Regardless of a match people and couples go through different periods in life when they are tested and Swami Ram Charran can help you to make the journey a little lighter.

TABLE 8.1: COMPATIBILITY TABLE OF LOVE MATCH/MARRIAGE CODES									
YOUR LIFECODE	*PARTNER'S LIFECODE*								
	1	*2*	*3*	*4*	*5*	*6*	*7*	*8*	*9*
7	8	9	1	2	3	4	5	6	7

Now look up your Love code number in the paragraphs below and read the forecast given

Love Code 1: Neutral match

If not independent, you will feel lonely in marriage or in relationship. Do not be demanding or controlling. Avoid forcing people. Respect all.

Love Code 2: Excellent match

A happy married life or relationship only if words and excess desires are under control. Watch your words you could get into trouble.

Love Code 3: Excellent match

You will enjoy a marriage life of comfort and will prosper only through your children. Make them great in life. This relationship has a lot of ego each partner wants to be heard.

Love Code 4: Neutral match

You will have to work hard to please your partner. You will have a great deal of stress, but you must not complain. Just do it.

Love Code 5: Excellent match

If you do not TRUST your partner, the marriage or relationship will be tough for both. Become friends. Do not be possessive.

Love Code 6: A Negative match

You will have to keep your ego down or separation will take placed, be humble and avoid high temper and criticizing others.

Love Code 7: Neutral match

You will have a difficult love life, but being spiritual will overcome all obstacles. People will become jealous of you quickly.

Love Code 8: Excellent match

You will enjoy a prosperous marriage life; money will be your test in marriage. Relationship will be business like, more material than spiritual and this can make you lose each other.

Love Code 9: A Negative match

Struggle, tests, and abuse are the characteristics of this marriage life. You will need a lot of faith.

What Is A Good Year To Marry?

After you find out that you make a good match with your partner and take the next step and decide to marry, it is important to choose a year that is suitable for you and your significant other. Following is a table with the effects of the marriage year for your LifeCode. On the next page you will find the table for the best days to marry. Since marriage is such an important step it is also recommended that you verify the dates with a knowledgeable Pundit.

GOOD YEARS TO MARRY: 1980, 1981, 1984, 1985, 1989, 1990, 1993, 1994, 1998, 1999, 2002, 2003, 2007, 2008, 2011, 2012, 2016, 2017, 2020 and 2021 before the middle of September.

FAIR YEARS TO MARRY: 1983, 1986, 1987, 1992, 1995, 1996, 2001, 2004, 2005, 2010, 2013, 2014, 2019, 2022, 2023 before the middle of September.

BAD YEARS TO MARRY: 1982, 1988, 1991, 1997, 2000, 2006, 2009, 2015, 2018, 2024 before the middle of September.

What Is A Good Day To Marry?

GOOD DAYS TO MARRY: 1, 4, 5, 9, 10, 13, 14, 18, 19, 22, 23, 27, 28 and 31.
FAIR DAYS TO MARRY: 3, 6, 7, 12, 15, 16, 21, 24, 25 and 30.
BAD DAYS TO MARRY: 2, 8, 11, 17, 20, 26 and 29.

The above information applies to the day of any month in any year. For the most appropriate date for marriage a competent priest should be consulted.

Section 9

ADVICE FOR MARRIED COUPLES

IF YOUR MARRIAGE IS HAVING PROBLEMS THEN ONE OF THE FOLLOWING ARE NOT BEING FOLLOWED

1 If your husband or wife is suspected of having an affair the first question you must ask is why is this happening to yourself and the second question that should be asked is ....did you yourself help create this situation? Most of the time when a spouse is having an affair it is because the one who is suffering the loneliness did not cooperate with the feelings of the other. For example, if a husband is having an affair it is because the wife did not provide the bedroom attention that he needed. If for example, the wife is the one having an affair it is usually because she has lost all respect for her husband and no longer consider him important. Hence, usually, a good priest or astrologer would be able to find out the reason why and help the couple see the reality of the situation instead of heading for divorce. Denial of sexual attention is a major cause of divorce.

2 The second major cause of married couples heading for divorce or separation are family member interference. Unless a family member is sleeping in the same bedroom with the married couple, then that family member should have no comments about the marriage. Unless a mother-in-law accepts her daughter-in-law or son-in-law or vice versa there will be no peace in the family and married couple will continue to struggle with family members. In such a case married couples are advised to move far away from family or relatives and should really think of each other's welfare more. Either one should never seek the advice of family members about the other......this is consider betrayal and gossiping.

3 Be sure to check with you astrologer or Hindu priest to see if your marriage is a compatible one. If it is a milk and lemon marriage, then special rituals (Pujas) or ceremonies need to be performed to eliminate the negative influences of this relationship. There are certain people born on certain days that when they marry will create death,

sickness, or financial losses for the other partner   immediately after they have slept with each other.

4 Usually when the wife keeps saying "NO" to the husband in regards to SEX it is   because something is affecting her energy which causes her to have no feeling   for her husband. Usually she doesn't enjoy her love life when she's with her   husband. This is an indication that the chakras are holy centers in her body   which are impure. The first indication of this is when the female starts wearing   black clothes and starts having pains all over the body. In such a case she   needs to see the priest or Hindu astrologer to correct this problem so that the   couple could have a better love life.

Section 10

The Vedic Name Code

Your Life Controlled By The Cycles of Your Name

Names are sounds, and the Vedic Sciences recognizes that each one of us is a vibration at a specific frequency called a LifeCode. Letters forms sound or vibrations and so all languages are subject to sound or musical notes. All languages have "vocals" or vowels, which combine with consonants to form sounds or musical notes. Every name of a person will have these vowels and so the sound or vibration caused by the letters when combined would be part of the group of sounds that make up that name. In English it is sound that forms our unique frequency with the world, and so each one of us harmonizes in a unique way with the universe. When we are given a name by our parents, the feelings and emotional connection with the universe at that moment with the mother or father is embedded in the name of the baby when they give the baby its name. For example if a mother or father is going through a distressing time in their life, most likely the baby's name will start with an "I " or with an "R " as these letters represent distress at childhood. If the parents are happy and are doing well in life then the letter "E " or "C " or "L" will be the starting letter of the baby's name. This will affect any baby in any culture if the letter sound is the same as these letters mentioned.

You are unique! There will never be another YOU! A natal horoscope is not repeated for 25,000 years, because the planets all move at different speeds around our Sun. It is highly unlikely that two people would ever be born on the same date, in the same place, and be given the identically spelled name. An Astrologer needs your date, time, and place of birth. Vedic Mathematics needs only your birth certificate full name and birth date to tell who you are, what you have to work with and much, much more.

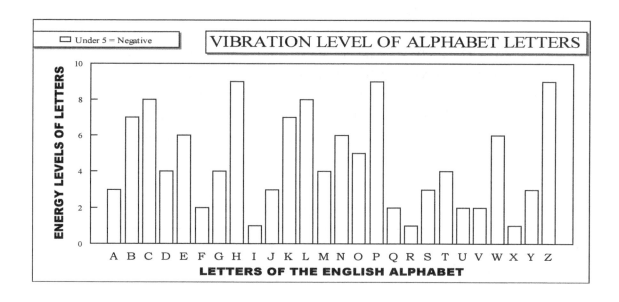

FORECAST YOUR LIFE BASED ON THE NAME GIVEN TO YOU

WHY DO I HAVE UNHAPPINESS? WHY AM I SUFFERING AND STRUGGLING? WHY AM I MARRIED TO THIS PERSON IN THIS LIFE? WHAT MADE ME CHOOSE THIS PERSON FOR MYSELF? WHY DID THIS PERSON ROB ME? WHY AM I HURT OR WHY AM I SICK THIS WAY? WILL I EVER HAVE HAPPINESS...?

Whenever you are unhappy or you are having problems, did you ever stop and think whether you had created this yourself or whether you have to experience this because of some action that you performed previously. When you are unhappy you should ask TWO important questions... First....Why ME?...that is Why am I the one having this problem?...and Secondly....WHAT did I do to create this situation now?....and then the subsequent questions follow.. KARMA is the name of the Universal record keeper of all actions a person creates in the universe. Besides being a record keeper, he is also a Bank that will provide the benefits or reaction according to the actions you deposited previously. So if you deposit good actions of great value then you will be able to withdraw these great values plus interest at a later date. There is an order in the universe in which we live and each of our actions has a profound effect on that order. The universe will move to correct itself depending upon the action performed. When we hate for instance, God devises a way to teach us love. This concept is akin to the scientific law of equilibrium. When a system which was functioning in an orderly manner is thrown into chaos by some action or force, the

41

system quickly reacts to restore that order and reverts back from a state of dis-equilibrium to its original state of equilibrium

Each letter controls 9 years of your life so insert you name in the following box and you can know how your name affects your life in the age you are in now, Insert you name into the following worksheet and then find your prosperity level according to your age. A high prosperity age brings all wealth and love and happiness in your life. If you are in a low prosperity age pray, give charity and fast until the next prosperity level. If all prosperity is low, then you need to change the spelling of your name,

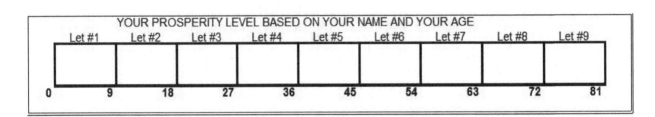

Section 11
The Vedic Name Sound Code

Create a Name That Will Bring You Success!

What is importance of your name or any name? How does your name control your life & experiences? Why are countries whose names start with an "I" suffering? Can your name tell the path of your life from birth to death? Are longer names better for longer lives? Can your name predict the type of career you will follow? Will your name forecast the diseases that will afflict you? All this and more can be answered in this book... Find out how changing your name can make the difference in your life YOUR NAME determines your death, your wealth, your health and your success in life.

There are in total 108 sounds in the universe. Each sound has a distinct vibration of its own, which foretells usually the karma that the baby has brought with it from the past lives. The name should always be chosen carefully since these are the key vibrations that will control your life path and the key actions that determine the karmic benefits in this life.

Here are some key points that you should consider when choosing a name for your child:

* -The letter 'I' brings distress, struggle, and worry, it should be replaced with the letters 'EE'
* The letter 'R' should not be used in the first or second position of the name or it will bring struggle and sickness
*- The letter 'O' should not be used in the naming of businesses
*- the letters 'U', 'E', 'L', 'C', 'P', 'N', 'S', 'A', 'H', 'K' and 'Z' are all good letters to start a name with for prosperity.

Karmic Energy Levels of the Name Letters

In the graph below you will find the karmic energy level of all the letters of the English alphabets. You can actually know if the letters are good in your name or not by matching the letters in your name against the letters in the graph. If there are many letters with measurement below the energy level of 5, you should change your name to a more positive one. This can be accomplished while STILL keeping the same SOUND. For example, the letter "I" can be replaced by "EE" thereby making a negative letter a positive one. For example "Ariana" can be changed to "Areeana".

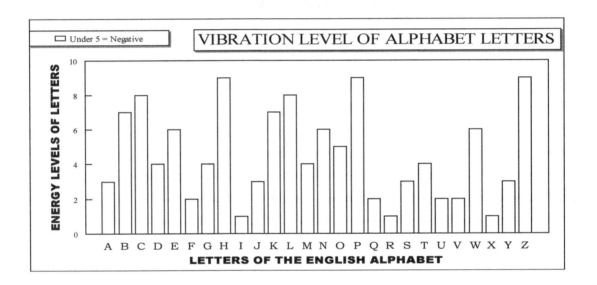

PLEASE NOTE:
IF YOU ARE NOT USING YOUR BIRTH NAME AND ARE USING A GIVEN NAME BY YOUR PARENTS OR A FRIEND OF THE FAMILY, CHANCES ARE THAT YOU MAY BE AFFECTING YOUR PROSPERITY. TO BE SURE THAT YOUR GIVEN NAME IS GOOD FOR YOU, YOU SHOULD GET A NAME CHART DONE BY SWAMI RAM AT THE CHAKRA SQUARE HEALING CENTER.

Section 12
Successful Business Names

If your business is failing or has become slow it is not because your customers do not want your products or services anymore. Most likely there is some cycle that is affecting you, your business location or your business names. We all know that to have a successful business, your sales must increase every so often and your costs or expenses should be minimized. If you are not ready to face the hard times and the good times when they come, then you are not prepared for business properly. This could result in your downfall and also in the complete loss of your business. This book prepares you to avoid these pitfalls in business

Some of the factors that affect your business are as follows:

1. The registered business name
2. Your date of birth and if needed your spouse's birth date
3. The address location of the business
4. If a partnership, the birthdays of all the people in the business.
5. The direction of the business entrance
6. A list of suggested business names. Avoid the letters I,O and R in the names.
7. The welcome mat at the front door
8. If you already have a business name then you will need the date of incorporation,
9. The business owner's birth date
10. if not some future dates you are planning to start the business
11. The day the business is started
12. The address, building number, the unit number of the business location as
13. The placement of the register as well as the city and state location
14. The partnership LifeCode combination
15. The square footage of the building space for use

16. The energy movement in the store
17. The type of business you will do in there
18. The front door, the register and you should face the east.

When you are experiencing low business sales how do you know when it will get better? How do you find out if the business you are planning will make money for you or if you will lose your total investment in this new business? Can you predict whether your partners in business will do well with you or will they cheat you? How can you increase the number of customers you presently have and make them buy more of your products?

Names are sounds, and the Vedic Sciences recognize that each one of us is a vibration at a specific frequency. The names of people and businesses are governed by these vibrations. Letters create sounds or vibrations and so all languages are subject to sound or musical notes. All languages have "vocals" or vowels, which combine with consonants to form sounds or musical notes. Every name of a business or person will have these vowels and so the sound or vibration caused by the letters when combined would be part of the group of sounds that make up that name. In English, it is sound that forms our unique frequency with the world, and so each business and each person harmonizes in a unique way with the universe

HOW IS THE COMPANY PROGRESS MEASURED BY VEDIC CODES?

The companies are rated according to their progress and profits on a scale of 1 to 10 ----10 being the highest in profits and sales and 1 being the lowest in profits and sales.

1   BAD - NOT RECOMMENDED
2   BAD - NOT RECOMMENDED
3   LOW PROFITS WILL BE LOW AND SLOW
4   NEUTRAL SALES AND GAINS WILL BE EQUAL
5   AVERAGE SALES AND PROFITS WILL BE AVERAGE
6   GOOD SALES AND PROFITS ARE HIGHER THAN EXPENSE
7   UP & DOWN SALES WILL BE UP AND DOWN
8   PROFITABLE INCOME IS HIGH AND COMPANY PROGRESSES
9   POWERFUL SALES, PROFITS, PROGRESS ALL HAPPENS
10   FORTUNE 500 SALES, PROFITS, PROGRESS ALL HAPPENS

BUSINESS NAMES AND THEIR RATINGS

I have found that certain name combinations create either a positive or negative energy for the company. I have included a list of the names of some business and I have ranked them based on their value in millions to evaluate the effect of the name.

Company names can determine the failure or success of its business progress. Profits are usually affected in negative years and productivity with profits increase in positive years. These points of progress and slow down in business profits can be anticipated ahead of time years or months before,. Just like the seasons, the vedic code can determine the spring, summer and winter of the cycles that affect a company.

Name	Rating	Name	Rating
Zenethmarketing.com	10	EBOOK GOOGLE ORG	4
Zenetheducation.com	10	Globalinformationacademy.com	6
Heendu Learning Center	4	Universalinformationclub.com	8
Hindu Astrology Society	5	UniversalWealthClub.com	7
Life Jyotish Ashram	3	UniversalCommerceClub.com	8
EXACT UNIVERSE COM HTTP	5	GlobalWealthClub.com	5
YOGI PHYSICIST COM HTTP	4	wealthglobal (suggested by swami)	8
QUANTUM LIFECODE COM HTTP	7	GlobalCommerceClub.com	7

Section 13
Buying a Business

1. Buying a Business Can Be a Disaster if not Checked Properly
2. The date of the launching or opening date business started. You must schedule a reopening of the business to select an appropriate date.
3. The location address or number on the building. If it is an office suite or warehouse number you need to check that number also
4. The first 3 letters cannot contain an "I" and "O" or the first 15 letters if it is an older business
5. The date that you plan to take over the business or the date you plan to start the business with your ownership
6. The direction that the front entrance face
7. The interior layout of the business
8. The colors that are used for the outside and inside

When buying a business, you are also buying the karma of the previous owner as a well as the good will.

MONTH OF INCORPORATION (BELOW)	DAY OF INCORPORATION								
	1 10 19 28	2 11 20 29	3 12 21 30	4 13 22 31	5 14 23	6 15 24	7 16 25	8 17 26	9 18 27
JANUARY	2	3	4	5	6	7	8	9	1
FEBRUARY	3	4	5	6	7	8	9	1	2
MARCH	4	5	6	7	8	9	1	2	3
APRIL	5	6	7	8	9	1	2	3	4
MAY	6	7	8	9	1	2	3	4	5

JUNE	7	8	9	1	2	3	4	5	6
JULY	8	9	1	2	3	4	5	6	7
AUGUST	9	1	2	3	4	5	6	7	8
SEPTEMBER	1	2	3	4	5	6	7	8	9
OCTOBER	2	3	4	5	6	7	8	9	1
NOVEMBER	3	4	5	6	7	8	9	1	2
DECEMBER	4	5	6	7	8	9	1	2	3

Opening Day Of Your Business

The Opening Day and Month You Choose Affects the Outcome of Your Business
The month and day you move into the business is very important, as this begins your life in the business. If the month or day is not a good then you can experience such things as sickness, money problems and employee problems etc. Below is a table to help you move into the business in a good month and after that you will find a table with the correct days to move into a business.

To use this table, look up your LifeCode number of the owner on the left and the month in question on the top rows, then cross them to find the answer.

YOUR LIFECODE	THE BEST MONTH TO MOVE INTO A BUSINESS								
	Jan Oct	Feb Nov	Mar Dec	Apr	May	Jun	Jul	Aug	Sep
1	2	3	4	5	6	7	8	9	1
2	3	4	5	6	7	8	9	1	2
3	4	5	6	7	8	9	1	2	3
4	5	6	7	8	9	1	2	3	4
5	6	7	8	9	1	2	3	4	5
6	7	8	9	1	2	3	4	5	6
7	8	9	1	2	3	4	5	6	7
8	9	1	2	3	4	5	6	7	8
9	1	2	3	4	5	6	7	8	9

In the table above the key numbers are interpreted as follows:
1. Fair Month   4. Fair Month   7.   Good Month

2. Excellent Month	5. Excellent Month	8. Excellent Month
3. Excellent Month	6. Bad Month	9. Bad Month

The day you move into the business is very important, as well. This begins your financial activity in the business. If the day is not a good day it can affect the business as long as you are in that location and you can experience difficulties with money and employees. Below is a table to help you move into the business on a good day. To use this table, look up your LifeCode number on the left and the day in question on the top rows, then cross them to find the number key that answers your question.

FOR MORE INFORMATION AND GREATER DETAILS ON OPENING YOUR OWN SUCCESSFUL BUSINESS, READ "THE BUSINESS LIFECODE" BY SWAMI RAM CHARRAN AVAILABLE FOR THE LOW PRICE OF $29.99 ON OUR WEBSITE: WWW.SHOP.SWAMIRAM.COM

Section 14

INVESTMENTS AND MONEY ADVICE FOR THIS YEAR

WHAT IS THE BEST WAY FOR ME TO INVEST MY MONEY?

HOW TO MAKE PROFITS ALWAYS

- Work with a set plan or chose a consistent system to follow
- Chose you trading cycle and do not change it in any way for that trading instrument
- Avoid being greedy when the stock reaches the targeted price - sell no matter what
- Do not get your emotions or feelings involved in the stock trading sequence

YOU MUST CHOOSE THE CYCLE FOR TRADING

TO USE THE VEDIC CODE SYSTEM OF TRADING …

You must choose a fixed trading cycle before you can trade successfully benefit from this trading system because everything in the universe moves in cycles and periods of Time. If you do not do this then your system will never have a beginning and end and so you will not have a system that can be understood at any point. You will not be able to choose a point of sale or buy and so can lose your investments quickly. Once you have chosen you cycle or trading period, you must stick to that period for that specific investment you have placed in the market. After you have cashed in your profits, you can change the cycle or trading period to a different one for another initial investment or trading instrument. The following are the types of TRADING CYCLES from which you can choose. You can also create your own period or cycle, as long as you stick with it and do not get greedy thinking you will make more if you go over the end point. There are some trading instruments that have odd opening and closing times. These can be dealt with as special systems.

TRADING CYCLES OR PERIODS

1   5-MINUTES TRADING :Only for a specific date chart with exact time beginning

2   HOURLY TRADING PERIOD :Any day with the specific beg hour and ending hour

3   DAILY TRADING PERIOD :From Market opening to closing

4   WEEKLY TRADING :From Mon to Fri or from Sunday night to Fri

5   BI-WEEKLY TRADING :From 15th to 15th or following Moon'd phases

6   MONTHLY TRADING :From the 1st to the 15th or from 1st to the 1st

7   QUARTERLY TRADING :Any three months or 90 day period

8   SEMI-ANNUAL TRADING :Any 6 months or 180 day periods

9   YEARLY TRADING :From any date to any date or 360 days period

10   5-YEAR TRADING :Any 60 months with a beginning date to an ending date

HOW TO READ THE INVESTMENT GRAPHS IN THE VEDIC CODE SYSTEM

The following graphs do not forecast the actual prices of the stocks, but they predict the movement of the prices in terms of energy trends. Each month the performance of the stock will be according to the energy trend of that particular company for that month. If the trend moves downward, then it indicates that the price could possible move downward or some bad news will come out about that company that month. If the trend moves upward then the price of the shares may move upward or the company news will. All movements of prices or profits are measured between the 1 and 10. If a company graph happens to reach the point of 10 that month, then chances are it would be wise to sell quickly as soon it could drop again also very quickly. When the points of the trends are below 3 then it would be advised to buy the stock or security to sell later. There are no guarantees offered by this system, but when used in the past, it has worked fairly well for most investors.

To become a successful investor one must invest with the movements of the universal energy cycles. For example you cannot say to yourself that you ae going to invest in a stock for returns in two weeks and then change your mind and sell after one week. This will surely create losses for you. In using Vedic Code wave theory to invest you must be sure of what TIME PERIOD you want to invest for. According to the Vedic Code Price Momentum Indicator, the lower end of the indicator below 2 begins to get oversold. Anything below 1 is extremely oversold.

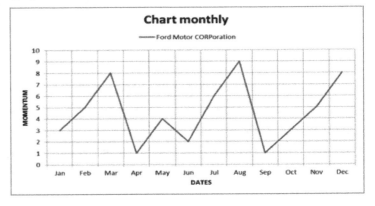

Section 15

Vedic Investment Codes for 2016

In the following table you will find a selected set of investment categories that matches your Vedic Birth Code.

VEDIC INVESTMENT CODES	
INVESTMENT TYPE	YOUR VEDIC BIRTH CODE #7
STOCK MARKET	2
MONEY	6
SAVINGS BANK	2
LAND	2
GAMBLING	6
MOVIES	1
PUBLISHING	1
JEWELRY	6
FARMING	7
REAL ESTATE	2
CONSTRUCTION	2
ROMANCE	9
IMPORT/EXPORT	3

#1 - INVESTMENT ADVICE
- You have to do it all by yourself – having a partner is trouble.
- To make this investment profitable you need to maintain and research all information about it.

- Try to seek leadership and creativity in this investment, as this helps you improve profits.
- Avoid becoming too dominant.

#2 - INVESTMENT ADVICE
- A good business doing partnership with spouse, friend or family member
- You always make profits as long as your relationship with the people involved is positive.
- Learn to be very cooperative with the people you meet in this investment and watch what you say, as this can cause you losses.

#3 - INVESTMENT ADVICE
- Many opportunities present themselves in this business for you.
- Always maintain constant knowledge about your investments, and then your profits will always be high.
- Try to maintain a good sense of humor as it brings profits.
- Avoid childishness or immature controlling of others.

#4 - INVESTMENT ADVICE
- This investment requires that you work very hard.
- No matter how hard you work, you have to work harder to make any profits with this investment.

#5 - INVESTMENT ADVICE
- A constant changing investment, which requires rapid thinking and action before you can become successful.
- Constant change and new ideas are needed to make this investment profitable.
- Watch out for fraudulent and deceptive people.

#6 - INVESTMENT ADVICE
- An investment that requires research, responsibility and power.
- This investment should never have a partnership.
- Avoid confrontation, conflicts and disagreements in this investment as you may lose your investment.
- Watch out for thieves and robbers.

#7 - INVESTMENT ADVICE
- This investment must be done with the utmost discretion and secrecy.
- All transactions in this investment should be done with caution, and profits will come to you slowly but surely.

· Research into the background of this investment, as there may be secret pitfalls awaiting you.

#8 - INVESTMENT ADVICE

· A very lucrative and profitable investment.
· Invest as much as you can and with good timing your sales will become profitable.
· Most of the people you contact regarding this investment will want to be paid their fair share.

#9 - INVESTMENT ADVICE

· You should avoid this type of investment.
· Extreme caution is needed with his investment or else you will lose a great deal of money.
· Try to invest as little as you can and do not spend too much money on improvements, as this will create very little profit.
· Buying and selling quickly is better as a sort term investment.
· Consult with a priest regarding your investment.

When people invest in a home – the American dream – the stock market or in a business of their own, and then surprisingly lose it in a few months or a few years, they and their friends often wonder what caused such a loss. Most of the time it is due to lack of knowledge of business strategies or the timing of when the investment was made.

What you need to know now is whether you will be successful in any particular type of investments and what investments are good for you. When you invest in a certain type of investment, your chances of gaining a profit may be greater than in certain other types. The most important factors that govern any investment are type, timing and matching with karmic Codes of Life. As Shakespeare said, "Some are born great. Some achieve greatness. And some have greatness thrust upon them."

Not everyone is suitable for certain types of investments; so knowing what types of investments are suitable for you increases your chances of making profits and becoming wealthy. On the previous Table, I have selected the most popular types of investments that can be compared to your Vedic Birth Code to help you understand the best types of investments that you can get into. However, it doesn't mean you should shut out other investments completely. Perhaps a partner, who is compatible with you, would be able to work with certain investments that are negative with your birth code but positive with your partner's.

Section 16
THE MONEY CODE

Like all things, money should be respected and treated as a divine energy that is used by all of us to enjoy this world. There are nine forms of money energy, which affect all of us according to our actions in life. For example, you may notice that if we fail to perform our duties properly to our employers, we will be denied raises. Or another example is if we steal money from others, we will lose our wealth in many different ways.

The nine forms of money are:

1. Creativity – money affecting the mind and desire
2. Sharing – money affecting relationship with others
3. Knowledge – money affecting children, education and comfort
4. Duty – money affecting your job and your foundation
5. Movement – money for pleasure and changes
6. Power – money affecting your status and your responsibilities
7. Emotion – money affecting your spiritual relationship with the Universe
8. Enjoyment – money that makes you enjoy power, luxury and beauty
9. Health – money affecting the condition of your life with regard to diseases, confinement and karma

Vedic Money Code #7 Applies to You
- You're very secretive about money.
- Even though money may not be important to you, you need it.
- Using money for real estate is lucky for you.
- You do not like when other people owe you money.
- You become very emotional about your savings and your earnings.
- Raises and bonuses come to you slowly but surely.
- You do well in business money wise.
- You may secretly spend or earn money from bars or clubhouses.
- Very few people know about your finance.

Section 17
The Vehicle Code

WHAT IS TYPE OF PROBLEMS I CAN HAVE WITH THE CAR THIS YEAR?

LIFECODE	VEHICLE OR MACHINERY MODEL YEAR								
	2008	2009	2010	2011	2012	2013	2014	2015	2016
7	8	9	1	2	3	4	5	6	7

PLEASE NOTE: There are other factors affecting this also such as the LifeCode of the person driving and what type of year they are running. Even if the year digit of the vehicle is a good one, once in a while, you will still have an accident or break down depending on the timing. However that is still better than a year digit 9 or 6 which presents breakdowns all the time.

To obtain the year digit of a vehicle or equipment check the year of manufacturing. Just add the year e.g. 1993 = 1 + 9 + 9 + 3 = 22 and reduce to single digit 2+2=4. If its 9 or 6, it's negative. Here it is 4 so it's somewhat troublesome. The following are the qualities of the number digits from 1 to 9.

1. Fairly good
2. Excellent
3. Excellent
4. Somewhat troublesome
5. Fair
6. Negative, Very Bad
7. Good
8. Excellent
9. Negative

The driver or operator in combination with the vehicle or equipment is also taken into consideration as that can affect performance of the vehicle. The following will show how the LifeCode of the driver or operator matches the year of the vehicle or equipment in bad or good energy in some of the years ahead

For example: Equipment produced in 1999 is 1: 1+9+9+9 = 28=> 2+8= 10=> 1+0= 1. A 2016 model is 9: 2+0+1+6= 9

The vehicle of course would respond with its own energy field together with the energy field of the human person. A measure of the resulting energy field would most likely tell how that Vehicle or equipment would respond to your energy field when you are in it. Use the person's LifeCode in combination with the year the automobile was manufactured to see the effects.

Vehicle Code 1:

This is a good car that will prove reliable, driving alone most of the time, problems with lights and ignition area. Usually have books and signs. Listen to talk shows.

Vehicle Code 2:

Car transports many people, shopping, music playing, romance, love and sex will be influenced by this car. Driver always has company. Problems are seats, crowded trunk and interior.

Vehicle Code 3:

Children will be transported, elaborate musical and speaker system. Most problems will be with the steering and guidance system.

Vehicle Code 4:

This car will be used mostly for job. Solid car, it could experience manufacturing problems. The engine is stronger than the body of the car.

Vehicle Code 5:

This car accumulates a lot of mileage. This car has wheel or transmission problems. This car will change many hands quickly.

Vehicle Code 6:

This car may have lots of repairs, tickets and possible accidents now and previously. You may experience loan payment problems and spend lots of money on body repairs or exhaust system.

Vehicle Code 7:

Car will be used for religious purposes. There will be oil or water problems. Driver thinks a lot. If negative owner used for drugs or alcohol, atmosphere will be quiet. Problems may be engine components.

Vehicle Code 8:

Car is luxurious and expensive, some custom made. Driver experiences comfort and may even have a chauffeur. The driver may be a businessman, designer or model.

Vehicle Code 9:

Car may have water and possible radiator, fuel pump problems. Possible accident will damage the car but little injury to the driver. Owner will spend lots of money on repairs and maintenance.

Section 18

EXPLANATION OF MONTHLY FORECAST FOR THE YEAR

DAILY INFLUENCE: (NEGATIVE, POSITIVE or NEUTRAL)

This tells you how the month is going to be in General. Some months are more negative than some, and some months are more positive than some others. You can enjoy the neutral months by doing activities that have been left back or those that do not require too much effort, as in neutral months your energy is on a middle level. It is good to pray more on your negative months. Do more meditation or Chanting of the Mantras. Perform Charity or spiritual work as this will make you more connected to the universe. On Positive months you will be able to relax more and you will have more energy to do what you want. It's good to set up interviews and important projects for those months. Court cases are postponed usually on negative months.

FORECAST AND ADVICE FOR THE MONTH:

This is a generally close description of the month. It helps you to assess your month accordingly and lets you have an idea of some of the things that may show up in your life that month.

KEYWORDS:

These are suggested words that will mostly affect your life that month. All may not apply, only some will apply. This is to let you know that some of these things may affect you. It prepares you to expect these.

They may be positive or negative according to the influence of the month.

BIBLE VERSES: (Proverbs)

These have been taken from the Book of Proverbs in the Christian St James Bible.

READ PSALMS #'s:

More than Five Psalms have been recommended, but you only need to read at least two of those given.

VEDIC MANTRAS FOR THE month:

These are special words which are designed to produce certain sounds and vibrations that will create positive changes in your life. Just like the bible says that "In the beginning it was the word, and the word was God and the word became one" so also the Hindus have the word "OM" which is known as the first word of Creation and is known as the vibration of birth. Dr. OZ on OPRAH recommends the Chanting of "OM" for relieving stress change mental energy- good or bad.

RULING PLANET:

The Planets acts as Timers in our life. Like the Moon controls the ovulation cycle in women, the planets affect our emotions and Moods, and our reaction to the Universal forces. SUN, MOON, MERCURY, VENUS and JUPITER are all Positive effects. The Negative ones are SATURN, RAHU, KETU, NEPTUNE, URANUS and PLUTO.

RULING DEITY:

Each of us is influences by cosmic forces and elements constantly in the Universe. The Deities are these forces and elements that affect our life every minute, hours, months, months and years. For example when there is a predominance of Salt in our body, then our energy is hyper and when there is a lot of sugar, our nerves become itchy. The deities which are all the elements in the periodic table such as odium, etc. can affect our health, money and more by the way our brains and bodies handle them.

PUJAS & CHARITABLE SUGGESTIONS FOR THE MONTH:

These are suggested charitable actions that will create good reactions in your life, as well as payoff your Karmic debts. Everything we do is a ritual in life. Puja simple means holy or Karmic rituals.

Jan-2016	Shiva	This is considered a POSITIVE month for you	Planet: Jupiter

ADVICE & DETAILS

LIFECODE FORECAST: Money is the main issue in your life this month. All aspects of your life connected with money may be affected such as your job, your mortgage, your prestige, your income and so on. Love and romance may be expensive but pleasurable if you are positive. Marriage this month may be very profitable to the female partner. You may be tempted to buy yourself that expensive item you have wanted to buy for a long time but never had the money. On the other hand if you have been negative this month may bring delay, disappointment, deception or trickery pertaining to finance. It is a good time to request a promotion from your superiors and also a good time to play the lottery. Try to save some of the money that will come your way this month as you will need it in emergency next month. Real estate opportunities may seem attractive for investment purposes. It is a good time to invest in the stock market, but very little. This is a positive month for money matters and for purchasing that expensive item that is needed. Income should be high now and money will be coming from unusual quarters. If you are negative expect unforeseen expenses this month. Save some of your money for next month as you will need it. Avoid extravagance or over spending.

MONEY	LOVE	CAREER	FAMILY	TRAVEL	WEDDING	MOVE	BUSINESS	HEALTH	Lotto #'s	play 3 #s
Excellent	Good	Excellent	Good	Good	Excellent	Good	Excellent	Excellent	45,46,31,23,17,38,38	719

SHOPPING	GAMBLE	SEX	KEYWORD	KEYWORD					
Excellent	Excellent	is excellent	MONEY	Business,Major Expense,Money - Profits,Income,Investments,Power,Promotion,Fame - TV					

STRESS LEVEL	LUCKY COLORS	JEWELERY	MOONS EFFECT	GRAHA EFFECT	MONTHLY DEITY
Low	Yellow/Silver	Diamonds/Gold/Pearls	Secretive	Money Graha	LAXMI

MONTHLY PUJA	MONTHLY PSALMS
Decorate Land, Feed the poor, Donate milk /products to all, Feed holy guests,	, 35 ,44, 53, 62, 80,

BODY PARTS	DISEASE /sickness	POSSIBLE HEALTH PROBLEMS	MONTHLY EFFECT ON...Intestines
Intestines	Disease of the colon	Constipation problems	Laxmi Affects You This Month – Your Wealth

MANTRA FOR MONTH
Om Hareem Nama Swaha..Shri Maha Laxmi Aye Namah swaha 12 times

SPECIAL MESSAGE FOR THIS MONTH:
RULES FOR SUCCESS ; Avoid spending so much. Control expenses - always keep track. You must have a specific amount consistantly every day, week, or month. Avoid being extravagant unless you can afford it. Play lotto with your head not over it. Do not create debts - avoid credit . Always use cash - you will be more successful.

NEGATIVE DAYS:.............	2*8*11*17*20*26*29	January

Feb-2016	Shiva	This is considered a NEGATIVE month for you	Planet: Saturn

ADVICE & DETAILS

LIFECODE FORECAST: Be careful of accidents, conflict with police officers, negative involvement with the court and worrisome problems from all sides. At all cost you are advised to keep a low profile this month and avoid confrontations with others who are negative. Your income may be low, expenses may be high and money may be short. You may also receive sad news from afar, or news of an illness. Your personal affairs may be delayed and opportunities that may seem great at first may not be attained successfully if started this month. Of course if you are religious and charitable most of these problems may be minimized. Control your temper. Do not speak harshly and avoid conflicts with co-workers. You must go to the temple as much as you can and meditate a great deal as all these will assist you safely through this month. Any activity this month should involve spirituality, or learning. Tension may be very high and sexual feelings may be very strong. If you are having an illicit affair, you must be careful of scandal. The key word is finish. Take care of unfinished business this month. Write your ideas down and keep it for next month. Don't think of changing jobs at this time. You may be prone to accidents or have worrisome problems from all sides. Keep a low profile and avoid confrontations of a negative nature with others. Income will be low and money may be short. There is possible sad news. Delay or deception in personal affairs and opportunities will not be attained successfully. If you are religious most of these problems will be minimized.

MONEY	LOVE	CAREER	FAMILY	TRAVEL	WEDDING	MOVE	BUSINESS	HEALTH	Lotto #'s	play 3 #s
Bad	Bad	Bad	Fair	Bad	Bad	Bad	Bad	Bad	61,12,41,63,29,24,5	350

SHOPPING	GAMBLE	SEX	KEYWORD	KEYWORD					
Bad	Bad	is very bad	KARMA	Destruction,Losses,Death,Sickness - cold,Legal matter,Abusive,Karmic debts,God - Karma					

STRESS LEVEL	LUCKY COLORS	JEWELERY	MOONS EFFECT	GRAHA EFFECT	MONTHLY DEITY
High	Gold/Brown//Green	Saphire/Hessonite	Ivestments	Evil Graha	PITREES

MONTHLY PUJA	MONTHLY PSALMS
Remembrance of family members who died, worship of older people. gifts to grand parents	9, 18, 36 63, 81,

BODY PARTS	DISEASE /sickness	POSSIBLE HEALTH PROBLEMS	MONTHLY EFFECT ON...Circulation
Circulation	Disease all kinds	General health is weak	Pitrees Affects You This Month – Your Problems

MANTRA FOR MONTH
Om Ganga mataye nama swaha Om Varuna Devta aye Pahimam 11 times

SPECIAL MESSAGE FOR THIS MONTH:
RULES FOR SUCCESS ; Become a student of the Universe Respect elder people and authority Follow all government laws and regulations Attend religious functions regularly Read and learn from others Avoid commanding others impulsively Seek advise for religious teachers Follow astrology and occult science Stop denying or doubting when facts are presented to you Avoid suspicion of loved ones Do not help others unless you are in a position to do so. Never! Never! Fight the government Always give to charity Avoid alcohol, drugs and cigarrettes

NEGATIVE DAYS:.............	2*8*11*17*20*26*29	February

Mar-2016	Shiva	This is considered a NEUTRAL month for you	Planet: Sun

ADVICE & DETAILS

LIFECODE FORECAST: You may be feeling quite independent this month and possibly lonely. You may be very busy attending to a lot of your projects, your career or your business. You may find yourself in conflict with others as a result of your becoming too commanding or too dominating. If you are married, tension may arise at the beginning of the month where you may be denied attention from your spouse or lover. Some of your personal projects or dreams may become a reality at this time. Your inventive abilities are extremely high and you may be congratulated or honored by persons in authority. A promotion may come about at your place of employment. Your health may be affected on the 8th or 17th of the month. Quarrels may occur on the 5th, 14th and 23rd of the month. A few opportunities for promotions and advancements in your ambitions may present themselves. Take advantage of these. If you are experiencing negative feelings of loneliness, perform meditative Puja. Concentrate on yourself this month and try to do everything that you have to do on your own without requesting help from others. People will not be as cooperative as you want them to be. You may feel lonely at times. However, any new opportunities presented will make you feel good about yourself. Do not be over-confident or too competitive with others. Do not expect many invitations until next month.

MONEY	LOVE	CAREER	FAMILY	TRAVEL	WEDDING	MOVE	BUSINESS	HEALTH	Lotto #'s	play 3 #s
Fair	Bad	Good	Bad	Fair	Bad	Fair	Fair	Fair	53,38,13,6,42,43,47	699

SHOPPING	GAMBLE	SEX	KEYWORD	KEYWORD						
Fair	Fair	is fair	MIND	Independence,Loneliness,Meditative,Worry,Dominating,Illness - Cold,On Your Own,Commanding						

STRESS LEVEL	LUCKY COLORS	JEWELERY	MOONS EFFECT	GRAHA EFFECT	MONTHLY DEITY
High	White/Yellow/	Pearl/Quartz	Arrogance	Status Graha	GURU

MONTHLY PUJA	MONTHLY PSALMS
Give Gifts to Priests, Invite holy ones to your home, Feed Swamis and Yogis, Do Shiva Puja.	1, 28 ,46, 73,,

BODY PARTS	DISEASE /sickness	POSSIBLE HEALTH PROBLEMS	MONTHLY EFFECT ON...Head
Head	Disease of the head	Nervousness caused by worrying	Guru Affects You This Month – Your Mind

MANTRA FOR MONTH
Om Namo Bhagawate Mukhtanandaya, 108 times

SPECIAL MESSAGE FOR THIS MONTH:
RULES FOR SUCCESS: Do not let your mind idle. Always try to be a leader. Meditate to slow down your mind. Do not be dominating or bossy to others. Only give advise when asked for it... When left alone by partner do not fight - pray instead. Avoid depression moments - meditate when feeling lonely. When accused of anything - rise above it When offered a leadership position at work - accept it

NEGATIVE DAYS:.............	2*8*11*17*20*26*29	March

Apr-2016	Shiva	This is considered a POSITIVE month for you	Planet: Moon

ADVICE & DETAILS

LIFECODE FORECAST: Romance and love may be predominant in your mind this month. If married you will be enjoying the pleasures of the opposite sex this month. If single you may be dating that favorite person you wanted to date for a while now. Expect quite a few visitors at home or through the telephone. Your emotion may be high and you may be asked to perform good deeds. If your partner is not properly matched astrologically with you then expect a great deal of disagreements this month. Your popularity may rise now so expect quite a few requests for service from others. That invitation you have been looking forward to may come now. Expect many friends to call you or visit you this month. You may meet some new contacts or some new interests in your love affairs. That special someone, you have been thinking about may enter your life now. Married couples will be spending much more time with each other this month. Business partnerships will be profitable.

MONEY	LOVE	CAREER	FAMILY	TRAVEL	WEDDING	MOVE	BUSINESS	HEALTH	Lotto #'s	play 3 #s
Good	Excellent	Good	Good	Excellent	Good	Good	Good	Good	68,20,61,43,38,24,42	940

SHOPPING	GAMBLE	SEX	KEYWORD	KEYWORD						
Good	Good	is good	LOVE	Romance,Popularity,Visitors,Shopping,Food, Drinks,Co-operation,Friendships,Affection						

STRESS LEVEL	LUCKY COLORS	JEWELERY	MOONS EFFECT	GRAHA EFFECT	MONTHLY DEITY
Low	Red/Yellow/Pink	Topaz/Diamonds	Conservative	Love Graha	KRISHNA

MONTHLY PUJA	MONTHLY PSALMS
Give Gifts to females andnMother, Serve milk Products, Worship Durga forms	, 29 ,38, 47, 56,

BODY PARTS	DISEASE /sickness	POSSIBLE HEALTH PROBLEMS	MONTHLY EFFECT ON...Speech
Speech	Disease of the mouth	Food poisoning problems	Krishna Affects You This Month – Love Life

MANTRA FOR MONTH
Kali Durge Namo Nama Om Durge aye nama swaha 108 times

SPECIAL MESSAGE FOR THIS MONTH:
RULES FOR SUCCESS;   Control your speech or words. Always be cooperative to others. learn to cook - you will be great. The more people you feed the more success in your life. Always offer guests something to drink or eat. Never! Never! Have an affair - it will ruin you. Learn to be religious - it will help. Listen to music when you are sad. Learn to sing - you have a great voice Always be well dressed and neat. Hug and embrace all close people - you will find peace quickly. Do not speak if your heart does not say it. Love for one person is your karmic test. Be diplomatic in business - do not let out all your plans or secrets. Your words can really becom reality so watch what you say.

NEGATIVE DAYS:.............	2*8*11*17*20*26*29	April

May-2016		Shiva		This is considered a POSITIVE month for you				Planet: Mercury		

ADVICE & DETAILS

LIFECODE FORECAST: If you are a female and not pregnant at this time then you may surely hear news of pregnancy from someone related to the family. Children may need your attention this month and may demand that you spend more time with them. You may find yourself studying or reading a great deal now and if you are a student you will be successful in your exams or courses at school. You may be spending a great deal of time on the telephone and may receive lots of calls from old friends who may surprise you. If you are in business for yourself expect a great deal of profits coming to you through the telephone and an increase in clientele, but be aware that is not how much money you make, but how much you get to keep. If you are negative then expect some distress through younger individuals. You should be doing a lot of entertaining or you are being entertained a great deal this month. Your creativity is high and you will be successful with many of your undertakings. Most of your wishes will be realized. Old friends will show up at your home. Enjoy the month.

MONEY	LOVE	CAREER	FAMILY	TRAVEL	WEDDING	MOVE	BUSINESS	HEALTH	Lotto #'s	play 3 #s
Good	Fair	Good	Good	Excellent	Good	Good	Good	Excellent	57,20,41,48,61,60,39	94

SHOPPING	GAMBLE	SEX	KEYWORD	KEYWORD						
Good	Good	Is great	SOCIAL	Children,Education,Astrology,Bargains,Social Functions,Childishness,Groups - Parties,Teacher						

STRESS LEVEL		LUCKY COLORS	JEWELERY	MOONS EFFECT	GRAHA EFFECT	MONTHLY DEITY
Low		Green/Sky Blue/	Diamonds/Silver	Enthusiastic	Social Graha	GAUREE

MONTHLY PUJA	MONTHLY PSALMS
Wash the feet of Children, Do Satnarayan Pooja, Read & chant Geeta	57, 75, 102, 120

BODY PARTS	DISEASE /sickness	POSSIBLE HEALTH PROBLEMS	MONTHLY EFFECT ON...Hips
Hips	Disease of sexual organs	Menstrual cycle problems (females)	Gauree Affects You This Month – Social Life

MANTRA FOR MONTH
Om hareem Kleem Hreem Aem Saraswataye namaha 21 times

SPECIAL MESSAGE FOR THIS MONTH:
RULES FOR SUCCESS; Avoid too much Television. Accept and love children always. Do not seat around too much. Avoid demanding too much attention from parents. Read a great deal - books will answer all questions. Never drop out of school or quit classes. Respect your teachers. Do not be too playful or immature. Be careful of abortions and miscarriages.

NEGATIVE DAYS:.............	2*8*11*17*20*26*29	May

Jun-2016		Shiva		This is considered a NEGATIVE month for you				Planet: Pluto		

ADVICE & DETAILS

LIFECODE FORECAST: Repairs in the home, pains in the joints, overwork, tiredness, sleepiness are the influences of this month. You may be feeling very lazy and may have to put in extra time at the job for your boss. It may be a very busy time in your business or occupation. Now is the time when you may be able to fix that broken appliance or wall in your home. If you are looking for a job this month you may not find one because wherever you go the salary may not be to your satisfaction. If you are employed presently you may feel at this time that the payment received does not compensate for the work you are performing. Owners of real estate or rental properties may experience difficulty with tenants this month. In the beginning of this month your car may also require some maintenance. Contact with your mother or a female mother figure may be expected soon. Purchase of antiques or articles of those who have died may come into your possession. This is a good time for constructive activities, exercise, diet and hard work. Expect to participate in community affairs. Accept all overtime given to you at your place of employment and put in extra hours to complete your personal duties. Cut down on expenses as money is low at this time. Watch your health. This is a good time to visit the doctor.

MONEY	LOVE	CAREER	FAMILY	TRAVEL	WEDDING	MOVE	BUSINESS	HEALTH	Lotto #'s	play 3 #s
Bad	Fair	Bad	Fair	Bad	Good	Bad	Bad	Bad	9,38,46,41,20,66,19	169

SHOPPING	GAMBLE	SEX	KEYWORD	KEYWORD						
Bad	Bad	Is tough	CAREER	Career,Hard Work,Co-workers,Low Payment,Job Problems,High Temper,Low Pay,Laziness						

STRESS LEVEL		LUCKY COLORS	JEWELERY	MOONS EFFECT	GRAHA EFFECT	MONTHLY DEITY
High		Dark Blue/ Purple/	Amethyst/Gold	Emotional	Job Graha	GANAPATI

MONTHLY PUJA	MONTHLY PSALMS
Worship Ganesh, Give gifts to father, and co -workers, Plant gardens, farms	4, 13, 31 ,40,

BODY PARTS	DISEASE /sickness	POSSIBLE HEALTH PROBLEMS	MONTHLY EFFECT ON...Stomach
Stomach	Disease of the belly	Bone problems and stomach problems	Ganapati Affects You This Month – Your Career

MANTRA FOR MONTH
Om Jai Viganeshwaraya.. Lambodaraya Namo Namaha 21 times

SPECIAL MESSAGE FOR THIS MONTH:
RULES FOR SUCCESS; Always work hard at your job Never demand a raise - it will come. Rest yourself well after a day's work. Keep an open mind - Don't be annoyant. Do not get angry at everybody.

NEGATIVE DAYS:.............	2*8*11*17*20*26*29	June

Jul-2016	Shiva	This is considered a POSITIVE month for you	Planet: Venus

ADVICE & DETAILS

LIFECODE FORECAST: Short travel or driving to a distant location is forecasted for you this month. If you are not taking a vacation, then you may be traveling as a result of your employment or personal business. Your romantic feelings may be extremely high at this time and single individuals may encounter an exciting month and find new romance. If married you will be enjoying the pleasures of the opposite sex this month. If single you may be dating that favorite person you wanted to date for a while now. You may be involved in a false situation where you may be accused of insincerity or you may be deceived by somebody close to you. All telephone calls coming to you from long distances should not be taken seriously. It is possible that the situation may not be as somber as you think it is. If you are negative be careful of affliction to the private organs. You must also be careful of loss of reputation. If you are making a trip you will enjoy meeting some interesting people. Your appearance may be a major topic this month. Sex, love and romance are prevalent in your mind this month. Also travel and long distance communications occupy most of your time now. You will be meeting with strangers or attractive members of the opposite sex. New changes or a possible move is the highlight of this month. Avoid impulsiveness, trickery, or dishonesty from others.

MONEY	LOVE	CAREER	FAMILY	TRAVEL	WEDDING	MOVE	BUSINESS	HEALTH	Lotto #'s	play 3 #s
Bad	Excellent	Fair	Good	Excellent	Good	Excellent	Good	Excellent	65,65,60,13,4,30,36	353

SHOPPING	GAMBLE	SEX	KEYWORD	KEYWORD				
Good	Good	is good	CHANGE	Sexuality,Travel,Change,Distant, far,Travel delays,Deception,Excercise,Illicit Affairs

STRESS LEVEL	LUCKY COLORS	JEWELERY	MOONS EFFECT	GRAHA EFFECT	MONTHLY DEITY
Fair	Tan/Green/ Beige	Pearl/Silver/quartz	Courageous	Travel Graha	NARADA

MONTHLY PUJA: Artistic gifts, Pray to Krishna, Do good deeds, do Spiritual trips

MONTHLY PSALMS: 5, 32 , 50, 77, 122

BODY PARTS	DISEASE /sickness	POSSIBLE HEALTH PROBLEMS	MONTHLY EFFECT ON...Feet
Feet	Disease of the feet	Blood poisoning and muscle problems	Narada Affects You This Month – Your Pleasures

MANTRA FOR MONTH
Om Graam Greem Graum Sa Gurave namah swaha 21 times

SPECIAL MESSAGE FOR THIS MONTH:
RULES FOR SUCCESS; Avoid illicit affairs or cheating. Being false or lying is prohibited as it will be negative karma. Sex and consistancy is your karmic test. Avoid doubting the existence of God. Never fight the Revenue Service or Government You think God is not watching you sometimes..Are your sure? You must admit when you are wrong - keep an open mind

NEGATIVE DAYS:............. 2*8*11*17*20*26*29   July

Aug-2016	Shiva	This is considered a NEGATIVE month for you	Planet: Mars

ADVICE & DETAILS

LIFECODE FORECAST: Control your anger or your temper. It is a very tense month and you may experience some delays and difficulties at your place of employment as well as at home. Equipments may break down and traveling may be difficult. It is advisable for you to stay together with family and relatives. Do worship and meditate with them and last but not least attend services at the temple. All this will serve to assist you from having many difficulties now. Be careful of accidents and possible pain or injury to the lower back. If any disagreements develop between you and your partner, it surely is your fault for not being able to control your temper. If positive you may be promoted at your place of employment or be given more responsibility with more pay. Avoid conflicts with co-workers or being involved in discussions that are argumentative. Most of all admit when you are wrong, if you are. Avoid aggressiveness. Accept all responsibilities given to you. There is the possibility of association with negative people who will try to take advantage of you. Be calm and patient as you will be torn between your love life and your job. Be prepared for a possible quarrel with your partner or the end of a friendship. Do not cry or get angry over petty annoyances or younger individuals. Sexual activity is low.

MONEY	LOVE	CAREER	FAMILY	TRAVEL	WEDDING	MOVE	BUSINESS	HEALTH	Lotto #'s	play 3 #s
Bad	Bad	Bad	Bad	Bad	Bad	Bad	Fair	Bad	33,27,74,68,26,20,24	151

SHOPPING	GAMBLE	SEX	KEYWORD	KEYWORD				
Fair	Bad	is frustrating	POWER	Responsibilty,Disagreement,Family,Back Pain,Family Conflicts,Traffic Ticket,Quarrels,Jealousy

STRESS LEVEL	LUCKY COLORS	JEWELERY	MOONS EFFECT	GRAHA EFFECT	MONTHLY DEITY
High	Purple/Blue/Rose	Emerald/Saphire	Educational	Family Graha	HANUMAN

MONTHLY PUJA: Meditate, Control temper, Pray to Hanuman, Chant Hanuman Chalisa

MONTHLY PSALMS: 6, 15, 33 ,42,

BODY PARTS	DISEASE /sickness	POSSIBLE HEALTH PROBLEMS	MONTHLY EFFECT ON...Back/Spine
Back/Spine	Disease of the bones	Broken bones, back pain, migraine headache	Hanuman Affects You This Month - Responsabilities

MANTRA FOR MONTH
Om Mana Swasti Shanti Kuru kuru Swaha Shivoham Shivoham 27 times

SPECIAL MESSAGE FOR THIS MONTH:
RULES FOR SUCCESS ; Avoid borrowing money or credit. Do not eat meat or fish everyday. Avoid red meat totally. Responsibility is your karmic test. obey all traffic laws - police sees you quickly. Respect your in-laws avoid conflict. Even if others are jealous - trust in God. Learn to be patient - you'll win. Do not command religious people. Avoid thinking that you know everything. Do not be hasty - you will loose in business. Respect Laxmi - do not waste your money.

NEGATIVE DAYS:............. 2*8*11*17*20*26*29   August

Sep-2016		Shiva		This is considered a NEUTRAL month for you					Planet: Uranus		

ADVICE & DETAILS

LIFECODE FORECAST: Avoid criticizing anyone or getting yourself involved in any gossip as this may become very damaging to your reputation this month. You may receive news of an older person dying far away or you may visit a sick person in the hospital or a prison. Income may be very low at this time. Do not start any business or project this month as it may be delayed. Admit your fault and apologize if necessary as this may prevent any serious confrontation with others. You may be feeling very sleepy or tired at this time. Rest and relax as much as you can as next month may be very hectic. Most of your money problems will disappear in a few weeks. If you are negative you may experience inner conflicts and worries. It is most important that you attend the temple or any religious functions this month as this will assist you in some of the problems you are experiencing. You may find the solution in those places. If you are positive you may find yourself among spiritual individuals who are very knowledgeable and who may be able to teach you a great deal about religion or spirituality. See an astrologer or Guru if you are having difficulties this month. Accept gracefully when others criticize you. Avoid being hasty or too secretive about your feelings. You may be feeling lonely. If so try to read or study or meditate. Write those letters that you had planned to write last month. Financial gains are low so avoid spending. Listen to religious people and be charitable to those in need of help. You will get into trouble because of gossip or criticism this month.

MONEY	LOVE	CAREER	FAMILY	TRAVEL	WEDDING	MOVE	BUSINESS	HEALTH	Lotto #'s	play 3 #s
Good	Good	Fair	Good	Good	Bad	Good	Bad	Fair	73,39,38,64,14,28,29	552

SHOPPING	GAMBLE	SEX	KEYWORD	KEYWORD			
Bad	Fair	is quiet	DIVINE	Spirituality,Religious,Astrology,Inner Conflicts,Religious ,Sleepiness,Advice given,Alcohol - drugs			

STRESS LEVEL	LUCKY COLORS	JEWELERY	MOONS EFFECT	GRAHA EFFECT	MONTHLY DEITY
Fair	Light Blue/Peach	Tiger's eye/Gold/Silver	Affectionate	God'S Graha	GANGA

MONTHLY PUJA	MONTHLY PSALMS
Chant Shiva Mantras, Take gifts to Ocean - Ganga Puja, Donate to Temple, Priests, etc.	61, 79, 106,

BODY PARTS	DISEASE /sickness	POSSIBLE HEALTH PROBLEMS	MONTHLY EFFECT ON...Emotions
Emotions	Disease of the blood	Heart problems, addiction to drugs and alcohol	Ganga Affects You This Month – Your Beliefs

MANTRA FOR MONTH
Jai Jai Shiva Shambo.(2) ...Mahadeva Shambo (2) 21 times 8

SPECIAL MESSAGE FOR THIS MONTH:
RULES FOR SUCCESS ; Avoid alcohol, drugs and smoking. you must learn to be religious Do Durga pooja Give respect to all women. Marriage is your karmic test. Too much sleep will be a drag in your life. Express your feelings without hurting others. Do not mix business with friendship. Pay respect to all religious people.

NEGATIVE DAYS:.............	2*8*11*17*20*26*29	September

Oct-2016		Shiva		This is considered a POSITIVE month for you					Planet: Jupiter		

ADVICE & DETAILS

LIFECODE FORECAST: Money is the main issue in your life this month. All aspects of your life connected with money may be affected such as your job, your mortgage, your prestige, your income and so on. Love and romance may be expensive but pleasurable if you are positive. Marriage this month may be very profitable to the female partner. You may be tempted to buy yourself that expensive item you have wanted to buy for a long time but never had the money. On the other hand if you have been negative this month may bring delay, disappointment, deception or trickery pertaining to finance. It is a good time to request a promotion from your superiors and also a good time to play the lottery. Try to save some of the money that will come your way this month as you will need it in emergency next month. Real estate opportunities may seem attractive for investment purposes. It is a good time to invest in the stock market, but very little. This is a positive month for money matters and for purchasing that expensive item that is needed. Income should be high now and money will be coming from unusual quarters. If you are negative expect unforeseen expenses this month. Save some of your money for next month as you will need it. Avoid extravagance or over spending.

MONEY	LOVE	CAREER	FAMILY	TRAVEL	WEDDING	MOVE	BUSINESS	HEALTH	Lotto #'s	play 3 #s
Excellent	Good	Excellent	Good	Good	Excellent	Good	Excellent	Excellent	13,52,31,48,27,6,31	985

SHOPPING	GAMBLE	SEX	KEYWORD	KEYWORD			
Excellent	Excellent	is excellent	MONEY	Business,Major Expense,Money - Profits,Income,Investments,Power,Promotion,Fame - TV			

STRESS LEVEL	LUCKY COLORS	JEWELERY	MOONS EFFECT	GRAHA EFFECT	MONTHLY DEITY
Low	Yellow/Silver	Diamonds/Gold/Pearls	Secretive	Money Graha	LAXMI

MONTHLY PUJA	MONTHLY PSALMS
Decorate Land, Feed the poor, Donate milk /products to all, Feed holy guests,	, 35 ,44, 53, 62, 80,

BODY PARTS	DISEASE /sickness	POSSIBLE HEALTH PROBLEMS	MONTHLY EFFECT ON...Intestines
Intestines	Disease of the colon	Constipation problems	Laxmi Affects You This Month – Your Wealth

MANTRA FOR MONTH
Om Hareem Nama Swaha..Shri Maha Laxmi Aye Namah swaha 12 times

SPECIAL MESSAGE FOR THIS MONTH:
RULES FOR SUCCESS ; Avoid spending so much. Control expenses - always keep track. You must have a specific amount consistantly every day, week, or month. Avoid being extravagant unless you can afford it. Play lotto with your head not over it. Do not create debts - avoid credit . Always use cash - you will be more successful.

NEGATIVE DAYS:.............	2*8*11*17*20*26*29	October

Nov-2016	Shiva	This is considered a NEGATIVE month for you	Planet: Saturn

ADVICE & DETAILS

LIFECODE FORECAST: Be careful of accidents, conflict with police officers, negative involvement with the court and worrisome problems from all sides. At all cost you are advised to keep a low profile this month and avoid confrontations with others who are negative. Your income may be low, expenses may be high and money may be short. You may also receive sad news from afar, or news of an illness. Your personal affairs may be delayed and opportunities that may seem great at first may not be attained successfully if started this month. Of course if you are religious and charitable most of these problems may be minimized. Control your temper. Do not speak harshly and avoid conflicts with co-workers. You must go to the temple as much as you can and meditate a great deal as all these will assist you safely through this month. Any activity this month should involve spirituality, or learning. Tension may be very high and sexual feelings may be very strong. If you are having an illicit affair, you must be careful of scandal. The key word is finish. Take care of unfinished business this month. Write your ideas down and keep it for next month. Don't think of changing jobs at this time. You may be prone to accidents or have worrisome problems from all sides. Keep a low profile and avoid confrontations of a negative nature with others. Income will be low and money may be short. There is possible sad news. Delay or deception in personal affairs and opportunities will not be attained successfully. If you are religious most of these problems will be minimized.

MONEY	LOVE	CAREER	FAMILY	TRAVEL	WEDDING	MOVE	BUSINESS	HEALTH	Lotto #'s	play 3 #s
Bad	Bad	Bad	Fair	Bad	Bad	Bad	Bad	Bad	3,32,57,48,36,64,21	799

SHOPPING	GAMBLE	SEX	KEYWORD	KEYWORD						
Bad	Bad	is very bad	KARMA	Destruction,Losses,Death,Sickness - cold,Legal matter,Abusive,Karmic debts,God - Karma						

STRESS LEVEL	LUCKY COLORS	JEWELERY	MOONS EFFECT	GRAHA EFFECT	MONTHLY DEITY
High	Gold/Brown//Green	Saphire/Hessonite	Ivestments	Evil Graha	PITREES

MONTHLY PUJA	MONTHLY PSALMS
Remembrance of family members who died, worship of older people. gifts to grand parents	9, 18, 36 63, 81,

BODY PARTS	DISEASE /sickness	POSSIBLE HEALTH PROBLEMS	MONTHLY EFFECT ON...Circulation
Circulation	Disease all kinds	General health is weak	Pitrees Affects You This Month – Your Problems

MANTRA FOR MONTH
Om Ganga mataye nama swaha Om Varuna Devta aye Pahimam 11 times

SPECIAL MESSAGE FOR THIS MONTH:
RULES FOR SUCCESS ; Become a student of the Universe Respect elder people and authority Follow all government laws and regulations Attend religious functions regularly Read and learn from others Avoid commanding others impulsively Seek advise for religious teachers Follow astrology and occult science Stop denying or doubting when facts are presented to you Avoid suspicion of loved ones Do not help others unless you are in a position to do so. Never! Never! Fight the government Always give to charity Avoid alcohol, drugs and cigarrettes

NEGATIVE DAYS:.............	2*8*11*17*20*26*29	November

Dec-2016	Shiva	This is considered a NEUTRAL month for you	Planet: Sun

ADVICE & DETAILS

LIFECODE FORECAST: You may be feeling quite independent this month and possibly lonely. You may be very busy attending to a lot of your projects, your career or your business. You may find yourself in conflict with others as a result of your becoming too commanding or too dominating. If you are married, tension may arise at the beginning of the month where you may be denied attention from your spouse or lover. Some of your personal projects or dreams may become a reality at this time. Your inventive abilities are extremely high and you may be congratulated or honored by persons in authority. A promotion may come about at your place of employment. Your health may be affected on the 8th or l7th of the month. Quarrels may occur on the 5th, 14th and 23rd of the month. A few opportunities for promotions and advancements in your ambitions may present themselves. Take advantage of these. If you are experiencing negative feelings of loneliness, perform meditative Puja. Concentrate on yourself this month and try to do everything that you have to do on your own without requesting help from others. People will not be as cooperative as you want them to be. You may feel lonely at times. However, any new opportunities presented will make you feel good about yourself. Do not be over-confident or too competitive with others. Do not expect many invitations until next month.

MONEY	LOVE	CAREER	FAMILY	TRAVEL	WEDDING	MOVE	BUSINESS	HEALTH	Lotto #'s	play 3 #s
Fair	Bad	Good	Bad	Fair	Bad	Fair	Fair	Fair	54,35,52,63,69,20,65	780

SHOPPING	GAMBLE	SEX	KEYWORD	KEYWORD						
Fair	Fair	is fair	MIND	Independence,Loneliness,Meditative,Worry,Dominating,Illness - Cold,On Your Own,Commanding						

STRESS LEVEL	LUCKY COLORS	JEWELERY	MOONS EFFECT	GRAHA EFFECT	MONTHLY DEITY
High	White/Yellow/	Pearl/Quartz	Arrogance	Status Graha	GURU

MONTHLY PUJA	MONTHLY PSALMS
Give Gifts to Priests, Invite holy ones to your home, Feed Swamis and Yogis, Do Shiva Puja.	1, 28 ,46, 73,,

BODY PARTS	DISEASE /sickness	POSSIBLE HEALTH PROBLEMS	MONTHLY EFFECT ON...Head
Head	Disease of the head	Nervousness caused by worrying	Guru Affects You This Month – Your Mind

MANTRA FOR MONTH
Om Namo Bhagawate Mukhtanandaya, 108 times

SPECIAL MESSAGE FOR THIS MONTH:
RULES FOR SUCCESS: Do not let your mind idle. Always try to be a leader. Meditate to slow down your mind. Do not be dominating or bossy to others. Only give advise when asked for it... When left alone by partner do not fight - pray instead. Avoid depression moments - meditate when feeling lonely. When accused of anything - rise above it When offered a leadership position at work - accept it

NEGATIVE DAYS:.............	2*8*11*17*20*26*29	December

Section 19
CONTROL THE POSITIVE AND NEGATIVE DAYS IN YOUR LIFE

How to Control the Positive and Negative Days or Months in Your Life

When I know I have a negative day, I do not go to an interview, or I do not take an operation or schedule a surgery. When I go on a date with a lover I do not plan it on a negative day, I would enjoy my romantic moments with my partner on positive days. I pick positive days when I take a trip in my car or travel on an airline. I check the number of the place where I visit and assess the effects of the place on my mind and body. If it is a negative place for me, I would be very careful of what I eat or drink. If I have food to eat, I would pray over my food before eating. At work, I would find out the LifeCode numbers of all the people around me and determine who will work well with me and who will disagree with me. I then will act accordingly with each person in a way that will not bring me in conflict with anyone there.

LOVE & MARRIAGE

If it is a negative day for your lover then wait for another day to discuss anything important. If it is a positive day and your lover wants to spend some time with you then accept the invitations. You will feel like a miserable dog on negative days, avoid getting angry that day, accept all insults or criticism without protest…you will have your day for that. Avoid excessive sexual contact on negative days. Once is enough. If you fail on a negative day, do not worry, you will do better in a positive day.

HEALTH & FOOD

On negative days, you will feel low energy, you will feel like you want to stay home and sleep, you will feel like others do not care for you, and you can feel depressed and lazy. Listen to some music or nice chants. If you are feeling any pain try to do something natural, as going to the doctor is not a good idea. Watch what you eat as you could get indigestion, or diarrhea or fevers. Resting is always a good idea. Do not complain about your negative feelings, tell God instead. Do not do anything without knowing how it is going to help you. On negative days, avoid anything acidic. On positive days, avoid too much sugar as the body is in low metabolism.

WEALTH & MONEY

On negative days, you will receive credit calls, they may ask you to pay a bill or you will have to lend money to others. Do not address it at this time; try to address those problems on the next day, as the whole energy will change. Do not get angry. On Positive days, investments, business, any purchases will be good. Do not buy any equipment on negative days it will break.

JOB & CAREER

Your boss and other co-workers will test you on negative days. Ignore their comments and wait for another day. Remember: "every dog has its day" and you will have your opportunities on positive days. On negative days, the boss will give you more work, do not protest, accept it with great heart; this will reward you with good karma on positive days.

TRAVEL & DRIVING

Do not plan your travels on negative days, as this will create delays, baggage problems and lost or stolen articles. You will be much happier travelling on positive days. Driving on negative days can cause accidents; you have to be more cautious, say your prayers before going. On positive days, you do not have to worry. If you are planning a vacation, do it in a positive month, as it will not be a real vacation on a negative month. If someone is visiting you and they arrive at your home on a negative day for you, prepare for some conflicts. You will not feel relieved until they are gone.

MEDITATION & PRAYER

On negative days, your mind will not be able to focus. Doubts and disbelief will constantly plague your mind about God. You will have doubts about your life, your goals, and your relationships. Pray, meditate, get your thoughts together and wait for positive day. Avoid excessive exercises or strenuous yoga practices on negative days. The best way to avoid mental nervousness and tension on negative is to chant soothing meditation mantras such as "KALI DURGE NAMO NAMA". While sitting in the meditative position, think about all the things that make you angry and solve it in your mind. Do not try to clear you mind, you will get frustrated. Do longer meditation on negative days and shorter meditations on Positive days.

Now you ask the question as how I know my positive and negative days, good year, bad year, or a negative or neutral month to expect. This is the knowledge I will present in this book. Planning your life successfully does not require you to battle uselessly with the universe, but to work with the universe. Equation of life offers you the opportunity to do so with such a joy and enthusiasm that is limitless and ecstatic in its rewards and glory.

Friday, January 1, 2016 — This is considered a POSITIVE day for you — Planet: Jupiter

ADVICE & DETAILS

If you can, take short trips and enjoy high pleasure. There will be lots of moving today.

MANTRA FOR TODAY

Om Hareem Nama Swaha..Shri Maha Laxmi Aye Namah swaha 12 times

MONEY	LOVE	CAREER	FAMILY	TRAVEL	WEDDING	MOVE	BUSINESS	HEALTH	Lotto #'s	play 3 #s
Excellent	Good	Excellent	Good	Good	Excellent	Good	Excellent	Excellent	11,68,7,54,45,33,70	956

SHOPPING	GAMBLE	SEX	KEYWORD	KEYWORD						
Excellent	Excellent	is excellent	MONEY	Business,Major Expense,Money - Profits,Income,Investments,Power,Promotion,Fame - TV						

STRESS LEVEL	LUCKY COLORS	JEWELERY	MOONS EFFECT	GRAHA EFFECT	DAILY DEITY
Low	Yellow/Silver	Diamonds/Gold/Pearls	Secretive	Money Graha	Mahalaxmi

DAILY PUJA
Decorate Land, Feed the poor, Donate milk /products to all, Feed holy guests,

DAILY PSALMS
8, 17, 35 ,44, 53, 62, 80, 107, 125

Saturday, January 2, 2016 — This is considered a NEGATIVE day for you — Planet: Saturn

ADVICE & DETAILS

Connect with the God within today so you can avoid the loneliness that can result from being boastful and criticizing others. Look at yourself first instead of trying to fix others.

MANTRA FOR TODAY

Om Ganga mataye nama swaha Om Varuna Devta aye Pahimam 11 times

MONEY	LOVE	CAREER	FAMILY	TRAVEL	WEDDING	MOVE	BUSINESS	HEALTH	Lotto #'s	play 3 #s
Bad	Bad	Bad	Fair	Bad	Bad	Bad	Bad	Bad	74,51,68,41,66,17,50	987

SHOPPING	GAMBLE	SEX	KEYWORD	KEYWORD						
Bad	Bad	is very bad	KARMA	Destruction,Losses,Death,Sickness - cold,Legal matter,Abusive,Karmic debts,God - Karma						

STRESS LEVEL	LUCKY COLORS	JEWELERY	MOONS EFFECT	GRAHA EFFECT	DAILY DEITY
High	Gold/Brown//Green	Saphire/Hessonite	Ivestments	Evil Graha	Agnidev

DAILY PUJA
Remembrance of family members who died, worship of older people. gifts to grand parents

DAILY PSALMS
9, 18, 36 ,45, 54, 63, 81, 108, 126

Sunday, January 3, 2016 — This is considered a NEUTRAL day for you — Planet: Sun

ADVICE & DETAILS

Today, you may be home alone, you may feel a bit confined, but at the same time you will have a sense of independence and the realization of your capabilities. This day may be influenced by dealings with the government, courts or legal institutions.

MANTRA FOR TODAY

Om Namo Bhagawate Mukhtanandaya, 108 times

MONEY	LOVE	CAREER	FAMILY	TRAVEL	WEDDING	MOVE	BUSINESS	HEALTH	Lotto #'s	play 3 #s
Fair	Bad	Good	Bad	Fair	Bad	Fair	Fair	Fair	73,1,17,28,42,8,60	304

SHOPPING	GAMBLE	SEX	KEYWORD	KEYWORD						
Fair	Fair	is fair	MIND	Independence,Loneliness,Meditative,Worry,Dominating,Illness - Cold,On Your Own,Commanding						

STRESS LEVEL	LUCKY COLORS	JEWELERY	MOONS EFFECT	GRAHA EFFECT	DAILY DEITY
High	White/Yellow/	Pearl/Quartz	Arrogance	Status Graha	Saraswaty

DAILY PUJA
Give Gifts to Priests, Invite holy ones to your home, Feed Swamis and Yogis, Do Shiva Puja.

DAILY PSALMS
1, 10, 28 ,37, 46, 55, 73, 100, 118

Monday, January 4, 2016 — This is considered a POSITIVE day for you — Planet: Moon

ADVICE & DETAILS

There will be opportunity for romantic dates or encounters. You will make money today and get profits. There is a good chance of promotion.

MANTRA FOR TODAY

Kali Durge Namo Nama Om Durge aye nama swaha 108 times

MONEY	LOVE	CAREER	FAMILY	TRAVEL	WEDDING	MOVE	BUSINESS	HEALTH	Lotto #'s	play 3 #s
Good	Excellent	Good	Good	Excellent	Good	Good	Good	Good	25,4,3,63,7,48,20	68

SHOPPING	GAMBLE	SEX	KEYWORD	KEYWORD						
Good	Good	is good	LOVE	Romance,Popularity,Visitors,Shopping,Food, Drinks,Co-operation,Friendships,Affection						

STRESS LEVEL	LUCKY COLORS	JEWELERY	MOONS EFFECT	GRAHA EFFECT	DAILY DEITY
Low	Red/Yellow/Pink	Topaz/Diamonds	Conservative	Love Graha	Gauri

DAILY PUJA
Give Gifts to females andnMother, Serve milk Products, Worship Durga forms

DAILY PSALMS
2, 11, 29 ,38, 47, 56, 74, 101, 119

Tuesday, January 5, 2016 — This is considered a POSITIVE day for you — Planet: Mercury

ADVICE & DETAILS

This is slow and lazy day, but for your karma you are advised to work and to be industrious. Your accomplishments today will be important for your personal growth.

MANTRA FOR TODAY

Om hareem Kleem Hreem Aem Saraswataye namaha 21 times

MONEY	LOVE	CAREER	FAMILY	TRAVEL	WEDDING	MOVE	BUSINESS	HEALTH	Lotto #'s	play 3 #s
Good	Fair	Good	Good	Excellent	Good	Good	Good	Excellent	1,66,34,31,63,70,11	286

SHOPPING	GAMBLE	SEX	KEYWORD	KEYWORD						
Good	Good	is great	SOCIAL	Children,Education,Astrology,Bargains,Social Functions,Childishness,Groups - Parties,Teacher						

STRESS LEVEL	LUCKY COLORS	JEWELERY	MOONS EFFECT	GRAHA EFFECT	DAILY DEITY
Low	Green/Sky Blue/	Diamonds/Silver	Enthusiastic	Social Graha	Vishnu

DAILY PUJA	DAILY PSALMS
Wash the feet of Children, Do Satnarayan Pooja, Read & chant Geeta	3, 12, 30 ,39, 48, 57, 75, 102, 120

Wednesday, January 6, 2016 — This is considered a NEGATIVE day for you — Planet: Pluto

ADVICE & DETAILS

If you can, take short trips and enjoy high pleasure. There will be lots of moving today.

MANTRA FOR TODAY

Om Jai Viganeshwaraya.. Lambodaraya Namo Namaha 21 times

MONEY	LOVE	CAREER	FAMILY	TRAVEL	WEDDING	MOVE	BUSINESS	HEALTH	Lotto #'s	play 3 #s
Bad	Fair	Bad	Fair	Bad	Good	Bad	Bad	Bad	70,35,75,68,16,21,24	805

SHOPPING	GAMBLE	SEX	KEYWORD	KEYWORD						
Bad	Bad	is tough	CAREER	Career,Hard Work,Co-workers,Low Payment,Job Problems,High Temper,Low Pay,Laziness						

STRESS LEVEL	LUCKY COLORS	JEWELERY	MOONS EFFECT	GRAHA EFFECT	DAILY DEITY
High	Dark Blue/ Purple/	Amethyst/Gold	Emotional	Job Graha	Lingam

DAILY PUJA	DAILY PSALMS
Worship Ganesh, Give gifts to father, and co -workers, Plant gardens, farms	4, 13, 31 ,40, 49, 58, 76, 103, 121

Thursday, January 7, 2016 — This is considered a POSITIVE day for you — Planet: Venus

ADVICE & DETAILS

Today is a positive day to spend with others. You will be surrounded by partners, friends, associates and teachers. The exchange is beneficial, even if it is not what you expect.

MANTRA FOR TODAY

Om Graam Greem Graum Sa Gurave namah swaha 21 times

MONEY	LOVE	CAREER	FAMILY	TRAVEL	WEDDING	MOVE	BUSINESS	HEALTH	Lotto #'s	play 3 #s
Bad	Excellent	Fair	Good	Excellent	Good	Excellent	Good	Excellent	37,3,40,58,57,41,2	619

SHOPPING	GAMBLE	SEX	KEYWORD	KEYWORD						
Good	Good	is good	CHANGE	Sexuality,Travel,Change,Distant, far,Travel delays,Deception,Excercise,Illicit Affairs						

STRESS LEVEL	LUCKY COLORS	JEWELERY	MOONS EFFECT	GRAHA EFFECT	DAILY DEITY
Fair	Tan/Green/ Beige	Pearl/Silver/quartz	Courageous	Travel Graha	Nataraja

DAILY PUJA	DAILY PSALMS
Artistic gifts, Pray to Krishna, Do good deeds, do Spiritual trips	5, 14, 32 ,41, 50, 59, 77, 104, 122

Friday, January 8, 2016 — This is considered a NEGATIVE day for you — Planet: Mars

ADVICE & DETAILS

You will feel in command of everything today, be careful not to be too bossy and to be careful with your expression. It is a good day for creative endeavors such as publishing or writing. You will have an opportunity to work or be in groups or to be invited to parties.

MANTRA FOR TODAY

Om Mana Swasti Shanti Kuru kuru Swaha Shivoham Shivoham 27 times

MONEY	LOVE	CAREER	FAMILY	TRAVEL	WEDDING	MOVE	BUSINESS	HEALTH	Lotto #'s	play 3 #s
Bad	Bad	Bad	Bad	Bad	Bad	Bad	Fair	Bad	37,65,16,49,41,2,12	27

SHOPPING	GAMBLE	SEX	KEYWORD	KEYWORD						
Fair	Bad	is frustrating	POWER	Responsibilty,Disagreement,Family,Back Pain,Family Conflicts,Traffic Ticket,Quarrels,Jealousy						

STRESS LEVEL	LUCKY COLORS	JEWELERY	MOONS EFFECT	GRAHA EFFECT	DAILY DEITY
High	Purple/Blue/Rose	Emerald/Saphire	Educational	Family Graha	Mahakali

DAILY PUJA	DAILY PSALMS
Meditate, Control temper, Pray to Hanuman, Chant Hanuman Chalisa	6, 15, 33 ,42, 51, 60, 78, 105, 123

Saturday, January 9, 2016 — This is considered a NEUTRAL day for you — Planet: Uranus

ADVICE & DETAILS

This is a day for expressing yourself in oral, visual or written form. Talk to others possibly in a group or at a gathering, paint or write a poem, book or article. This is also a day that if you are negative the use of alcohol or drugs will create danger for you, try to avoid it.

MANTRA FOR TODAY

Jai Jai Shiva Shambo.(2) ...Mahadeva Shambo (2) 21 times 8

MONEY	LOVE	CAREER	FAMILY	TRAVEL	WEDDING	MOVE	BUSINESS	HEALTH	Lotto #'s	play 3 #s
Good	Good	Fair	Good	Good	Bad	Good	Bad	Fair	71,62,67,60,8,8,21	697

SHOPPING	GAMBLE	SEX	KEYWORD	KEYWORD				
Bad	Fair	is quiet	DIVINE	Spirituality,Religious,Astrology,Inner Conflicts,Religious ,Sleepiness,Advice given,Alcohol - drugs				

STRESS LEVEL	LUCKY COLORS	JEWELERY	MOONS EFFECT	GRAHA EFFECT	DAILY DEITY
Fair	Light Blue/Peach	Tiger's eye/Gold/Silver	Affectionate	God'S Graha	Shesnaag

DAILY PUJA
Chant Shiva Mantras, Take gifts to Ocean - Ganga Puja, Donate to Temple, Priests, etc.

DAILY PSALMS
7, 16, 34 ,43, 52, 61, 79, 106, 124

Sunday, January 10, 2016 — This is considered a POSITIVE day for you — Planet: Jupiter

ADVICE & DETAILS

If you can, take short trips and enjoy high pleasure. There will be lots of moving today.

MANTRA FOR TODAY

Om Hareem Nama Swaha..Shri Maha Laxmi Aye Namah swaha 12 times

MONEY	LOVE	CAREER	FAMILY	TRAVEL	WEDDING	MOVE	BUSINESS	HEALTH	Lotto #'s	play 3 #s
Excellent	Good	Excellent	Good	Good	Excellent	Good	Excellent	Excellent	47,69,8,9,54,29,66	761

SHOPPING	GAMBLE	SEX	KEYWORD	KEYWORD				
Excellent	Excellent	is excellent	MONEY	Business,Major Expense,Money - Profits,Income,Investments,Power,Promotion,Fame - TV				

STRESS LEVEL	LUCKY COLORS	JEWELERY	MOONS EFFECT	GRAHA EFFECT	DAILY DEITY
Low	Yellow/Silver	Diamonds/Gold/Pearls	Secretive	Money Graha	Mahalaxmi

DAILY PUJA
Decorate Land, Feed the poor, Donate milk /products to all, Feed holy guests,

DAILY PSALMS
8, 17, 35 ,44, 53, 62, 80, 107, 125

Monday, January 11, 2016 — This is considered a NEGATIVE day for you — Planet: Saturn

ADVICE & DETAILS

Connect with the God within today so you can avoid the loneliness that can result from being boastful and criticizing others. Look at yourself first instead of trying to fix others.

MANTRA FOR TODAY

Om Ganga mataye nama swaha Om Varuna Devta aye Pahimam 11 times

MONEY	LOVE	CAREER	FAMILY	TRAVEL	WEDDING	MOVE	BUSINESS	HEALTH	Lotto #'s	play 3 #s
Bad	Bad	Bad	Fair	Bad	Bad	Bad	Bad	Bad	44,39,58,3,11,24,26	285

SHOPPING	GAMBLE	SEX	KEYWORD	KEYWORD				
Bad	Bad	is very bad	KARMA	Destruction,Losses,Death,Sickness - cold,Legal matter,Abusive,Karmic debts,God - Karma				

STRESS LEVEL	LUCKY COLORS	JEWELERY	MOONS EFFECT	GRAHA EFFECT	DAILY DEITY
High	Gold/Brown//Green	Saphire/Hessonite	Ivestments	Evil Graha	Agnidev

DAILY PUJA
Remembrance of family members who died, worship of older people. gifts to grand parents

DAILY PSALMS
9, 18, 36 ,45, 54, 63, 81, 108, 126

Tuesday, January 12, 2016 — This is considered a NEUTRAL day for you — Planet: Sun

ADVICE & DETAILS

Today, you may be home alone, you may feel a bit confined, but at the same time you will have a sense of independence and the realization of your capabilities. This day may be influenced by dealings with the government, courts or legal institutions.

MANTRA FOR TODAY

Om Namo Bhagawate Mukhtanandaya, 108 times

MONEY	LOVE	CAREER	FAMILY	TRAVEL	WEDDING	MOVE	BUSINESS	HEALTH	Lotto #'s	play 3 #s
Fair	Bad	Good	Bad	Fair	Bad	Fair	Fair	Fair	12,74,16,41,41,27,62	244

SHOPPING	GAMBLE	SEX	KEYWORD	KEYWORD				
Fair	Fair	is fair	MIND	Independence,Loneliness,Meditative,Worry,Dominating,Illness - Cold,On Your Own,Commanding				

STRESS LEVEL	LUCKY COLORS	JEWELERY	MOONS EFFECT	GRAHA EFFECT	DAILY DEITY
High	White/Yellow/	Pearl/Quartz	Arrogance	Status Graha	Saraswaty

DAILY PUJA
Give Gifts to Priests, Invite holy ones to your home, Feed Swamis and Yogis, Do Shiva Puja.

DAILY PSALMS
1, 10, 28 ,37, 46, 55, 73, 100, 118

Wednesday, January 13, 2016 | This is considered a POSITIVE day for you | Planet: Moon

ADVICE & DETAILS	MANTRA FOR TODAY
There will be opportunity for romantic dates or encounters. You will make money today and get profits. There is a good chance of promotion.	Kali Durge Namo Nama Om Durge aye nama swaha 108 times

MONEY	LOVE	CAREER	FAMILY	TRAVEL	WEDDING	MOVE	BUSINESS	HEALTH	Lotto #'s	play 3 #s
Good	Excellent	Good	Good	Excellent	Good	Good	Good	Good	40,59,53,20,12,47,45	140

SHOPPING	GAMBLE	SEX	KEYWORD	KEYWORD						
Good	Good	is good	LOVE	Romance,Popularity,Visitors,Shopping,Food, Drinks,Co-operation,Friendships,Affection						

STRESS LEVEL		LUCKY COLORS	JEWELERY	MOONS EFFECT	GRAHA EFFECT	DAILY DEITY
Low		Red/Yellow/Pink	Topaz/Diamonds	Conservative	Love Graha	Gauri

DAILY PUJA	DAILY PSALMS
Give Gifts to females andnMother, Serve milk Products, Worship Durga forms	2, 11, 29 ,38, 47, 56, 74, 101, 119

Thursday, January 14, 2016 | This is considered a POSITIVE day for you | Planet: Mercury

ADVICE & DETAILS	MANTRA FOR TODAY
This is slow and lazy day, but for your karma you are advised to work and to be industrious. Your accomplishments today will be important for your personal growth.	Om hareem Kleem Hreem Aem Saraswataye namaha 21 times

MONEY	LOVE	CAREER	FAMILY	TRAVEL	WEDDING	MOVE	BUSINESS	HEALTH	Lotto #'s	play 3 #s
Good	Fair	Good	Good	Excellent	Good	Good	Good	Excellent	18,22,54,56,6,15,51	465

SHOPPING	GAMBLE	SEX	KEYWORD	KEYWORD						
Good	Good	is great	SOCIAL	Children,Education,Astrology,Bargains,Social Functions,Childishness,Groups - Parties,Teacher						

STRESS LEVEL		LUCKY COLORS	JEWELERY	MOONS EFFECT	GRAHA EFFECT	DAILY DEITY
Low		Green/Sky Blue/	Diamonds/Silver	Enthusiastic	Social Graha	Vishnu

DAILY PUJA	DAILY PSALMS
Wash the feet of Children, Do Satnarayan Pooja, Read & chant Geeta	3, 12, 30 ,39, 48, 57, 75, 102, 120

Friday, January 15, 2016 | This is considered a NEGATIVE day for you | Planet: Pluto

ADVICE & DETAILS	MANTRA FOR TODAY
If you can, take short trips and enjoy high pleasure. There will be lots of moving today.	Om Jai Viganeshwaraya.. Lambodaraya Namo Namaha 21 times

MONEY	LOVE	CAREER	FAMILY	TRAVEL	WEDDING	MOVE	BUSINESS	HEALTH	Lotto #'s	play 3 #s
Bad	Fair	Bad	Fair	Bad	Good	Bad	Bad	Bad	8,69,47,29,42,40,45	700

SHOPPING	GAMBLE	SEX	KEYWORD	KEYWORD						
Bad	Bad	is tough	CAREER	Career,Hard Work,Co-workers,Low Payment,Job Problems,High Temper,Low Pay,Laziness						

STRESS LEVEL		LUCKY COLORS	JEWELERY	MOONS EFFECT	GRAHA EFFECT	DAILY DEITY
High		Dark Blue/ Purple/	Amethyst/Gold	Emotional	Job Graha	Lingam

DAILY PUJA	DAILY PSALMS
Worship Ganesh, Give gifts to father, and co -workers, Plant gardens, farms	4, 13, 31 ,40, 49, 58, 76, 103, 121

Saturday, January 16, 2016 | This is considered a POSITIVE day for you | Planet: Venus

ADVICE & DETAILS	MANTRA FOR TODAY
Today is a positive day to spend with others. You will be surrounded by partners, friends, associates and teachers. The exchange is beneficial, even if it is not what you expect.	Om Graam Greem Graum Sa Gurave namah swaha 21 times

MONEY	LOVE	CAREER	FAMILY	TRAVEL	WEDDING	MOVE	BUSINESS	HEALTH	Lotto #'s	play 3 #s
Bad	Excellent	Fair	Good	Excellent	Good	Excellent	Good	Excellent	74,22,44,55,25,27,58	884

SHOPPING	GAMBLE	SEX	KEYWORD	KEYWORD						
Good	Good	is good	CHANGE	Sexuality,Travel,Change,Distant, far,Travel delays,Deception,Excercise,Illicit Affairs						

STRESS LEVEL		LUCKY COLORS	JEWELERY	MOONS EFFECT	GRAHA EFFECT	DAILY DEITY
Fair		Tan/Green/ Beige	Pearl/Silver/quartz	Courageous	Travel Graha	Nataraja

DAILY PUJA	DAILY PSALMS
Artistic gifts, Pray to Krishna, Do good deeds, do Spiritual trips	5, 14, 32 ,41, 50, 59, 77, 104, 122

Sunday, January 17, 2016 — This is considered a NEGATIVE day for you — Planet: Mars

ADVICE & DETAILS

You will feel in command of everything today, be careful not to be too bossy and to be careful with your expression. It is a good day for creative endeavors such as publishing or writing. You will have an opportunity to work or be in groups or to be invited to parties.

MANTRA FOR TODAY

Om Mana Swasti Shanti Kuru kuru Swaha Shivoham Shivoham 27 times

MONEY	LOVE	CAREER	FAMILY	TRAVEL	WEDDING	MOVE	BUSINESS	HEALTH	Lotto #'s	play 3 #s
Bad	Bad	Bad	Bad	Bad	Bad	Bad	Fair	Bad	61,44,57,73,65,18,68	21

SHOPPING	GAMBLE	SEX	KEYWORD	KEYWORD						
Fair	Bad	is frustrating	POWER	Responsibilty,Disagreement,Family,Back Pain,Family Conflicts,Traffic Ticket,Quarrels,Jealousy						

STRESS LEVEL		LUCKY COLORS		JEWELERY		MOONS EFFECT		GRAHA EFFECT		DAILY DEITY
High		Purple/Blue/Rose		Emerald/Saphire		Educational		Family Graha		Mahakali

DAILY PUJA
Meditate, Control temper, Pray to Hanuman, Chant Hanuman Chalisa

DAILY PSALMS
6, 15, 33 ,42, 51, 60, 78, 105, 123

Monday, January 18, 2016 — This is considered a NEUTRAL day for you — Planet: Uranus

ADVICE & DETAILS

This is a day for expressing yourself in oral, visual or written form. Talk to others possibly in a group or at a gathering, paint or write a poem, book or article. This is also a day that if you are negative the use of alcohol or drugs will create danger for you, try to avoid it.

MANTRA FOR TODAY

Jai Jai Shiva Shambo.(2) ...Mahadeva Shambo (2) 21 times 8

MONEY	LOVE	CAREER	FAMILY	TRAVEL	WEDDING	MOVE	BUSINESS	HEALTH	Lotto #'s	play 3 #s
Good	Good	Fair	Good	Good	Bad	Good	Bad	Fair	41,7,25,38,8,56,14	471

SHOPPING	GAMBLE	SEX	KEYWORD	KEYWORD						
Bad	Fair	is quiet	DIVINE	Spirituality,Religious,Astrology,Inner Conflicts,Religious ,Sleepiness,Advice given,Alcohol - drugs						

STRESS LEVEL		LUCKY COLORS		JEWELERY		MOONS EFFECT		GRAHA EFFECT		DAILY DEITY
Fair		Light Blue/Peach		Tiger's eye/Gold/Silver		Affectionate		God'S Graha		Shesnaag

DAILY PUJA
Chant Shiva Mantras, Take gifts to Ocean - Ganga Puja, Donate to Temple, Priests, etc.

DAILY PSALMS
7, 16, 34 ,43, 52, 61, 79, 106, 124

Tuesday, January 19, 2016 — This is considered a POSITIVE day for you — Planet: Jupiter

ADVICE & DETAILS

If you can, take short trips and enjoy high pleasure. There will be lots of moving today.

MANTRA FOR TODAY

Om Hareem Nama Swaha..Shri Maha Laxmi Aye Namah swaha 12 times

MONEY	LOVE	CAREER	FAMILY	TRAVEL	WEDDING	MOVE	BUSINESS	HEALTH	Lotto #'s	play 3 #s
Excellent	Good	Excellent	Good	Good	Excellent	Good	Excellent	Excellent	71,35,36,62,62,51,72	334

SHOPPING	GAMBLE	SEX	KEYWORD	KEYWORD						
Excellent	Excellent	is excellent	MONEY	Business,Major Expense,Money - Profits,Income,Investments,Power,Promotion,Fame - TV						

STRESS LEVEL		LUCKY COLORS		JEWELERY		MOONS EFFECT		GRAHA EFFECT		DAILY DEITY
Low		Yellow/Silver		Diamonds/Gold/Pearls		Secretive		Money Graha		Mahalaxmi

DAILY PUJA
Decorate Land, Feed the poor, Donate milk /products to all, Feed holy guests,

DAILY PSALMS
8, 17, 35 ,44, 53, 62, 80, 107, 125

Wednesday, January 20, 2016 — This is considered a NEGATIVE day for you — Planet: Saturn

ADVICE & DETAILS

Connect with the God within today so you can avoid the loneliness that can result from being boastful and criticizing others. Look at yourself first instead of trying to fix others.

MANTRA FOR TODAY

Om Ganga mataye nama swaha Om Varuna Devta aye Pahimam 11 times

MONEY	LOVE	CAREER	FAMILY	TRAVEL	WEDDING	MOVE	BUSINESS	HEALTH	Lotto #'s	play 3 #s
Bad	Bad	Bad	Fair	Bad	Bad	Bad	Bad	Bad	75,73,31,7,20,16,10	694

SHOPPING	GAMBLE	SEX	KEYWORD	KEYWORD						
Bad	Bad	is very bad	KARMA	Destruction,Losses,Death,Sickness - cold,Legal matter,Abusive,Karmic debts,God - Karma						

STRESS LEVEL		LUCKY COLORS		JEWELERY		MOONS EFFECT		GRAHA EFFECT		DAILY DEITY
High		Gold/Brown//Green		Saphire/Hessonite		Ivestments		Evil Graha		Agnidev

DAILY PUJA
Remembrance of family members who died, worship of older people. gifts to grand parents

DAILY PSALMS
9, 18, 36 ,45, 54, 63, 81, 108, 126

Thursday, January 21, 2016 — This is considered a NEUTRAL day for you — Planet: Sun

ADVICE & DETAILS

Today, you may be home alone, you may feel a bit confined, but at the same time you will have a sense of independence and the realization of your capabilities. This day may be influenced by dealings with the government, courts or legal institutions.

MANTRA FOR TODAY

Om Namo Bhagawate Mukhtanandaya, 108 times

MONEY	LOVE	CAREER	FAMILY	TRAVEL	WEDDING	MOVE	BUSINESS	HEALTH	Lotto #'s	play 3 #s
Fair	Bad	Good	Bad	Fair	Bad	Fair	Fair	Fair	18,8,39,46,7,52,68	686

SHOPPING	GAMBLE	SEX	KEYWORD	KEYWORD
Fair	Fair	is fair	MIND	Independence,Loneliness,Meditative,Worry,Dominating,Illness - Cold,On Your Own,Commanding

STRESS LEVEL	LUCKY COLORS	JEWELERY	MOONS EFFECT	GRAHA EFFECT	DAILY DEITY
High	White/Yellow/	Pearl/Quartz	Arrogance	Status Graha	Saraswaty

DAILY PUJA
Give Gifts to Priests, Invite holy ones to your home, Feed Swamis and Yogis, Do Shiva Puja.

DAILY PSALMS
1, 10, 28 ,37, 46, 55, 73, 100, 118

Friday, January 22, 2016 — This is considered a POSITIVE day for you — Planet: Moon

ADVICE & DETAILS

There will be opportunity for romantic dates or encounters. You will make money today and get profits. There is a good chance of promotion.

MANTRA FOR TODAY

Kali Durge Namo Nama Om Durge aye nama swaha 108 times

MONEY	LOVE	CAREER	FAMILY	TRAVEL	WEDDING	MOVE	BUSINESS	HEALTH	Lotto #'s	play 3 #s
Good	Excellent	Good	Good	Excellent	Good	Good	Good	Good	70,15,49,32,5,55,50	780

SHOPPING	GAMBLE	SEX	KEYWORD	KEYWORD
Good	Good	is good	LOVE	Romance,Popularity,Visitors,Shopping,Food, Drinks,Co-operation,Friendships,Affection

STRESS LEVEL	LUCKY COLORS	JEWELERY	MOONS EFFECT	GRAHA EFFECT	DAILY DEITY
Low	Red/Yellow/Pink	Topaz/Diamonds	Conservative	Love Graha	Gauri

DAILY PUJA
Give Gifts to females andnMother, Serve milk Products, Worship Durga forms

DAILY PSALMS
2, 11, 29 ,38, 47, 56, 74, 101, 119

Saturday, January 23, 2016 — This is considered a POSITIVE day for you — Planet: Mercury

ADVICE & DETAILS

This is slow and lazy day, but for your karma you are advised to work and to be industrious. Your accomplishments today will be important for your personal growth.

MANTRA FOR TODAY

Om hareem Kleem Hreem Aem Saraswataye namaha 21 times

MONEY	LOVE	CAREER	FAMILY	TRAVEL	WEDDING	MOVE	BUSINESS	HEALTH	Lotto #'s	play 3 #s
Good	Fair	Good	Good	Excellent	Good	Good	Good	Excellent	74,47,59,12,67,19,13	935

SHOPPING	GAMBLE	SEX	KEYWORD	KEYWORD
Good	Good	is great	SOCIAL	Children,Education,Astrology,Bargains,Social Functions,Childishness,Groups - Parties,Teacher

STRESS LEVEL	LUCKY COLORS	JEWELERY	MOONS EFFECT	GRAHA EFFECT	DAILY DEITY
Low	Green/Sky Blue/	Diamonds/Silver	Enthusiastic	Social Graha	Vishnu

DAILY PUJA
Wash the feet of Children, Do Satnarayan Pooja, Read & chant Geeta

DAILY PSALMS
3, 12, 30 ,39, 48, 57, 75, 102, 120

Sunday, January 24, 2016 — This is considered a NEGATIVE day for you — Planet: Pluto

ADVICE & DETAILS

If you can, take short trips and enjoy high pleasure. There will be lots of moving today.

MANTRA FOR TODAY

Om Jai Viganeshwaraya.. Lambodaraya Namo Namaha 21 times

MONEY	LOVE	CAREER	FAMILY	TRAVEL	WEDDING	MOVE	BUSINESS	HEALTH	Lotto #'s	play 3 #s
Bad	Fair	Bad	Fair	Bad	Good	Bad	Bad	Bad	56,62,70,73,6,17,31	813

SHOPPING	GAMBLE	SEX	KEYWORD	KEYWORD
Bad	Bad	is tough	CAREER	Career,Hard Work,Co-workers,Low Payment,Job Problems,High Temper,Low Pay,Laziness

STRESS LEVEL	LUCKY COLORS	JEWELERY	MOONS EFFECT	GRAHA EFFECT	DAILY DEITY
High	Dark Blue/ Purple/	Amethyst/Gold	Emotional	Job Graha	Lingam

DAILY PUJA
Worship Ganesh, Give gifts to father, and co -workers, Plant gardens, farms

DAILY PSALMS
4, 13, 31 ,40, 49, 58, 76, 103, 121

Monday, January 25, 2016 — This is considered a POSITIVE day for you — Planet: Venus

ADVICE & DETAILS

Today is a positive day to spend with others. You will be surrounded by partners, friends, associates and teachers. The exchange is beneficial, even if it is not what you expect.

MANTRA FOR TODAY

Om Graam Greem Graum Sa Gurave namah swaha 21 times

MONEY	LOVE	CAREER	FAMILY	TRAVEL	WEDDING	MOVE	BUSINESS	HEALTH	Lotto #'s	play 3 #s
Bad	Excellent	Fair	Good	Excellent	Good	Excellent	Good	Excellent	32,71,67,8,26,25,39	359

SHOPPING	GAMBLE	SEX	KEYWORD	KEYWORD						
Good	Good	is good	CHANGE	Sexuality,Travel,Change,Distant, far,Travel delays,Deception,Excercise,Illicit Affairs						

STRESS LEVEL	LUCKY COLORS	JEWELERY	MOONS EFFECT	GRAHA EFFECT	DAILY DEITY
Fair	Tan/Green/ Beige	Pearl/Silver/quartz	Courageous	Travel Graha	Nataraja

DAILY PUJA
Artistic gifts, Pray to Krishna, Do good deeds, do Spiritual trips

DAILY PSALMS
5, 14, 32 ,41, 50, 59, 77, 104, 122

Tuesday, January 26, 2016 — This is considered a NEGATIVE day for you — Planet: Mars

ADVICE & DETAILS

You will feel in command of everything today, be careful not to be too bossy and to be careful with your expression. It is a good day for creative endeavors such as publishing or writing. You will have an opportunity to work or be in groups or to be invited to parties.

MANTRA FOR TODAY

Om Mana Swasti Shanti Kuru kuru Swaha Shivoham Shivoham 27 times

MONEY	LOVE	CAREER	FAMILY	TRAVEL	WEDDING	MOVE	BUSINESS	HEALTH	Lotto #'s	play 3 #s
Bad	Bad	Bad	Bad	Bad	Bad	Bad	Fair	Bad	34,64,9,34,56,53,38	505

SHOPPING	GAMBLE	SEX	KEYWORD	KEYWORD						
Fair	Bad	is frustrating	POWER	Responsibilty,Disagreement,Family,Back Pain,Family Conflicts,Traffic Ticket,Quarrels,Jealousy						

STRESS LEVEL	LUCKY COLORS	JEWELERY	MOONS EFFECT	GRAHA EFFECT	DAILY DEITY
High	Purple/Blue/Rose	Emerald/Saphire	Educational	Family Graha	Mahakali

DAILY PUJA
Meditate, Control temper, Pray to Hanuman, Chant Hanuman Chalisa

DAILY PSALMS
6, 15, 33 ,42, 51, 60, 78, 105, 123

Wednesday, January 27, 2016 — This is considered a NEUTRAL day for you — Planet: Uranus

ADVICE & DETAILS

This is a day for expressing yourself in oral, visual or written form. Talk to others possibly in a group or at a gathering, paint or write a poem, book or article. This is also a day that if you are negative the use of alcohol or drugs will create danger for you, try to avoid it.

MANTRA FOR TODAY

Jai Jai Shiva Shambo.(2) ...Mahadeva Shambo (2) 21 times 8

MONEY	LOVE	CAREER	FAMILY	TRAVEL	WEDDING	MOVE	BUSINESS	HEALTH	Lotto #'s	play 3 #s
Good	Good	Fair	Good	Good	Bad	Good	Bad	Fair	39,16,3,25,18,27,20	402

SHOPPING	GAMBLE	SEX	KEYWORD	KEYWORD						
Bad	Fair	is quiet	DIVINE	Spirituality,Religious,Astrology,Inner Conflicts,Religious ,Sleepiness,Advice given,Alcohol - drugs						

STRESS LEVEL	LUCKY COLORS	JEWELERY	MOONS EFFECT	GRAHA EFFECT	DAILY DEITY
Fair	Light Blue/Peach	Tiger's eye/Gold/Silver	Affectionate	God'S Graha	Shesnaag

DAILY PUJA
Chant Shiva Mantras, Take gifts to Ocean - Ganga Puja, Donate to Temple, Priests, etc.

DAILY PSALMS
7, 16, 34 ,43, 52, 61, 79, 106, 124

Thursday, January 28, 2016 — This is considered a POSITIVE day for you — Planet: Jupiter

ADVICE & DETAILS

If you can, take short trips and enjoy high pleasure. There will be lots of moving today.

MANTRA FOR TODAY

Om Hareem Nama Swaha..Shri Maha Laxmi Aye Namah swaha 12 times

MONEY	LOVE	CAREER	FAMILY	TRAVEL	WEDDING	MOVE	BUSINESS	HEALTH	Lotto #'s	play 3 #s
Excellent	Good	Excellent	Good	Good	Excellent	Good	Excellent	Excellent	75,21,54,33,8,11,37	277

SHOPPING	GAMBLE	SEX	KEYWORD	KEYWORD						
Excellent	Excellent	is excellent	MONEY	Business,Major Expense,Money - Profits,Income,Investments,Power,Promotion,Fame - TV						

STRESS LEVEL	LUCKY COLORS	JEWELERY	MOONS EFFECT	GRAHA EFFECT	DAILY DEITY
Low	Yellow/Silver	Diamonds/Gold/Pearls	Secretive	Money Graha	Mahalaxmi

DAILY PUJA
Decorate Land, Feed the poor, Donate milk /products to all, Feed holy guests,

DAILY PSALMS
8, 17, 35 ,44, 53, 62, 80, 107, 125

Friday, January 29, 2016 — This is considered a NEGATIVE day for you — Planet: Saturn

ADVICE & DETAILS	MANTRA FOR TODAY
Connect with the God within today so you can avoid the loneliness that can result from being boastful and criticizing others. Look at yourself first instead of trying to fix others.	Om Ganga mataye nama swaha Om Varuna Devta aye Pahimam 11 times

MONEY	LOVE	CAREER	FAMILY	TRAVEL	WEDDING	MOVE	BUSINESS	HEALTH	Lotto #'s	play 3 #s
Bad	Bad	Bad	Fair	Bad	Bad	Bad	Bad	Bad	2,73,29,16,47,31,33	180

SHOPPING	GAMBLE	SEX	KEYWORD	KEYWORD
Bad	Bad	is very bad	KARMA	Destruction,Losses,Death,Sickness - cold,Legal matter,Abusive,Karmic debts,God - Karma

STRESS LEVEL	LUCKY COLORS	JEWELERY	MOONS EFFECT	GRAHA EFFECT	DAILY DEITY
High	Gold/Brown//Green	Saphire/Hessonite	Ivestments	Evil Graha	Agnidev

DAILY PUJA	DAILY PSALMS
Remembrance of family members who died, worship of older people. gifts to grand parents	9, 18, 36 ,45, 54, 63, 81, 108, 126

Saturday, January 30, 2016 — This is considered a NEUTRAL day for you — Planet: Sun

ADVICE & DETAILS	MANTRA FOR TODAY
Today, you may be home alone, you may feel a bit confined, but at the same time you will have a sense of independence and the realization of your capabilities. This day may be influenced by dealings with the government, courts or legal institutions.	Om Namo Bhagawate Mukhtanandaya, 108 times

MONEY	LOVE	CAREER	FAMILY	TRAVEL	WEDDING	MOVE	BUSINESS	HEALTH	Lotto #'s	play 3 #s
Fair	Bad	Good	Bad	Fair	Bad	Fair	Fair	Fair	59,4,27,31,44,23,49	199

SHOPPING	GAMBLE	SEX	KEYWORD	KEYWORD
Fair	Fair	is fair	MIND	Independence,Loneliness,Meditative,Worry,Dominating,Illness - Cold,On Your Own,Commanding

STRESS LEVEL	LUCKY COLORS	JEWELERY	MOONS EFFECT	GRAHA EFFECT	DAILY DEITY
High	White/Yellow/	Pearl/Quartz	Arrogance	Status Graha	Saraswaty

DAILY PUJA	DAILY PSALMS
Give Gifts to Priests, Invite holy ones to your home, Feed Swamis and Yogis, Do Shiva Puja.	1, 10, 28 ,37, 46, 55, 73, 100, 118

Sunday, January 31, 2016 — This is considered a POSITIVE day for you — Planet: Moon

ADVICE & DETAILS	MANTRA FOR TODAY
There will be opportunity for romantic dates or encounters. You will make money today and get profits. There is a good chance of promotion.	Kali Durge Namo Nama Om Durge aye nama swaha 108 times

MONEY	LOVE	CAREER	FAMILY	TRAVEL	WEDDING	MOVE	BUSINESS	HEALTH	Lotto #'s	play 3 #s
Good	Excellent	Good	Good	Excellent	Good	Good	Good	Good	44,64,62,37,24,49,3	975

SHOPPING	GAMBLE	SEX	KEYWORD	KEYWORD
Good	Good	is good	LOVE	Romance,Popularity,Visitors,Shopping,Food, Drinks,Co-operation,Friendships,Affection

STRESS LEVEL	LUCKY COLORS	JEWELERY	MOONS EFFECT	GRAHA EFFECT	DAILY DEITY
Low	Red/Yellow/Pink	Topaz/Diamonds	Conservative	Love Graha	Gauri

DAILY PUJA	DAILY PSALMS
Give Gifts to females andnMother, Serve milk Products, Worship Durga forms	2, 11, 29 ,38, 47, 56, 74, 101, 119

Monday, February 1, 2016 — This is considered a POSITIVE day for you — Planet: Jupiter

ADVICE & DETAILS	MANTRA FOR TODAY
You will probably be taking short trips today or you will be moving. You will feel like moving and exercising and you should do it! There will be opportunity for illicit affairs, stay aware of how this affects you and others around you.	Om Hareem Nama Swaha..Shri Maha Laxmi Aye Namah swaha 12 times

MONEY	LOVE	CAREER	FAMILY	TRAVEL	WEDDING	MOVE	BUSINESS	HEALTH	Lotto #'s	play 3 #s
Excellent	Good	Excellent	Good	Good	Excellent	Good	Excellent	Excellent	3,46,6,59,35,56,20	433

SHOPPING	GAMBLE	SEX	KEYWORD	KEYWORD
Excellent	Excellent	is excellent	MONEY	Business,Major Expense,Money - Profits,Income,Investments,Power,Promotion,Fame - TV

STRESS LEVEL	LUCKY COLORS	JEWELERY	MOONS EFFECT	GRAHA EFFECT	DAILY DEITY
Low	Yellow/Silver	Diamonds/Gold/Pearls	Secretive	Money Graha	Mahalaxmi

DAILY PUJA	DAILY PSALMS
Decorate Land, Feed the poor, Donate milk /products to all, Feed holy guests,	8, 17, 35 ,44, 53, 62, 80, 107, 125

Tuesday, February 2, 2016 — This is considered a NEGATIVE day for you — Planet: Saturn

ADVICE & DETAILS

Try to remember that when you criticize others, you are seeing in others what you think you are missing, be kind and concentrate on the positive characteristics of others not in what you perceive are negatives. The influence of this day will make you introspective and thoughts about your spiritual self will arise. Remember that loves heals all, try to have loving, healing thoughts as much as possible. Rest today if you can.

MANTRA FOR TODAY

Om Ganga mataye nama swaha Om Varuna Devta aye Pahimam 11 times

MONEY	LOVE	CAREER	FAMILY	TRAVEL	WEDDING	MOVE	BUSINESS	HEALTH	Lotto #'s	play 3 #s
Bad	Bad	Bad	Fair	Bad	Bad	Bad	Bad	Bad	75,57,24,65,14,50,65	140

SHOPPING	GAMBLE	SEX	KEYWORD	KEYWORD				
Bad	Bad	is very bad	KARMA	Destruction,Losses,Death,Sickness - cold,Legal matter,Abusive,Karmic debts,God - Karma				

STRESS LEVEL	LUCKY COLORS	JEWELERY	MOONS EFFECT	GRAHA EFFECT	DAILY DEITY
High	Gold/Brown//Green	Saphire/Hessonite	Ivestments	Evil Graha	Agnidev

DAILY PUJA
Remembrance of family members who died, worship of older people. gifts to grand parents

DAILY PSALMS
9, 18, 36 ,45, 54, 63, 81, 108, 126

Wednesday, February 3, 2016 — This is considered a NEUTRAL day for you — Planet: Sun

ADVICE & DETAILS

The only obstacle to this very positive day is your speech. If you are careful and kind with your words expect money, romance and positive outlook for partnerships in any area.

MANTRA FOR TODAY

Om Namo Bhagawate Mukhtanandaya, 108 times

MONEY	LOVE	CAREER	FAMILY	TRAVEL	WEDDING	MOVE	BUSINESS	HEALTH	Lotto #'s	play 3 #s
Fair	Bad	Good	Bad	Fair	Bad	Fair	Fair	Fair	27,41,37,46,28,4,20	717

SHOPPING	GAMBLE	SEX	KEYWORD	KEYWORD				
Fair	Fair	is fair	MIND	Independence,Loneliness,Meditative,Worry,Dominating,Illness - Cold,On Your Own,Commanding				

STRESS LEVEL	LUCKY COLORS	JEWELERY	MOONS EFFECT	GRAHA EFFECT	DAILY DEITY
High	White/Yellow/	Pearl/Quartz	Arrogance	Status Graha	Saraswaty

DAILY PUJA
Give Gifts to Priests, Invite holy ones to your home, Feed Swamis and Yogis, Do Shiva Puja.

DAILY PSALMS
1, 10, 28 ,37, 46, 55, 73, 100, 118

Thursday, February 4, 2016 — This is considered a POSITIVE day for you — Planet: Moon

ADVICE & DETAILS

Every word your lips utter today have great power and they must be used with love and positive intention to avoid conflict. You will have the opportunity to serve and cooperate with others today, use it. Listen to music or express your feelings through music to get blessings today.

MANTRA FOR TODAY

Kali Durge Namo Nama Om Durge aye nama swaha 108 times

MONEY	LOVE	CAREER	FAMILY	TRAVEL	WEDDING	MOVE	BUSINESS	HEALTH	Lotto #'s	play 3 #s
Good	Excellent	Good	Good	Excellent	Good	Good	Good	Good	68,54,60,65,23,50,51	821

SHOPPING	GAMBLE	SEX	KEYWORD	KEYWORD				
Good	Good	is good	LOVE	Romance,Popularity,Visitors,Shopping,Food, Drinks,Co-operation,Friendships,Affection				

STRESS LEVEL	LUCKY COLORS	JEWELERY	MOONS EFFECT	GRAHA EFFECT	DAILY DEITY
Low	Red/Yellow/Pink	Topaz/Diamonds	Conservative	Love Graha	Gauri

DAILY PUJA
Give Gifts to females andnMother, Serve milk Products, Worship Durga forms

DAILY PSALMS
2, 11, 29 ,38, 47, 56, 74, 101, 119

Friday, February 5, 2016 — This is considered a POSITIVE day for you — Planet: Mercury

ADVICE & DETAILS

You may spend your day at home alone watching TV or may instead opt for luxurious and pleasurable activities that may bring you around fame or famous people. You will be influenced by money, so you will worry about it, make it or spend it.

MANTRA FOR TODAY

Om hareem Kleem Hreem Aem Saraswataye namaha 21 times

MONEY	LOVE	CAREER	FAMILY	TRAVEL	WEDDING	MOVE	BUSINESS	HEALTH	Lotto #'s	play 3 #s
Good	Fair	Good	Good	Excellent	Good	Good	Good	Excellent	24,49,28,65,36,7,30	526

SHOPPING	GAMBLE	SEX	KEYWORD	KEYWORD				
Good	Good	is great	SOCIAL	Children,Education,Astrology,Bargains,Social Functions,Childishness,Groups - Parties,Teacher				

STRESS LEVEL	LUCKY COLORS	JEWELERY	MOONS EFFECT	GRAHA EFFECT	DAILY DEITY
Low	Green/Sky Blue/	Diamonds/Silver	Enthusiastic	Social Graha	Vishnu

DAILY PUJA
Wash the feet of Children, Do Satnarayan Pooja, Read & chant Geeta

DAILY PSALMS
3, 12, 30 ,39, 48, 57, 75, 102, 120

Saturday, February 6, 2016 — This is considered a NEGATIVE day for you — Planet: Pluto

ADVICE & DETAILS

This will be a positive day if you can control your tongue and do not criticize anyone, particularly your loved ones and especially your partner. The influences are love and marriage. This is the opportunity to create a special surprise meal for your partner and share it with love in a romantic setting with soothing music as background.

MANTRA FOR TODAY

Om Jai Viganeshwaraya.. Lambodaraya Namo Namaha 21 times

MONEY	LOVE	CAREER	FAMILY	TRAVEL	WEDDING	MOVE	BUSINESS	HEALTH	Lotto #'s	play 3 #s
Bad	Fair	Bad	Fair	Bad	Good	Bad	Bad	Bad	38,21,70,61,51,51,29	458

SHOPPING	GAMBLE	SEX	KEYWORD	KEYWORD						
Bad	Bad	is tough	CAREER	Career,Hard Work,Co-workers,Low Payment,Job Problems,High Temper,Low Pay,Laziness						

STRESS LEVEL	LUCKY COLORS	JEWELERY	MOONS EFFECT	GRAHA EFFECT	DAILY DEITY
High	Dark Blue/ Purple/	Amethyst/Gold	Emotional	Job Graha	Lingam

DAILY PUJA	DAILY PSALMS
Worship Ganesh, Give gifts to father, and co -workers, Plant gardens, farms	4, 13, 31 ,40, 49, 58, 76, 103, 121

Sunday, February 7, 2016 — This is considered a POSITIVE day for you — Planet: Venus

ADVICE & DETAILS

Show your affection, cooperate with others and listen to music today; these activities will help you with the paymente of some karmic debts that may become overdue this day.

MANTRA FOR TODAY

Om Graam Greem Graum Sa Gurave namah swaha 21 times

MONEY	LOVE	CAREER	FAMILY	TRAVEL	WEDDING	MOVE	BUSINESS	HEALTH	Lotto #'s	play 3 #s
Bad	Excellent	Fair	Good	Excellent	Good	Excellent	Good	Excellent	66,74,73,22,57,24,46	733

SHOPPING	GAMBLE	SEX	KEYWORD	KEYWORD						
Good	Good	is good	CHANGE	Sexuality,Travel,Change,Distant, far,Travel delays,Deception,Excercise,Illicit Affairs						

STRESS LEVEL	LUCKY COLORS	JEWELERY	MOONS EFFECT	GRAHA EFFECT	DAILY DEITY
Fair	Tan/Green/ Beige	Pearl/Silver/quartz	Courageous	Travel Graha	Nataraja

DAILY PUJA	DAILY PSALMS
Artistic gifts, Pray to Krishna, Do good deeds, do Spiritual trips	5, 14, 32 ,41, 50, 59, 77, 104, 122

Monday, February 8, 2016 — This is considered a NEGATIVE day for you — Planet: Mars

ADVICE & DETAILS

You must watch out for misleading statements from others. There will be many changes today. Your sexual energy will be high. You will be thinking a great deal today about very deep and profound subjects.

MANTRA FOR TODAY

Om Mana Swasti Shanti Kuru kuru Swaha Shivoham Shivoham 27 times

MONEY	LOVE	CAREER	FAMILY	TRAVEL	WEDDING	MOVE	BUSINESS	HEALTH	Lotto #'s	play 3 #s
Bad	Bad	Bad	Bad	Bad	Bad	Bad	Fair	Bad	72,7,43,64,4,14,51	575

SHOPPING	GAMBLE	SEX	KEYWORD	KEYWORD						
Fair	Bad	is frustrating	POWER	Responsibilty,Disagreement,Family,Back Pain,Family Conflicts,Traffic Ticket,Quarrels,Jealousy						

STRESS LEVEL	LUCKY COLORS	JEWELERY	MOONS EFFECT	GRAHA EFFECT	DAILY DEITY
High	Purple/Blue/Rose	Emerald/Saphire	Educational	Family Graha	Mahakali

DAILY PUJA	DAILY PSALMS
Meditate, Control temper, Pray to Hanuman, Chant Hanuman Chalisa	6, 15, 33 ,42, 51, 60, 78, 105, 123

Tuesday, February 9, 2016 — This is considered a NEUTRAL day for you — Planet: Uranus

ADVICE & DETAILS

You will feel like watching television and would probably prefer the company of children today. You may be acting somewhat immaturely today so be careful of choices and words that may have long term consequences. Today will be a good day for creativity related to writing and publishing.

MANTRA FOR TODAY

Jai Jai Shiva Shambo.(2) ...Mahadeva Shambo (2) 21 times 8

MONEY	LOVE	CAREER	FAMILY	TRAVEL	WEDDING	MOVE	BUSINESS	HEALTH	Lotto #'s	play 3 #s
Good	Good	Fair	Good	Good	Bad	Good	Bad	Fair	63,16,66,28,52,7,28	712

SHOPPING	GAMBLE	SEX	KEYWORD	KEYWORD						
Bad	Fair	is quiet	DIVINE	Spirituality,Religious,Astrology,Inner Conflicts,Religious ,Sleepiness,Advice given,Alcohol - drugs						

STRESS LEVEL	LUCKY COLORS	JEWELERY	MOONS EFFECT	GRAHA EFFECT	DAILY DEITY
Fair	Light Blue/Peach	Tiger's eye/Gold/Silver	Affectionate	God'S Graha	Shesnaag

DAILY PUJA	DAILY PSALMS
Chant Shiva Mantras, Take gifts to Ocean - Ganga Puja, Donate to Temple, Priests, etc.	7, 16, 34 ,43, 52, 61, 79, 106, 124

Wednesday, February 10, 2016 — This is considered a POSITIVE day for you — Planet: Jupiter

ADVICE & DETAILS	MANTRA FOR TODAY
You will probably be taking short trips today or you will be moving. You will feel like moving and exercising and you should do it! There will be opportunity for illicit affairs, stay aware of how this affects you and others around you.	Om Hareem Nama Swaha..Shri Maha Laxmi Aye Namah swaha 12 times

MONEY	LOVE	CAREER	FAMILY	TRAVEL	WEDDING	MOVE	BUSINESS	HEALTH	Lotto #'s	play 3 #s
Excellent	Good	Excellent	Good	Good	Excellent	Good	Excellent	Excellent	2,28,19,32,50,23,36	339

SHOPPING	GAMBLE	SEX	KEYWORD	KEYWORD				
Excellent	Excellent	is excellent	MONEY	Business,Major Expense,Money - Profits,Income,Investments,Power,Promotion,Fame - TV				

STRESS LEVEL		LUCKY COLORS	JEWELERY	MOONS EFFECT	GRAHA EFFECT	DAILY DEITY
Low		Yellow/Silver	Diamonds/Gold/Pearls	Secretive	Money Graha	Mahalaxmi

DAILY PUJA	DAILY PSALMS
Decorate Land, Feed the poor, Donate milk /products to all, Feed holy guests,	8, 17, 35 ,44, 53, 62, 80, 107, 125

Thursday, February 11, 2016 — This is considered a NEGATIVE day for you — Planet: Saturn

ADVICE & DETAILS	MANTRA FOR TODAY
Try to remember that when you criticize others, you are seeing in others what you think you are missing, be kind and concentrate on the positive characteristics of others not in what you perceive are negatives. The influence of this day will make you introspective and thoughts about your spiritual self will arise. Remember that loves heals all, try to have loving, healing thoughts as much as possible. Rest today if you can.	Om Ganga mataye nama swaha Om Varuna Devta aye Pahimam 11 times

MONEY	LOVE	CAREER	FAMILY	TRAVEL	WEDDING	MOVE	BUSINESS	HEALTH	Lotto #'s	play 3 #s
Bad	Bad	Bad	Fair	Bad	Bad	Bad	Bad	Bad	58,52,24,72,21,20,36	497

SHOPPING	GAMBLE	SEX	KEYWORD	KEYWORD				
Bad	Bad	is very bad	KARMA	Destruction,Losses,Death,Sickness - cold,Legal matter,Abusive,Karmic debts,God - Karma				

STRESS LEVEL		LUCKY COLORS	JEWELERY	MOONS EFFECT	GRAHA EFFECT	DAILY DEITY
High		Gold/Brown//Green	Saphire/Hessonite	Ivestments	Evil Graha	Agnidev

DAILY PUJA	DAILY PSALMS
Remembrance of family members who died, worship of older people. gifts to grand parents	9, 18, 36 ,45, 54, 63, 81, 108, 126

Friday, February 12, 2016 — This is considered a NEUTRAL day for you — Planet: Sun

ADVICE & DETAILS	MANTRA FOR TODAY
The only obstacle to this very positive day is your speech. If you are careful and kind with your words expect money, romance and positive outlook for partnerships in any area.	Om Namo Bhagawate Mukhtanandaya, 108 times

MONEY	LOVE	CAREER	FAMILY	TRAVEL	WEDDING	MOVE	BUSINESS	HEALTH	Lotto #'s	play 3 #s
Fair	Bad	Good	Bad	Fair	Bad	Fair	Fair	Fair	43,4,23,28,73,29,2	393

SHOPPING	GAMBLE	SEX	KEYWORD	KEYWORD				
Fair	Fair	is fair	MIND	Independence,Loneliness,Meditative,Worry,Dominating,Illness - Cold,On Your Own,Commanding				

STRESS LEVEL		LUCKY COLORS	JEWELERY	MOONS EFFECT	GRAHA EFFECT	DAILY DEITY
High		White/Yellow/	Pearl/Quartz	Arrogance	Status Graha	Saraswaty

DAILY PUJA	DAILY PSALMS
Give Gifts to Priests, Invite holy ones to your home, Feed Swamis and Yogis, Do Shiva Puja.	1, 10, 28 ,37, 46, 55, 73, 100, 118

Saturday, February 13, 2016 — This is considered a POSITIVE day for you — Planet: Moon

ADVICE & DETAILS	MANTRA FOR TODAY
Every word your lips utter today have great power and they must be used with love and positive intention to avoid conflict. You will have the opportunity to serve and cooperate with others today, use it. Listen to music or express your feelings through music to get blessings today.	Kali Durge Namo Nama Om Durge aye nama swaha 108 times

MONEY	LOVE	CAREER	FAMILY	TRAVEL	WEDDING	MOVE	BUSINESS	HEALTH	Lotto #'s	play 3 #s
Good	Excellent	Good	Good	Excellent	Good	Good	Good	Good	6,75,27,74,52,37,13	373

SHOPPING	GAMBLE	SEX	KEYWORD	KEYWORD				
Good	Good	is good	LOVE	Romance,Popularity,Visitors,Shopping,Food, Drinks,Co-operation,Friendships,Affection				

STRESS LEVEL		LUCKY COLORS	JEWELERY	MOONS EFFECT	GRAHA EFFECT	DAILY DEITY
Low		Red/Yellow/Pink	Topaz/Diamonds	Conservative	Love Graha	Gauri

DAILY PUJA	DAILY PSALMS
Give Gifts to females andnMother, Serve milk Products, Worship Durga forms	2, 11, 29 ,38, 47, 56, 74, 101, 119

Sunday, February 14, 2016 — This is considered a POSITIVE day for you — Planet: Mercury

ADVICE & DETAILS

You may spend your day at home alone watching TV or may instead opt for luxurious and pleasurable activities that may bring you around fame or famous people. You will be influenced by money, so you will worry about it, make it or spend it.

MANTRA FOR TODAY

Om hareem Kleem Hreem Aem Saraswataye namaha 21 times

MONEY	LOVE	CAREER	FAMILY	TRAVEL	WEDDING	MOVE	BUSINESS	HEALTH	Lotto #'s	play 3 #s
Good	Fair	Good	Good	Excellent	Good	Good	Good	Excellent	69,63,43,61,47,12,32	36

SHOPPING	GAMBLE	SEX	KEYWORD	KEYWORD						
Good	Good	is great	SOCIAL	Children,Education,Astrology,Bargains,Social Functions,Childishness,Groups - Parties,Teacher						

STRESS LEVEL	LUCKY COLORS	JEWELERY	MOONS EFFECT	GRAHA EFFECT	DAILY DEITY
Low	Green/Sky Blue/	Diamonds/Silver	Enthusiastic	Social Graha	Vishnu

DAILY PUJA
Wash the feet of Children, Do Satnarayan Pooja, Read & chant Geeta

DAILY PSALMS
3, 12, 30 ,39, 48, 57, 75, 102, 120

Monday, February 15, 2016 — This is considered a NEGATIVE day for you — Planet: Pluto

ADVICE & DETAILS

This will be a positive day if you can control your tongue and do not criticize anyone, particularly your loved ones and especially your partner. The influences are love and marriage. This is the opportunity to create a special surprise meal for your partner and share it with love in a romantic setting with soothing music as background.

MANTRA FOR TODAY

Om Jai Viganeshwaraya.. Lambodaraya Namo Namaha 21 times

MONEY	LOVE	CAREER	FAMILY	TRAVEL	WEDDING	MOVE	BUSINESS	HEALTH	Lotto #'s	play 3 #s
Bad	Fair	Bad	Fair	Bad	Good	Bad	Bad	Bad	26,72,16,22,68,6,44	999

SHOPPING	GAMBLE	SEX	KEYWORD	KEYWORD						
Bad	Bad	is tough	CAREER	Career,Hard Work,Co-workers,Low Payment,Job Problems,High Temper,Low Pay,Laziness						

STRESS LEVEL	LUCKY COLORS	JEWELERY	MOONS EFFECT	GRAHA EFFECT	DAILY DEITY
High	Dark Blue/ Purple/	Amethyst/Gold	Emotional	Job Graha	Lingam

DAILY PUJA
Worship Ganesh, Give gifts to father, and co -workers, Plant gardens, farms

DAILY PSALMS
4, 13, 31 ,40, 49, 58, 76, 103, 121

Tuesday, February 16, 2016 — This is considered a POSITIVE day for you — Planet: Venus

ADVICE & DETAILS

Show your affection, cooperate with others and listen to music today; these activities will help you with the paymente of some karmic debts that may become overdue this day.

MANTRA FOR TODAY

Om Graam Greem Graum Sa Gurave namah swaha 21 times

MONEY	LOVE	CAREER	FAMILY	TRAVEL	WEDDING	MOVE	BUSINESS	HEALTH	Lotto #'s	play 3 #s
Bad	Excellent	Fair	Good	Excellent	Good	Excellent	Good	Excellent	31,35,60,65,54,35,13	517

SHOPPING	GAMBLE	SEX	KEYWORD	KEYWORD						
Good	Good	is good	CHANGE	Sexuality,Travel,Change,Distant, far,Travel delays,Deception,Excercise,Illicit Affairs						

STRESS LEVEL	LUCKY COLORS	JEWELERY	MOONS EFFECT	GRAHA EFFECT	DAILY DEITY
Fair	Tan/Green/ Beige	Pearl/Silver/quartz	Courageous	Travel Graha	Nataraja

DAILY PUJA
Artistic gifts, Pray to Krishna, Do good deeds, do Spiritual trips

DAILY PSALMS
5, 14, 32 ,41, 50, 59, 77, 104, 122

Wednesday, February 17, 2016 — This is considered a NEGATIVE day for you — Planet: Mars

ADVICE & DETAILS

You must watch out for misleading statements from others. There will be many changes today. Your sexual energy will be high. You will be thinking a great deal today about very deep and profound subjects.

MANTRA FOR TODAY

Om Mana Swasti Shanti Kuru kuru Swaha Shivoham Shivoham 27 times

MONEY	LOVE	CAREER	FAMILY	TRAVEL	WEDDING	MOVE	BUSINESS	HEALTH	Lotto #'s	play 3 #s
Bad	Bad	Bad	Bad	Bad	Bad	Bad	Fair	Bad	65,12,5,75,25,7,9	777

SHOPPING	GAMBLE	SEX	KEYWORD	KEYWORD						
Fair	Bad	is frustrating	POWER	Responsibilty,Disagreement,Family,Back Pain,Family Conflicts,Traffic Ticket,Quarrels,Jealousy						

STRESS LEVEL	LUCKY COLORS	JEWELERY	MOONS EFFECT	GRAHA EFFECT	DAILY DEITY
High	Purple/Blue/Rose	Emerald/Saphire	Educational	Family Graha	Mahakali

DAILY PUJA
Meditate, Control temper, Pray to Hanuman, Chant Hanuman Chalisa

DAILY PSALMS
6, 15, 33 ,42, 51, 60, 78, 105, 123

Thursday, February 18, 2016 — This is considered a NEUTRAL day for you — Planet: Uranus

ADVICE & DETAILS

You will feel like watching television and would probably prefer the company of children today. You may be acting somewhat immaturely today so be careful of choices and words that may have long term consequences. Today will be a good day for creativity related to writing and publishing.

MANTRA FOR TODAY

Jai Jai Shiva Shambo.(2) ...Mahadeva Shambo (2) 21 times 8

MONEY	LOVE	CAREER	FAMILY	TRAVEL	WEDDING	MOVE	BUSINESS	HEALTH	Lotto #'s	play 3 #s
Good	Good	Fair	Good	Good	Bad	Good	Bad	Fair	51,68,44,47,69,5,41	809

SHOPPING	GAMBLE	SEX	KEYWORD	KEYWORD						
Bad	Fair	is quiet	DIVINE	Spirituality,Religious,Astrology,Inner Conflicts,Religious ,Sleepiness,Advice given,Alcohol - drugs						

STRESS LEVEL	LUCKY COLORS	JEWELERY	MOONS EFFECT	GRAHA EFFECT	DAILY DEITY
Fair	Light Blue/Peach	Tiger's eye/Gold/Silver	Affectionate	God'S Graha	Shesnaag

DAILY PUJA	DAILY PSALMS
Chant Shiva Mantras, Take gifts to Ocean - Ganga Puja, Donate to Temple, Priests, etc.	7, 16, 34 ,43, 52, 61, 79, 106, 124

Friday, February 19, 2016 — This is considered a POSITIVE day for you — Planet: Jupiter

ADVICE & DETAILS

You will probably be taking short trips today or you will be moving. You will feel like moving and exercising and you should do it! There will be opportunity for illicit affairs, stay aware of how this affects you and others around you.

MANTRA FOR TODAY

Om Hareem Nama Swaha..Shri Maha Laxmi Aye Namah swaha 12 times

MONEY	LOVE	CAREER	FAMILY	TRAVEL	WEDDING	MOVE	BUSINESS	HEALTH	Lotto #'s	play 3 #s
Excellent	Good	Excellent	Good	Good	Excellent	Good	Excellent	Excellent	49,20,8,34,72,75,28	299

SHOPPING	GAMBLE	SEX	KEYWORD	KEYWORD						
Excellent	Excellent	is excellent	MONEY	Business,Major Expense,Money - Profits,Income,Investments,Power,Promotion,Fame - TV						

STRESS LEVEL	LUCKY COLORS	JEWELERY	MOONS EFFECT	GRAHA EFFECT	DAILY DEITY
Low	Yellow/Silver	Diamonds/Gold/Pearls	Secretive	Money Graha	Mahalaxmi

DAILY PUJA	DAILY PSALMS
Decorate Land, Feed the poor, Donate milk /products to all, Feed holy guests,	8, 17, 35 ,44, 53, 62, 80, 107, 125

Saturday, February 20, 2016 — This is considered a NEGATIVE day for you — Planet: Saturn

ADVICE & DETAILS

Try to remember that when you criticize others, you are seeing in others what you think you are missing, be kind and concentrate on the positive characteristics of others not in what you perceive are negatives. The influence of this day will make you introspective and thoughts about your spiritual self will arise. Remember that loves heals all, try to have loving, healing thoughts as much as possible. Rest today if you can.

MANTRA FOR TODAY

Om Ganga mataye nama swaha Om Varuna Devta aye Pahimam 11 times

MONEY	LOVE	CAREER	FAMILY	TRAVEL	WEDDING	MOVE	BUSINESS	HEALTH	Lotto #'s	play 3 #s
Bad	Bad	Bad	Fair	Bad	Bad	Bad	Bad	Bad	64,35,2,12,28,13,48	186

SHOPPING	GAMBLE	SEX	KEYWORD	KEYWORD						
Bad	Bad	is very bad	KARMA	Destruction,Losses,Death,Sickness - cold,Legal matter,Abusive,Karmic debts,God - Karma						

STRESS LEVEL	LUCKY COLORS	JEWELERY	MOONS EFFECT	GRAHA EFFECT	DAILY DEITY
High	Gold/Brown//Green	Saphire/Hessonite	Ivestments	Evil Graha	Agnidev

DAILY PUJA	DAILY PSALMS
Remembrance of family members who died, worship of older people. gifts to grand parents	9, 18, 36 ,45, 54, 63, 81, 108, 126

Sunday, February 21, 2016 — This is considered a NEUTRAL day for you — Planet: Sun

ADVICE & DETAILS

The only obstacle to this very positive day is your speech. If you are careful and kind with your words expect money, romance and positive outlook for partnerships in any area.

MANTRA FOR TODAY

Om Namo Bhagawate Mukhtanandaya, 108 times

MONEY	LOVE	CAREER	FAMILY	TRAVEL	WEDDING	MOVE	BUSINESS	HEALTH	Lotto #'s	play 3 #s
Fair	Bad	Good	Bad	Fair	Bad	Fair	Fair	Fair	75,8,42,41,42,71,73	546

SHOPPING	GAMBLE	SEX	KEYWORD	KEYWORD						
Fair	Fair	is fair	MIND	Independence,Loneliness,Meditative,Worry,Dominating,Illness - Cold,On Your Own,Commanding						

STRESS LEVEL	LUCKY COLORS	JEWELERY	MOONS EFFECT	GRAHA EFFECT	DAILY DEITY
High	White/Yellow/	Pearl/Quartz	Arrogance	Status Graha	Saraswaty

DAILY PUJA	DAILY PSALMS
Give Gifts to Priests, Invite holy ones to your home, Feed Swamis and Yogis, Do Shiva Puja.	1, 10, 28 ,37, 46, 55, 73, 100, 118

Monday, February 22, 2016 — This is considered a POSITIVE day for you — Planet: Moon

ADVICE & DETAILS

Every word your lips utter today have great power and they must be used with love and positive intention to avoid conflict. You will have the opportunity to serve and cooperate with others today, use it. Listen to music or express your feelings through music to get blessings today.

MANTRA FOR TODAY

Kali Durge Namo Nama Om Durge aye nama swaha 108 times

MONEY	LOVE	CAREER	FAMILY	TRAVEL	WEDDING	MOVE	BUSINESS	HEALTH	Lotto #'s	play 3 #s
Good	Excellent	Good	Good	Excellent	Good	Good	Good	Good	17,4,36,30,59,19,47	85

SHOPPING	GAMBLE	SEX	KEYWORD	KEYWORD						
Good	Good	is good	LOVE	Romance,Popularity,Visitors,Shopping,Food, Drinks,Co-operation,Friendships,Affection						

STRESS LEVEL	LUCKY COLORS	JEWELERY	MOONS EFFECT	GRAHA EFFECT	DAILY DEITY
Low	Red/Yellow/Pink	Topaz/Diamonds	Conservative	Love Graha	Gauri

DAILY PUJA	DAILY PSALMS
Give Gifts to females andnMother, Serve milk Products, Worship Durga forms	2, 11, 29 ,38, 47, 56, 74, 101, 119

Tuesday, February 23, 2016 — This is considered a POSITIVE day for you — Planet: Mercury

ADVICE & DETAILS

You may spend your day at home alone watching TV or may instead opt for luxurious and pleasurable activities that may bring you around fame or famous people. You will be influenced by money, so you will worry about it, make it or spend it.

MANTRA FOR TODAY

Om hareem Kleem Hreem Aem Saraswataye namaha 21 times

MONEY	LOVE	CAREER	FAMILY	TRAVEL	WEDDING	MOVE	BUSINESS	HEALTH	Lotto #'s	play 3 #s
Good	Fair	Good	Good	Excellent	Good	Good	Good	Excellent	4,28,31,70,3,52,45	369

SHOPPING	GAMBLE	SEX	KEYWORD	KEYWORD						
Good	Good	is great	SOCIAL	Children,Education,Astrology,Bargains,Social Functions,Childishness,Groups - Parties,Teacher						

STRESS LEVEL	LUCKY COLORS	JEWELERY	MOONS EFFECT	GRAHA EFFECT	DAILY DEITY
Low	Green/Sky Blue/	Diamonds/Silver	Enthusiastic	Social Graha	Vishnu

DAILY PUJA	DAILY PSALMS
Wash the feet of Children, Do Satnarayan Pooja, Read & chant Geeta	3, 12, 30 ,39, 48, 57, 75, 102, 120

Wednesday, February 24, 2016 — This is considered a NEGATIVE day for you — Planet: Pluto

ADVICE & DETAILS

This will be a positive day if you can control your tongue and do not criticize anyone, particularly your loved ones and especially your partner. The influences are love and marriage. This is the opportunity to create a special surprise meal for your partner and share it with love in a romantic setting with soothing music as background.

MANTRA FOR TODAY

Om Jai Viganeshwaraya.. Lambodaraya Namo Namaha 21 times

MONEY	LOVE	CAREER	FAMILY	TRAVEL	WEDDING	MOVE	BUSINESS	HEALTH	Lotto #'s	play 3 #s
Bad	Fair	Bad	Fair	Bad	Good	Bad	Bad	Bad	7,3,57,40,14,12,38	915

SHOPPING	GAMBLE	SEX	KEYWORD	KEYWORD						
Bad	Bad	is tough	CAREER	Career,Hard Work,Co-workers,Low Payment,Job Problems,High Temper,Low Pay,Laziness						

STRESS LEVEL	LUCKY COLORS	JEWELERY	MOONS EFFECT	GRAHA EFFECT	DAILY DEITY
High	Dark Blue/ Purple/	Amethyst/Gold	Emotional	Job Graha	Lingam

DAILY PUJA	DAILY PSALMS
Worship Ganesh, Give gifts to father, and co -workers, Plant gardens, farms	4, 13, 31 ,40, 49, 58, 76, 103, 121

Thursday, February 25, 2016 — This is considered a POSITIVE day for you — Planet: Venus

ADVICE & DETAILS

Show your affection, cooperate with others and listen to music today; these activities will help you with the paymente of some karmic debts that may become overdue this day.

MANTRA FOR TODAY

Om Graam Greem Graum Sa Gurave namah swaha 21 times

MONEY	LOVE	CAREER	FAMILY	TRAVEL	WEDDING	MOVE	BUSINESS	HEALTH	Lotto #'s	play 3 #s
Bad	Excellent	Fair	Good	Excellent	Good	Excellent	Good	Excellent	49,60,27,48,9,11,70	851

SHOPPING	GAMBLE	SEX	KEYWORD	KEYWORD						
Good	Good	is good	CHANGE	Sexuality,Travel,Change,Distant, far,Travel delays,Deception,Excercise,Illicit Affairs						

STRESS LEVEL	LUCKY COLORS	JEWELERY	MOONS EFFECT	GRAHA EFFECT	DAILY DEITY
Fair	Tan/Green/ Beige	Pearl/Silver/quartz	Courageous	Travel Graha	Nataraja

DAILY PUJA	DAILY PSALMS
Artistic gifts, Pray to Krishna, Do good deeds, do Spiritual trips	5, 14, 32 ,41, 50, 59, 77, 104, 122

Friday, February 26, 2016 — This is considered a NEGATIVE day for you — Planet: Mars

ADVICE & DETAILS	MANTRA FOR TODAY
You must watch out for misleading statements from others. There will be many changes today. Your sexual energy will be high. You will be thinking a great deal today about very deep and profound subjects.	Om Mana Swasti Shanti Kuru kuru Swaha Shivoham Shivoham 27 times

MONEY	LOVE	CAREER	FAMILY	TRAVEL	WEDDING	MOVE	BUSINESS	HEALTH	Lotto #'s	play 3 #s
Bad	Bad	Bad	Bad	Bad	Bad	Bad	Fair	Bad	21,64,50,56,70,53,63	549

SHOPPING	GAMBLE	SEX	KEYWORD	KEYWORD
Fair	Bad	is frustrating	POWER	Responsibilty,Disagreement,Family,Back Pain,Family Conflicts,Traffic Ticket,Quarrels,Jealousy

STRESS LEVEL	LUCKY COLORS	JEWELERY	MOONS EFFECT	GRAHA EFFECT	DAILY DEITY
High	Purple/Blue/Rose	Emerald/Saphire	Educational	Family Graha	Mahakali

DAILY PUJA	DAILY PSALMS
Meditate, Control temper, Pray to Hanuman, Chant Hanuman Chalisa	6, 15, 33 ,42, 51, 60, 78, 105, 123

Saturday, February 27, 2016 — This is considered a NEUTRAL day for you — Planet: Uranus

ADVICE & DETAILS	MANTRA FOR TODAY
You will feel like watching television and would probably prefer the company of children today. You may be acting somewhat immaturely today so be careful of choices and words that may have long term consequences. Today will be a good day for creativity related to writing and publishing.	Jai Jai Shiva Shambo.(2) ...Mahadeva Shambo (2) 21 times 8

MONEY	LOVE	CAREER	FAMILY	TRAVEL	WEDDING	MOVE	BUSINESS	HEALTH	Lotto #'s	play 3 #s
Good	Good	Fair	Good	Good	Bad	Good	Bad	Fair	40,62,49,71,67,7,29	819

SHOPPING	GAMBLE	SEX	KEYWORD	KEYWORD
Bad	Fair	is quiet	DIVINE	Spirituality,Religious,Astrology,Inner Conflicts,Religious ,Sleepiness,Advice given,Alcohol - drugs

STRESS LEVEL	LUCKY COLORS	JEWELERY	MOONS EFFECT	GRAHA EFFECT	DAILY DEITY
Fair	Light Blue/Peach	Tiger's eye/Gold/Silver	Affectionate	God'S Graha	Shesnaag

DAILY PUJA	DAILY PSALMS
Chant Shiva Mantras, Take gifts to Ocean - Ganga Puja, Donate to Temple, Priests, etc.	7, 16, 34 ,43, 52, 61, 79, 106, 124

Sunday, February 28, 2016 — This is considered A POSITIVE day for you — Planet: Jupiter

ADVICE & DETAILS	MANTRA FOR TODAY
You will probably be taking short trips today or you will be moving. You will feel like moving and exercising and you should do it! There will be opportunity for illicit affairs, stay aware of how this affects you and others around you.	Om Hareem Nama Swaha..Shri Maha Laxmi Aye Namah swaha 12 times

MONEY	LOVE	CAREER	FAMILY	TRAVEL	WEDDING	MOVE	BUSINESS	HEALTH	Lotto #'s	play 3 #s
Excellent	Good	Excellent	Good	Good	Excellent	Good	Excellent	Excellent	1,10,55,6,49,6,26	14

SHOPPING	GAMBLE	SEX	KEYWORD	KEYWORD
Excellent	Excellent	is excellent	MONEY	Business,Major Expense,Money - Profits,Income,Investments,Power,Promotion,Fame - TV

STRESS LEVEL	LUCKY COLORS	JEWELERY	MOONS EFFECT	GRAHA EFFECT	DAILY DEITY
Low	Yellow/Silver	Diamonds/Gold/Pearls	Secretive	Money Graha	Mahalaxmi

DAILY PUJA	DAILY PSALMS
Decorate Land, Feed the poor, Donate milk /products to all, Feed holy guests,	8, 17, 35 ,44, 53, 62, 80, 107, 125

Monday, February 29, 2016 — This is considered a NEGATIVE day for you — Planet: Saturn

ADVICE & DETAILS	MANTRA FOR TODAY
Try to remember that when you criticize others, you are seeing in others what you think you are missing, be kind and concentrate on the positive characteristics of others not in what you perceive are negatives. The influence of this day will make you introspective and thoughts about your spiritual self will arise. Remember that loves heals all, try to have loving, healing thoughts as much as possible. Rest today if you can.	Om Ganga mataye nama swaha Om Varuna Devta aye Pahimam 11 times

MONEY	LOVE	CAREER	FAMILY	TRAVEL	WEDDING	MOVE	BUSINESS	HEALTH	Lotto #'s	play 3 #s
Bad	Bad	Bad	Fair	Bad	Bad	Bad	Bad	Bad	44,47,38,63,21,39,21	566

SHOPPING	GAMBLE	SEX	KEYWORD	KEYWORD
Bad	Bad	is very bad	KARMA	Destruction,Losses,Death,Sickness - cold,Legal matter,Abusive,Karmic debts,God - Karma

STRESS LEVEL	LUCKY COLORS	JEWELERY	MOONS EFFECT	GRAHA EFFECT	DAILY DEITY
High	Gold/Brown//Green	Saphire/Hessonite	Ivestments	Evil Graha	Agnidev

DAILY PUJA	DAILY PSALMS
Remembrance of family members who died, worship of older people. gifts to grand parents	9, 18, 36 ,45, 54, 63, 81, 108, 126

Tuesday, March 1, 2016 — This is considered a POSITIVE day for you — Planet: Jupiter

ADVICE & DETAILS

The power of your expression today is great. Use this power to communicate with others, to write and publish or to entertain others when in groups or parties. There is the influence of someone that is jealous of you, be aware of it and try to be modest.

MANTRA FOR TODAY

Om Hareem Nama Swaha..Shri Maha Laxmi Aye Namah swaha 12 times

MONEY	LOVE	CAREER	FAMILY	TRAVEL	WEDDING	MOVE	BUSINESS	HEALTH	Lotto #'s	play 3 #s
Excellent	Good	Excellent	Good	Good	Excellent	Good	Excellent	Excellent	48,60,4,34,71,1,14	640

SHOPPING	GAMBLE	SEX	KEYWORD	KEYWORD				
Excellent	Excellent	is excellent	MONEY	Business,Major Expense,Money - Profits,Income,Investments,Power,Promotion,Fame - TV				

STRESS LEVEL	LUCKY COLORS	JEWELERY	MOONS EFFECT	GRAHA EFFECT	DAILY DEITY
Low	Yellow/Silver	Diamonds/Gold/Pearls	Secretive	Money Graha	Mahalaxmi

DAILY PUJA
Decorate Land, Feed the poor, Donate milk /products to all, Feed holy guests,

DAILY PSALMS
8, 17, 35 ,44, 53, 62, 80, 107, 125

Wednesday, March 2, 2016 — This is considered a NEGATIVE day for you — Planet: Saturn

ADVICE & DETAILS

Although this will be a day open for you to socialize with others, you must avoid extremes and parties with alcohol and drugs. Your enemies will take advantage of you today when they see you in your weakest state. Try to rest, you will be sleepy.

MANTRA FOR TODAY

Om Ganga mataye nama swaha Om Varuna Devta aye Pahimam 11 times

MONEY	LOVE	CAREER	FAMILY	TRAVEL	WEDDING	MOVE	BUSINESS	HEALTH	Lotto #'s	play 3 #s
Bad	Bad	Bad	Fair	Bad	Bad	Bad	Bad	Bad	49,15,14,9,3,20,37	989

SHOPPING	GAMBLE	SEX	KEYWORD	KEYWORD				
Bad	Bad	is very bad	KARMA	Destruction,Losses,Death,Sickness - cold,Legal matter,Abusive,Karmic debts,God - Karma				

STRESS LEVEL	LUCKY COLORS	JEWELERY	MOONS EFFECT	GRAHA EFFECT	DAILY DEITY
High	Gold/Brown//Green	Saphire/Hessonite	Ivestments	Evil Graha	Agnidev

DAILY PUJA
Remembrance of family members who died, worship of older people. gifts to grand parents

DAILY PSALMS
9, 18, 36 ,45, 54, 63, 81, 108, 126

Thursday, March 3, 2016 — This is considered a NEUTRAL day for you — Planet: Sun

ADVICE & DETAILS

There may be sickness of children or you may be getting sick. There will be losses and sadness.

MANTRA FOR TODAY

Om Namo Bhagawate Mukhtanandaya, 108 times

MONEY	LOVE	CAREER	FAMILY	TRAVEL	WEDDING	MOVE	BUSINESS	HEALTH	Lotto #'s	play 3 #s
Fair	Bad	Good	Bad	Fair	Bad	Fair	Fair	Fair	41,51,71,71,28,28,23	906

SHOPPING	GAMBLE	SEX	KEYWORD	KEYWORD				
Fair	Fair	is fair	MIND	Independence,Loneliness,Meditative,Worry,Dominating,Illness - Cold,On Your Own,Commanding				

STRESS LEVEL	LUCKY COLORS	JEWELERY	MOONS EFFECT	GRAHA EFFECT	DAILY DEITY
High	White/Yellow/	Pearl/Quartz	Arrogance	Status Graha	Saraswaty

DAILY PUJA
Give Gifts to Priests, Invite holy ones to your home, Feed Swamis and Yogis, Do Shiva Puja.

DAILY PSALMS
1, 10, 28 ,37, 46, 55, 73, 100, 118

Friday, March 4, 2016 — This is considered a POSITIVE day for you — Planet: Moon

ADVICE & DETAILS

Express your thoughts, opinions or information to partners and/or children. Day is influenced by children and ability to acquire information by reading or other means.

MANTRA FOR TODAY

Kali Durge Namo Nama Om Durge aye nama swaha 108 times

MONEY	LOVE	CAREER	FAMILY	TRAVEL	WEDDING	MOVE	BUSINESS	HEALTH	Lotto #'s	play 3 #s
Good	Excellent	Good	Good	Excellent	Good	Good	Good	Good	43,39,56,23,7,39,10	479

SHOPPING	GAMBLE	SEX	KEYWORD	KEYWORD				
Good	Good	is good	LOVE	Romance,Popularity,Visitors,Shopping,Food, Drinks,Co-operation,Friendships,Affection				

STRESS LEVEL	LUCKY COLORS	JEWELERY	MOONS EFFECT	GRAHA EFFECT	DAILY DEITY
Low	Red/Yellow/Pink	Topaz/Diamonds	Conservative	Love Graha	Gauri

DAILY PUJA
Give Gifts to females andnMother, Serve milk Products, Worship Durga forms

DAILY PSALMS
2, 11, 29 ,38, 47, 56, 74, 101, 119

Saturday, March 5, 2016 — This is considered a POSITIVE day for you — Planet: Mercury

ADVICE & DETAILS

Reading will benefit you today. You will have to hone your communication skills and speak clearly and listen carefully, especially when dealing with Real Estate and teachers of any type.

MANTRA FOR TODAY

Om hareem Kleem Hreem Aem Saraswataye namaha 21 times

MONEY	LOVE	CAREER	FAMILY	TRAVEL	WEDDING	MOVE	BUSINESS	HEALTH	Lotto #'s	play 3 #s
Good	Fair	Good	Good	Excellent	Good	Good	Good	Excellent	20,8,26,24,28,68,64	638

SHOPPING	GAMBLE	SEX	KEYWORD	KEYWORD						
Good	Good	is great	SOCIAL	Children,Education,Astrology,Bargains,Social Functions,Childishness,Groups - Parties,Teacher						

STRESS LEVEL	LUCKY COLORS	JEWELERY	MOONS EFFECT	GRAHA EFFECT	DAILY DEITY
Low	Green/Sky Blue/	Diamonds/Silver	Enthusiastic	Social Graha	Vishnu

DAILY PUJA
Wash the feet of Children, Do Satnarayan Pooja, Read & chant Geeta

DAILY PSALMS
3, 12, 30 ,39, 48, 57, 75, 102, 120

Sunday, March 6, 2016 — This is considered a NEGATIVE day for you — Planet: Pluto

ADVICE & DETAILS

Overcome laziness and low pay today and improve your karma by being industrious, hard working and controlling your high temper.

MANTRA FOR TODAY

Om Jai Viganeshwaraya.. Lambodaraya Namo Namaha 21 times

MONEY	LOVE	CAREER	FAMILY	TRAVEL	WEDDING	MOVE	BUSINESS	HEALTH	Lotto #'s	play 3 #s
Bad	Fair	Bad	Fair	Bad	Good	Bad	Bad	Bad	32,26,52,71,65,25,75	710

SHOPPING	GAMBLE	SEX	KEYWORD	KEYWORD						
Bad	Bad	is tough	CAREER	Career,Hard Work,Co-workers,Low Payment,Job Problems,High Temper,Low Pay,Laziness						

STRESS LEVEL	LUCKY COLORS	JEWELERY	MOONS EFFECT	GRAHA EFFECT	DAILY DEITY
High	Dark Blue/ Purple/	Amethyst/Gold	Emotional	Job Graha	Lingam

DAILY PUJA
Worship Ganesh, Give gifts to father, and co -workers, Plant gardens, farms

DAILY PSALMS
4, 13, 31 ,40, 49, 58, 76, 103, 121

Monday, March 7, 2016 — This is considered a POSITIVE day for you — Planet: Venus

ADVICE & DETAILS

Although this will be a day open for you to socialize with others, you must avoid extremes and parties with alcohol and drugs. Your enemies will take advantage of you today when they see you in your weakest state. Try to rest, you will be sleepy.

MANTRA FOR TODAY

Om Graam Greem Graum Sa Gurave namah swaha 21 times

MONEY	LOVE	CAREER	FAMILY	TRAVEL	WEDDING	MOVE	BUSINESS	HEALTH	Lotto #'s	play 3 #s
Bad	Excellent	Fair	Good	Excellent	Good	Excellent	Good	Excellent	21,21,24,8,54,22,8	503

SHOPPING	GAMBLE	SEX	KEYWORD	KEYWORD						
Good	Good	is good	CHANGE	Sexuality,Travel,Change,Distant, far,Travel delays,Deception,Excercise,Illicit Affairs						

STRESS LEVEL	LUCKY COLORS	JEWELERY	MOONS EFFECT	GRAHA EFFECT	DAILY DEITY
Fair	Tan/Green/ Beige	Pearl/Silver/quartz	Courageous	Travel Graha	Nataraja

DAILY PUJA
Artistic gifts, Pray to Krishna, Do good deeds, do Spiritual trips

DAILY PSALMS
5, 14, 32 ,41, 50, 59, 77, 104, 122

Tuesday, March 8, 2016 — This is considered a NEGATIVE day for you — Planet: Mars

ADVICE & DETAILS

Children will be prevalent today. This day is marked with a great deal of creativity ideal for areas related to the left side of the brain such as writing, painting, handcrafts, baking, cooking or needlework.

MANTRA FOR TODAY

Om Mana Swasti Shanti Kuru kuru Swaha Shivoham Shivoham 27 times

MONEY	LOVE	CAREER	FAMILY	TRAVEL	WEDDING	MOVE	BUSINESS	HEALTH	Lotto #'s	play 3 #s
Bad	Bad	Bad	Bad	Bad	Bad	Bad	Fair	Bad	27,5,68,49,8,45,3	522

SHOPPING	GAMBLE	SEX	KEYWORD	KEYWORD						
Fair	Bad	is frustrating	POWER	Responsibilty,Disagreement,Family,Back Pain,Family Conflicts,Traffic Ticket,Quarrels,Jealousy						

STRESS LEVEL	LUCKY COLORS	JEWELERY	MOONS EFFECT	GRAHA EFFECT	DAILY DEITY
High	Purple/Blue/Rose	Emerald/Saphire	Educational	Family Graha	Mahakali

DAILY PUJA
Meditate, Control temper, Pray to Hanuman, Chant Hanuman Chalisa

DAILY PSALMS
6, 15, 33 ,42, 51, 60, 78, 105, 123

Wednesday, March 9, 2016 — This is considered a NEUTRAL day for you — Planet: Uranus

ADVICE & DETAILS

The thought of watching TV is very appealing today. Spending time with children will benefit your creativity, but you must refrain from allowing immaturity to control your actions today.

MANTRA FOR TODAY

Jai Jai Shiva Shambo.(2) ...Mahadeva Shambo (2) 21 times 8

MONEY	LOVE	CAREER	FAMILY	TRAVEL	WEDDING	MOVE	BUSINESS	HEALTH	Lotto #'s	play 3 #s
Good	Good	Fair	Good	Good	Bad	Good	Bad	Fair	23,23,64,72,20,53,22	771

SHOPPING	GAMBLE	SEX	KEYWORD	KEYWORD						
Bad	Fair	is quiet	DIVINE	Spirituality,Religious,Astrology,Inner Conflicts,Religious ,Sleepiness,Advice given,Alcohol - drugs						

STRESS LEVEL	LUCKY COLORS	JEWELERY	MOONS EFFECT	GRAHA EFFECT	DAILY DEITY
Fair	Light Blue/Peach	Tiger's eye/Gold/Silver	Affectionate	God'S Graha	Shesnaag

DAILY PUJA	DAILY PSALMS
Chant Shiva Mantras, Take gifts to Ocean - Ganga Puja, Donate to Temple, Priests, etc.	7, 16, 34 ,43, 52, 61, 79, 106, 124

Thursday, March 10, 2016 — This is considered a POSITIVE day for you — Planet: Jupiter

ADVICE & DETAILS

The power of your expression today is great. Use this power to communicate with others, to write and publish or to entertain others when in groups or parties. There is the influence of someone that is jealous of you, be aware of it and try to be modest.

MANTRA FOR TODAY

Om Hareem Nama Swaha..Shri Maha Laxmi Aye Namah swaha 12 times

MONEY	LOVE	CAREER	FAMILY	TRAVEL	WEDDING	MOVE	BUSINESS	HEALTH	Lotto #'s	play 3 #s
Excellent	Good	Excellent	Good	Good	Excellent	Good	Excellent	Excellent	21,36,54,43,62,4,75	658

SHOPPING	GAMBLE	SEX	KEYWORD	KEYWORD						
Excellent	Excellent	is excellent	MONEY	Business,Major Expense,Money - Profits,Income,Investments,Power,Promotion,Fame - TV						

STRESS LEVEL	LUCKY COLORS	JEWELERY	MOONS EFFECT	GRAHA EFFECT	DAILY DEITY
Low	Yellow/Silver	Diamonds/Gold/Pearls	Secretive	Money Graha	Mahalaxmi

DAILY PUJA	DAILY PSALMS
Decorate Land, Feed the poor, Donate milk /products to all, Feed holy guests,	8, 17, 35 ,44, 53, 62, 80, 107, 125

Friday, March 11, 2016 — This is considered a NEGATIVE day for you — Planet: Saturn

ADVICE & DETAILS

Although this will be a day open for you to socialize with others, you must avoid extremes and parties with alcohol and drugs. Your enemies will take advantage of you today when they see you in your weakest state. Try to rest, you will be sleepy.

MANTRA FOR TODAY

Om Ganga mataye nama swaha Om Varuna Devta aye Pahimam 11 times

MONEY	LOVE	CAREER	FAMILY	TRAVEL	WEDDING	MOVE	BUSINESS	HEALTH	Lotto #'s	play 3 #s
Bad	Bad	Bad	Fair	Bad	Bad	Bad	Bad	Bad	6,49,36,26,41,38,60	341

SHOPPING	GAMBLE	SEX	KEYWORD	KEYWORD						
Bad	Bad	is very bad	KARMA	Destruction,Losses,Death,Sickness - cold,Legal matter,Abusive,Karmic debts,God - Karma						

STRESS LEVEL	LUCKY COLORS	JEWELERY	MOONS EFFECT	GRAHA EFFECT	DAILY DEITY
High	Gold/Brown//Green	Saphire/Hessonite	Ivestments	Evil Graha	Agnidev

DAILY PUJA	DAILY PSALMS
Remembrance of family members who died, worship of older people. gifts to grand parents	9, 18, 36 ,45, 54, 63, 81, 108, 126

Saturday, March 12, 2016 — This is considered a NEUTRAL day for you — Planet: Sun

ADVICE & DETAILS

There may be sickness of children or you may be getting sick. There will be losses and sadness.

MANTRA FOR TODAY

Om Namo Bhagawate Mukhtanandaya, 108 times

MONEY	LOVE	CAREER	FAMILY	TRAVEL	WEDDING	MOVE	BUSINESS	HEALTH	Lotto #'s	play 3 #s
Fair	Bad	Good	Bad	Fair	Bad	Fair	Fair	Fair	23,40,9,32,27,74,24	239

SHOPPING	GAMBLE	SEX	KEYWORD	KEYWORD						
Fair	Fair	is fair	MIND	Independence,Loneliness,Meditative,Worry,Dominating,Illness - Cold,On Your Own,Commanding						

STRESS LEVEL	LUCKY COLORS	JEWELERY	MOONS EFFECT	GRAHA EFFECT	DAILY DEITY
High	White/Yellow/	Pearl/Quartz	Arrogance	Status Graha	Saraswaty

DAILY PUJA	DAILY PSALMS
Give Gifts to Priests, Invite holy ones to your home, Feed Swamis and Yogis, Do Shiva Puja.	1, 10, 28 ,37, 46, 55, 73, 100, 118

Sunday, March 13, 2016 — This is considered a POSITIVE day for you — Planet: Moon

ADVICE & DETAILS

Express your thoughts, opinions or information to partners and/or children. Day is influenced by children and ability to acquire information by reading or other means.

MANTRA FOR TODAY

Kali Durge Namo Nama Om Durge aye nama swaha 108 times

MONEY	LOVE	CAREER	FAMILY	TRAVEL	WEDDING	MOVE	BUSINESS	HEALTH	Lotto #'s	play 3 #s
Good	Excellent	Good	Good	Excellent	Good	Good	Good	Good	39,29,13,32,62,33,62	454

SHOPPING	GAMBLE	SEX	KEYWORD	KEYWORD						
Good	Good	is good	LOVE	Romance,Popularity,Visitors,Shopping,Food, Drinks,Co-operation,Friendships,Affection						

STRESS LEVEL	LUCKY COLORS	JEWELERY	MOONS EFFECT	GRAHA EFFECT	DAILY DEITY
Low	Red/Yellow/Pink	Topaz/Diamonds	Conservative	Love Graha	Gauri

DAILY PUJA	DAILY PSALMS
Give Gifts to females andnMother, Serve milk Products, Worship Durga forms	2, 11, 29 ,38, 47, 56, 74, 101, 119

Monday, March 14, 2016 — This is considered a POSITIVE day for you — Planet: Mercury

ADVICE & DETAILS

Reading will benefit you today. You will have to hone your communication skills and speak clearly and listen carefully, especially when dealing with Real Estate and teachers of any type.

MANTRA FOR TODAY

Om hareem Kleem Hreem Aem Saraswataye namaha 21 times

MONEY	LOVE	CAREER	FAMILY	TRAVEL	WEDDING	MOVE	BUSINESS	HEALTH	Lotto #'s	play 3 #s
Good	Fair	Good	Good	Excellent	Good	Good	Good	Excellent	29,43,20,73,1,26,1	536

SHOPPING	GAMBLE	SEX	KEYWORD	KEYWORD						
Good	Good	is great	SOCIAL	Children,Education,Astrology,Bargains,Social Functions,Childishness,Groups - Parties,Teacher						

STRESS LEVEL	LUCKY COLORS	JEWELERY	MOONS EFFECT	GRAHA EFFECT	DAILY DEITY
Low	Green/Sky Blue/	Diamonds/Silver	Enthusiastic	Social Graha	Vishnu

DAILY PUJA	DAILY PSALMS
Wash the feet of Children, Do Satnarayan Pooja, Read & chant Geeta	3, 12, 30 ,39, 48, 57, 75, 102, 120

Tuesday, March 15, 2016 — This is considered a NEGATIVE day for you — Planet: Pluto

ADVICE & DETAILS

Overcome laziness and low pay today and improve your karma by being industrious, hard working and controlling your high temper.

MANTRA FOR TODAY

Om Jai Viganeshwaraya.. Lambodaraya Namo Namaha 21 times

MONEY	LOVE	CAREER	FAMILY	TRAVEL	WEDDING	MOVE	BUSINESS	HEALTH	Lotto #'s	play 3 #s
Bad	Fair	Bad	Fair	Bad	Good	Bad	Bad	Bad	24,45,61,28,34,68,13	131

SHOPPING	GAMBLE	SEX	KEYWORD	KEYWORD						
Bad	Bad	is tough	CAREER	Career,Hard Work,Co-workers,Low Payment,Job Problems,High Temper,Low Pay,Laziness						

STRESS LEVEL	LUCKY COLORS	JEWELERY	MOONS EFFECT	GRAHA EFFECT	DAILY DEITY
High	Dark Blue/ Purple/	Amethyst/Gold	Emotional	Job Graha	Lingam

DAILY PUJA	DAILY PSALMS
Worship Ganesh, Give gifts to father, and co -workers, Plant gardens, farms	4, 13, 31 ,40, 49, 58, 76, 103, 121

Wednesday, March 16, 2016 — This is considered a POSITIVE day for you — Planet: Venus

ADVICE & DETAILS

Although this will be a day open for you to socialize with others, you must avoid extremes and parties with alcohol and drugs. Your enemies will take advantage of you today when they see you in your weakest state. Try to rest, you will be sleepy.

MANTRA FOR TODAY

Om Graam Greem Graum Sa Gurave namah swaha 21 times

MONEY	LOVE	CAREER	FAMILY	TRAVEL	WEDDING	MOVE	BUSINESS	HEALTH	Lotto #'s	play 3 #s
Bad	Excellent	Fair	Good	Excellent	Good	Excellent	Good	Excellent	27,58,47,45,75,66,13	497

SHOPPING	GAMBLE	SEX	KEYWORD	KEYWORD						
Good	Good	is good	CHANGE	Sexuality,Travel,Change,Distant, far,Travel delays,Deception,Excercise,Illicit Affairs						

STRESS LEVEL	LUCKY COLORS	JEWELERY	MOONS EFFECT	GRAHA EFFECT	DAILY DEITY
Fair	Tan/Green/ Beige	Pearl/Silver/quartz	Courageous	Travel Graha	Nataraja

DAILY PUJA	DAILY PSALMS
Artistic gifts, Pray to Krishna, Do good deeds, do Spiritual trips	5, 14, 32 ,41, 50, 59, 77, 104, 122

Thursday, March 17, 2016 — This is considered a NEGATIVE day for you — Planet: Mars

ADVICE & DETAILS

Children will be prevalent today. This day is marked with a great deal of creativity ideal for areas related to the left side of the brain such as writing, painting, handcrafts, baking, cooking or needlework.

MANTRA FOR TODAY

Om Mana Swasti Shanti Kuru kuru Swaha Shivoham Shivoham 27 times

MONEY	LOVE	CAREER	FAMILY	TRAVEL	WEDDING	MOVE	BUSINESS	HEALTH	Lotto #'s	play 3 #s
Bad	Bad	Bad	Bad	Bad	Bad	Bad	Fair	Bad	39,29,33,67,67,8,61	139

SHOPPING	GAMBLE	SEX	KEYWORD	KEYWORD						
Fair	Bad	is frustrating	POWER	Responsibilty,Disagreement,Family,Back Pain,Family Conflicts,Traffic Ticket,Quarrels,Jealousy						

STRESS LEVEL	LUCKY COLORS	JEWELERY	MOONS EFFECT	GRAHA EFFECT	DAILY DEITY
High	Purple/Blue/Rose	Emerald/Saphire	Educational	Family Graha	Mahakali

DAILY PUJA
Meditate, Control temper, Pray to Hanuman, Chant Hanuman Chalisa

DAILY PSALMS
6, 15, 33 ,42, 51, 60, 78, 105, 123

Friday, March 18, 2016 — This is considered a NEUTRAL day for you — Planet: Uranus

ADVICE & DETAILS

The thought of watching TV is very appealing today. Spending time with children will benefit your creativity, but you must refrain from allowing immaturity to control your actions today.

MANTRA FOR TODAY

Jai Jai Shiva Shambo.(2) ...Mahadeva Shambo (2) 21 times 8

MONEY	LOVE	CAREER	FAMILY	TRAVEL	WEDDING	MOVE	BUSINESS	HEALTH	Lotto #'s	play 3 #s
Good	Good	Fair	Good	Good	Bad	Good	Bad	Fair	22,68,69,65,23,32,11	964

SHOPPING	GAMBLE	SEX	KEYWORD	KEYWORD						
Bad	Fair	is quiet	DIVINE	Spirituality,Religious,Astrology,Inner Conflicts,Religious ,Sleepiness,Advice given,Alcohol - drugs						

STRESS LEVEL	LUCKY COLORS	JEWELERY	MOONS EFFECT	GRAHA EFFECT	DAILY DEITY
Fair	Light Blue/Peach	Tiger's eye/Gold/Silver	Affectionate	God'S Graha	Shesnaag

DAILY PUJA
Chant Shiva Mantras, Take gifts to Ocean - Ganga Puja, Donate to Temple, Priests, etc.

DAILY PSALMS
7, 16, 34 ,43, 52, 61, 79, 106, 124

Saturday, March 19, 2016 — This is considered a POSITIVE day for you — Planet: Jupiter

ADVICE & DETAILS

The power of your expression today is great. Use this power to communicate with others, to write and publish or to entertain others when in groups or parties. There is the influence of someone that is jealous of you, be aware of it and try to be modest.

MANTRA FOR TODAY

Om Hareem Nama Swaha..Shri Maha Laxmi Aye Namah swaha 12 times

MONEY	LOVE	CAREER	FAMILY	TRAVEL	WEDDING	MOVE	BUSINESS	HEALTH	Lotto #'s	play 3 #s
Excellent	Good	Excellent	Good	Good	Excellent	Good	Excellent	Excellent	46,46,15,70,2,1,63	458

SHOPPING	GAMBLE	SEX	KEYWORD	KEYWORD						
Excellent	Excellent	is excellent	MONEY	Business,Major Expense,Money - Profits,Income,Investments,Power,Promotion,Fame - TV						

STRESS LEVEL	LUCKY COLORS	JEWELERY	MOONS EFFECT	GRAHA EFFECT	DAILY DEITY
Low	Yellow/Silver	Diamonds/Gold/Pearls	Secretive	Money Graha	Mahalaxmi

DAILY PUJA
Decorate Land, Feed the poor, Donate milk /products to all, Feed holy guests,

DAILY PSALMS
8, 17, 35 ,44, 53, 62, 80, 107, 125

Sunday, March 20, 2016 — This is considered a NEGATIVE day for you — Planet: Saturn

ADVICE & DETAILS

Although this will be a day open for you to socialize with others, you must avoid extremes and parties with alcohol and drugs. Your enemies will take advantage of you today when they see you in your weakest state. Try to rest, you will be sleepy.

MANTRA FOR TODAY

Om Ganga mataye nama swaha Om Varuna Devta aye Pahimam 11 times

MONEY	LOVE	CAREER	FAMILY	TRAVEL	WEDDING	MOVE	BUSINESS	HEALTH	Lotto #'s	play 3 #s
Bad	Bad	Bad	Fair	Bad	Bad	Bad	Bad	Bad	63,51,42,26,7,9,55	573

SHOPPING	GAMBLE	SEX	KEYWORD	KEYWORD						
Bad	Bad	is very bad	KARMA	Destruction,Losses,Death,Sickness - cold,Legal matter,Abusive,Karmic debts,God - Karma						

STRESS LEVEL	LUCKY COLORS	JEWELERY	MOONS EFFECT	GRAHA EFFECT	DAILY DEITY
High	Gold/Brown//Green	Saphire/Hessonite	Ivestments	Evil Graha	Agnidev

DAILY PUJA
Remembrance of family members who died, worship of older people. gifts to grand parents

DAILY PSALMS
9, 18, 36 ,45, 54, 63, 81, 108, 126

Monday, March 21, 2016 — This is considered a NEUTRAL day for you — Planet: Sun

ADVICE & DETAILS

There may be sickness of children or you may be getting sick. There will be losses and sadness.

MANTRA FOR TODAY

Om Namo Bhagawate Mukhtanandaya, 108 times

MONEY	LOVE	CAREER	FAMILY	TRAVEL	WEDDING	MOVE	BUSINESS	HEALTH	Lotto #'s	play 3 #s
Fair	Bad	Good	Bad	Fair	Bad	Fair	Fair	Fair	3,45,46,33,66,31,57	620

SHOPPING	GAMBLE	SEX	KEYWORD	KEYWORD
Fair	Fair	is fair	MIND	Independence,Loneliness,Meditative,Worry,Dominating,Illness - Cold,On Your Own,Commanding

STRESS LEVEL	LUCKY COLORS	JEWELERY	MOONS EFFECT	GRAHA EFFECT	DAILY DEITY
High	White/Yellow/	Pearl/Quartz	Arrogance	Status Graha	Saraswaty

DAILY PUJA
Give Gifts to Priests, Invite holy ones to your home, Feed Swamis and Yogis, Do Shiva Puja.

DAILY PSALMS
1, 10, 28 ,37, 46, 55, 73, 100, 118

Tuesday, March 22, 2016 — This is considered a POSITIVE day for you — Planet: Moon

ADVICE & DETAILS

Express your thoughts, opinions or information to partners and/or children. Day is influenced by children and ability to acquire information by reading or other means.

MANTRA FOR TODAY

Kali Durge Namo Nama Om Durge aye nama swaha 108 times

MONEY	LOVE	CAREER	FAMILY	TRAVEL	WEDDING	MOVE	BUSINESS	HEALTH	Lotto #'s	play 3 #s
Good	Excellent	Good	Good	Excellent	Good	Good	Good	Good	53,27,9,14,71,24,51	317

SHOPPING	GAMBLE	SEX	KEYWORD	KEYWORD
Good	Good	is good	LOVE	Romance,Popularity,Visitors,Shopping,Food, Drinks,Co-operation,Friendships,Affection

STRESS LEVEL	LUCKY COLORS	JEWELERY	MOONS EFFECT	GRAHA EFFECT	DAILY DEITY
Low	Red/Yellow/Pink	Topaz/Diamonds	Conservative	Love Graha	Gauri

DAILY PUJA
Give Gifts to females andnMother, Serve milk Products, Worship Durga forms

DAILY PSALMS
2, 11, 29 ,38, 47, 56, 74, 101, 119

Wednesday, March 23, 2016 — This is considered a POSITIVE day for you — Planet: Mercury

ADVICE & DETAILS

Reading will benefit you today. You will have to hone your communication skills and speak clearly and listen carefully, especially when dealing with Real Estate and teachers of any type.

MANTRA FOR TODAY

Om hareem Kleem Hreem Aem Saraswataye namaha 21 times

MONEY	LOVE	CAREER	FAMILY	TRAVEL	WEDDING	MOVE	BUSINESS	HEALTH	Lotto #'s	play 3 #s
Good	Fair	Good	Good	Excellent	Good	Good	Good	Excellent	65,72,5,4,29,10,24	597

SHOPPING	GAMBLE	SEX	KEYWORD	KEYWORD
Good	Good	is great	SOCIAL	Children,Education,Astrology,Bargains,Social Functions,Childishness,Groups - Parties,Teacher

STRESS LEVEL	LUCKY COLORS	JEWELERY	MOONS EFFECT	GRAHA EFFECT	DAILY DEITY
Low	Green/Sky Blue/	Diamonds/Silver	Enthusiastic	Social Graha	Vishnu

DAILY PUJA
Wash the feet of Children, Do Satnarayan Pooja, Read & chant Geeta

DAILY PSALMS
3, 12, 30 ,39, 48, 57, 75, 102, 120

Thursday, March 24, 2016 — This is considered a NEGATIVE day for you — Planet: Pluto

ADVICE & DETAILS

Overcome laziness and low pay today and improve your karma by being industrious, hard working and controlling your high temper.

MANTRA FOR TODAY

Om Jai Viganeshwaraya.. Lambodaraya Namo Namaha 21 times

MONEY	LOVE	CAREER	FAMILY	TRAVEL	WEDDING	MOVE	BUSINESS	HEALTH	Lotto #'s	play 3 #s
Bad	Fair	Bad	Fair	Bad	Good	Bad	Bad	Bad	67,21,6,41,59,5,12	824

SHOPPING	GAMBLE	SEX	KEYWORD	KEYWORD
Bad	Bad	is tough	CAREER	Career,Hard Work,Co-workers,Low Payment,Job Problems,High Temper,Low Pay,Laziness

STRESS LEVEL	LUCKY COLORS	JEWELERY	MOONS EFFECT	GRAHA EFFECT	DAILY DEITY
High	Dark Blue/ Purple/	Amethyst/Gold	Emotional	Job Graha	Lingam

DAILY PUJA
Worship Ganesh, Give gifts to father, and co -workers, Plant gardens, farms

DAILY PSALMS
4, 13, 31 ,40, 49, 58, 76, 103, 121

Friday, March 25, 2016 — This is considered a POSITIVE day for you — Planet: Venus

ADVICE & DETAILS

Although this will be a day open for you to socialize with others, you must avoid extremes and parties with alcohol and drugs. Your enemies will take advantage of you today when they see you in your weakest state. Try to rest, you will be sleepy.

MANTRA FOR TODAY

Om Graam Greem Graum Sa Gurave namah swaha 21 times

MONEY	LOVE	CAREER	FAMILY	TRAVEL	WEDDING	MOVE	BUSINESS	HEALTH	Lotto #'s	play 3 #s
Bad	Excellent	Fair	Good	Excellent	Good	Excellent	Good	Excellent	12,19,53,23,56,61,54	627

SHOPPING	GAMBLE	SEX	KEYWORD	KEYWORD						
Good	Good	is good	CHANGE	Sexuality,Travel,Change,Distant, far,Travel delays,Deception,Excercise,Illicit Affairs						

STRESS LEVEL	LUCKY COLORS	JEWELERY	MOONS EFFECT	GRAHA EFFECT	DAILY DEITY
Fair	Tan/Green/ Beige	Pearl/Silver/quartz	Courageous	Travel Graha	Nataraja

DAILY PUJA	DAILY PSALMS
Artistic gifts, Pray to Krishna, Do good deeds, do Spiritual trips	5, 14, 32 ,41, 50, 59, 77, 104, 122

Saturday, March 26, 2016 — This is considered a NEGATIVE day for you — Planet: Mars

ADVICE & DETAILS

Children will be prevalent today. This day is marked with a great deal of creativity ideal for areas related to the left side of the brain such as writing, painting, handcrafts, baking, cooking or needlework.

MANTRA FOR TODAY

Om Mana Swasti Shanti Kuru kuru Swaha Shivoham Shivoham 27 times

MONEY	LOVE	CAREER	FAMILY	TRAVEL	WEDDING	MOVE	BUSINESS	HEALTH	Lotto #'s	play 3 #s
Bad	Bad	Bad	Bad	Bad	Bad	Bad	Fair	Bad	23,55,11,34,20,44,67	368

SHOPPING	GAMBLE	SEX	KEYWORD	KEYWORD						
Fair	Bad	is frustrating	POWER	Responsibilty,Disagreement,Family,Back Pain,Family Conflicts,Traffic Ticket,Quarrels,Jealousy						

STRESS LEVEL	LUCKY COLORS	JEWELERY	MOONS EFFECT	GRAHA EFFECT	DAILY DEITY
High	Purple/Blue/Rose	Emerald/Saphire	Educational	Family Graha	Mahakali

DAILY PUJA	DAILY PSALMS
Meditate, Control temper, Pray to Hanuman, Chant Hanuman Chalisa	6, 15, 33 ,42, 51, 60, 78, 105, 123

Sunday, March 27, 2016 — This is considered a NEUTRAL day for you — Planet: Uranus

ADVICE & DETAILS

The thought of watching TV is very appealing today. Spending time with children will benefit your creativity, but you must refrain from allowing immaturity to control your actions today.

MANTRA FOR TODAY

Jai Jai Shiva Shambo.(2) ...Mahadeva Shambo (2) 21 times 8

MONEY	LOVE	CAREER	FAMILY	TRAVEL	WEDDING	MOVE	BUSINESS	HEALTH	Lotto #'s	play 3 #s
Good	Good	Fair	Good	Good	Bad	Good	Bad	Fair	67,68,54,54,1,59,22	999

SHOPPING	GAMBLE	SEX	KEYWORD	KEYWORD						
Bad	Fair	is quiet	DIVINE	Spirituality,Religious,Astrology,Inner Conflicts,Religious ,Sleepiness,Advice given,Alcohol - drugs						

STRESS LEVEL	LUCKY COLORS	JEWELERY	MOONS EFFECT	GRAHA EFFECT	DAILY DEITY
Fair	Light Blue/Peach	Tiger's eye/Gold/Silver	Affectionate	God'S Graha	Shesnaag

DAILY PUJA	DAILY PSALMS
Chant Shiva Mantras, Take gifts to Ocean - Ganga Puja, Donate to Temple, Priests, etc.	7, 16, 34 ,43, 52, 61, 79, 106, 124

Monday, March 28, 2016 — This is considered a POSITIVE day for you — Planet: Jupiter

ADVICE & DETAILS

The power of your expression today is great. Use this power to communicate with others, to write and publish or to entertain others when in groups or parties. There is the influence of someone that is jealous of you, be aware of it and try to be modest.

MANTRA FOR TODAY

Om Hareem Nama Swaha..Shri Maha Laxmi Aye Namah swaha 12 times

MONEY	LOVE	CAREER	FAMILY	TRAVEL	WEDDING	MOVE	BUSINESS	HEALTH	Lotto #'s	play 3 #s
Excellent	Good	Excellent	Good	Good	Excellent	Good	Excellent	Excellent	57,33,8,58,31,63,34	390

SHOPPING	GAMBLE	SEX	KEYWORD	KEYWORD						
Excellent	Excellent	is excellent	MONEY	Business,Major Expense,Money - Profits,Income,Investments,Power,Promotion,Fame - TV						

STRESS LEVEL	LUCKY COLORS	JEWELERY	MOONS EFFECT	GRAHA EFFECT	DAILY DEITY
Low	Yellow/Silver	Diamonds/Gold/Pearls	Secretive	Money Graha	Mahalaxmi

DAILY PUJA	DAILY PSALMS
Decorate Land, Feed the poor, Donate milk /products to all, Feed holy guests,	8, 17, 35 ,44, 53, 62, 80, 107, 125

Tuesday, March 29, 2016 — This is considered a NEGATIVE day for you — Planet: Saturn

ADVICE & DETAILS	MANTRA FOR TODAY
Although this will be a day open for you to socialize with others, you must avoid extremes and parties with alcohol and drugs. Your enemies will take advantage of you today when they see you in your weakest state. Try to rest, you will be sleepy.	Om Ganga mataye nama swaha Om Varuna Devta aye Pahimam 11 times

MONEY	LOVE	CAREER	FAMILY	TRAVEL	WEDDING	MOVE	BUSINESS	HEALTH	Lotto #'s	play 3 #s
Bad	Bad	Bad	Fair	Bad	Bad	Bad	Bad	Bad	29,35,64,63,64,62,34	118

SHOPPING	GAMBLE	SEX	KEYWORD	KEYWORD				
Bad	Bad	is very bad	KARMA	Destruction,Losses,Death,Sickness - cold,Legal matter,Abusive,Karmic debts,God - Karma				

STRESS LEVEL	LUCKY COLORS	JEWELERY	MOONS EFFECT	GRAHA EFFECT	DAILY DEITY
High	Gold/Brown//Green	Saphire/Hessonite	Ivestments	Evil Graha	Agnidev

DAILY PUJA	DAILY PSALMS
Remembrance of family members who died, worship of older people. gifts to grand parents	9, 18, 36 ,45, 54, 63, 81, 108, 126

Wednesday, March 30, 2016 — This is considered a NEUTRAL day for you — Planet: Sun

ADVICE & DETAILS	MANTRA FOR TODAY
There may be sickness of children or you may be getting sick. There will be losses and sadness.	Om Namo Bhagawate Mukhtanandaya, 108 times

MONEY	LOVE	CAREER	FAMILY	TRAVEL	WEDDING	MOVE	BUSINESS	HEALTH	Lotto #'s	play 3 #s
Fair	Bad	Good	Bad	Fair	Bad	Fair	Fair	Fair	36,23,44,34,52,10,72	16

SHOPPING	GAMBLE	SEX	KEYWORD	KEYWORD				
Fair	Fair	is fair	MIND	Independence,Loneliness,Meditative,Worry,Dominating,Illness - Cold,On Your Own,Commanding				

STRESS LEVEL	LUCKY COLORS	JEWELERY	MOONS EFFECT	GRAHA EFFECT	DAILY DEITY
High	White/Yellow/	Pearl/Quartz	Arrogance	Status Graha	Saraswaty

DAILY PUJA	DAILY PSALMS
Give Gifts to Priests, Invite holy ones to your home, Feed Swamis and Yogis, Do Shiva Puja.	1, 10, 28 ,37, 46, 55, 73, 100, 118

Thursday, March 31, 2016 — This is considered a POSITIVE day for you — Planet: Moon

ADVICE & DETAILS	MANTRA FOR TODAY
Express your thoughts, opinions or information to partners and/or children. Day is influenced by children and ability to acquire information by reading or other means.	Kali Durge Namo Nama Om Durge aye nama swaha 108 times

MONEY	LOVE	CAREER	FAMILY	TRAVEL	WEDDING	MOVE	BUSINESS	HEALTH	Lotto #'s	play 3 #s
Good	Excellent	Good	Good	Excellent	Good	Good	Good	Good	52,52,11,70,63,20,58	155

SHOPPING	GAMBLE	SEX	KEYWORD	KEYWORD				
Good	Good	is good	LOVE	Romance,Popularity,Visitors,Shopping,Food, Drinks,Co-operation,Friendships,Affection				

STRESS LEVEL	LUCKY COLORS	JEWELERY	MOONS EFFECT	GRAHA EFFECT	DAILY DEITY
Low	Red/Yellow/Pink	Topaz/Diamonds	Conservative	Love Graha	Gauri

DAILY PUJA	DAILY PSALMS
Give Gifts to females andnMother, Serve milk Products, Worship Durga forms	2, 11, 29 ,38, 47, 56, 74, 101, 119

Friday, April 1, 2016 — This is considered a POSITIVE day for you — Planet: Jupiter

ADVICE & DETAILS	MANTRA FOR TODAY
Dealings with Real Estate of things related to your professional life may bring beauty and sex into your realm. You will feel fatigued during the day.	Om Hareem Nama Swaha..Shri Maha Laxmi Aye Namah swaha 12 times

MONEY	LOVE	CAREER	FAMILY	TRAVEL	WEDDING	MOVE	BUSINESS	HEALTH	Lotto #'s	play 3 #s
Excellent	Good	Excellent	Good	Good	Excellent	Good	Excellent	Excellent	26,8,1,44,52,58,72	141

SHOPPING	GAMBLE	SEX	KEYWORD	KEYWORD				
Excellent	Excellent	is excellent	MONEY	Business,Major Expense,Money - Profits,Income,Investments,Power,Promotion,Fame - TV				

STRESS LEVEL	LUCKY COLORS	JEWELERY	MOONS EFFECT	GRAHA EFFECT	DAILY DEITY
Low	Yellow/Silver	Diamonds/Gold/Pearls	Secretive	Money Graha	Mahalaxmi

DAILY PUJA	DAILY PSALMS
Decorate Land, Feed the poor, Donate milk /products to all, Feed holy guests,	8, 17, 35 ,44, 53, 62, 80, 107, 125

Saturday, April 2, 2016 — This is considered a NEGATIVE day for you — Planet: Saturn

ADVICE & DETAILS

Be ready to face job difficulties that may come to you today centered in your godliness not your ego. Remember this day is part of your career and the long-term goals you have.

MANTRA FOR TODAY

Om Ganga mataye nama swaha
Om Varuna Devta aye Pahimam 11 times

MONEY	LOVE	CAREER	FAMILY	TRAVEL	WEDDING	MOVE	BUSINESS	HEALTH	Lotto #'s	play 3 #s
Bad	Bad	Bad	Fair	Bad	Bad	Bad	Bad	Bad	68,67,10,8,11,47,12	498

SHOPPING	GAMBLE	SEX	KEYWORD	KEYWORD				
Bad	Bad	is very bad	KARMA	Destruction,Losses,Death,Sickness - cold,Legal matter,Abusive,Karmic debts,God - Karma				

STRESS LEVEL	LUCKY COLORS	JEWELERY	MOONS EFFECT	GRAHA EFFECT	DAILY DEITY
High	Gold/Brown//Green	Saphire/Hessonite	Ivestments	Evil Graha	Agnidev

DAILY PUJA
Remembrance of family members who died, worship of older people. gifts to grand parents

DAILY PSALMS
9, 18, 36 ,45, 54, 63, 81, 108, 126

Sunday, April 3, 2016 — This is considered a NEUTRAL day for you — Planet: Sun

ADVICE & DETAILS

Assiduous dedication to your tasks and responsibilities will be rewarded today. It will be a day when you are busy, but being indolent today will cost you dearly in financial opportunities.

MANTRA FOR TODAY

Om Namo Bhagawate Mukhtanandaya, 108 times

MONEY	LOVE	CAREER	FAMILY	TRAVEL	WEDDING	MOVE	BUSINESS	HEALTH	Lotto #'s	play 3 #s
Fair	Bad	Good	Bad	Fair	Bad	Fair	Fair	Fair	26,62,53,24,39,65,20	237

SHOPPING	GAMBLE	SEX	KEYWORD	KEYWORD				
Fair	Fair	is fair	MIND	Independence,Loneliness,Meditative,Worry,Dominating,Illness - Cold,On Your Own,Commanding				

STRESS LEVEL	LUCKY COLORS	JEWELERY	MOONS EFFECT	GRAHA EFFECT	DAILY DEITY
High	White/Yellow/	Pearl/Quartz	Arrogance	Status Graha	Saraswaty

DAILY PUJA
Give Gifts to Priests, Invite holy ones to your home, Feed Swamis and Yogis, Do Shiva Puja.

DAILY PSALMS
1, 10, 28 ,37, 46, 55, 73, 100, 118

Monday, April 4, 2016 — This is considered a POSITIVE day for you — Planet: Moon

ADVICE & DETAILS

Your karma for today requires you to be industrious and work very hard. You must put your laziness away. Associates will give you positive input and/or help.

MANTRA FOR TODAY

Kali Durge Namo Nama Om Durge aye nama swaha 108 times

MONEY	LOVE	CAREER	FAMILY	TRAVEL	WEDDING	MOVE	BUSINESS	HEALTH	Lotto #'s	play 3 #s
Good	Excellent	Good	Good	Excellent	Good	Good	Good	Good	10,73,12,75,51,47,53	999

SHOPPING	GAMBLE	SEX	KEYWORD	KEYWORD				
Good	Good	is good	LOVE	Romance,Popularity,Visitors,Shopping,Food, Drinks,Co-operation,Friendships,Affection				

STRESS LEVEL	LUCKY COLORS	JEWELERY	MOONS EFFECT	GRAHA EFFECT	DAILY DEITY
Low	Red/Yellow/Pink	Topaz/Diamonds	Conservative	Love Graha	Gauri

DAILY PUJA
Give Gifts to females andnMother, Serve milk Products, Worship Durga forms

DAILY PSALMS
2, 11, 29 ,38, 47, 56, 74, 101, 119

Tuesday, April 5, 2016 — This is considered a POSITIVE day for you — Planet: Mercury

ADVICE & DETAILS

Today is a day to work and work even if you feel lazy. You need to be industrious and achieve all tasks that you can today. You will be in association with others while doing these projects, accept the input.

MANTRA FOR TODAY

Om hareem Kleem Hreem Aem Saraswataye namaha 21 times

MONEY	LOVE	CAREER	FAMILY	TRAVEL	WEDDING	MOVE	BUSINESS	HEALTH	Lotto #'s	play 3 #s
Good	Fair	Good	Good	Excellent	Good	Good	Good	Excellent	52,54,67,1,34,57,60	253

SHOPPING	GAMBLE	SEX	KEYWORD	KEYWORD				
Good	Good	is great	SOCIAL	Children,Education,Astrology,Bargains,Social Functions,Childishness,Groups - Parties,Teacher				

STRESS LEVEL	LUCKY COLORS	JEWELERY	MOONS EFFECT	GRAHA EFFECT	DAILY DEITY
Low	Green/Sky Blue/	Diamonds/Silver	Enthusiastic	Social Graha	Vishnu

DAILY PUJA
Wash the feet of Children, Do Satnarayan Pooja, Read & chant Geeta

DAILY PSALMS
3, 12, 30 ,39, 48, 57, 75, 102, 120

Wednesday, April 6, 2016 — This is considered a NEGATIVE day for you — Planet: Pluto

ADVICE & DETAILS

Today you feel lazy, but you will need to work, be industrious and accomplish as much as possible. You will need to control your high temper and accept that today you will feel like they do not pay you enough to do your job.

MANTRA FOR TODAY

Om Jai Viganeshwaraya.. Lambodaraya Namo Namaha 21 times

MONEY	LOVE	CAREER	FAMILY	TRAVEL	WEDDING	MOVE	BUSINESS	HEALTH	Lotto #'s	play 3 #s
Bad	Fair	Bad	Fair	Bad	Good	Bad	Bad	Bad	7,58,21,11,16,23,56	938

SHOPPING	GAMBLE	SEX	KEYWORD	KEYWORD
Bad	Bad	is tough	CAREER	Career,Hard Work,Co-workers,Low Payment,Job Problems,High Temper,Low Pay,Laziness

STRESS LEVEL	LUCKY COLORS	JEWELERY	MOONS EFFECT	GRAHA EFFECT	DAILY DEITY
High	Dark Blue/ Purple/	Amethyst/Gold	Emotional	Job Graha	Lingam

DAILY PUJA
Worship Ganesh, Give gifts to father, and co -workers, Plant gardens, farms

DAILY PSALMS
4, 13, 31 ,40, 49, 58, 76, 103, 121

Thursday, April 7, 2016 — This is considered a POSITIVE day for you — Planet: Venus

ADVICE & DETAILS

Do not allow the job problems that you may have today to affect your long-term career plans. Remember the foundation of your career is built on a day per day basis at your job. Act and think conscious of your godliness.

MANTRA FOR TODAY

Om Graam Greem Graum Sa Gurave namah swaha 21 times

MONEY	LOVE	CAREER	FAMILY	TRAVEL	WEDDING	MOVE	BUSINESS	HEALTH	Lotto #'s	play 3 #s
Bad	Excellent	Fair	Good	Excellent	Good	Excellent	Good	Excellent	55,16,29,37,75,57,11	726

SHOPPING	GAMBLE	SEX	KEYWORD	KEYWORD
Good	Good	is good	CHANGE	Sexuality,Travel,Change,Distant, far,Travel delays,Deception,Excercise,Illicit Affairs

STRESS LEVEL	LUCKY COLORS	JEWELERY	MOONS EFFECT	GRAHA EFFECT	DAILY DEITY
Fair	Tan/Green/ Beige	Pearl/Silver/quartz	Courageous	Travel Graha	Nataraja

DAILY PUJA
Artistic gifts, Pray to Krishna, Do good deeds, do Spiritual trips

DAILY PSALMS
5, 14, 32 ,41, 50, 59, 77, 104, 122

Friday, April 8, 2016 — This is considered a NEGATIVE day for you — Planet: Mars

ADVICE & DETAILS

You are going to feel very lazy today, but you must push through this feeling and devote your day to work with others and work diligently.

MANTRA FOR TODAY

Om Mana Swasti Shanti Kuru kuru Swaha Shivoham Shivoham 27 times

MONEY	LOVE	CAREER	FAMILY	TRAVEL	WEDDING	MOVE	BUSINESS	HEALTH	Lotto #'s	play 3 #s
Bad	Bad	Bad	Bad	Bad	Bad	Bad	Fair	Bad	25,22,3,13,15,62,28	216

SHOPPING	GAMBLE	SEX	KEYWORD	KEYWORD
Fair	Bad	is frustrating	POWER	Responsibilty,Disagreement,Family,Back Pain,Family Conflicts,Traffic Ticket,Quarrels,Jealousy

STRESS LEVEL	LUCKY COLORS	JEWELERY	MOONS EFFECT	GRAHA EFFECT	DAILY DEITY
High	Purple/Blue/Rose	Emerald/Saphire	Educational	Family Graha	Mahakali

DAILY PUJA
Meditate, Control temper, Pray to Hanuman, Chant Hanuman Chalisa

DAILY PSALMS
6, 15, 33 ,42, 51, 60, 78, 105, 123

Saturday, April 9, 2016 — This is considered a NEUTRAL day for you — Planet: Uranus

ADVICE & DETAILS

Find a reprieve from the weariness of everyday building your professional life by finding a book and reading about something that interests you and makes you happy.

MANTRA FOR TODAY

Jai Jai Shiva Shambo.(2) ...Mahadeva Shambo (2) 21 times 8

MONEY	LOVE	CAREER	FAMILY	TRAVEL	WEDDING	MOVE	BUSINESS	HEALTH	Lotto #'s	play 3 #s
Good	Good	Fair	Good	Good	Bad	Good	Bad	Fair	73,45,13,42,39,38,74	304

SHOPPING	GAMBLE	SEX	KEYWORD	KEYWORD
Bad	Fair	is quiet	DIVINE	Spirituality,Religious,Astrology,Inner Conflicts,Religious ,Sleepiness,Advice given,Alcohol - drugs

STRESS LEVEL	LUCKY COLORS	JEWELERY	MOONS EFFECT	GRAHA EFFECT	DAILY DEITY
Fair	Light Blue/Peach	Tiger's eye/Gold/Silver	Affectionate	God'S Graha	Shesnaag

DAILY PUJA
Chant Shiva Mantras, Take gifts to Ocean - Ganga Puja, Donate to Temple, Priests, etc.

DAILY PSALMS
7, 16, 34 ,43, 52, 61, 79, 106, 124

Sunday, April 10, 2016 — This is considered a POSITIVE day for you — Planet: Jupiter

ADVICE & DETAILS

Dealings with Real Estate of things related to your professional life may bring beauty and sex into your realm. You will feel fatigued during the day.

MANTRA FOR TODAY

Om Hareem Nama Swaha..Shri Maha Laxmi Aye Namah swaha 12 times

MONEY	LOVE	CAREER	FAMILY	TRAVEL	WEDDING	MOVE	BUSINESS	HEALTH	Lotto #'s	play 3 #s
Excellent	Good	Excellent	Good	Good	Excellent	Good	Excellent	Excellent	21,19,26,69,74,18,33	648

SHOPPING	GAMBLE	SEX	KEYWORD	KEYWORD						
Excellent	Excellent	is excellent	MONEY	Business,Major Expense,Money - Profits,Income,Investments,Power,Promotion,Fame - TV						

STRESS LEVEL	LUCKY COLORS	JEWELERY	MOONS EFFECT	GRAHA EFFECT	DAILY DEITY
Low	Yellow/Silver	Diamonds/Gold/Pearls	Secretive	Money Graha	Mahalaxmi

DAILY PUJA	DAILY PSALMS
Decorate Land, Feed the poor, Donate milk /products to all, Feed holy guests,	8, 17, 35 ,44, 53, 62, 80, 107, 125

Monday, April 11, 2016 — This is considered a NEGATIVE day for you — Planet: Saturn

ADVICE & DETAILS

Be ready to face job difficulties that may come to you today centered in your godliness not your ego. Remember this day is part of your career and the long-term goals you have.

MANTRA FOR TODAY

Om Ganga mataye nama swaha Om Varuna Devta aye Pahimam 11 times

MONEY	LOVE	CAREER	FAMILY	TRAVEL	WEDDING	MOVE	BUSINESS	HEALTH	Lotto #'s	play 3 #s
Bad	Bad	Bad	Fair	Bad	Bad	Bad	Bad	Bad	29,38,44,11,52,9,25	532

SHOPPING	GAMBLE	SEX	KEYWORD	KEYWORD						
Bad	Bad	is very bad	KARMA	Destruction,Losses,Death,Sickness - cold,Legal matter,Abusive,Karmic debts,God - Karma						

STRESS LEVEL	LUCKY COLORS	JEWELERY	MOONS EFFECT	GRAHA EFFECT	DAILY DEITY
High	Gold/Brown//Green	Saphire/Hessonite	Ivestments	Evil Graha	Agnidev

DAILY PUJA	DAILY PSALMS
Remembrance of family members who died, worship of older people. gifts to grand parents	9, 18, 36 ,45, 54, 63, 81, 108, 126

Tuesday, April 12, 2016 — This is considered a NEUTRAL day for you — Planet: Sun

ADVICE & DETAILS

Assiduous dedication to your tasks and responsibilities will be rewarded today. It will be a day when you are busy, but being indolent today will cost you dearly in financial opportunities.

MANTRA FOR TODAY

Om Namo Bhagawate Mukhtanandaya, 108 times

MONEY	LOVE	CAREER	FAMILY	TRAVEL	WEDDING	MOVE	BUSINESS	HEALTH	Lotto #'s	play 3 #s
Fair	Bad	Good	Bad	Fair	Bad	Fair	Fair	Fair	63,40,24,48,30,55,40	416

SHOPPING	GAMBLE	SEX	KEYWORD	KEYWORD						
Fair	Fair	is fair	MIND	Independence,Loneliness,Meditative,Worry,Dominating,Illness - Cold,On Your Own,Commanding						

STRESS LEVEL	LUCKY COLORS	JEWELERY	MOONS EFFECT	GRAHA EFFECT	DAILY DEITY
High	White/Yellow/	Pearl/Quartz	Arrogance	Status Graha	Saraswaty

DAILY PUJA	DAILY PSALMS
Give Gifts to Priests, Invite holy ones to your home, Feed Swamis and Yogis, Do Shiva Puja.	1, 10, 28 ,37, 46, 55, 73, 100, 118

Wednesday, April 13, 2016 — This is considered a POSITIVE day for you — Planet: Moon

ADVICE & DETAILS

Your karma for today requires you to be industrious and work very hard. You must put your laziness away. Associates will give you positive input and/or help.

MANTRA FOR TODAY

Kali Durge Namo Nama Om Durge aye nama swaha 108 times

MONEY	LOVE	CAREER	FAMILY	TRAVEL	WEDDING	MOVE	BUSINESS	HEALTH	Lotto #'s	play 3 #s
Good	Excellent	Good	Good	Excellent	Good	Good	Good	Good	6,27,25,16,11,42,36	222

SHOPPING	GAMBLE	SEX	KEYWORD	KEYWORD						
Good	Good	is good	LOVE	Romance,Popularity,Visitors,Shopping,Food, Drinks,Co-operation,Friendships,Affection						

STRESS LEVEL	LUCKY COLORS	JEWELERY	MOONS EFFECT	GRAHA EFFECT	DAILY DEITY
Low	Red/Yellow/Pink	Topaz/Diamonds	Conservative	Love Graha	Gauri

DAILY PUJA	DAILY PSALMS
Give Gifts to females andnMother, Serve milk Products, Worship Durga forms	2, 11, 29 ,38, 47, 56, 74, 101, 119

Thursday, April 14, 2016 — This is considered a POSITIVE day for you — Planet: Mercury

ADVICE & DETAILS

Today is a day to work and work even if you feel lazy. You need to be industrious and achieve all tasks that you can today. You will be in association with others while doing these projects, accept the input.

MANTRA FOR TODAY

Om hareem Kleem Hreem Aem Saraswataye namaha 21 times

MONEY	LOVE	CAREER	FAMILY	TRAVEL	WEDDING	MOVE	BUSINESS	HEALTH	Lotto #'s	play 3 #s
Good	Fair	Good	Good	Excellent	Good	Good	Good	Excellent	61,56,61,14,63,18,68	708

SHOPPING	GAMBLE	SEX	KEYWORD	KEYWORD						
Good	Good	is great	SOCIAL	Children,Education,Astrology,Bargains,Social Functions,Childishness,Groups - Parties,Teacher						

STRESS LEVEL	LUCKY COLORS	JEWELERY	MOONS EFFECT	GRAHA EFFECT	DAILY DEITY
Low	Green/Sky Blue/	Diamonds/Silver	Enthusiastic	Social Graha	Vishnu

DAILY PUJA	DAILY PSALMS
Wash the feet of Children, Do Satnarayan Pooja, Read & chant Geeta	3, 12, 30 ,39, 48, 57, 75, 102, 120

Friday, April 15, 2016 — This is considered a NEGATIVE day for you — Planet: Pluto

ADVICE & DETAILS

Today you feel lazy, but you will need to work, be industrious and accomplish as much as possible. You will need to control your high temper and accept that today you will feel like they do not pay you enough to do your job.

MANTRA FOR TODAY

Om Jai Viganeshwaraya.. Lambodaraya Namo Namaha 21 times

MONEY	LOVE	CAREER	FAMILY	TRAVEL	WEDDING	MOVE	BUSINESS	HEALTH	Lotto #'s	play 3 #s
Bad	Fair	Bad	Fair	Bad	Good	Bad	Bad	Bad	73,43,71,8,35,27,54	102

SHOPPING	GAMBLE	SEX	KEYWORD	KEYWORD						
Bad	Bad	is tough	CAREER	Career,Hard Work,Co-workers,Low Payment,Job Problems,High Temper,Low Pay,Laziness						

STRESS LEVEL	LUCKY COLORS	JEWELERY	MOONS EFFECT	GRAHA EFFECT	DAILY DEITY
High	Dark Blue/ Purple/	Amethyst/Gold	Emotional	Job Graha	Lingam

DAILY PUJA	DAILY PSALMS
Worship Ganesh, Give gifts to father, and co -workers, Plant gardens, farms	4, 13, 31 ,40, 49, 58, 76, 103, 121

Saturday, April 16, 2016 — This is considered a POSITIVE day for you — Planet: Venus

ADVICE & DETAILS

Do not allow the job problems that you may have today to affect your long-term career plans. Remember the foundation of your career is built on a day per day basis at your job. Act and think conscious of your godliness.

MANTRA FOR TODAY

Om Graam Greem Graum Sa Gurave namah swaha 21 times

MONEY	LOVE	CAREER	FAMILY	TRAVEL	WEDDING	MOVE	BUSINESS	HEALTH	Lotto #'s	play 3 #s
Bad	Excellent	Fair	Good	Excellent	Good	Excellent	Good	Excellent	26,61,63,53,10,63,1	856

SHOPPING	GAMBLE	SEX	KEYWORD	KEYWORD						
Good	Good	is good	CHANGE	Sexuality,Travel,Change,Distant, far,Travel delays,Deception,Excercise,Illicit Affairs						

STRESS LEVEL	LUCKY COLORS	JEWELERY	MOONS EFFECT	GRAHA EFFECT	DAILY DEITY
Fair	Tan/Green/ Beige	Pearl/Silver/quartz	Courageous	Travel Graha	Nataraja

DAILY PUJA	DAILY PSALMS
Artistic gifts, Pray to Krishna, Do good deeds, do Spiritual trips	5, 14, 32 ,41, 50, 59, 77, 104, 122

Sunday, April 17, 2016 — This is considered a NEGATIVE day for you — Planet: Mars

ADVICE & DETAILS

You are going to feel very lazy today, but you must push through this feeling and devote your day to work with others and work diligently.

MANTRA FOR TODAY

Om Mana Swasti Shanti Kuru kuru Swaha Shivoham Shivoham 27 times

MONEY	LOVE	CAREER	FAMILY	TRAVEL	WEDDING	MOVE	BUSINESS	HEALTH	Lotto #'s	play 3 #s
Bad	Bad	Bad	Bad	Bad	Bad	Bad	Fair	Bad	65,61,44,60,62,5,14	861

SHOPPING	GAMBLE	SEX	KEYWORD	KEYWORD						
Fair	Bad	is frustrating	POWER	Responsibilty,Disagreement,Family,Back Pain,Family Conflicts,Traffic Ticket,Quarrels,Jealousy						

STRESS LEVEL	LUCKY COLORS	JEWELERY	MOONS EFFECT	GRAHA EFFECT	DAILY DEITY
High	Purple/Blue/Rose	Emerald/Saphire	Educational	Family Graha	Mahakali

DAILY PUJA	DAILY PSALMS
Meditate, Control temper, Pray to Hanuman, Chant Hanuman Chalisa	6, 15, 33 ,42, 51, 60, 78, 105, 123

Monday, April 18, 2016 — This is considered a NEUTRAL day for you — Planet: Uranus

ADVICE & DETAILS

Find a reprieve from the weariness of everyday building your professional life by finding a book and reading about something that interests you and makes you happy.

MANTRA FOR TODAY

Jai Jai Shiva Shambo.(2) ...Mahadeva Shambo (2) 21 times 8

MONEY	LOVE	CAREER	FAMILY	TRAVEL	WEDDING	MOVE	BUSINESS	HEALTH	Lotto #'s	play 3 #s
Good	Good	Fair	Good	Good	Bad	Good	Bad	Fair	54,67,34,1,3,74,33	839

SHOPPING	GAMBLE	SEX	KEYWORD	KEYWORD						
Bad	Fair	is quiet	DIVINE	Spirituality,Religious,Astrology,Inner Conflicts,Religious ,Sleepiness,Advice given,Alcohol - drugs						

STRESS LEVEL	LUCKY COLORS	JEWELERY	MOONS EFFECT	GRAHA EFFECT	DAILY DEITY
Fair	Light Blue/Peach	Tiger's eye/Gold/Silver	Affectionate	God'S Graha	Shesnaag

DAILY PUJA
Chant Shiva Mantras, Take gifts to Ocean - Ganga Puja, Donate to Temple, Priests, etc.

DAILY PSALMS
7, 16, 34 ,43, 52, 61, 79, 106, 124

Tuesday, April 19, 2016 — This is considered a POSITIVE day for you — Planet: Jupiter

ADVICE & DETAILS

Dealings with Real Estate of things related to your professional life may bring beauty and sex into your realm. You will feel fatigued during the day.

MANTRA FOR TODAY

Om Hareem Nama Swaha..Shri Maha Laxmi Aye Namah swaha 12 times

MONEY	LOVE	CAREER	FAMILY	TRAVEL	WEDDING	MOVE	BUSINESS	HEALTH	Lotto #'s	play 3 #s
Excellent	Good	Excellent	Good	Good	Excellent	Good	Excellent	Excellent	24,11,39,60,20,39,10	314

SHOPPING	GAMBLE	SEX	KEYWORD	KEYWORD						
Excellent	Excellent	is excellent	MONEY	Business,Major Expense,Money - Profits,Income,Investments,Power,Promotion,Fame - TV						

STRESS LEVEL	LUCKY COLORS	JEWELERY	MOONS EFFECT	GRAHA EFFECT	DAILY DEITY
Low	Yellow/Silver	Diamonds/Gold/Pearls	Secretive	Money Graha	Mahalaxmi

DAILY PUJA
Decorate Land, Feed the poor, Donate milk /products to all, Feed holy guests,

DAILY PSALMS
8, 17, 35 ,44, 53, 62, 80, 107, 125

Wednesday, April 20, 2016 — This is considered a NEGATIVE day for you — Planet: Saturn

ADVICE & DETAILS

Be ready to face job difficulties that may come to you today centered in your godliness not your ego. Remember this day is part of your career and the long-term goals you have.

MANTRA FOR TODAY

Om Ganga mataye nama swaha Om Varuna Devta aye Pahimam 11 times

MONEY	LOVE	CAREER	FAMILY	TRAVEL	WEDDING	MOVE	BUSINESS	HEALTH	Lotto #'s	play 3 #s
Bad	Bad	Bad	Fair	Bad	Bad	Bad	Bad	Bad	75,65,9,1,70,62,43	511

SHOPPING	GAMBLE	SEX	KEYWORD	KEYWORD						
Bad	Bad	is very bad	KARMA	Destruction,Losses,Death,Sickness - cold,Legal matter,Abusive,Karmic debts,God - Karma						

STRESS LEVEL	LUCKY COLORS	JEWELERY	MOONS EFFECT	GRAHA EFFECT	DAILY DEITY
High	Gold/Brown//Green	Saphire/Hessonite	Ivestments	Evil Graha	Agnidev

DAILY PUJA
Remembrance of family members who died, worship of older people. gifts to grand parents

DAILY PSALMS
9, 18, 36 ,45, 54, 63, 81, 108, 126

Thursday, April 21, 2016 — This is considered a NEUTRAL day for you — Planet: Sun

ADVICE & DETAILS

Assiduous dedication to your tasks and responsibilities will be rewarded today. It will be a day when you are busy, but being indolent today will cost you dearly in financial opportunities.

MANTRA FOR TODAY

Om Namo Bhagawate Mukhtanandaya, 108 times

MONEY	LOVE	CAREER	FAMILY	TRAVEL	WEDDING	MOVE	BUSINESS	HEALTH	Lotto #'s	play 3 #s
Fair	Bad	Good	Bad	Fair	Bad	Fair	Fair	Fair	11,49,57,44,5,4,43	233

SHOPPING	GAMBLE	SEX	KEYWORD	KEYWORD						
Fair	Fair	is fair	MIND	Independence,Loneliness,Meditative,Worry,Dominating,Illness - Cold,On Your Own,Commanding						

STRESS LEVEL	LUCKY COLORS	JEWELERY	MOONS EFFECT	GRAHA EFFECT	DAILY DEITY
High	White/Yellow/	Pearl/Quartz	Arrogance	Status Graha	Saraswaty

DAILY PUJA
Give Gifts to Priests, Invite holy ones to your home, Feed Swamis and Yogis, Do Shiva Puja.

DAILY PSALMS
1, 10, 28 ,37, 46, 55, 73, 100, 118

Friday, April 22, 2016 | This is considered a POSITIVE day for you | Planet: Moon

ADVICE & DETAILS	MANTRA FOR TODAY
Your karma for today requires you to be industrious and work very hard. You must put your laziness away. Associates will give you positive input and/or help.	Kali Durge Namo Nama Om Durge aye nama swaha 108 times

MONEY	LOVE	CAREER	FAMILY	TRAVEL	WEDDING	MOVE	BUSINESS	HEALTH	Lotto #'s	play 3 #s
Good	Excellent	Good	Good	Excellent	Good	Good	Good	Good	64,17,3,10,23,11,11	243

SHOPPING	GAMBLE	SEX	KEYWORD	KEYWORD						
Good	Good	is good	LOVE	Romance,Popularity,Visitors,Shopping,Food, Drinks,Co-operation,Friendships,Affection						

STRESS LEVEL	LUCKY COLORS	JEWELERY	MOONS EFFECT	GRAHA EFFECT	DAILY DEITY
Low	Red/Yellow/Pink	Topaz/Diamonds	Conservative	Love Graha	Gauri

DAILY PUJA	DAILY PSALMS
Give Gifts to females andnMother, Serve milk Products, Worship Durga forms	2, 11, 29 ,38, 47, 56, 74, 101, 119

Saturday, April 23, 2016 | This is considered a POSITIVE day for you | Planet: Mercury

ADVICE & DETAILS	MANTRA FOR TODAY
Today is a day to work and work even if you feel lazy. You need to be industrious and achieve all tasks that you can today. You will be in association with others while doing these projects, accept the input.	Om hareem Kleem Hreem Aem Saraswataye namaha 21 times

MONEY	LOVE	CAREER	FAMILY	TRAVEL	WEDDING	MOVE	BUSINESS	HEALTH	Lotto #'s	play 3 #s
Good	Fair	Good	Good	Excellent	Good	Good	Good	Excellent	51,27,42,10,49,44,20	454

SHOPPING	GAMBLE	SEX	KEYWORD	KEYWORD						
Good	Good	is great	SOCIAL	Children,Education,Astrology,Bargains,Social Functions,Childishness,Groups - Parties,Teacher						

STRESS LEVEL	LUCKY COLORS	JEWELERY	MOONS EFFECT	GRAHA EFFECT	DAILY DEITY
Low	Green/Sky Blue/	Diamonds/Silver	Enthusiastic	Social Graha	Vishnu

DAILY PUJA	DAILY PSALMS
Wash the feet of Children, Do Satnarayan Pooja, Read & chant Geeta	3, 12, 30 ,39, 48, 57, 75, 102, 120

Sunday, April 24, 2016 | This is considered a NEGATIVE day for you | Planet: Pluto

ADVICE & DETAILS	MANTRA FOR TODAY
Today you feel lazy, but you will need to work, be industrious and accomplish as much as possible. You will need to control your high temper and accept that today you will feel like they do not pay you enough to do your job.	Om Jai Viganeshwaraya.. Lambodaraya Namo Namaha 21 times

MONEY	LOVE	CAREER	FAMILY	TRAVEL	WEDDING	MOVE	BUSINESS	HEALTH	Lotto #'s	play 3 #s
Bad	Fair	Bad	Fair	Bad	Good	Bad	Bad	Bad	4,33,42,21,29,15,51	303

SHOPPING	GAMBLE	SEX	KEYWORD	KEYWORD						
Bad	Bad	is tough	CAREER	Career,Hard Work,Co-workers,Low Payment,Job Problems,High Temper,Low Pay,Laziness						

STRESS LEVEL	LUCKY COLORS	JEWELERY	MOONS EFFECT	GRAHA EFFECT	DAILY DEITY
High	Dark Blue/ Purple/	Amethyst/Gold	Emotional	Job Graha	Lingam

DAILY PUJA	DAILY PSALMS
Worship Ganesh, Give gifts to father, and co -workers, Plant gardens, farms	4, 13, 31 ,40, 49, 58, 76, 103, 121

Monday, April 25, 2016 | This is considered a POSITIVE day for you | Planet: Venus

ADVICE & DETAILS	MANTRA FOR TODAY
Do not allow the job problems that you may have today to affect your long-term career plans. Remember the foundation of your career is built on a day per day basis at your job. Act and think conscious of your godliness.	Om Graam Greem Graum Sa Gurave namah swaha 21 times

MONEY	LOVE	CAREER	FAMILY	TRAVEL	WEDDING	MOVE	BUSINESS	HEALTH	Lotto #'s	play 3 #s
Bad	Excellent	Fair	Good	Excellent	Good	Excellent	Good	Excellent	4,60,11,32,33,60,72	791

SHOPPING	GAMBLE	SEX	KEYWORD	KEYWORD						
Good	Good	is good	CHANGE	Sexuality,Travel,Change,Distant, far,Travel delays,Deception,Excercise,Illicit Affairs						

STRESS LEVEL	LUCKY COLORS	JEWELERY	MOONS EFFECT	GRAHA EFFECT	DAILY DEITY
Fair	Tan/Green/ Beige	Pearl/Silver/quartz	Courageous	Travel Graha	Nataraja

DAILY PUJA	DAILY PSALMS
Artistic gifts, Pray to Krishna, Do good deeds, do Spiritual trips	5, 14, 32 ,41, 50, 59, 77, 104, 122

Tuesday, April 26, 2016 — This is considered a NEGATIVE day for you — Planet: Mars

ADVICE & DETAILS

You are going to feel very lazy today, but you must push through this feeling and devote your day to work with others and work diligently.

MANTRA FOR TODAY

Om Mana Swasti Shanti Kuru kuru Swaha Shivoham Shivoham 27 times

MONEY	LOVE	CAREER	FAMILY	TRAVEL	WEDDING	MOVE	BUSINESS	HEALTH	Lotto #'s	play 3 #s
Bad	Bad	Bad	Bad	Bad	Bad	Bad	Fair	Bad	14,18,33,44,53,42,72	798

SHOPPING	GAMBLE	SEX	KEYWORD	KEYWORD
Fair	Bad	is frustrating	POWER	Responsibilty,Disagreement,Family,Back Pain,Family Conflicts,Traffic Ticket,Quarrels,Jealousy

STRESS LEVEL	LUCKY COLORS	JEWELERY	MOONS EFFECT	GRAHA EFFECT	DAILY DEITY
High	Purple/Blue/Rose	Emerald/Saphire	Educational	Family Graha	Mahakali

DAILY PUJA	DAILY PSALMS
Meditate, Control temper, Pray to Hanuman, Chant Hanuman Chalisa	6, 15, 33 ,42, 51, 60, 78, 105, 123

Wednesday, April 27, 2016 — This is considered a NEUTRAL day for you — Planet: Uranus

ADVICE & DETAILS

Find a reprieve from the weariness of everyday building your professional life by finding a book and reading about something that interests you and makes you happy.

MANTRA FOR TODAY

Jai Jai Shiva Shambo.(2) ...Mahadeva Shambo (2) 21 times 8

MONEY	LOVE	CAREER	FAMILY	TRAVEL	WEDDING	MOVE	BUSINESS	HEALTH	Lotto #'s	play 3 #s
Good	Good	Fair	Good	Good	Bad	Good	Bad	Fair	3,63,44,16,72,27,56	571

SHOPPING	GAMBLE	SEX	KEYWORD	KEYWORD
Bad	Fair	is quiet	DIVINE	Spirituality,Religious,Astrology,Inner Conflicts,Religious ,Sleepiness,Advice given,Alcohol - drugs

STRESS LEVEL	LUCKY COLORS	JEWELERY	MOONS EFFECT	GRAHA EFFECT	DAILY DEITY
Fair	Light Blue/Peach	Tiger's eye/Gold/Silver	Affectionate	God'S Graha	Shesnaag

DAILY PUJA	DAILY PSALMS
Chant Shiva Mantras, Take gifts to Ocean - Ganga Puja, Donate to Temple, Priests, etc.	7, 16, 34 ,43, 52, 61, 79, 106, 124

Thursday, April 28, 2016 — This is considered a POSITIVE day for you — Planet: Jupiter

ADVICE & DETAILS

Dealings with Real Estate of things related to your professional life may bring beauty and sex into your realm. You will feel fatigued during the day.

MANTRA FOR TODAY

Om Hareem Nama Swaha..Shri Maha Laxmi Aye Namah swaha 12 times

MONEY	LOVE	CAREER	FAMILY	TRAVEL	WEDDING	MOVE	BUSINESS	HEALTH	Lotto #'s	play 3 #s
Excellent	Good	Excellent	Good	Good	Excellent	Good	Excellent	Excellent	2,68,38,14,41,66,2	193

SHOPPING	GAMBLE	SEX	KEYWORD	KEYWORD
Excellent	Excellent	is excellent	MONEY	Business,Major Expense,Money - Profits,Income,Investments,Power,Promotion,Fame - TV

STRESS LEVEL	LUCKY COLORS	JEWELERY	MOONS EFFECT	GRAHA EFFECT	DAILY DEITY
Low	Yellow/Silver	Diamonds/Gold/Pearls	Secretive	Money Graha	Mahalaxmi

DAILY PUJA	DAILY PSALMS
Decorate Land, Feed the poor, Donate milk /products to all, Feed holy guests,	8, 17, 35 ,44, 53, 62, 80, 107, 125

Friday, April 29, 2016 — This is considered a NEGATIVE day for you — Planet: Saturn

ADVICE & DETAILS

Be ready to face job difficulties that may come to you today centered in your godliness not your ego. Remember this day is part of your career and the long-term goals you have.

MANTRA FOR TODAY

Om Ganga mataye nama swaha Om Varuna Devta aye Pahimam 11 times

MONEY	LOVE	CAREER	FAMILY	TRAVEL	WEDDING	MOVE	BUSINESS	HEALTH	Lotto #'s	play 3 #s
Bad	Bad	Bad	Fair	Bad	Bad	Bad	Bad	Bad	48,25,51,22,70,53,27	581

SHOPPING	GAMBLE	SEX	KEYWORD	KEYWORD
Bad	Bad	is very bad	KARMA	Destruction,Losses,Death,Sickness - cold,Legal matter,Abusive,Karmic debts,God - Karma

STRESS LEVEL	LUCKY COLORS	JEWELERY	MOONS EFFECT	GRAHA EFFECT	DAILY DEITY
High	Gold/Brown//Green	Saphire/Hessonite	Ivestments	Evil Graha	Agnidev

DAILY PUJA	DAILY PSALMS
Remembrance of family members who died, worship of older people. gifts to grand parents	9, 18, 36 ,45, 54, 63, 81, 108, 126

Saturday, April 30, 2016 — This is considered a NEUTRAL day for you — Planet: Sun

ADVICE & DETAILS

Assiduous dedication to your tasks and responsibilities will be rewarded today. It will be a day when you are busy, but being indolent today will cost you dearly in financial opportunities.

MANTRA FOR TODAY

Om Namo Bhagawate Mukhtanandaya, 108 times

MONEY	LOVE	CAREER	FAMILY	TRAVEL	WEDDING	MOVE	BUSINESS	HEALTH	Lotto #'s	play 3 #s
Fair	Bad	Good	Bad	Fair	Bad	Fair	Fair	Fair	4,54,17,57,69,20,6	297

SHOPPING	GAMBLE	SEX	KEYWORD	KEYWORD						
Fair	Fair	is fair	MIND	Independence,Loneliness,Meditative,Worry,Dominating,Illness - Cold,On Your Own,Commanding						

STRESS LEVEL	LUCKY COLORS	JEWELERY	MOONS EFFECT	GRAHA EFFECT	DAILY DEITY
High	White/Yellow/	Pearl/Quartz	Arrogance	Status Graha	Saraswaty

DAILY PUJA	DAILY PSALMS
Give Gifts to Priests, Invite holy ones to your home, Feed Swamis and Yogis, Do Shiva Puja.	1, 10, 28 ,37, 46, 55, 73, 100, 118

Sunday, May 1, 2016 — This is considered a POSITIVE day for you — Planet: Jupiter

ADVICE & DETAILS

There will be moving to and from today. You will experience great pleasure today and will also have to deal with money either receiving it or paying it out. You may be watching TV or meeting someone known related to the entertainment industry.

MANTRA FOR TODAY

Om Hareem Nama Swaha..Shri Maha Laxmi Aye Namah swaha 12 times

MONEY	LOVE	CAREER	FAMILY	TRAVEL	WEDDING	MOVE	BUSINESS	HEALTH	Lotto #'s	play 3 #s
Excellent	Good	Excellent	Good	Good	Excellent	Good	Excellent	Excellent	61,26,30,20,75,1,3	892

SHOPPING	GAMBLE	SEX	KEYWORD	KEYWORD						
Excellent	Excellent	is excellent	MONEY	Business,Major Expense,Money - Profits,Income,Investments,Power,Promotion,Fame - TV						

STRESS LEVEL	LUCKY COLORS	JEWELERY	MOONS EFFECT	GRAHA EFFECT	DAILY DEITY
Low	Yellow/Silver	Diamonds/Gold/Pearls	Secretive	Money Graha	Mahalaxmi

DAILY PUJA	DAILY PSALMS
Decorate Land, Feed the poor, Donate milk /products to all, Feed holy guests,	8, 17, 35 ,44, 53, 62, 80, 107, 125

Monday, May 2, 2016 — This is considered a NEGATIVE day for you — Planet: Saturn

ADVICE & DETAILS

This day is influenced by changes, moves and trips to close by locations. You will change your mind often and this lack of focus may cause you to get into an accident. Try to stay focused on your goals and minimize the multitasking especially when driving from one place to another.

MANTRA FOR TODAY

Om Ganga mataye nama swaha Om Varuna Devta aye Pahimam 11 times

MONEY	LOVE	CAREER	FAMILY	TRAVEL	WEDDING	MOVE	BUSINESS	HEALTH	Lotto #'s	play 3 #s
Bad	Bad	Bad	Fair	Bad	Bad	Bad	Bad	Bad	50,25,48,67,18,46,44	488

SHOPPING	GAMBLE	SEX	KEYWORD	KEYWORD						
Bad	Bad	is very bad	KARMA	Destruction,Losses,Death,Sickness - cold,Legal matter,Abusive,Karmic debts,God - Karma						

STRESS LEVEL	LUCKY COLORS	JEWELERY	MOONS EFFECT	GRAHA EFFECT	DAILY DEITY
High	Gold/Brown//Green	Saphire/Hessonite	Ivestments	Evil Graha	Agnidev

DAILY PUJA	DAILY PSALMS
Remembrance of family members who died, worship of older people. gifts to grand parents	9, 18, 36 ,45, 54, 63, 81, 108, 126

Tuesday, May 3, 2016 — This is considered a NEUTRAL day for you — Planet: Sun

ADVICE & DETAILS

Sex appeal and beauty are important to you today. You must control your ego-based anger and try to understand that every thing in the universe is in perfect order. You will experience travel and changes today

MANTRA FOR TODAY

Om Namo Bhagawate Mukhtanandaya, 108 times

MONEY	LOVE	CAREER	FAMILY	TRAVEL	WEDDING	MOVE	BUSINESS	HEALTH	Lotto #'s	play 3 #s
Fair	Bad	Good	Bad	Fair	Bad	Fair	Fair	Fair	75,64,63,69,52,29,47	38

SHOPPING	GAMBLE	SEX	KEYWORD	KEYWORD						
Fair	Fair	is fair	MIND	Independence,Loneliness,Meditative,Worry,Dominating,Illness - Cold,On Your Own,Commanding						

STRESS LEVEL	LUCKY COLORS	JEWELERY	MOONS EFFECT	GRAHA EFFECT	DAILY DEITY
High	White/Yellow/	Pearl/Quartz	Arrogance	Status Graha	Saraswaty

DAILY PUJA	DAILY PSALMS
Give Gifts to Priests, Invite holy ones to your home, Feed Swamis and Yogis, Do Shiva Puja.	1, 10, 28 ,37, 46, 55, 73, 100, 118

Wednesday, May 4, 2016 — This is considered a POSITIVE day for you — Planet: Moon

ADVICE & DETAILS

Sexual energy is very high today. It is a good time to enjoy the company of your lover. Do not trust the words of others that may be deceiving, and make sure you are not deceiving others with your words. Accept all changes in your life gracefully.

MANTRA FOR TODAY

Kali Durge Namo Nama Om Durge aye nama swaha 108 times

MONEY	LOVE	CAREER	FAMILY	TRAVEL	WEDDING	MOVE	BUSINESS	HEALTH	Lotto #'s	play 3 #s
Good	Excellent	Good	Good	Excellent	Good	Good	Good	Good	54,36,73,66,14,40,75	262

SHOPPING	GAMBLE	SEX	KEYWORD	KEYWORD
Good	Good	is good	LOVE	Romance,Popularity,Visitors,Shopping,Food, Drinks,Co-operation,Friendships,Affection

STRESS LEVEL	LUCKY COLORS	JEWELERY	MOONS EFFECT	GRAHA EFFECT	DAILY DEITY
Low	Red/Yellow/Pink	Topaz/Diamonds	Conservative	Love Graha	Gauri

DAILY PUJA	DAILY PSALMS
Give Gifts to females andnMother, Serve milk Products, Worship Durga forms	2, 11, 29 ,38, 47, 56, 74, 101, 119

Thursday, May 5, 2016 — This is considered a POSITIVE day for you — Planet: Mercury

ADVICE & DETAILS

You will probably experience some type of short trip and/or moving today. Communication is important today so think carefully, speak clearly and listen with intent to transfer messages correctly.

MANTRA FOR TODAY

Om hareem Kleem Hreem Aem Saraswataye namaha 21 times

MONEY	LOVE	CAREER	FAMILY	TRAVEL	WEDDING	MOVE	BUSINESS	HEALTH	Lotto #'s	play 3 #s
Good	Fair	Good	Good	Excellent	Good	Good	Good	Excellent	19,56,43,72,31,36,5	743

SHOPPING	GAMBLE	SEX	KEYWORD	KEYWORD
Good	Good	is great	SOCIAL	Children,Education,Astrology,Bargains,Social Functions,Childishness,Groups - Parties,Teacher

STRESS LEVEL	LUCKY COLORS	JEWELERY	MOONS EFFECT	GRAHA EFFECT	DAILY DEITY
Low	Green/Sky Blue/	Diamonds/Silver	Enthusiastic	Social Graha	Vishnu

DAILY PUJA	DAILY PSALMS
Wash the feet of Children, Do Satnarayan Pooja, Read & chant Geeta	3, 12, 30 ,39, 48, 57, 75, 102, 120

Friday, May 6, 2016 — This is considered a NEGATIVE day for you — Planet: Pluto

ADVICE & DETAILS

You may be deceived today perhaps by a sexual partner or someone else. Use your words carefully today, they are powerful and will have serious consequences. There will be many changes today, make sure you stay truthful regardless.

MANTRA FOR TODAY

Om Jai Viganeshwaraya.. Lambodaraya Namo Namaha 21 times

MONEY	LOVE	CAREER	FAMILY	TRAVEL	WEDDING	MOVE	BUSINESS	HEALTH	Lotto #'s	play 3 #s
Bad	Fair	Bad	Fair	Bad	Good	Bad	Bad	Bad	20,56,52,36,42,51,75	167

SHOPPING	GAMBLE	SEX	KEYWORD	KEYWORD
Bad	Bad	is tough	CAREER	Career,Hard Work,Co-workers,Low Payment,Job Problems,High Temper,Low Pay,Laziness

STRESS LEVEL	LUCKY COLORS	JEWELERY	MOONS EFFECT	GRAHA EFFECT	DAILY DEITY
High	Dark Blue/ Purple/	Amethyst/Gold	Emotional	Job Graha	Lingam

DAILY PUJA	DAILY PSALMS
Worship Ganesh, Give gifts to father, and co -workers, Plant gardens, farms	4, 13, 31 ,40, 49, 58, 76, 103, 121

Saturday, May 7, 2016 — This is considered a POSITIVE day for you — Planet: Venus

ADVICE & DETAILS

This day is influenced by changes, moves and trips to close by locations. You will change your mind often and this lack of focus may cause you to get into an accident. Try to stay focused on your goals and minimize the multitasking especially when driving from one place to another.

MANTRA FOR TODAY

Om Graam Greem Graum Sa Gurave namah swaha 21 times

MONEY	LOVE	CAREER	FAMILY	TRAVEL	WEDDING	MOVE	BUSINESS	HEALTH	Lotto #'s	play 3 #s
Bad	Excellent	Fair	Good	Excellent	Good	Excellent	Good	Excellent	69,62,49,52,1,68,18	698

SHOPPING	GAMBLE	SEX	KEYWORD	KEYWORD
Good	Good	is good	CHANGE	Sexuality,Travel,Change,Distant, far,Travel delays,Deception,Excercise,Illicit Affairs

STRESS LEVEL	LUCKY COLORS	JEWELERY	MOONS EFFECT	GRAHA EFFECT	DAILY DEITY
Fair	Tan/Green/ Beige	Pearl/Silver/quartz	Courageous	Travel Graha	Nataraja

DAILY PUJA	DAILY PSALMS
Artistic gifts, Pray to Krishna, Do good deeds, do Spiritual trips	5, 14, 32 ,41, 50, 59, 77, 104, 122

Sunday, May 8, 2016 — This is considered a NEGATIVE day for you — Planet: Mars

ADVICE & DETAILS	MANTRA FOR TODAY
This day you may feel a bit sad and depressed over health matters and some other type of personal losses. Center your thougts in divine spiritual and religious ideas and try to have an attitude of gratitude to receive blessings.	Om Mana Swasti Shanti Kuru kuru Swaha Shivoham Shivoham 27 times

MONEY	LOVE	CAREER	FAMILY	TRAVEL	WEDDING	MOVE	BUSINESS	HEALTH	Lotto #'s	play 3 #s
Bad	Bad	Bad	Bad	Bad	Bad	Bad	Fair	Bad	38,29,57,47,27,51,3	925

SHOPPING	GAMBLE	SEX	KEYWORD	KEYWORD						
Fair	Bad	is frustrating	POWER	Responsibilty,Disagreement,Family,Back Pain,Family Conflicts,Traffic Ticket,Quarrels,Jealousy						

STRESS LEVEL	LUCKY COLORS	JEWELERY	MOONS EFFECT	GRAHA EFFECT	DAILY DEITY
High	Purple/Blue/Rose	Emerald/Saphire	Educational	Family Graha	Mahakali

DAILY PUJA	DAILY PSALMS
Meditate, Control temper, Pray to Hanuman, Chant Hanuman Chalisa	6, 15, 33 ,42, 51, 60, 78, 105, 123

Monday, May 9, 2016 — This is considered a NEUTRAL day for you — Planet: Uranus

ADVICE & DETAILS	MANTRA FOR TODAY
This is a day of great movement and many short trips. There may be changes in mood, ideas, location, etc. Communication is very important today, make sure other understand what you are trying to say and verify that what you understood is what was said to you.	Jai Jai Shiva Shambo.(2) ...Mahadeva Shambo (2) 21 times 8

MONEY	LOVE	CAREER	FAMILY	TRAVEL	WEDDING	MOVE	BUSINESS	HEALTH	Lotto #'s	play 3 #s
Good	Good	Fair	Good	Good	Bad	Good	Bad	Fair	22,61,10,63,19,13,8	360

SHOPPING	GAMBLE	SEX	KEYWORD	KEYWORD						
Bad	Fair	is quiet	DIVINE	Spirituality,Religious,Astrology,Inner Conflicts,Religious ,Sleepiness,Advice given,Alcohol - drugs						

STRESS LEVEL	LUCKY COLORS	JEWELERY	MOONS EFFECT	GRAHA EFFECT	DAILY DEITY
Fair	Light Blue/Peach	Tiger's eye/Gold/Silver	Affectionate	God'S Graha	Shesnaag

DAILY PUJA	DAILY PSALMS
Chant Shiva Mantras, Take gifts to Ocean - Ganga Puja, Donate to Temple, Priests, etc.	7, 16, 34 ,43, 52, 61, 79, 106, 124

Tuesday, May 10, 2016 — This is considered a POSITIVE day for you — Planet: Jupiter

ADVICE & DETAILS	MANTRA FOR TODAY
There will be moving to and from today. You will experience great pleasure today and will also have to deal with money either receiving it or paying it out. You may be watching TV or meeting someone known related to the entertainment industry.	Om Hareem Nama Swaha..Shri Maha Laxmi Aye Namah swaha 12 times

MONEY	LOVE	CAREER	FAMILY	TRAVEL	WEDDING	MOVE	BUSINESS	HEALTH	Lotto #'s	play 3 #s
Excellent	Good	Excellent	Good	Good	Excellent	Good	Excellent	Excellent	23,67,64,65,63,69,49	277

SHOPPING	GAMBLE	SEX	KEYWORD	KEYWORD						
Excellent	Excellent	is excellent	MONEY	Business,Major Expense,Money - Profits,Income,Investments,Power,Promotion,Fame - TV						

STRESS LEVEL	LUCKY COLORS	JEWELERY	MOONS EFFECT	GRAHA EFFECT	DAILY DEITY
Low	Yellow/Silver	Diamonds/Gold/Pearls	Secretive	Money Graha	Mahalaxmi

DAILY PUJA	DAILY PSALMS
Decorate Land, Feed the poor, Donate milk /products to all, Feed holy guests,	8, 17, 35 ,44, 53, 62, 80, 107, 125

Wednesday, May 11, 2016 — This is considered a NEGATIVE day for you — Planet: Saturn

ADVICE & DETAILS	MANTRA FOR TODAY
This day is influenced by changes, moves and trips to close by locations. You will change your mind often and this lack of focus may cause you to get into an accident. Try to stay focused on your goals and minimize the multitasking especially when driving from one place to another.	Om Ganga mataye nama swaha Om Varuna Devta aye Pahimam 11 times

MONEY	LOVE	CAREER	FAMILY	TRAVEL	WEDDING	MOVE	BUSINESS	HEALTH	Lotto #'s	play 3 #s
Bad	Bad	Bad	Fair	Bad	Bad	Bad	Bad	Bad	14,11,8,71,69,60,55	501

SHOPPING	GAMBLE	SEX	KEYWORD	KEYWORD						
Bad	Bad	is very bad	KARMA	Destruction,Losses,Death,Sickness - cold,Legal matter,Abusive,Karmic debts,God - Karma						

STRESS LEVEL	LUCKY COLORS	JEWELERY	MOONS EFFECT	GRAHA EFFECT	DAILY DEITY
High	Gold/Brown//Green	Saphire/Hessonite	Ivestments	Evil Graha	Agnidev

DAILY PUJA	DAILY PSALMS
Remembrance of family members who died, worship of older people. gifts to grand parents	9, 18, 36 ,45, 54, 63, 81, 108, 126

Thursday, May 12, 2016 — This is considered a NEUTRAL day for you — Planet: Sun

ADVICE & DETAILS

Sex appeal and beauty are important to you today. You must control your ego-based anger and try to understand that every thing in the universe is in perfect order. You will experience travel and changes today

MANTRA FOR TODAY

Om Namo Bhagawate Mukhtanandaya, 108 times

MONEY	LOVE	CAREER	FAMILY	TRAVEL	WEDDING	MOVE	BUSINESS	HEALTH	Lotto #'s	play 3 #s
Fair	Bad	Good	Bad	Fair	Bad	Fair	Fair	Fair	28,69,34,51,7,5,36	668

SHOPPING	GAMBLE	SEX	KEYWORD	KEYWORD
Fair	Fair	is fair	MIND	Independence,Loneliness,Meditative,Worry,Dominating,Illness - Cold,On Your Own,Commanding

STRESS LEVEL	LUCKY COLORS	JEWELERY	MOONS EFFECT	GRAHA EFFECT	DAILY DEITY
High	White/Yellow/	Pearl/Quartz	Arrogance	Status Graha	Saraswaty

DAILY PUJA
Give Gifts to Priests, Invite holy ones to your home, Feed Swamis and Yogis, Do Shiva Puja.

DAILY PSALMS
1, 10, 28 ,37, 46, 55, 73, 100, 118

Friday, May 13, 2016 — This is considered a POSITIVE day for you — Planet: Moon

ADVICE & DETAILS

Sexual energy is very high today. It is a good time to enjoy the company of your lover. Do not trust the words of others that may be deceiving, and make sure you are not deceiving others with your words. Accept all changes in your life gracefully.

MANTRA FOR TODAY

Kali Durge Namo Nama Om Durge aye nama swaha 108 times

MONEY	LOVE	CAREER	FAMILY	TRAVEL	WEDDING	MOVE	BUSINESS	HEALTH	Lotto #'s	play 3 #s
Good	Excellent	Good	Good	Excellent	Good	Good	Good	Good	51,24,3,3,51,64,23	297

SHOPPING	GAMBLE	SEX	KEYWORD	KEYWORD
Good	Good	is good	LOVE	Romance,Popularity,Visitors,Shopping,Food, Drinks,Co-operation,Friendships,Affection

STRESS LEVEL	LUCKY COLORS	JEWELERY	MOONS EFFECT	GRAHA EFFECT	DAILY DEITY
Low	Red/Yellow/Pink	Topaz/Diamonds	Conservative	Love Graha	Gauri

DAILY PUJA
Give Gifts to females andnMother, Serve milk Products, Worship Durga forms

DAILY PSALMS
2, 11, 29 ,38, 47, 56, 74, 101, 119

Saturday, May 14, 2016 — This is considered a POSITIVE day for you — Planet: Mercury

ADVICE & DETAILS

You will probably experience some type of short trip and/or moving today. Communication is important today so think carefully, speak clearly and listen with intent to transfer messages correctly.

MANTRA FOR TODAY

Om hareem Kleem Hreem Aem Saraswataye namaha 21 times

MONEY	LOVE	CAREER	FAMILY	TRAVEL	WEDDING	MOVE	BUSINESS	HEALTH	Lotto #'s	play 3 #s
Good	Fair	Good	Good	Excellent	Good	Good	Good	Excellent	75,74,30,70,15,51,36	256

SHOPPING	GAMBLE	SEX	KEYWORD	KEYWORD
Good	Good	is great	SOCIAL	Children,Education,Astrology,Bargains,Social Functions,Childishness,Groups - Parties,Teacher

STRESS LEVEL	LUCKY COLORS	JEWELERY	MOONS EFFECT	GRAHA EFFECT	DAILY DEITY
Low	Green/Sky Blue/	Diamonds/Silver	Enthusiastic	Social Graha	Vishnu

DAILY PUJA
Wash the feet of Children, Do Satnarayan Pooja, Read & chant Geeta

DAILY PSALMS
3, 12, 30 ,39, 48, 57, 75, 102, 120

Sunday, May 15, 2016 — This is considered a NEGATIVE day for you — Planet: Pluto

ADVICE & DETAILS

You may be deceived today perhaps by a sexual partner or someone else. Use your words carefully today, they are powerful and will have serious consequences. There will be many changes today, make sure you stay truthful regardless.

MANTRA FOR TODAY

Om Jai Viganeshwaraya.. Lambodaraya Namo Namaha 21 times

MONEY	LOVE	CAREER	FAMILY	TRAVEL	WEDDING	MOVE	BUSINESS	HEALTH	Lotto #'s	play 3 #s
Bad	Fair	Bad	Fair	Bad	Good	Bad	Bad	Bad	61,50,29,8,42,69,51	506

SHOPPING	GAMBLE	SEX	KEYWORD	KEYWORD
Bad	Bad	is tough	CAREER	Career,Hard Work,Co-workers,Low Payment,Job Problems,High Temper,Low Pay,Laziness

STRESS LEVEL	LUCKY COLORS	JEWELERY	MOONS EFFECT	GRAHA EFFECT	DAILY DEITY
High	Dark Blue/ Purple/	Amethyst/Gold	Emotional	Job Graha	Lingam

DAILY PUJA
Worship Ganesh, Give gifts to father, and co -workers, Plant gardens, farms

DAILY PSALMS
4, 13, 31 ,40, 49, 58, 76, 103, 121

Monday, May 16, 2016 — This is considered a POSITIVE day for you — Planet: Venus

ADVICE & DETAILS

This day is influenced by changes, moves and trips to close by locations. You will change your mind often and this lack of focus may cause you to get into an accident. Try to stay focused on your goals and minimize the multitasking especially when driving from one place to another.

MANTRA FOR TODAY

Om Graam Greem Graum Sa Gurave namah swaha 21 times

MONEY	LOVE	CAREER	FAMILY	TRAVEL	WEDDING	MOVE	BUSINESS	HEALTH	Lotto #'s	play 3 #s
Bad	Excellent	Fair	Good	Excellent	Good	Excellent	Good	Excellent	49,47,68,71,4,3,46	838

SHOPPING	GAMBLE	SEX	KEYWORD	KEYWORD				
Good	Good	is good	CHANGE	Sexuality,Travel,Change,Distant, far,Travel delays,Deception,Excercise,Illicit Affairs				

STRESS LEVEL	LUCKY COLORS	JEWELERY	MOONS EFFECT	GRAHA EFFECT	DAILY DEITY
Fair	Tan/Green/ Beige	Pearl/Silver/quartz	Courageous	Travel Graha	Nataraja

DAILY PUJA
Artistic gifts, Pray to Krishna, Do good deeds, do Spiritual trips

DAILY PSALMS
5, 14, 32 ,41, 50, 59, 77, 104, 122

Tuesday, May 17, 2016 — This is considered a NEGATIVE day for you — Planet: Mars

ADVICE & DETAILS

This day you may feel a bit sad and depressed over health matters and some other type of personal losses. Center your thougts in divine spiritual and religious ideas and try to have an attitude of gratitude to receive blessings.

MANTRA FOR TODAY

Om Mana Swasti Shanti Kuru kuru Swaha Shivoham Shivoham 27 times

MONEY	LOVE	CAREER	FAMILY	TRAVEL	WEDDING	MOVE	BUSINESS	HEALTH	Lotto #'s	play 3 #s
Bad	Bad	Bad	Bad	Bad	Bad	Bad	Fair	Bad	75,7,33,73,3,9,48	469

SHOPPING	GAMBLE	SEX	KEYWORD	KEYWORD				
Fair	Bad	is frustrating	POWER	Responsibilty,Disagreement,Family,Back Pain,Family Conflicts,Traffic Ticket,Quarrels,Jealousy				

STRESS LEVEL	LUCKY COLORS	JEWELERY	MOONS EFFECT	GRAHA EFFECT	DAILY DEITY
High	Purple/Blue/Rose	Emerald/Saphire	Educational	Family Graha	Mahakali

DAILY PUJA
Meditate, Control temper, Pray to Hanuman, Chant Hanuman Chalisa

DAILY PSALMS
6, 15, 33 ,42, 51, 60, 78, 105, 123

Wednesday, May 18, 2016 — This is considered a NEUTRAL day for you — Planet: Uranus

ADVICE & DETAILS

This is a day of great movement and many short trips. There may be changes in mood, ideas, location, etc. Communication is very important today, make sure other understand what you are trying to say and verify that what you understood is what was said to you.

MANTRA FOR TODAY

Jai Jai Shiva Shambo.(2) ...Mahadeva Shambo (2) 21 times 8

MONEY	LOVE	CAREER	FAMILY	TRAVEL	WEDDING	MOVE	BUSINESS	HEALTH	Lotto #'s	play 3 #s
Good	Good	Fair	Good	Good	Bad	Good	Bad	Fair	36,25,41,66,10,6,38	968

SHOPPING	GAMBLE	SEX	KEYWORD	KEYWORD				
Bad	Fair	is quiet	DIVINE	Spirituality,Religious,Astrology,Inner Conflicts,Religious ,Sleepiness,Advice given,Alcohol - drugs				

STRESS LEVEL	LUCKY COLORS	JEWELERY	MOONS EFFECT	GRAHA EFFECT	DAILY DEITY
Fair	Light Blue/Peach	Tiger's eye/Gold/Silver	Affectionate	God'S Graha	Shesnaag

DAILY PUJA
Chant Shiva Mantras, Take gifts to Ocean - Ganga Puja, Donate to Temple, Priests, etc.

DAILY PSALMS
7, 16, 34 ,43, 52, 61, 79, 106, 124

Thursday, May 19, 2016 — This is considered a POSITIVE day for you — Planet: Jupiter

ADVICE & DETAILS

There will be moving to and from today. You will experience great pleasure today and will also have to deal with money either receiving it or paying it out. You may be watching TV or meeting someone known related to the entertainment industry.

MANTRA FOR TODAY

Om Hareem Nama Swaha..Shri Maha Laxmi Aye Namah swaha 12 times

MONEY	LOVE	CAREER	FAMILY	TRAVEL	WEDDING	MOVE	BUSINESS	HEALTH	Lotto #'s	play 3 #s
Excellent	Good	Excellent	Good	Good	Excellent	Good	Excellent	Excellent	44,18,33,59,28,49,68	114

SHOPPING	GAMBLE	SEX	KEYWORD	KEYWORD				
Excellent	Excellent	is excellent	MONEY	Business,Major Expense,Money - Profits,Income,Investments,Power,Promotion,Fame - TV				

STRESS LEVEL	LUCKY COLORS	JEWELERY	MOONS EFFECT	GRAHA EFFECT	DAILY DEITY
Low	Yellow/Silver	Diamonds/Gold/Pearls	Secretive	Money Graha	Mahalaxmi

DAILY PUJA
Decorate Land, Feed the poor, Donate milk /products to all, Feed holy guests,

DAILY PSALMS
8, 17, 35 ,44, 53, 62, 80, 107, 125

Friday, May 20, 2016 — This is considered a NEGATIVE day for you — Planet: Saturn

ADVICE & DETAILS

This day is influenced by changes, moves and trips to close by locations. You will change your mind often and this lack of focus may cause you to get into an accident. Try to stay focused on your goals and minimize the multitasking especially when driving from one place to another.

MANTRA FOR TODAY

Om Ganga mataye nama swaha
Om Varuna Devta aye Pahimam 11 times

MONEY	LOVE	CAREER	FAMILY	TRAVEL	WEDDING	MOVE	BUSINESS	HEALTH	Lotto #'s	play 3 #s
Bad	Bad	Bad	Fair	Bad	Bad	Bad	Bad	Bad	11,49,11,52,66,23,28	631

SHOPPING	GAMBLE	SEX	KEYWORD	KEYWORD						
Bad	Bad	is very bad	KARMA	Destruction,Losses,Death,Sickness - cold,Legal matter,Abusive,Karmic debts,God - Karma						

STRESS LEVEL	LUCKY COLORS	JEWELERY	MOONS EFFECT	GRAHA EFFECT	DAILY DEITY
High	Gold/Brown//Green	Saphire/Hessonite	Ivestments	Evil Graha	Agnidev

DAILY PUJA: Remembrance of family members who died, worship of older people. gifts to grand parents

DAILY PSALMS: 9, 18, 36 ,45, 54, 63, 81, 108, 126

Saturday, May 21, 2016 — This is considered a NEUTRAL day for you — Planet: Sun

ADVICE & DETAILS

Sex appeal and beauty are important to you today. You must control your ego-based anger and try to understand that every thing in the universe is in perfect order. You will experience travel and changes today

MANTRA FOR TODAY

Om Namo Bhagawate Mukhtanandaya, 108 times

MONEY	LOVE	CAREER	FAMILY	TRAVEL	WEDDING	MOVE	BUSINESS	HEALTH	Lotto #'s	play 3 #s
Fair	Bad	Good	Bad	Fair	Bad	Fair	Fair	Fair	27,56,45,20,6,64,47	367

SHOPPING	GAMBLE	SEX	KEYWORD	KEYWORD						
Fair	Fair	is fair	MIND	Independence,Loneliness,Meditative,Worry,Dominating,Illness - Cold,On Your Own,Commanding						

STRESS LEVEL	LUCKY COLORS	JEWELERY	MOONS EFFECT	GRAHA EFFECT	DAILY DEITY
High	White/Yellow/	Pearl/Quartz	Arrogance	Status Graha	Saraswaty

DAILY PUJA: Give Gifts to Priests, Invite holy ones to your home, Feed Swamis and Yogis, Do Shiva Puja.

DAILY PSALMS: 1, 10, 28 ,37, 46, 55, 73, 100, 118

Sunday, May 22, 2016 — This is considered a POSITIVE day for you — Planet: Moon

ADVICE & DETAILS

Sexual energy is very high today. It is a good time to enjoy the company of your lover. Do not trust the words of others that may be deceiving, and make sure you are not deceiving others with your words. Accept all changes in your life gracefully.

MANTRA FOR TODAY

Kali Durge Namo Nama Om Durge aye nama swaha 108 times

MONEY	LOVE	CAREER	FAMILY	TRAVEL	WEDDING	MOVE	BUSINESS	HEALTH	Lotto #'s	play 3 #s
Good	Excellent	Good	Good	Excellent	Good	Good	Good	Good	60,22,74,14,40,12,2	690

SHOPPING	GAMBLE	SEX	KEYWORD	KEYWORD						
Good	Good	is good	LOVE	Romance,Popularity,Visitors,Shopping,Food, Drinks,Co-operation,Friendships,Affection						

STRESS LEVEL	LUCKY COLORS	JEWELERY	MOONS EFFECT	GRAHA EFFECT	DAILY DEITY
Low	Red/Yellow/Pink	Topaz/Diamonds	Conservative	Love Graha	Gauri

DAILY PUJA: Give Gifts to females andnMother, Serve milk Products, Worship Durga forms

DAILY PSALMS: 2, 11, 29 ,38, 47, 56, 74, 101, 119

Monday, May 23, 2016 — This is considered a POSITIVE day for you — Planet: Mercury

ADVICE & DETAILS

You will probably experience some type of short trip and/or moving today. Communication is important today so think carefully, speak clearly and listen with intent to transfer messages correctly.

MANTRA FOR TODAY

Om hareem Kleem Hreem Aem Saraswataye namaha 21 times

MONEY	LOVE	CAREER	FAMILY	TRAVEL	WEDDING	MOVE	BUSINESS	HEALTH	Lotto #'s	play 3 #s
Good	Fair	Good	Good	Excellent	Good	Good	Good	Excellent	59,61,25,55,46,73,44	473

SHOPPING	GAMBLE	SEX	KEYWORD	KEYWORD						
Good	Good	is great	SOCIAL	Children,Education,Astrology,Bargains,Social Functions,Childishness,Groups - Parties,Teacher						

STRESS LEVEL	LUCKY COLORS	JEWELERY	MOONS EFFECT	GRAHA EFFECT	DAILY DEITY
Low	Green/Sky Blue/	Diamonds/Silver	Enthusiastic	Social Graha	Vishnu

DAILY PUJA: Wash the feet of Children, Do Satnarayan Pooja, Read & chant Geeta

DAILY PSALMS: 3, 12, 30 ,39, 48, 57, 75, 102, 120

Tuesday, May 24, 2016 — This is considered a NEGATIVE day for you — Planet: Pluto

ADVICE & DETAILS

You may be deceived today perhaps by a sexual partner or someone else. Use your words carefully today, they are powerful and will have serious consequences. There will be many changes today, make sure you stay truthful regardless.

MANTRA FOR TODAY

Om Jai Viganeshwaraya.. Lambodaraya Namo Namaha 21 times

MONEY	LOVE	CAREER	FAMILY	TRAVEL	WEDDING	MOVE	BUSINESS	HEALTH	Lotto #'s	play 3 #s
Bad	Fair	Bad	Fair	Bad	Good	Bad	Bad	Bad	60,60,18,27,69,46,22	774

SHOPPING	GAMBLE	SEX	KEYWORD	KEYWORD						
Bad	Bad	is tough	CAREER	Career,Hard Work,Co-workers,Low Payment,Job Problems,High Temper,Low Pay,Laziness						

STRESS LEVEL	LUCKY COLORS	JEWELERY	MOONS EFFECT	GRAHA EFFECT	DAILY DEITY
High	Dark Blue/ Purple/	Amethyst/Gold	Emotional	Job Graha	Lingam

DAILY PUJA
Worship Ganesh, Give gifts to father, and co-workers, Plant gardens, farms

DAILY PSALMS
4, 13, 31 ,40, 49, 58, 76, 103, 121

Wednesday, May 25, 2016 — This is considered a POSITIVE day for you — Planet: Venus

ADVICE & DETAILS

This day is influenced by changes, moves and trips to close by locations. You will change your mind often and this lack of focus may cause you to get into an accident. Try to stay focused on your goals and minimize the multitasking especially when driving from one place to another.

MANTRA FOR TODAY

Om Graam Greem Graum Sa Gurave namah swaha 21 times

MONEY	LOVE	CAREER	FAMILY	TRAVEL	WEDDING	MOVE	BUSINESS	HEALTH	Lotto #'s	play 3 #s
Bad	Excellent	Fair	Good	Excellent	Good	Excellent	Good	Excellent	8,34,32,51,46,18,16	161

SHOPPING	GAMBLE	SEX	KEYWORD	KEYWORD						
Good	Good	is good	CHANGE	Sexuality,Travel,Change,Distant, far,Travel delays,Deception,Excercise,Illicit Affairs						

STRESS LEVEL	LUCKY COLORS	JEWELERY	MOONS EFFECT	GRAHA EFFECT	DAILY DEITY
Fair	Tan/Green/ Beige	Pearl/Silver/quartz	Courageous	Travel Graha	Nataraja

DAILY PUJA
Artistic gifts, Pray to Krishna, Do good deeds, do Spiritual trips

DAILY PSALMS
5, 14, 32 ,41, 50, 59, 77, 104, 122

Thursday, May 26, 2016 — This is considered a NEGATIVE day for you — Planet: Mars

ADVICE & DETAILS

This day you may feel a bit sad and depressed over health matters and some other type of personal losses. Center your thougts in divine spiritual and religious ideas and try to have an attitude of gratitude to receive blessings.

MANTRA FOR TODAY

Om Mana Swasti Shanti Kuru kuru Swaha Shivoham Shivoham 27 times

MONEY	LOVE	CAREER	FAMILY	TRAVEL	WEDDING	MOVE	BUSINESS	HEALTH	Lotto #'s	play 3 #s
Bad	Bad	Bad	Bad	Bad	Bad	Bad	Fair	Bad	4,14,31,68,51,34,63	234

SHOPPING	GAMBLE	SEX	KEYWORD	KEYWORD						
Fair	Bad	is frustrating	POWER	Responsibilty,Disagreement,Family,Back Pain,Family Conflicts,Traffic Ticket,Quarrels,Jealousy						

STRESS LEVEL	LUCKY COLORS	JEWELERY	MOONS EFFECT	GRAHA EFFECT	DAILY DEITY
High	Purple/Blue/Rose	Emerald/Saphire	Educational	Family Graha	Mahakali

DAILY PUJA
Meditate, Control temper, Pray to Hanuman, Chant Hanuman Chalisa

DAILY PSALMS
6, 15, 33 ,42, 51, 60, 78, 105, 123

Friday, May 27, 2016 — This is considered a NEUTRAL day for you — Planet: Uranus

ADVICE & DETAILS

This is a day of great movement and many short trips. There may be changes in mood, ideas, location, etc. Communication is very important today, make sure other understand what you are trying to say and verify that what you understood is what was said to you.

MANTRA FOR TODAY

Jai Jai Shiva Shambo.(2) ...Mahadeva Shambo (2) 21 times 8

MONEY	LOVE	CAREER	FAMILY	TRAVEL	WEDDING	MOVE	BUSINESS	HEALTH	Lotto #'s	play 3 #s
Good	Good	Fair	Good	Good	Bad	Good	Bad	Fair	29,64,41,47,52,19,15	253

SHOPPING	GAMBLE	SEX	KEYWORD	KEYWORD						
Bad	Fair	is quiet	DIVINE	Spirituality,Religious,Astrology,Inner Conflicts,Religious ,Sleepiness,Advice given,Alcohol - drugs						

STRESS LEVEL	LUCKY COLORS	JEWELERY	MOONS EFFECT	GRAHA EFFECT	DAILY DEITY
Fair	Light Blue/Peach	Tiger's eye/Gold/Silver	Affectionate	God'S Graha	Shesnaag

DAILY PUJA
Chant Shiva Mantras, Take gifts to Ocean - Ganga Puja, Donate to Temple, Priests, etc.

DAILY PSALMS
7, 16, 34 ,43, 52, 61, 79, 106, 124

Saturday, May 28, 2016 — This is considered a POSITIVE day for you — Planet: Jupiter

ADVICE & DETAILS	MANTRA FOR TODAY
There will be moving to and from today. You will experience great pleasure today and will also have to deal with money either receiving it or paying it out. You may be watching TV or meeting someone known related to the entertainment industry.	Om Hareem Nama Swaha..Shri Maha Laxmi Aye Namah swaha 12 times

MONEY	LOVE	CAREER	FAMILY	TRAVEL	WEDDING	MOVE	BUSINESS	HEALTH	Lotto #'s	play 3 #s
Excellent	Good	Excellent	Good	Good	Excellent	Good	Excellent	Excellent	71,49,27,66,73,17,16	364

SHOPPING	GAMBLE	SEX	KEYWORD	KEYWORD						
Excellent	Excellent	is excellent	MONEY	Business,Major Expense,Money - Profits,Income,Investments,Power,Promotion,Fame - TV						

STRESS LEVEL	LUCKY COLORS	JEWELERY	MOONS EFFECT	GRAHA EFFECT	DAILY DEITY
Low	Yellow/Silver	Diamonds/Gold/Pearls	Secretive	Money Graha	Mahalaxmi

DAILY PUJA	DAILY PSALMS
Decorate Land, Feed the poor, Donate milk /products to all, Feed holy guests,	8, 17, 35 ,44, 53, 62, 80, 107, 125

Sunday, May 29, 2016 — This is considered a NEGATIVE day for you — Planet: Saturn

ADVICE & DETAILS	MANTRA FOR TODAY
This day is influenced by changes, moves and trips to close by locations. You will change your mind often and this lack of focus may cause you to get into an accident. Try to stay focused on your goals and minimize the multitasking especially when driving from one place to another.	Om Ganga mataye nama swaha Om Varuna Devta aye Pahimam 11 times

MONEY	LOVE	CAREER	FAMILY	TRAVEL	WEDDING	MOVE	BUSINESS	HEALTH	Lotto #'s	play 3 #s
Bad	Bad	Bad	Fair	Bad	Bad	Bad	Bad	Bad	26,6,45,11,1,39,73	317

SHOPPING	GAMBLE	SEX	KEYWORD	KEYWORD						
Bad	Bad	is very bad	KARMA	Destruction,Losses,Death,Sickness - cold,Legal matter,Abusive,Karmic debts,God - Karma						

STRESS LEVEL	LUCKY COLORS	JEWELERY	MOONS EFFECT	GRAHA EFFECT	DAILY DEITY
High	Gold/Brown//Green	Saphire/Hessonite	Ivestments	Evil Graha	Agnidev

DAILY PUJA	DAILY PSALMS
Remembrance of family members who died, worship of older people. gifts to grand parents	9, 18, 36 ,45, 54, 63, 81, 108, 126

Monday, May 30, 2016 — This is considered a NEUTRAL day for you — Planet: Sun

ADVICE & DETAILS	MANTRA FOR TODAY
Sex appeal and beauty are important to you today. You must control your ego-based anger and try to understand that every thing in the universe is in perfect order. You will experience travel and changes today	Om Namo Bhagawate Mukhtanandaya, 108 times

MONEY	LOVE	CAREER	FAMILY	TRAVEL	WEDDING	MOVE	BUSINESS	HEALTH	Lotto #'s	play 3 #s
Fair	Bad	Good	Bad	Fair	Bad	Fair	Fair	Fair	40,18,67,3,19,55,30	994

SHOPPING	GAMBLE	SEX	KEYWORD	KEYWORD						
Fair	Fair	is fair	MIND	Independence,Loneliness,Meditative,Worry,Dominating,Illness - Cold,On Your Own,Commanding						

STRESS LEVEL	LUCKY COLORS	JEWELERY	MOONS EFFECT	GRAHA EFFECT	DAILY DEITY
High	White/Yellow/	Pearl/Quartz	Arrogance	Status Graha	Saraswaty

DAILY PUJA	DAILY PSALMS
Give Gifts to Priests, Invite holy ones to your home, Feed Swamis and Yogis, Do Shiva Puja.	1, 10, 28 ,37, 46, 55, 73, 100, 118

Tuesday, May 31, 2016 — This is considered a POSITIVE day for you — Planet: Moon

ADVICE & DETAILS	MANTRA FOR TODAY
Sexual energy is very high today. It is a good time to enjoy the company of your lover. Do not trust the words of others that may be deceiving, and make sure you are not deceiving others with your words. Accept all changes in your life gracefully.	Kali Durge Namo Nama Om Durge aye nama swaha 108 times

MONEY	LOVE	CAREER	FAMILY	TRAVEL	WEDDING	MOVE	BUSINESS	HEALTH	Lotto #'s	play 3 #s
Good	Excellent	Good	Good	Excellent	Good	Good	Good	Good	12,40,61,18,10,18,26	525

SHOPPING	GAMBLE	SEX	KEYWORD	KEYWORD						
Good	Good	is good	LOVE	Romance,Popularity,Visitors,Shopping,Food, Drinks,Co-operation,Friendships,Affection						

STRESS LEVEL	LUCKY COLORS	JEWELERY	MOONS EFFECT	GRAHA EFFECT	DAILY DEITY
Low	Red/Yellow/Pink	Topaz/Diamonds	Conservative	Love Graha	Gauri

DAILY PUJA	DAILY PSALMS
Give Gifts to females andnMother, Serve milk Products, Worship Durga forms	2, 11, 29 ,38, 47, 56, 74, 101, 119

Wednesday, June 1, 2016 | This is considered a POSITIVE day for you | Planet: Jupiter

ADVICE & DETAILS	MANTRA FOR TODAY
Government and police agencies may cross paths with you today; try to follow the law so the encounters are more pleasurable. You will be the target of jealousy today so try to stay humble about your accomplishments or your belongings and remember that the good times also pass what remains is only the purity in your heart. You will have to confront many responsibilities today do it with surrender and service in your heart.	Om Hareem Nama Swaha..Shri Maha Laxmi Aye Namah swaha 12 times

MONEY	LOVE	CAREER	FAMILY	TRAVEL	WEDDING	MOVE	BUSINESS	HEALTH	Lotto #'s	play 3 #s
Excellent	Good	Excellent	Good	Good	Excellent	Good	Excellent	Excellent	7,58,35,64,28,37,73	856

SHOPPING	GAMBLE	SEX	KEYWORD	KEYWORD				
Excellent	Excellent	is excellent	MONEY	Business,Major Expense,Money - Profits,Income,Investments,Power,Promotion,Fame - TV				

STRESS LEVEL	LUCKY COLORS	JEWELERY	MOONS EFFECT	GRAHA EFFECT	DAILY DEITY
Low	Yellow/Silver	Diamonds/Gold/Pearls	Secretive	Money Graha	Mahalaxmi

DAILY PUJA	DAILY PSALMS
Decorate Land, Feed the poor, Donate milk /products to all, Feed holy guests,	8, 17, 35 ,44, 53, 62, 80, 107, 125

Thursday, June 2, 2016 | This is considered a NEGATIVE day for you | Planet: Saturn

ADVICE & DETAILS	MANTRA FOR TODAY
You have to deal with a great deal of responsibilities today; regardless of this others will feel jealous and envious of you. There are possible encounters with police and/or government officials.	Om Ganga mataye nama swaha Om Varuna Devta aye Pahimam 11 times

MONEY	LOVE	CAREER	FAMILY	TRAVEL	WEDDING	MOVE	BUSINESS	HEALTH	Lotto #'s	play 3 #s
Bad	Bad	Bad	Fair	Bad	Bad	Bad	Bad	Bad	63,64,39,47,46,35,57	429

SHOPPING	GAMBLE	SEX	KEYWORD	KEYWORD				
Bad	Bad	is very bad	KARMA	Destruction,Losses,Death,Sickness - cold,Legal matter,Abusive,Karmic debts,God - Karma				

STRESS LEVEL	LUCKY COLORS	JEWELERY	MOONS EFFECT	GRAHA EFFECT	DAILY DEITY
High	Gold/Brown//Green	Saphire/Hessonite	Ivestments	Evil Graha	Agnidev

DAILY PUJA	DAILY PSALMS
Remembrance of family members who died, worship of older people. gifts to grand parents	9, 18, 36 ,45, 54, 63, 81, 108, 126

Friday, June 3, 2016 | This is considered a NEUTRAL day for you | Planet: Sun

ADVICE & DETAILS	MANTRA FOR TODAY
Your authoritative attitude mixed with arrogance and the need to feel superior may bring you difficulties with government or any of its agencies and may also make you feel lonely. Being humble today will be beneficial.	Om Namo Bhagawate Mukhtanandaya, 108 times

MONEY	LOVE	CAREER	FAMILY	TRAVEL	WEDDING	MOVE	BUSINESS	HEALTH	Lotto #'s	play 3 #s
Fair	Bad	Good	Bad	Fair	Bad	Fair	Fair	Fair	35,58,44,29,17,6,9	237

SHOPPING	GAMBLE	SEX	KEYWORD	KEYWORD				
Fair	Fair	is fair	MIND	Independence,Loneliness,Meditative,Worry,Dominating,Illness - Cold,On Your Own,Commanding				

STRESS LEVEL	LUCKY COLORS	JEWELERY	MOONS EFFECT	GRAHA EFFECT	DAILY DEITY
High	White/Yellow/	Pearl/Quartz	Arrogance	Status Graha	Saraswaty

DAILY PUJA	DAILY PSALMS
Give Gifts to Priests, Invite holy ones to your home, Feed Swamis and Yogis, Do Shiva Puja.	1, 10, 28 ,37, 46, 55, 73, 100, 118

Saturday, June 4, 2016 | This is considered a POSITIVE day for you | Planet: Moon

ADVICE & DETAILS	MANTRA FOR TODAY
Some of the negative influences for this day may be quarrels with loved ones and trouble with government. The positive influences are cooperation, affection and music that can help you counter the negative influences.	Kali Durge Namo Nama Om Durge aye nama swaha 108 times

MONEY	LOVE	CAREER	FAMILY	TRAVEL	WEDDING	MOVE	BUSINESS	HEALTH	Lotto #'s	play 3 #s
Good	Excellent	Good	Good	Excellent	Good	Good	Good	Good	39,62,25,44,50,39,45	854

SHOPPING	GAMBLE	SEX	KEYWORD	KEYWORD				
Good	Good	is good	LOVE	Romance,Popularity,Visitors,Shopping,Food, Drinks,Co-operation,Friendships,Affection				

STRESS LEVEL	LUCKY COLORS	JEWELERY	MOONS EFFECT	GRAHA EFFECT	DAILY DEITY
Low	Red/Yellow/Pink	Topaz/Diamonds	Conservative	Love Graha	Gauri

DAILY PUJA	DAILY PSALMS
Give Gifts to females andnMother, Serve milk Products, Worship Durga forms	2, 11, 29 ,38, 47, 56, 74, 101, 119

Sunday, June 5, 2016

| | | This is considered a POSITIVE day for you | | | | | | | Planet: Mercury | |

ADVICE & DETAILS

You may feel the exertion from your job and from building the life you have created for you and your family. Take a deep breath, try to take some time for yourself, reading would be beneficial.

MANTRA FOR TODAY

Om hareem Kleem Hreem Aem Saraswataye namaha 21 times

MONEY	LOVE	CAREER	FAMILY	TRAVEL	WEDDING	MOVE	BUSINESS	HEALTH	Lotto #'s	play 3 #s
Good	Fair	Good	Good	Excellent	Good	Good	Good	Excellent	30,25,22,50,35,63,70	803

SHOPPING	GAMBLE	SEX	KEYWORD	KEYWORD						
Good	Good	is great	SOCIAL	Children,Education,Astrology,Bargains,Social Functions,Childishness,Groups - Parties,Teacher						

STRESS LEVEL	LUCKY COLORS	JEWELERY	MOONS EFFECT	GRAHA EFFECT	DAILY DEITY
Low	Green/Sky Blue/	Diamonds/Silver	Enthusiastic	Social Graha	Vishnu

DAILY PUJA	DAILY PSALMS
Wash the feet of Children, Do Satnarayan Pooja, Read & chant Geeta	3, 12, 30 ,39, 48, 57, 75, 102, 120

Monday, June 6, 2016

| | | This is considered a NEGATIVE day for you | | | | | | | Planet: Pluto | |

ADVICE & DETAILS

Your high temper may get the best of you today; try to control it to avoid further karmas. You will have to work today even though you will feel lazy and have the nagging feeling that your pay is very low.

MANTRA FOR TODAY

Om Jai Viganeshwaraya.. Lambodaraya Namo Namaha 21 times

MONEY	LOVE	CAREER	FAMILY	TRAVEL	WEDDING	MOVE	BUSINESS	HEALTH	Lotto #'s	play 3 #s
Bad	Fair	Bad	Fair	Bad	Good	Bad	Bad	Bad	8,18,37,68,15,72,7	675

SHOPPING	GAMBLE	SEX	KEYWORD	KEYWORD						
Bad	Bad	is tough	CAREER	Career,Hard Work,Co-workers,Low Payment,Job Problems,High Temper,Low Pay,Laziness						

STRESS LEVEL	LUCKY COLORS	JEWELERY	MOONS EFFECT	GRAHA EFFECT	DAILY DEITY
High	Dark Blue/ Purple/	Amethyst/Gold	Emotional	Job Graha	Lingam

DAILY PUJA	DAILY PSALMS
Worship Ganesh, Give gifts to father, and co -workers, Plant gardens, farms	4, 13, 31 ,40, 49, 58, 76, 103, 121

Tuesday, June 7, 2016

| | | This is considered a POSITIVE day for you | | | | | | | Planet: Venus | |

ADVICE & DETAILS

You will feel a great deal of frustration today if your financial matters related to job promotion, profits and money do not work out in the manner that you expect them to. Be patient and try to understand that the universe only send you what you can handle. You have been given what you need the brain and the brawn to work and accomplish your desires.

MANTRA FOR TODAY

Om Graam Greem Graum Sa Gurave namah swaha 21 times

MONEY	LOVE	CAREER	FAMILY	TRAVEL	WEDDING	MOVE	BUSINESS	HEALTH	Lotto #'s	play 3 #s
Bad	Excellent	Fair	Good	Excellent	Good	Excellent	Good	Excellent	23,57,46,20,66,17,58	776

SHOPPING	GAMBLE	SEX	KEYWORD	KEYWORD						
Good	Good	is good	CHANGE	Sexuality,Travel,Change,Distant, far,Travel delays,Deception,Excercise,Illicit Affairs						

STRESS LEVEL	LUCKY COLORS	JEWELERY	MOONS EFFECT	GRAHA EFFECT	DAILY DEITY
Fair	Tan/Green/ Beige	Pearl/Silver/quartz	Courageous	Travel Graha	Nataraja

DAILY PUJA	DAILY PSALMS
Artistic gifts, Pray to Krishna, Do good deeds, do Spiritual trips	5, 14, 32 ,41, 50, 59, 77, 104, 122

Wednesday, June 8, 2016

| | | This is considered a NEGATIVE day for you | | | | | | | Planet: Mars | |

ADVICE & DETAILS

Although you feel powerful today, you must connect with your inner intelligence and give and receive advice with an open heart and mind. You will have to opportunity to experience high pleasure today and be around or be part of things related to TV or fame.

MANTRA FOR TODAY

Om Mana Swasti Shanti Kuru kuru Swaha Shivoham Shivoham 27 times

MONEY	LOVE	CAREER	FAMILY	TRAVEL	WEDDING	MOVE	BUSINESS	HEALTH	Lotto #'s	play 3 #s
Bad	Bad	Bad	Bad	Bad	Bad	Bad	Fair	Bad	64,58,26,21,54,75,54	786

SHOPPING	GAMBLE	SEX	KEYWORD	KEYWORD						
Fair	Bad	is frustrating	POWER	Responsibilty,Disagreement,Family,Back Pain,Family Conflicts,Traffic Ticket,Quarrels,Jealousy						

STRESS LEVEL	LUCKY COLORS	JEWELERY	MOONS EFFECT	GRAHA EFFECT	DAILY DEITY
High	Purple/Blue/Rose	Emerald/Saphire	Educational	Family Graha	Mahakali

DAILY PUJA	DAILY PSALMS
Meditate, Control temper, Pray to Hanuman, Chant Hanuman Chalisa	6, 15, 33 ,42, 51, 60, 78, 105, 123

Thursday, June 9, 2016 — This is considered a NEUTRAL day for you — Planet: Uranus

ADVICE & DETAILS

There will be a feeling of excitement and anticipation, but changes in plans or ideas may leave you feeling frustrated. Use your internal power to overcome the frustration and flow with the changes that at the end will be beneficial.

MANTRA FOR TODAY

Jai Jai Shiva Shambo.(2) ...Mahadeva Shambo (2) 21 times 8

MONEY	LOVE	CAREER	FAMILY	TRAVEL	WEDDING	MOVE	BUSINESS	HEALTH	Lotto #'s	play 3 #s
Good	Good	Fair	Good	Good	Bad	Good	Bad	Fair	10,41,14,38,24,11,4	468

SHOPPING	GAMBLE	SEX	KEYWORD	KEYWORD						
Bad	Fair	is quiet	DIVINE	Spirituality,Religious,Astrology,Inner Conflicts,Religious ,Sleepiness,Advice given,Alcohol - drugs						

STRESS LEVEL	LUCKY COLORS	JEWELERY	MOONS EFFECT	GRAHA EFFECT	DAILY DEITY
Fair	Light Blue/Peach	Tiger's eye/Gold/Silver	Affectionate	God'S Graha	Shesnaag

DAILY PUJA	DAILY PSALMS
Chant Shiva Mantras, Take gifts to Ocean - Ganga Puja, Donate to Temple, Priests, etc.	7, 16, 34 ,43, 52, 61, 79, 106, 124

Friday, June 10, 2016 — This is considered A POSITIVE day for you — Planet: Jupiter

ADVICE & DETAILS

Government and police agencies may cross paths with you today; try to follow the law so the encounters are more pleasurable. You will be the target of jealousy today so try to stay humble about your accomplishments or your belongings and remember that the good times also pass what remains is only the purity in your heart. You will have to confront many responsibilities today do it with surrender and service in your heart.

MANTRA FOR TODAY

Om Hareem Nama Swaha..Shri Maha Laxmi Aye Namah swaha 12 times

MONEY	LOVE	CAREER	FAMILY	TRAVEL	WEDDING	MOVE	BUSINESS	HEALTH	Lotto #'s	play 3 #s
Excellent	Good	Excellent	Good	Good	Excellent	Good	Excellent	Excellent	10,68,21,29,6,39,18	61

SHOPPING	GAMBLE	SEX	KEYWORD	KEYWORD						
Excellent	Excellent	is excellent	MONEY	Business,Major Expense,Money - Profits,Income,Investments,Power,Promotion,Fame - TV						

STRESS LEVEL	LUCKY COLORS	JEWELERY	MOONS EFFECT	GRAHA EFFECT	DAILY DEITY
Low	Yellow/Silver	Diamonds/Gold/Pearls	Secretive	Money Graha	Mahalaxmi

DAILY PUJA	DAILY PSALMS
Decorate Land, Feed the poor, Donate milk /products to all, Feed holy guests,	8, 17, 35 ,44, 53, 62, 80, 107, 125

Saturday, June 11, 2016 — This is considered a NEGATIVE day for you — Planet: Saturn

ADVICE & DETAILS

You have to deal with a great deal of responsibilities today; regardless of this others will feel jealous and envious of you. There are possible encounters with police and/or government officials.

MANTRA FOR TODAY

Om Ganga mataye nama swaha Om Varuna Devta aye Pahimam 11 times

MONEY	LOVE	CAREER	FAMILY	TRAVEL	WEDDING	MOVE	BUSINESS	HEALTH	Lotto #'s	play 3 #s
Bad	Bad	Bad	Fair	Bad	Bad	Bad	Bad	Bad	27,30,23,75,68,23,40	8

SHOPPING	GAMBLE	SEX	KEYWORD	KEYWORD						
Bad	Bad	is very bad	KARMA	Destruction,Losses,Death,Sickness - cold,Legal matter,Abusive,Karmic debts,God - Karma						

STRESS LEVEL	LUCKY COLORS	JEWELERY	MOONS EFFECT	GRAHA EFFECT	DAILY DEITY
High	Gold/Brown//Green	Saphire/Hessonite	Ivestments	Evil Graha	Agnidev

DAILY PUJA	DAILY PSALMS
Remembrance of family members who died, worship of older people. gifts to grand parents	9, 18, 36 ,45, 54, 63, 81, 108, 126

Sunday, June 12, 2016 — This is considered a NEUTRAL day for you — Planet: Sun

ADVICE & DETAILS

Your authoritative attitude mixed with arrogance and the need to feel superior may bring you difficulties with government or any of its agencies and may also make you feel lonely. Being humble today will be beneficial.

MANTRA FOR TODAY

Om Namo Bhagawate Mukhtanandaya, 108 times

MONEY	LOVE	CAREER	FAMILY	TRAVEL	WEDDING	MOVE	BUSINESS	HEALTH	Lotto #'s	play 3 #s
Fair	Bad	Good	Bad	Fair	Bad	Fair	Fair	Fair	71,18,8,31,60,24,13	504

SHOPPING	GAMBLE	SEX	KEYWORD	KEYWORD						
Fair	Fair	is fair	MIND	Independence,Loneliness,Meditative,Worry,Dominating,Illness - Cold,On Your Own,Commanding						

STRESS LEVEL	LUCKY COLORS	JEWELERY	MOONS EFFECT	GRAHA EFFECT	DAILY DEITY
High	White/Yellow/	Pearl/Quartz	Arrogance	Status Graha	Saraswaty

DAILY PUJA	DAILY PSALMS
Give Gifts to Priests, Invite holy ones to your home, Feed Swamis and Yogis, Do Shiva Puja.	1, 10, 28 ,37, 46, 55, 73, 100, 118

Monday, June 13, 2016 — This is considered a POSITIVE day for you — Planet: Moon

ADVICE & DETAILS

Some of the negative influences for this day may be quarrels with loved ones and trouble with government. The positive influences are cooperation, affection and music that can help you counter the negative influences.

MANTRA FOR TODAY

Kali Durge Namo Nama Om Durge aye nama swaha 108 times

MONEY	LOVE	CAREER	FAMILY	TRAVEL	WEDDING	MOVE	BUSINESS	HEALTH	Lotto #'s	play 3 #s
Good	Excellent	Good	Good	Excellent	Good	Good	Good	Good	32,62,67,74,72,54,18	945

SHOPPING	GAMBLE	SEX	KEYWORD	KEYWORD				
Good	Good	is good	LOVE	Romance,Popularity,Visitors,Shopping,Food, Drinks,Co-operation,Friendships,Affection				

STRESS LEVEL	LUCKY COLORS	JEWELERY	MOONS EFFECT	GRAHA EFFECT	DAILY DEITY
Low	Red/Yellow/Pink	Topaz/Diamonds	Conservative	Love Graha	Gauri

DAILY PUJA	DAILY PSALMS
Give Gifts to females andnMother, Serve milk Products, Worship Durga forms	2, 11, 29 ,38, 47, 56, 74, 101, 119

Tuesday, June 14, 2016 — This is considered a POSITIVE day for you — Planet: Mercury

ADVICE & DETAILS

You may feel the exertion from your job and from building the life you have created for you and your family. Take a deep breath, try to take some time for yourself, reading would be beneficial.

MANTRA FOR TODAY

Om hareem Kleem Hreem Aem Saraswataye namaha 21 times

MONEY	LOVE	CAREER	FAMILY	TRAVEL	WEDDING	MOVE	BUSINESS	HEALTH	Lotto #'s	play 3 #s
Good	Fair	Good	Good	Excellent	Good	Good	Good	Excellent	28,38,3,34,46,69,3	901

SHOPPING	GAMBLE	SEX	KEYWORD	KEYWORD				
Good	Good	is great	SOCIAL	Children,Education,Astrology,Bargains,Social Functions,Childishness,Groups - Parties,Teacher				

STRESS LEVEL	LUCKY COLORS	JEWELERY	MOONS EFFECT	GRAHA EFFECT	DAILY DEITY
Low	Green/Sky Blue/	Diamonds/Silver	Enthusiastic	Social Graha	Vishnu

DAILY PUJA	DAILY PSALMS
Wash the feet of Children, Do Satnarayan Pooja, Read & chant Geeta	3, 12, 30 ,39, 48, 57, 75, 102, 120

Wednesday, June 15, 2016 — This is considered a NEGATIVE day for you — Planet: Pluto

ADVICE & DETAILS

Your high temper may get the best of you today; try to control it to avoid further karmas. You will have to work today even though you will feel lazy and have the nagging feeling that your pay is very low.

MANTRA FOR TODAY

Om Jai Viganeshwaraya.. Lambodaraya Namo Namaha 21 times

MONEY	LOVE	CAREER	FAMILY	TRAVEL	WEDDING	MOVE	BUSINESS	HEALTH	Lotto #'s	play 3 #s
Bad	Fair	Bad	Fair	Bad	Good	Bad	Bad	Bad	37,37,57,33,37,22,64	833

SHOPPING	GAMBLE	SEX	KEYWORD	KEYWORD				
Bad	Bad	is tough	CAREER	Career,Hard Work,Co-workers,Low Payment,Job Problems,High Temper,Low Pay,Laziness				

STRESS LEVEL	LUCKY COLORS	JEWELERY	MOONS EFFECT	GRAHA EFFECT	DAILY DEITY
High	Dark Blue/ Purple/	Amethyst/Gold	Emotional	Job Graha	Lingam

DAILY PUJA	DAILY PSALMS
Worship Ganesh, Give gifts to father, and co -workers, Plant gardens, farms	4, 13, 31 ,40, 49, 58, 76, 103, 121

Thursday, June 16, 2016 — This is considered a POSITIVE day for you — Planet: Venus

ADVICE & DETAILS

You will feel a great deal of frustration today if your financial matters related to job promotion, profits and money do not work out in the manner that you expect them to. Be patient and try to understand that the universe only send you what you can handle. You have been given what you need the brain and the brawn to work and accomplish your desires.

MANTRA FOR TODAY

Om Graam Greem Graum Sa Gurave namah swaha 21 times

MONEY	LOVE	CAREER	FAMILY	TRAVEL	WEDDING	MOVE	BUSINESS	HEALTH	Lotto #'s	play 3 #s
Bad	Excellent	Fair	Good	Excellent	Good	Excellent	Good	Excellent	69,48,64,60,51,31,74	636

SHOPPING	GAMBLE	SEX	KEYWORD	KEYWORD				
Good	Good	is good	CHANGE	Sexuality,Travel,Change,Distant, far,Travel delays,Deception,Excercise,Illicit Affairs				

STRESS LEVEL	LUCKY COLORS	JEWELERY	MOONS EFFECT	GRAHA EFFECT	DAILY DEITY
Fair	Tan/Green/ Beige	Pearl/Silver/quartz	Courageous	Travel Graha	Nataraja

DAILY PUJA	DAILY PSALMS
Artistic gifts, Pray to Krishna, Do good deeds, do Spiritual trips	5, 14, 32 ,41, 50, 59, 77, 104, 122

Friday, June 17, 2016 — This is considered a NEGATIVE day for you — Planet: Mars

ADVICE & DETAILS

Although you feel powerful today, you must connect with your inner intelligence and give and receive advice with an open heart and mind. You will have to opportunity to experience high pleasure today and be around or be part of things related to TV or fame.

MANTRA FOR TODAY

Om Mana Swasti Shanti Kuru kuru Swaha Shivoham Shivoham 27 times

MONEY	LOVE	CAREER	FAMILY	TRAVEL	WEDDING	MOVE	BUSINESS	HEALTH	Lotto #'s	play 3 #s
Bad	Bad	Bad	Bad	Bad	Bad	Bad	Fair	Bad	34,6,12,25,36,1,55	491

SHOPPING	GAMBLE	SEX	KEYWORD	KEYWORD						
Fair	Bad	is frustrating	POWER	Responsibilty,Disagreement,Family,Back Pain,Family Conflicts,Traffic Ticket,Quarrels,Jealousy						

STRESS LEVEL	LUCKY COLORS	JEWELERY	MOONS EFFECT	GRAHA EFFECT	DAILY DEITY
High	Purple/Blue/Rose	Emerald/Saphire	Educational	Family Graha	Mahakali

DAILY PUJA	DAILY PSALMS
Meditate, Control temper, Pray to Hanuman, Chant Hanuman Chalisa	6, 15, 33 ,42, 51, 60, 78, 105, 123

Saturday, June 18, 2016 — This is considered a NEUTRAL day for you — Planet: Uranus

ADVICE & DETAILS

There will be a feeling of excitement and anticipation, but changes in plans or ideas may leave you feeling frustrated. Use your internal power to overcome the frustration and flow with the changes that at the end will be beneficial.

MANTRA FOR TODAY

Jai Jai Shiva Shambo.(2) ...Mahadeva Shambo (2) 21 times 8

MONEY	LOVE	CAREER	FAMILY	TRAVEL	WEDDING	MOVE	BUSINESS	HEALTH	Lotto #'s	play 3 #s
Good	Good	Fair	Good	Good	Bad	Good	Bad	Fair	26,38,63,7,54,50,43	761

SHOPPING	GAMBLE	SEX	KEYWORD	KEYWORD						
Bad	Fair	is quiet	DIVINE	Spirituality,Religious,Astrology,Inner Conflicts,Religious ,Sleepiness,Advice given,Alcohol - drugs						

STRESS LEVEL	LUCKY COLORS	JEWELERY	MOONS EFFECT	GRAHA EFFECT	DAILY DEITY
Fair	Light Blue/Peach	Tiger's eye/Gold/Silver	Affectionate	God'S Graha	Shesnaag

DAILY PUJA	DAILY PSALMS
Chant Shiva Mantras, Take gifts to Ocean - Ganga Puja, Donate to Temple, Priests, etc.	7, 16, 34 ,43, 52, 61, 79, 106, 124

Sunday, June 19, 2016 — This is considered a POSITIVE day for you — Planet: Jupiter

ADVICE & DETAILS

Government and police agencies may cross paths with you today; try to follow the law so the encounters are more pleasurable. You will be the target of jealousy today so try to stay humble about your accomplishments or your belongings and remember that the good times also pass what remains is only the purity in your heart. You will have to confront many responsibilities today do it with surrender and service in your heart.

MANTRA FOR TODAY

Om Hareem Nama Swaha..Shri Maha Laxmi Aye Namah swaha 12 times

MONEY	LOVE	CAREER	FAMILY	TRAVEL	WEDDING	MOVE	BUSINESS	HEALTH	Lotto #'s	play 3 #s
Excellent	Good	Excellent	Good	Good	Excellent	Good	Excellent	Excellent	30,40,32,14,40,53,49	270

SHOPPING	GAMBLE	SEX	KEYWORD	KEYWORD						
Excellent	Excellent	is excellent	MONEY	Business,Major Expense,Money - Profits,Income,Investments,Power,Promotion,Fame - TV						

STRESS LEVEL	LUCKY COLORS	JEWELERY	MOONS EFFECT	GRAHA EFFECT	DAILY DEITY
Low	Yellow/Silver	Diamonds/Gold/Pearls	Secretive	Money Graha	Mahalaxmi

DAILY PUJA	DAILY PSALMS
Decorate Land, Feed the poor, Donate milk /products to all, Feed holy guests,	8, 17, 35 ,44, 53, 62, 80, 107, 125

Monday, June 20, 2016 — This is considered a NEGATIVE day for you — Planet: Saturn

ADVICE & DETAILS

You have to deal with a great deal of responsibilities today; regardless of this others will feel jealous and envious of you. There are possible encounters with police and/or government officials.

MANTRA FOR TODAY

Om Ganga mataye nama swaha Om Varuna Devta aye Pahimam 11 times

MONEY	LOVE	CAREER	FAMILY	TRAVEL	WEDDING	MOVE	BUSINESS	HEALTH	Lotto #'s	play 3 #s
Bad	Bad	Bad	Fair	Bad	Bad	Bad	Bad	Bad	24,44,45,29,38,2,39	777

SHOPPING	GAMBLE	SEX	KEYWORD	KEYWORD						
Bad	Bad	is very bad	KARMA	Destruction,Losses,Death,Sickness - cold,Legal matter,Abusive,Karmic debts,God - Karma						

STRESS LEVEL	LUCKY COLORS	JEWELERY	MOONS EFFECT	GRAHA EFFECT	DAILY DEITY
High	Gold/Brown//Green	Saphire/Hessonite	Ivestments	Evil Graha	Agnidev

DAILY PUJA	DAILY PSALMS
Remembrance of family members who died, worship of older people. gifts to grand parents	9, 18, 36 ,45, 54, 63, 81, 108, 126

Tuesday, June 21, 2016 — This is considered a NEUTRAL day for you — Planet: Sun

ADVICE & DETAILS	MANTRA FOR TODAY
Your authoritative attitude mixed with arrogance and the need to feel superior may bring you difficulties with government or any of its agencies and may also make you feel lonely. Being humble today will be beneficial.	Om Namo Bhagawate Mukhtanandaya, 108 times

MONEY	LOVE	CAREER	FAMILY	TRAVEL	WEDDING	MOVE	BUSINESS	HEALTH	Lotto #'s	play 3 #s
Fair	Bad	Good	Bad	Fair	Bad	Fair	Fair	Fair	47,35,58,9,47,56,50	269

SHOPPING	GAMBLE	SEX	KEYWORD	KEYWORD						
Fair	Fair	is fair	MIND	Independence,Loneliness,Meditative,Worry,Dominating,Illness - Cold,On Your Own,Commanding						

STRESS LEVEL		LUCKY COLORS	JEWELERY	MOONS EFFECT	GRAHA EFFECT	DAILY DEITY
High		White/Yellow/	Pearl/Quartz	Arrogance	Status Graha	Saraswaty

DAILY PUJA	DAILY PSALMS
Give Gifts to Priests, Invite holy ones to your home, Feed Swamis and Yogis, Do Shiva Puja.	1, 10, 28 ,37, 46, 55, 73, 100, 118

Wednesday, June 22, 2016 — This is considered a POSITIVE day for you — Planet: Moon

ADVICE & DETAILS	MANTRA FOR TODAY
Some of the negative influences for this day may be quarrels with loved ones and trouble with government. The positive influences are cooperation, affection and music that can help you counter the negative influences.	Kali Durge Namo Nama Om Durge aye nama swaha 108 times

MONEY	LOVE	CAREER	FAMILY	TRAVEL	WEDDING	MOVE	BUSINESS	HEALTH	Lotto #'s	play 3 #s
Good	Excellent	Good	Good	Excellent	Good	Good	Good	Good	12,72,45,16,65,57,7	409

SHOPPING	GAMBLE	SEX	KEYWORD	KEYWORD						
Good	Good	is good	LOVE	Romance,Popularity,Visitors,Shopping,Food, Drinks,Co-operation,Friendships,Affection						

STRESS LEVEL		LUCKY COLORS	JEWELERY	MOONS EFFECT	GRAHA EFFECT	DAILY DEITY
Low		Red/Yellow/Pink	Topaz/Diamonds	Conservative	Love Graha	Gauri

DAILY PUJA	DAILY PSALMS
Give Gifts to females andnMother, Serve milk Products, Worship Durga forms	2, 11, 29 ,38, 47, 56, 74, 101, 119

Thursday, June 23, 2016 — This is considered a POSITIVE day for you — Planet: Mercury

ADVICE & DETAILS	MANTRA FOR TODAY
You may feel the exertion from your job and from building the life you have created for you and your family. Take a deep breath, try to take some time for yourself, reading would be beneficial.	Om hareem Kleem Hreem Aem Saraswataye namaha 21 times

MONEY	LOVE	CAREER	FAMILY	TRAVEL	WEDDING	MOVE	BUSINESS	HEALTH	Lotto #'s	play 3 #s
Good	Fair	Good	Good	Excellent	Good	Good	Good	Excellent	47,49,25,63,13,29,53	941

SHOPPING	GAMBLE	SEX	KEYWORD	KEYWORD						
Good	Good	is great	SOCIAL	Children,Education,Astrology,Bargains,Social Functions,Childishness,Groups - Parties,Teacher						

STRESS LEVEL		LUCKY COLORS	JEWELERY	MOONS EFFECT	GRAHA EFFECT	DAILY DEITY
Low		Green/Sky Blue/	Diamonds/Silver	Enthusiastic	Social Graha	Vishnu

DAILY PUJA	DAILY PSALMS
Wash the feet of Children, Do Satnarayan Pooja, Read & chant Geeta	3, 12, 30 ,39, 48, 57, 75, 102, 120

Friday, June 24, 2016 — This is considered a NEGATIVE day for you — Planet: Pluto

ADVICE & DETAILS	MANTRA FOR TODAY
Your high temper may get the best of you today; try to control it to avoid further karmas. You will have to work today even though you will feel lazy and have the nagging feeling that your pay is very low.	Om Jai Viganeshwaraya.. Lambodaraya Namo Namaha 21 times

MONEY	LOVE	CAREER	FAMILY	TRAVEL	WEDDING	MOVE	BUSINESS	HEALTH	Lotto #'s	play 3 #s
Bad	Fair	Bad	Fair	Bad	Good	Bad	Bad	Bad	4,11,5,38,57,60,18	265

SHOPPING	GAMBLE	SEX	KEYWORD	KEYWORD						
Bad	Bad	is tough	CAREER	Career,Hard Work,Co-workers,Low Payment,Job Problems,High Temper,Low Pay,Laziness						

STRESS LEVEL		LUCKY COLORS	JEWELERY	MOONS EFFECT	GRAHA EFFECT	DAILY DEITY
High		Dark Blue/ Purple/	Amethyst/Gold	Emotional	Job Graha	Lingam

DAILY PUJA	DAILY PSALMS
Worship Ganesh, Give gifts to father, and co -workers, Plant gardens, farms	4, 13, 31 ,40, 49, 58, 76, 103, 121

Saturday, June 25, 2016 — This is considered a POSITIVE day for you — Planet: Venus

ADVICE & DETAILS	MANTRA FOR TODAY
You will feel a great deal of frustration today if your financial matters related to job promotion, profits and money do not work out in the manner that you expect them to. Be patient and try to understand that the universe only send you what you can handle. You have been given what you need the brain and the brawn to work and accomplish your desires.	Om Graam Greem Graum Sa Gurave namah swaha 21 times

MONEY	LOVE	CAREER	FAMILY	TRAVEL	WEDDING	MOVE	BUSINESS	HEALTH	Lotto #'s	play 3 #s
Bad	Excellent	Fair	Good	Excellent	Good	Excellent	Good	Excellent	30,47,65,20,37,22,14	738

SHOPPING	GAMBLE	SEX	KEYWORD	KEYWORD						
Good	Good	is good	CHANGE	Sexuality,Travel,Change,Distant, far,Travel delays,Deception,Excercise,Illicit Affairs						

STRESS LEVEL	LUCKY COLORS	JEWELERY	MOONS EFFECT	GRAHA EFFECT	DAILY DEITY
Fair	Tan/Green/ Beige	Pearl/Silver/quartz	Courageous	Travel Graha	Nataraja

DAILY PUJA	DAILY PSALMS
Artistic gifts, Pray to Krishna, Do good deeds, do Spiritual trips	5, 14, 32 ,41, 50, 59, 77, 104, 122

Sunday, June 26, 2016 — This is considered a NEGATIVE day for you — Planet: Mars

ADVICE & DETAILS	MANTRA FOR TODAY
Although you feel powerful today, you must connect with your inner intelligence and give and receive advice with an open heart and mind. You will have to opportunity to experience high pleasure today and be around or be part of things related to TV or fame.	Om Mana Swasti Shanti Kuru kuru Swaha Shivoham Shivoham 27 times

MONEY	LOVE	CAREER	FAMILY	TRAVEL	WEDDING	MOVE	BUSINESS	HEALTH	Lotto #'s	play 3 #s
Bad	Bad	Bad	Bad	Bad	Bad	Bad	Fair	Bad	58,19,34,49,49,61,11	293

SHOPPING	GAMBLE	SEX	KEYWORD	KEYWORD						
Fair	Bad	is frustrating	POWER	Responsibilty,Disagreement,Family,Back Pain,Family Conflicts,Traffic Ticket,Quarrels,Jealousy						

STRESS LEVEL	LUCKY COLORS	JEWELERY	MOONS EFFECT	GRAHA EFFECT	DAILY DEITY
High	Purple/Blue/Rose	Emerald/Saphire	Educational	Family Graha	Mahakali

DAILY PUJA	DAILY PSALMS
Meditate, Control temper, Pray to Hanuman, Chant Hanuman Chalisa	6, 15, 33 ,42, 51, 60, 78, 105, 123

Monday, June 27, 2016 — This is considered a NEUTRAL day for you — Planet: Uranus

ADVICE & DETAILS	MANTRA FOR TODAY
There will be a feeling of excitement and anticipation, but changes in plans or ideas may leave you feeling frustrated. Use your internal power to overcome the frustration and flow with the changes that at the end will be beneficial.	Jai Jai Shiva Shambo.(2) ...Mahadeva Shambo (2) 21 times 8

MONEY	LOVE	CAREER	FAMILY	TRAVEL	WEDDING	MOVE	BUSINESS	HEALTH	Lotto #'s	play 3 #s
Good	Good	Fair	Good	Good	Bad	Good	Bad	Fair	24,66,20,8,26,50,65	14

SHOPPING	GAMBLE	SEX	KEYWORD	KEYWORD						
Bad	Fair	is quiet	DIVINE	Spirituality,Religious,Astrology,Inner Conflicts,Religious ,Sleepiness,Advice given,Alcohol - drugs						

STRESS LEVEL	LUCKY COLORS	JEWELERY	MOONS EFFECT	GRAHA EFFECT	DAILY DEITY
Fair	Light Blue/Peach	Tiger's eye/Gold/Silver	Affectionate	God'S Graha	Shesnaag

DAILY PUJA	DAILY PSALMS
Chant Shiva Mantras, Take gifts to Ocean - Ganga Puja, Donate to Temple, Priests, etc.	7, 16, 34 ,43, 52, 61, 79, 106, 124

Tuesday, June 28, 2016 — This is considered a POSITIVE day for you — Planet: Jupiter

ADVICE & DETAILS	MANTRA FOR TODAY
Government and police agencies may cross paths with you today; try to follow the law so the encounters are more pleasurable. You will be the target of jealousy today so try to stay humble about your accomplishments or your belongings and remember that the good times also pass what remains is only the purity in your heart. You will have to confront many responsibilities today do it with surrender and service in your heart.	Om Hareem Nama Swaha..Shri Maha Laxmi Aye Namah swaha 12 times

MONEY	LOVE	CAREER	FAMILY	TRAVEL	WEDDING	MOVE	BUSINESS	HEALTH	Lotto #'s	play 3 #s
Excellent	Good	Excellent	Good	Good	Excellent	Good	Excellent	Excellent	69,71,25,36,66,49,1	186

SHOPPING	GAMBLE	SEX	KEYWORD	KEYWORD						
Excellent	Excellent	is excellent	MONEY	Business,Major Expense,Money - Profits,Income,Investments,Power,Promotion,Fame - TV						

STRESS LEVEL	LUCKY COLORS	JEWELERY	MOONS EFFECT	GRAHA EFFECT	DAILY DEITY
Low	Yellow/Silver	Diamonds/Gold/Pearls	Secretive	Money Graha	Mahalaxmi

DAILY PUJA	DAILY PSALMS
Decorate Land, Feed the poor, Donate milk /products to all, Feed holy guests,	8, 17, 35 ,44, 53, 62, 80, 107, 125

Wednesday, June 29, 2016 — This is considered a NEGATIVE day for you — Planet: Saturn

ADVICE & DETAILS

You have to deal with a great deal of responsibilities today; regardless of this others will feel jealous and envious of you. There are possible encounters with police and/or government officials.

MANTRA FOR TODAY

Om Ganga mataye nama swaha
Om Varuna Devta aye Pahimam 11 times

MONEY	LOVE	CAREER	FAMILY	TRAVEL	WEDDING	MOVE	BUSINESS	HEALTH	Lotto #'s	play 3 #s
Bad	Bad	Bad	Fair	Bad	Bad	Bad	Bad	Bad	4,25,2,37,51,24,40	202

SHOPPING	GAMBLE	SEX	KEYWORD	KEYWORD
Bad	Bad	is very bad	KARMA	Destruction,Losses,Death,Sickness - cold,Legal matter,Abusive,Karmic debts,God - Karma

STRESS LEVEL	LUCKY COLORS	JEWELERY	MOONS EFFECT	GRAHA EFFECT	DAILY DEITY
High	Gold/Brown//Green	Saphire/Hessonite	Ivestments	Evil Graha	Agnidev

DAILY PUJA	DAILY PSALMS
Remembrance of family members who died, worship of older people. gifts to grand parents	9, 18, 36 ,45, 54, 63, 81, 108, 126

Thursday, June 30, 2016 — This is considered a NEUTRAL day for you — Planet: Sun

ADVICE & DETAILS

Your authoritative attitude mixed with arrogance and the need to feel superior may bring you difficulties with government or any of its agencies and may also make you feel lonely. Being humble today will be beneficial.

MANTRA FOR TODAY

Om Namo Bhagawate Mukhtanandaya, 108 times

MONEY	LOVE	CAREER	FAMILY	TRAVEL	WEDDING	MOVE	BUSINESS	HEALTH	Lotto #'s	play 3 #s
Fair	Bad	Good	Bad	Fair	Bad	Fair	Fair	Fair	30,13,34,19,20,25,41	285

SHOPPING	GAMBLE	SEX	KEYWORD	KEYWORD
Fair	Fair	is fair	MIND	Independence,Loneliness,Meditative,Worry,Dominating,Illness - Cold,On Your Own,Commanding

STRESS LEVEL	LUCKY COLORS	JEWELERY	MOONS EFFECT	GRAHA EFFECT	DAILY DEITY
High	White/Yellow/	Pearl/Quartz	Arrogance	Status Graha	Saraswaty

DAILY PUJA	DAILY PSALMS
Give Gifts to Priests, Invite holy ones to your home, Feed Swamis and Yogis, Do Shiva Puja.	1, 10, 28 ,37, 46, 55, 73, 100, 118

Friday, July 1, 2016 — This is considered a POSITIVE day for you — Planet: Jupiter

ADVICE & DETAILS

It is important to follow God-like ways in order to receive protection from deceitful people that may want to take advantage of you today. Today you should expect short trips or some movement of some sort either places, people or things.

MANTRA FOR TODAY

Om Hareem Nama Swaha..Shri Maha Laxmi Aye Namah swaha 12 times

MONEY	LOVE	CAREER	FAMILY	TRAVEL	WEDDING	MOVE	BUSINESS	HEALTH	Lotto #'s	play 3 #s
Excellent	Good	Excellent	Good	Good	Excellent	Good	Excellent	Excellent	22,60,27,60,29,23,75	282

SHOPPING	GAMBLE	SEX	KEYWORD	KEYWORD
Excellent	Excellent	is excellent	MONEY	Business,Major Expense,Money - Profits,Income,Investments,Power,Promotion,Fame - TV

STRESS LEVEL	LUCKY COLORS	JEWELERY	MOONS EFFECT	GRAHA EFFECT	DAILY DEITY
Low	Yellow/Silver	Diamonds/Gold/Pearls	Secretive	Money Graha	Mahalaxmi

DAILY PUJA	DAILY PSALMS
Decorate Land, Feed the poor, Donate milk /products to all, Feed holy guests,	8, 17, 35 ,44, 53, 62, 80, 107, 125

Saturday, July 2, 2016 — This is considered a NEGATIVE day for you — Planet: Saturn

ADVICE & DETAILS

Make sure that the seeds you sow in your life are those of spirituality, devotion, love and understanding so you may reap the same bounty. Prepare yourself for possible accident or sudden changes in your life that give you an opportunity for rebirth .

MANTRA FOR TODAY

Om Ganga mataye nama swaha
Om Varuna Devta aye Pahimam 11 times

MONEY	LOVE	CAREER	FAMILY	TRAVEL	WEDDING	MOVE	BUSINESS	HEALTH	Lotto #'s	play 3 #s
Bad	Bad	Bad	Fair	Bad	Bad	Bad	Bad	Bad	59,72,29,37,39,28,60	378

SHOPPING	GAMBLE	SEX	KEYWORD	KEYWORD
Bad	Bad	is very bad	KARMA	Destruction,Losses,Death,Sickness - cold,Legal matter,Abusive,Karmic debts,God - Karma

STRESS LEVEL	LUCKY COLORS	JEWELERY	MOONS EFFECT	GRAHA EFFECT	DAILY DEITY
High	Gold/Brown//Green	Saphire/Hessonite	Ivestments	Evil Graha	Agnidev

DAILY PUJA	DAILY PSALMS
Remembrance of family members who died, worship of older people. gifts to grand parents	9, 18, 36 ,45, 54, 63, 81, 108, 126

Sunday, July 3, 2016 — This is considered a NEUTRAL day for you — Planet: Sun

ADVICE & DETAILS

A religious or spiritual demeanor will help you deal today with losses and lack of health. Be grateful for your blessings and offer the difficult lessons to the gods.

MANTRA FOR TODAY

Om Namo Bhagawate Mukhtanandaya, 108 times

MONEY	LOVE	CAREER	FAMILY	TRAVEL	WEDDING	MOVE	BUSINESS	HEALTH	Lotto #'s	play 3 #s
Fair	Bad	Good	Bad	Fair	Bad	Fair	Fair	Fair	35,58,46,60,63,18,26	304

SHOPPING	GAMBLE	SEX	KEYWORD	KEYWORD						
Fair	Fair	is fair	MIND	Independence,Loneliness,Meditative,Worry,Dominating,Illness - Cold,On Your Own,Commanding						

STRESS LEVEL	LUCKY COLORS	JEWELERY	MOONS EFFECT	GRAHA EFFECT	DAILY DEITY
High	White/Yellow/	Pearl/Quartz	Arrogance	Status Graha	Saraswaty

DAILY PUJA	DAILY PSALMS
Give Gifts to Priests, Invite holy ones to your home, Feed Swamis and Yogis, Do Shiva Puja.	1, 10, 28 ,37, 46, 55, 73, 100, 118

Monday, July 4, 2016 — This is considered A POSITIVE day for you — Planet: Moon

ADVICE & DETAILS

Instead of criticism, offer advice from the heart; not ego. It will be a slow day, but you will feel your connection to God. Do positive actions for good karma.

MANTRA FOR TODAY

Kali Durge Namo Nama Om Durge aye nama swaha 108 times

MONEY	LOVE	CAREER	FAMILY	TRAVEL	WEDDING	MOVE	BUSINESS	HEALTH	Lotto #'s	play 3 #s
Good	Excellent	Good	Good	Excellent	Good	Good	Good	Good	46,9,48,29,69,33,20	115

SHOPPING	GAMBLE	SEX	KEYWORD	KEYWORD						
Good	Good	is good	LOVE	Romance,Popularity,Visitors,Shopping,Food, Drinks,Co-operation,Friendships,Affection						

STRESS LEVEL	LUCKY COLORS	JEWELERY	MOONS EFFECT	GRAHA EFFECT	DAILY DEITY
Low	Red/Yellow/Pink	Topaz/Diamonds	Conservative	Love Graha	Gauri

DAILY PUJA	DAILY PSALMS
Give Gifts to females andnMother, Serve milk Products, Worship Durga forms	2, 11, 29 ,38, 47, 56, 74, 101, 119

Tuesday, July 5, 2016 — This is considered a POSITIVE day for you — Planet: Mercury

ADVICE & DETAILS

Today working and communicating with others may further your plans to publish that book you have been thinking about writing. It is a day when expression in any form will be fruitful. You must avoid negative influences of others with such things as alcohol and drugs served in gatherings.

MANTRA FOR TODAY

Om hareem Kleem Hreem Aem Saraswataye namaha 21 times

MONEY	LOVE	CAREER	FAMILY	TRAVEL	WEDDING	MOVE	BUSINESS	HEALTH	Lotto #'s	play 3 #s
Good	Fair	Good	Good	Excellent	Good	Good	Good	Excellent	35,37,60,59,19,5,69	278

SHOPPING	GAMBLE	SEX	KEYWORD	KEYWORD						
Good	Good	is great	SOCIAL	Children,Education,Astrology,Bargains,Social Functions,Childishness,Groups - Parties,Teacher						

STRESS LEVEL	LUCKY COLORS	JEWELERY	MOONS EFFECT	GRAHA EFFECT	DAILY DEITY
Low	Green/Sky Blue/	Diamonds/Silver	Enthusiastic	Social Graha	Vishnu

DAILY PUJA	DAILY PSALMS
Wash the feet of Children, Do Satnarayan Pooja, Read & chant Geeta	3, 12, 30 ,39, 48, 57, 75, 102, 120

Wednesday, July 6, 2016 — This is considered a NEGATIVE day for you — Planet: Pluto

ADVICE & DETAILS

It is important to follow God-like ways in order to receive protection from deceitful people that may want to take advantage of you today. Today you should expect short trips or some movement of some sort either places, people or things.

MANTRA FOR TODAY

Om Jai Viganeshwaraya.. Lambodaraya Namo Namaha 21 times

MONEY	LOVE	CAREER	FAMILY	TRAVEL	WEDDING	MOVE	BUSINESS	HEALTH	Lotto #'s	play 3 #s
Bad	Fair	Bad	Fair	Bad	Good	Bad	Bad	Bad	31,32,45,26,65,56,12	973

SHOPPING	GAMBLE	SEX	KEYWORD	KEYWORD						
Bad	Bad	is tough	CAREER	Career,Hard Work,Co-workers,Low Payment,Job Problems,High Temper,Low Pay,Laziness						

STRESS LEVEL	LUCKY COLORS	JEWELERY	MOONS EFFECT	GRAHA EFFECT	DAILY DEITY
High	Dark Blue/ Purple/	Amethyst/Gold	Emotional	Job Graha	Lingam

DAILY PUJA	DAILY PSALMS
Worship Ganesh, Give gifts to father, and co -workers, Plant gardens, farms	4, 13, 31 ,40, 49, 58, 76, 103, 121

Thursday, July 7, 2016 — This is considered a POSITIVE day for you — Planet: Venus

ADVICE & DETAILS	MANTRA FOR TODAY
Make sure that the seeds you sow in your life are those of spirituality, devotion, love and understanding so you may reap the same bounty. Prepare yourself for possible accident or sudden changes in your life that give you an opportunity for rebirth .	Om Graam Greem Graum Sa Gurave namah swaha 21 times

MONEY	LOVE	CAREER	FAMILY	TRAVEL	WEDDING	MOVE	BUSINESS	HEALTH	Lotto #'s	play 3 #s
Bad	Excellent	Fair	Good	Excellent	Good	Excellent	Good	Excellent	72,66,70,46,16,71,50	109

SHOPPING	GAMBLE	SEX	KEYWORD	KEYWORD						
Good	Good	is good	CHANGE	Sexuality,Travel,Change,Distant, far,Travel delays,Deception,Excercise,Illicit Affairs						

STRESS LEVEL		LUCKY COLORS		JEWELERY		MOONS EFFECT		GRAHA EFFECT		DAILY DEITY
Fair		Tan/Green/ Beige		Pearl/Silver/quartz		Courageous		Travel Graha		Nataraja

DAILY PUJA	DAILY PSALMS
Artistic gifts, Pray to Krishna, Do good deeds, do Spiritual trips	5, 14, 32 ,41, 50, 59, 77, 104, 122

Friday, July 8, 2016 — This is considered a NEGATIVE day for you — Planet: Mars

ADVICE & DETAILS	MANTRA FOR TODAY
Your manner of expression today may be commanding, make sure you do not go overboard and become bossy or overbearing. Enjoy the company of others in groups or parties. Use this time to work on creative projects like publishing, art or music.	Om Mana Swasti Shanti Kuru kuru Swaha Shivoham Shivoham 27 times

MONEY	LOVE	CAREER	FAMILY	TRAVEL	WEDDING	MOVE	BUSINESS	HEALTH	Lotto #'s	play 3 #s
Bad	Bad	Bad	Bad	Bad	Bad	Bad	Fair	Bad	26,70,9,61,35,55,49	156

SHOPPING	GAMBLE	SEX	KEYWORD	KEYWORD						
Fair	Bad	is frustrating	POWER	Responsibilty,Disagreement,Family,Back Pain,Family Conflicts,Traffic Ticket,Quarrels,Jealousy						

STRESS LEVEL		LUCKY COLORS		JEWELERY		MOONS EFFECT		GRAHA EFFECT		DAILY DEITY
High		Purple/Blue/Rose		Emerald/Saphire		Educational		Family Graha		Mahakali

DAILY PUJA	DAILY PSALMS
Meditate, Control temper, Pray to Hanuman, Chant Hanuman Chalisa	6, 15, 33 ,42, 51, 60, 78, 105, 123

Saturday, July 9, 2016 — This is considered a NEUTRAL day for you — Planet: Uranus

ADVICE & DETAILS	MANTRA FOR TODAY
Today working and communicating with others may further your plans to publish that book you have been thinking about writing. It is a day when expression in any form will be fruitful. You must avoid negative influences of others with such things as alcohol and drugs served in gatherings.	Jai Jai Shiva Shambo.(2) ...Mahadeva Shambo (2) 21 times 8

MONEY	LOVE	CAREER	FAMILY	TRAVEL	WEDDING	MOVE	BUSINESS	HEALTH	Lotto #'s	play 3 #s
Good	Good	Fair	Good	Good	Bad	Good	Bad	Fair	6,15,8,31,12,31,47	550

SHOPPING	GAMBLE	SEX	KEYWORD	KEYWORD						
Bad	Fair	is quiet	DIVINE	Spirituality,Religious,Astrology,Inner Conflicts,Religious ,Sleepiness,Advice given,Alcohol - drugs						

STRESS LEVEL		LUCKY COLORS		JEWELERY		MOONS EFFECT		GRAHA EFFECT		DAILY DEITY
Fair		Light Blue/Peach		Tiger's eye/Gold/Silver		Affectionate		God'S Graha		Shesnaag

DAILY PUJA	DAILY PSALMS
Chant Shiva Mantras, Take gifts to Ocean - Ganga Puja, Donate to Temple, Priests, etc.	7, 16, 34 ,43, 52, 61, 79, 106, 124

Sunday, July 10, 2016 — This is considered a POSITIVE day for you — Planet: Jupiter

ADVICE & DETAILS	MANTRA FOR TODAY
It is important to follow God-like ways in order to receive protection from deceitful people that may want to take advantage of you today. Today you should expect short trips or some movement of some sort either places, people or things.	Om Hareem Nama Swaha..Shri Maha Laxmi Aye Namah swaha 12 times

MONEY	LOVE	CAREER	FAMILY	TRAVEL	WEDDING	MOVE	BUSINESS	HEALTH	Lotto #'s	play 3 #s
Excellent	Good	Excellent	Good	Good	Excellent	Good	Excellent	Excellent	9,52,60,27,26,28,38	714

SHOPPING	GAMBLE	SEX	KEYWORD	KEYWORD						
Excellent	Excellent	is excellent	MONEY	Business,Major Expense,Money - Profits,Income,Investments,Power,Promotion,Fame - TV						

STRESS LEVEL		LUCKY COLORS		JEWELERY		MOONS EFFECT		GRAHA EFFECT		DAILY DEITY
Low		Yellow/Silver		Diamonds/Gold/Pearls		Secretive		Money Graha		Mahalaxmi

DAILY PUJA	DAILY PSALMS
Decorate Land, Feed the poor, Donate milk /products to all, Feed holy guests,	8, 17, 35 ,44, 53, 62, 80, 107, 125

Monday, July 11, 2016 — This is considered a NEGATIVE day for you — Planet: Saturn

ADVICE & DETAILS	MANTRA FOR TODAY
Make sure that the seeds you sow in your life are those of spirituality, devotion, love and understanding so you may reap the same bounty. Prepare yourself for possible accident or sudden changes in your life that give you an opportunity for rebirth .	Om Ganga mataye nama swaha Om Varuna Devta aye Pahimam 11 times

MONEY	LOVE	CAREER	FAMILY	TRAVEL	WEDDING	MOVE	BUSINESS	HEALTH	Lotto #'s	play 3 #s
Bad	Bad	Bad	Fair	Bad	Bad	Bad	Bad	Bad	32,2,62,10,28,15,46	952

SHOPPING	GAMBLE	SEX	KEYWORD	KEYWORD
Bad	Bad	is very bad	KARMA	Destruction,Losses,Death,Sickness - cold,Legal matter,Abusive,Karmic debts,God - Karma

STRESS LEVEL	LUCKY COLORS	JEWELERY	MOONS EFFECT	GRAHA EFFECT	DAILY DEITY
High	Gold/Brown//Green	Saphire/Hessonite	Ivestments	Evil Graha	Agnidev

DAILY PUJA	DAILY PSALMS
Remembrance of family members who died, worship of older people. gifts to grand parents	9, 18, 36 ,45, 54, 63, 81, 108, 126

Tuesday, July 12, 2016 — This is considered a NEUTRAL day for you — Planet: Sun

ADVICE & DETAILS	MANTRA FOR TODAY
A religious or spiritual demeanor will help you deal today with losses and lack of health. Be grateful for your blessings and offer the difficult lessons to the gods.	Om Namo Bhagawate Mukhtanandaya, 108 times

MONEY	LOVE	CAREER	FAMILY	TRAVEL	WEDDING	MOVE	BUSINESS	HEALTH	Lotto #'s	play 3 #s
Fair	Bad	Good	Bad	Fair	Bad	Fair	Fair	Fair	66,29,19,7,3,16,39	740

SHOPPING	GAMBLE	SEX	KEYWORD	KEYWORD
Fair	Fair	is fair	MIND	Independence,Loneliness,Meditative,Worry,Dominating,Illness - Cold,On Your Own,Commanding

STRESS LEVEL	LUCKY COLORS	JEWELERY	MOONS EFFECT	GRAHA EFFECT	DAILY DEITY
High	White/Yellow/	Pearl/Quartz	Arrogance	Status Graha	Saraswaty

DAILY PUJA	DAILY PSALMS
Give Gifts to Priests, Invite holy ones to your home, Feed Swamis and Yogis, Do Shiva Puja.	1, 10, 28 ,37, 46, 55, 73, 100, 118

Wednesday, July 13, 2016 — This is considered a POSITIVE day for you — Planet: Moon

ADVICE & DETAILS	MANTRA FOR TODAY
Instead of criticism, offer advice from the heart; not ego. It will be a slow day, but you will feel your connection to God. Do positive actions for good karma.	Kali Durge Namo Nama Om Durge aye nama swaha 108 times

MONEY	LOVE	CAREER	FAMILY	TRAVEL	WEDDING	MOVE	BUSINESS	HEALTH	Lotto #'s	play 3 #s
Good	Excellent	Good	Good	Excellent	Good	Good	Good	Good	32,23,53,21,13,39,19	234

SHOPPING	GAMBLE	SEX	KEYWORD	KEYWORD
Good	Good	is good	LOVE	Romance,Popularity,Visitors,Shopping,Food, Drinks,Co-operation,Friendships,Affection

STRESS LEVEL	LUCKY COLORS	JEWELERY	MOONS EFFECT	GRAHA EFFECT	DAILY DEITY
Low	Red/Yellow/Pink	Topaz/Diamonds	Conservative	Love Graha	Gauri

DAILY PUJA	DAILY PSALMS
Give Gifts to females andnMother, Serve milk Products, Worship Durga forms	2, 11, 29 ,38, 47, 56, 74, 101, 119

Thursday, July 14, 2016 — This is considered a POSITIVE day for you — Planet: Mercury

ADVICE & DETAILS	MANTRA FOR TODAY
Today working and communicating with others may further your plans to publish that book you have been thinking about writing. It is a day when expression in any form will be fruitful. You must avoid negative influences of others with such things as alcohol and drugs served in gatherings.	Om hareem Kleem Hreem Aem Saraswataye namaha 21 times

MONEY	LOVE	CAREER	FAMILY	TRAVEL	WEDDING	MOVE	BUSINESS	HEALTH	Lotto #'s	play 3 #s
Good	Fair	Good	Good	Excellent	Good	Good	Good	Excellent	58,50,26,9,17,61,39	970

SHOPPING	GAMBLE	SEX	KEYWORD	KEYWORD
Good	Good	is great	SOCIAL	Children,Education,Astrology,Bargains,Social Functions,Childishness,Groups - Parties,Teacher

STRESS LEVEL	LUCKY COLORS	JEWELERY	MOONS EFFECT	GRAHA EFFECT	DAILY DEITY
Low	Green/Sky Blue/	Diamonds/Silver	Enthusiastic	Social Graha	Vishnu

DAILY PUJA	DAILY PSALMS
Wash the feet of Children, Do Satnarayan Pooja, Read & chant Geeta	3, 12, 30 ,39, 48, 57, 75, 102, 120

Friday, July 15, 2016 — This is considered a NEGATIVE day for you — Planet: Pluto

ADVICE & DETAILS

It is important to follow God-like ways in order to receive protection from deceitful people that may want to take advantage of you today. Today you should expect short trips or some movement of some sort either places, people or things.

MANTRA FOR TODAY

Om Jai Viganeshwaraya.. Lambodaraya Namo Namaha 21 times

MONEY	LOVE	CAREER	FAMILY	TRAVEL	WEDDING	MOVE	BUSINESS	HEALTH	Lotto #'s	play 3 #s
Bad	Fair	Bad	Fair	Bad	Good	Bad	Bad	Bad	8,71,48,41,5,43,19	581

SHOPPING	GAMBLE	SEX	KEYWORD	KEYWORD						
Bad	Bad	is tough	CAREER	Career,Hard Work,Co-workers,Low Payment,Job Problems,High Temper,Low Pay,Laziness						

STRESS LEVEL	LUCKY COLORS	JEWELERY	MOONS EFFECT	GRAHA EFFECT	DAILY DEITY
High	Dark Blue/ Purple/	Amethyst/Gold	Emotional	Job Graha	Lingam

DAILY PUJA
Worship Ganesh, Give gifts to father, and co -workers, Plant gardens, farms

DAILY PSALMS
4, 13, 31 ,40, 49, 58, 76, 103, 121

Saturday, July 16, 2016 — This is considered a POSITIVE day for you — Planet: Venus

ADVICE & DETAILS

Make sure that the seeds you sow in your life are those of spirituality, devotion, love and understanding so you may reap the same bounty. Prepare yourself for possible accident or sudden changes in your life that give you an opportunity for rebirth .

MANTRA FOR TODAY

Om Graam Greem Graum Sa Gurave namah swaha 21 times

MONEY	LOVE	CAREER	FAMILY	TRAVEL	WEDDING	MOVE	BUSINESS	HEALTH	Lotto #'s	play 3 #s
Bad	Excellent	Fair	Good	Excellent	Good	Excellent	Good	Excellent	4,64,54,2,13,69,64	705

SHOPPING	GAMBLE	SEX	KEYWORD	KEYWORD						
Good	Good	is good	CHANGE	Sexuality,Travel,Change,Distant, far,Travel delays,Deception,Excercise,Illicit Affairs						

STRESS LEVEL	LUCKY COLORS	JEWELERY	MOONS EFFECT	GRAHA EFFECT	DAILY DEITY
Fair	Tan/Green/ Beige	Pearl/Silver/quartz	Courageous	Travel Graha	Nataraja

DAILY PUJA
Artistic gifts, Pray to Krishna, Do good deeds, do Spiritual trips

DAILY PSALMS
5, 14, 32 ,41, 50, 59, 77, 104, 122

Sunday, July 17, 2016 — This is considered a NEGATIVE day for you — Planet: Mars

ADVICE & DETAILS

Your manner of expression today may be commanding, make sure you do not go overboard and become bossy or overbearing. Enjoy the company of others in groups or parties. Use this time to work on creative projects like publishing, art or music.

MANTRA FOR TODAY

Om Mana Swasti Shanti Kuru kuru Swaha Shivoham Shivoham 27 times

MONEY	LOVE	CAREER	FAMILY	TRAVEL	WEDDING	MOVE	BUSINESS	HEALTH	Lotto #'s	play 3 #s
Bad	Bad	Bad	Bad	Bad	Bad	Bad	Fair	Bad	3,58,47,4,29,21,31	831

SHOPPING	GAMBLE	SEX	KEYWORD	KEYWORD						
Fair	Bad	is frustrating	POWER	Responsibilty,Disagreement,Family,Back Pain,Family Conflicts,Traffic Ticket,Quarrels,Jealousy						

STRESS LEVEL	LUCKY COLORS	JEWELERY	MOONS EFFECT	GRAHA EFFECT	DAILY DEITY
High	Purple/Blue/Rose	Emerald/Saphire	Educational	Family Graha	Mahakali

DAILY PUJA
Meditate, Control temper, Pray to Hanuman, Chant Hanuman Chalisa

DAILY PSALMS
6, 15, 33 ,42, 51, 60, 78, 105, 123

Monday, July 18, 2016 — This is considered a NEUTRAL day for you — Planet: Uranus

ADVICE & DETAILS

Today working and communicating with others may further your plans to publish that book you have been thinking about writing. It is a day when expression in any form will be fruitful. You must avoid negative influences of others with such things as alcohol and drugs served in gatherings.

MANTRA FOR TODAY

Jai Jai Shiva Shambo.(2) ...Mahadeva Shambo (2) 21 times 8

MONEY	LOVE	CAREER	FAMILY	TRAVEL	WEDDING	MOVE	BUSINESS	HEALTH	Lotto #'s	play 3 #s
Good	Good	Fair	Good	Good	Bad	Good	Bad	Fair	4,40,58,19,61,20,72	607

SHOPPING	GAMBLE	SEX	KEYWORD	KEYWORD						
Bad	Fair	is quiet	DIVINE	Spirituality,Religious,Astrology,Inner Conflicts,Religious ,Sleepiness,Advice given,Alcohol - drugs						

STRESS LEVEL	LUCKY COLORS	JEWELERY	MOONS EFFECT	GRAHA EFFECT	DAILY DEITY
Fair	Light Blue/Peach	Tiger's eye/Gold/Silver	Affectionate	God'S Graha	Shesnaag

DAILY PUJA
Chant Shiva Mantras, Take gifts to Ocean - Ganga Puja, Donate to Temple, Priests, etc.

DAILY PSALMS
7, 16, 34 ,43, 52, 61, 79, 106, 124

Tuesday, July 19, 2016 — This is considered a POSITIVE day for you — Planet: Jupiter

ADVICE & DETAILS	MANTRA FOR TODAY
It is important to follow God-like ways in order to receive protection from deceitful people that may want to take advantage of you today. Today you should expect short trips or some movement of some sort either places, people or things.	Om Hareem Nama Swaha..Shri Maha Laxmi Aye Namah swaha 12 times

MONEY	LOVE	CAREER	FAMILY	TRAVEL	WEDDING	MOVE	BUSINESS	HEALTH	Lotto #'s	play 3 #s
Excellent	Good	Excellent	Good	Good	Excellent	Good	Excellent	Excellent	59,17,4,16,54,38,33	805

SHOPPING	GAMBLE	SEX	KEYWORD	KEYWORD						
Excellent	Excellent	is excellent	MONEY	Business,Major Expense,Money - Profits,Income,Investments,Power,Promotion,Fame - TV						

STRESS LEVEL		LUCKY COLORS	JEWELERY	MOONS EFFECT	GRAHA EFFECT	DAILY DEITY
Low		Yellow/Silver	Diamonds/Gold/Pearls	Secretive	Money Graha	Mahalaxmi

DAILY PUJA	DAILY PSALMS
Decorate Land, Feed the poor, Donate milk /products to all, Feed holy guests,	8, 17, 35 ,44, 53, 62, 80, 107, 125

Wednesday, July 20, 2016 — This is considered a NEGATIVE day for you — Planet: Saturn

ADVICE & DETAILS	MANTRA FOR TODAY
Make sure that the seeds you sow in your life are those of spirituality, devotion, love and understanding so you may reap the same bounty. Prepare yourself for possible accident or sudden changes in your life that give you an opportunity for rebirth .	Om Ganga mataye nama swaha Om Varuna Devta aye Pahimam 11 times

MONEY	LOVE	CAREER	FAMILY	TRAVEL	WEDDING	MOVE	BUSINESS	HEALTH	Lotto #'s	play 3 #s
Bad	Bad	Bad	Fair	Bad	Bad	Bad	Bad	Bad	52,15,35,27,5,48,41	350

SHOPPING	GAMBLE	SEX	KEYWORD	KEYWORD						
Bad	Bad	is very bad	KARMA	Destruction,Losses,Death,Sickness - cold,Legal matter,Abusive,Karmic debts,God - Karma						

STRESS LEVEL		LUCKY COLORS	JEWELERY	MOONS EFFECT	GRAHA EFFECT	DAILY DEITY
High		Gold/Brown//Green	Saphire/Hessonite	Ivestments	Evil Graha	Agnidev

DAILY PUJA	DAILY PSALMS
Remembrance of family members who died, worship of older people. gifts to grand parents	9, 18, 36 ,45, 54, 63, 81, 108, 126

Thursday, July 21, 2016 — This is considered a NEUTRAL day for you — Planet: Sun

ADVICE & DETAILS	MANTRA FOR TODAY
A religious or spiritual demeanor will help you deal today with losses and lack of health. Be grateful for your blessings and offer the difficult lessons to the gods.	Om Namo Bhagawate Mukhtanandaya, 108 times

MONEY	LOVE	CAREER	FAMILY	TRAVEL	WEDDING	MOVE	BUSINESS	HEALTH	Lotto #'s	play 3 #s
Fair	Bad	Good	Bad	Fair	Bad	Fair	Fair	Fair	23,26,49,14,52,23,53	508

SHOPPING	GAMBLE	SEX	KEYWORD	KEYWORD						
Fair	Fair	is fair	MIND	Independence,Loneliness,Meditative,Worry,Dominating,Illness - Cold,On Your Own,Commanding						

STRESS LEVEL		LUCKY COLORS	JEWELERY	MOONS EFFECT	GRAHA EFFECT	DAILY DEITY
High		White/Yellow/	Pearl/Quartz	Arrogance	Status Graha	Saraswaty

DAILY PUJA	DAILY PSALMS
Give Gifts to Priests, Invite holy ones to your home, Feed Swamis and Yogis, Do Shiva Puja.	1, 10, 28 ,37, 46, 55, 73, 100, 118

Friday, July 22, 2016 — This is considered a POSITIVE day for you — Planet: Moon

ADVICE & DETAILS	MANTRA FOR TODAY
Instead of criticism, offer advice from the heart; not ego. It will be a slow day, but you will feel your connection to God. Do positive actions for good karma.	Kali Durge Namo Nama Om Durge aye nama swaha 108 times

MONEY	LOVE	CAREER	FAMILY	TRAVEL	WEDDING	MOVE	BUSINESS	HEALTH	Lotto #'s	play 3 #s
Good	Excellent	Good	Good	Excellent	Good	Good	Good	Good	8,36,23,18,25,13,1	591

SHOPPING	GAMBLE	SEX	KEYWORD	KEYWORD						
Good	Good	is good	LOVE	Romance,Popularity,Visitors,Shopping,Food, Drinks,Co-operation,Friendships,Affection						

STRESS LEVEL		LUCKY COLORS	JEWELERY	MOONS EFFECT	GRAHA EFFECT	DAILY DEITY
Low		Red/Yellow/Pink	Topaz/Diamonds	Conservative	Love Graha	Gauri

DAILY PUJA	DAILY PSALMS
Give Gifts to females andnMother, Serve milk Products, Worship Durga forms	2, 11, 29 ,38, 47, 56, 74, 101, 119

Saturday, July 23, 2016 — This is considered a POSITIVE day for you — Planet: Mercury

ADVICE & DETAILS

Today working and communicating with others may further your plans to publish that book you have been thinking about writing. It is a day when expression in any form will be fruitful. You must avoid negative influences of others with such things as alcohol and drugs served in gatherings.

MANTRA FOR TODAY

Om hareem Kleem Hreem Aem Saraswataye namaha 21 times

MONEY	LOVE	CAREER	FAMILY	TRAVEL	WEDDING	MOVE	BUSINESS	HEALTH	Lotto #'s	play 3 #s
Good	Fair	Good	Good	Excellent	Good	Good	Good	Excellent	45,6,26,16,11,35,75	860

SHOPPING	GAMBLE	SEX	KEYWORD	KEYWORD						
Good	Good	is great	SOCIAL	Children,Education,Astrology,Bargains,Social Functions,Childishness,Groups - Parties,Teacher						

STRESS LEVEL	LUCKY COLORS	JEWELERY	MOONS EFFECT	GRAHA EFFECT	DAILY DEITY
Low	Green/Sky Blue/	Diamonds/Silver	Enthusiastic	Social Graha	Vishnu

DAILY PUJA	DAILY PSALMS
Wash the feet of Children, Do Satnarayan Pooja, Read & chant Geeta	3, 12, 30 ,39, 48, 57, 75, 102, 120

Sunday, July 24, 2016 — This is considered a NEGATIVE day for you — Planet: Pluto

ADVICE & DETAILS

It is important to follow God-like ways in order to receive protection from deceitful people that may want to take advantage of you today. Today you should expect short trips or some movement of some sort either places, people or things.

MANTRA FOR TODAY

Om Jai Viganeshwaraya.. Lambodaraya Namo Namaha 21 times

MONEY	LOVE	CAREER	FAMILY	TRAVEL	WEDDING	MOVE	BUSINESS	HEALTH	Lotto #'s	play 3 #s
Bad	Fair	Bad	Fair	Bad	Good	Bad	Bad	Bad	4,71,14,53,75,26,31	56

SHOPPING	GAMBLE	SEX	KEYWORD	KEYWORD						
Bad	Bad	is tough	CAREER	Career,Hard Work,Co-workers,Low Payment,Job Problems,High Temper,Low Pay,Laziness						

STRESS LEVEL	LUCKY COLORS	JEWELERY	MOONS EFFECT	GRAHA EFFECT	DAILY DEITY
High	Dark Blue/ Purple/	Amethyst/Gold	Emotional	Job Graha	Lingam

DAILY PUJA	DAILY PSALMS
Worship Ganesh, Give gifts to father, and co -workers, Plant gardens, farms	4, 13, 31 ,40, 49, 58, 76, 103, 121

Monday, July 25, 2016 — This is considered a POSITIVE day for you — Planet: Venus

ADVICE & DETAILS

Make sure that the seeds you sow in your life are those of spirituality, devotion, love and understanding so you may reap the same bounty. Prepare yourself for possible accident or sudden changes in your life that give you an opportunity for rebirth .

MANTRA FOR TODAY

Om Graam Greem Graum Sa Gurave namah swaha 21 times

MONEY	LOVE	CAREER	FAMILY	TRAVEL	WEDDING	MOVE	BUSINESS	HEALTH	Lotto #'s	play 3 #s
Bad	Excellent	Fair	Good	Excellent	Good	Excellent	Good	Excellent	18,43,40,11,46,32,71	297

SHOPPING	GAMBLE	SEX	KEYWORD	KEYWORD						
Good	Good	is good	CHANGE	Sexuality,Travel,Change,Distant, far,Travel delays,Deception,Excercise,Illicit Affairs						

STRESS LEVEL	LUCKY COLORS	JEWELERY	MOONS EFFECT	GRAHA EFFECT	DAILY DEITY
Fair	Tan/Green/ Beige	Pearl/Silver/quartz	Courageous	Travel Graha	Nataraja

DAILY PUJA	DAILY PSALMS
Artistic gifts, Pray to Krishna, Do good deeds, do Spiritual trips	5, 14, 32 ,41, 50, 59, 77, 104, 122

Tuesday, July 26, 2016 — This is considered a NEGATIVE day for you — Planet: Mars

ADVICE & DETAILS

Your manner of expression today may be commanding, make sure you do not go overboard and become bossy or overbearing. Enjoy the company of others in groups or parties. Use this time to work on creative projects like publishing, art or music.

MANTRA FOR TODAY

Om Mana Swasti Shanti Kuru kuru Swaha Shivoham Shivoham 27 times

MONEY	LOVE	CAREER	FAMILY	TRAVEL	WEDDING	MOVE	BUSINESS	HEALTH	Lotto #'s	play 3 #s
Bad	Bad	Bad	Bad	Bad	Bad	Bad	Fair	Bad	15,74,68,26,75,55,71	581

SHOPPING	GAMBLE	SEX	KEYWORD	KEYWORD						
Fair	Bad	is frustrating	POWER	Responsibilty,Disagreement,Family,Back Pain,Family Conflicts,Traffic Ticket,Quarrels,Jealousy						

STRESS LEVEL	LUCKY COLORS	JEWELERY	MOONS EFFECT	GRAHA EFFECT	DAILY DEITY
High	Purple/Blue/Rose	Emerald/Saphire	Educational	Family Graha	Mahakali

DAILY PUJA	DAILY PSALMS
Meditate, Control temper, Pray to Hanuman, Chant Hanuman Chalisa	6, 15, 33 ,42, 51, 60, 78, 105, 123

Wednesday, July 27, 2016 — This is considered a NEUTRAL day for you — Planet: Uranus

ADVICE & DETAILS	MANTRA FOR TODAY
Today working and communicating with others may further your plans to publish that book you have been thinking about writing. It is a day when expression in any form will be fruitful. You must avoid negative influences of others with such things as alcohol and drugs served in gatherings.	Jai Jai Shiva Shambo.(2) ...Mahadeva Shambo (2) 21 times 8

MONEY	LOVE	CAREER	FAMILY	TRAVEL	WEDDING	MOVE	BUSINESS	HEALTH	Lotto #'s	play 3 #s
Good	Good	Fair	Good	Good	Bad	Good	Bad	Fair	35,24,58,64,45,70,61	11

SHOPPING	GAMBLE	SEX	KEYWORD	KEYWORD
Bad	Fair	is quiet	DIVINE	Spirituality,Religious,Astrology,Inner Conflicts,Religious ,Sleepiness,Advice given,Alcohol - drugs

STRESS LEVEL	LUCKY COLORS	JEWELERY	MOONS EFFECT	GRAHA EFFECT	DAILY DEITY
Fair	Light Blue/Peach	Tiger's eye/Gold/Silver	Affectionate	God'S Graha	Shesnaag

DAILY PUJA	DAILY PSALMS
Chant Shiva Mantras, Take gifts to Ocean - Ganga Puja, Donate to Temple, Priests, etc.	7, 16, 34 ,43, 52, 61, 79, 106, 124

Thursday, July 28, 2016 — This is considered a POSITIVE day for you — Planet: Jupiter

ADVICE & DETAILS	MANTRA FOR TODAY
It is important to follow God-like ways in order to receive protection from deceitful people that may want to take advantage of you today. Today you should expect short trips or some movement of some sort either places, people or things.	Om Hareem Nama Swaha..Shri Maha Laxmi Aye Namah swaha 12 times

MONEY	LOVE	CAREER	FAMILY	TRAVEL	WEDDING	MOVE	BUSINESS	HEALTH	Lotto #'s	play 3 #s
Excellent	Good	Excellent	Good	Good	Excellent	Good	Excellent	Excellent	67,20,44,60,48,46,63	602

SHOPPING	GAMBLE	SEX	KEYWORD	KEYWORD
Excellent	Excellent	is excellent	MONEY	Business,Major Expense,Money - Profits,Income,Investments,Power,Promotion,Fame - TV

STRESS LEVEL	LUCKY COLORS	JEWELERY	MOONS EFFECT	GRAHA EFFECT	DAILY DEITY
Low	Yellow/Silver	Diamonds/Gold/Pearls	Secretive	Money Graha	Mahalaxmi

DAILY PUJA	DAILY PSALMS
Decorate Land, Feed the poor, Donate milk /products to all, Feed holy guests,	8, 17, 35 ,44, 53, 62, 80, 107, 125

Friday, July 29, 2016 — This is considered a NEGATIVE day for you — Planet: Saturn

ADVICE & DETAILS	MANTRA FOR TODAY
Make sure that the seeds you sow in your life are those of spirituality, devotion, love and understanding so you may reap the same bounty. Prepare yourself for possible accident or sudden changes in your life that give you an opportunity for rebirth .	Om Ganga mataye nama swaha Om Varuna Devta aye Pahimam 11 times

MONEY	LOVE	CAREER	FAMILY	TRAVEL	WEDDING	MOVE	BUSINESS	HEALTH	Lotto #'s	play 3 #s
Bad	Bad	Bad	Fair	Bad	Bad	Bad	Bad	Bad	31,41,30,44,41,74,58	655

SHOPPING	GAMBLE	SEX	KEYWORD	KEYWORD
Bad	Bad	is very bad	KARMA	Destruction,Losses,Death,Sickness - cold,Legal matter,Abusive,Karmic debts,God - Karma

STRESS LEVEL	LUCKY COLORS	JEWELERY	MOONS EFFECT	GRAHA EFFECT	DAILY DEITY
High	Gold/Brown//Green	Saphire/Hessonite	Ivestments	Evil Graha	Agnidev

DAILY PUJA	DAILY PSALMS
Remembrance of family members who died, worship of older people. gifts to grand parents	9, 18, 36 ,45, 54, 63, 81, 108, 126

Saturday, July 30, 2016 — This is considered a NEUTRAL day for you — Planet: Sun

ADVICE & DETAILS	MANTRA FOR TODAY
A religious or spiritual demeanor will help you deal today with losses and lack of health. Be grateful for your blessings and offer the difficult lessons to the gods.	Om Namo Bhagawate Mukhtanandaya, 108 times

MONEY	LOVE	CAREER	FAMILY	TRAVEL	WEDDING	MOVE	BUSINESS	HEALTH	Lotto #'s	play 3 #s
Fair	Bad	Good	Bad	Fair	Bad	Fair	Fair	Fair	24,42,71,48,58,23,42	368

SHOPPING	GAMBLE	SEX	KEYWORD	KEYWORD
Fair	Fair	is fair	MIND	Independence,Loneliness,Meditative,Worry,Dominating,Illness - Cold,On Your Own,Commanding

STRESS LEVEL	LUCKY COLORS	JEWELERY	MOONS EFFECT	GRAHA EFFECT	DAILY DEITY
High	White/Yellow/	Pearl/Quartz	Arrogance	Status Graha	Saraswaty

DAILY PUJA	DAILY PSALMS
Give Gifts to Priests, Invite holy ones to your home, Feed Swamis and Yogis, Do Shiva Puja.	1, 10, 28 ,37, 46, 55, 73, 100, 118

Sunday, July 31, 2016 — This is considered a POSITIVE day for you — Planet: Moon

ADVICE & DETAILS	MANTRA FOR TODAY
Instead of criticism, offer advice from the heart; not ego. It will be a slow day, but you will feel your connection to God. Do positive actions for good karma.	Kali Durge Namo Nama Om Durge aye nama swaha 108 times

MONEY	LOVE	CAREER	FAMILY	TRAVEL	WEDDING	MOVE	BUSINESS	HEALTH	Lotto #'s	play 3 #s
Good	Excellent	Good	Good	Excellent	Good	Good	Good	Good	15,7,53,19,60,40,52	834

SHOPPING	GAMBLE	SEX	KEYWORD	KEYWORD						
Good	Good	is good	LOVE	Romance,Popularity,Visitors,Shopping,Food, Drinks,Co-operation,Friendships,Affection						

STRESS LEVEL	LUCKY COLORS	JEWELERY	MOONS EFFECT	GRAHA EFFECT	DAILY DEITY
Low	Red/Yellow/Pink	Topaz/Diamonds	Conservative	Love Graha	Gauri

DAILY PUJA	DAILY PSALMS
Give Gifts to females andnMother, Serve milk Products, Worship Durga forms	2, 11, 29 ,38, 47, 56, 74, 101, 119

Monday, August 1, 2016 — This is considered a POSITIVE day for you — Planet: Jupiter

ADVICE & DETAILS	MANTRA FOR TODAY
Money is coming and/or going out today, but it will be pleasurable. You may be changing locations and enjoying the company of someone known or famous from TV or the entertainment industry.	Om Hareem Nama Swaha..Shri Maha Laxmi Aye Namah swaha 12 times

MONEY	LOVE	CAREER	FAMILY	TRAVEL	WEDDING	MOVE	BUSINESS	HEALTH	Lotto #'s	play 3 #s
Excellent	Good	Excellent	Good	Good	Excellent	Good	Excellent	Excellent	50,2,28,21,52,44,6	878

SHOPPING	GAMBLE	SEX	KEYWORD	KEYWORD						
Excellent	Excellent	is excellent	MONEY	Business,Major Expense,Money - Profits,Income,Investments,Power,Promotion,Fame - TV						

STRESS LEVEL	LUCKY COLORS	JEWELERY	MOONS EFFECT	GRAHA EFFECT	DAILY DEITY
Low	Yellow/Silver	Diamonds/Gold/Pearls	Secretive	Money Graha	Mahalaxmi

DAILY PUJA	DAILY PSALMS
Decorate Land, Feed the poor, Donate milk /products to all, Feed holy guests,	8, 17, 35 ,44, 53, 62, 80, 107, 125

Tuesday, August 2, 2016 — This is considered a NEGATIVE day for you — Planet: Saturn

ADVICE & DETAILS	MANTRA FOR TODAY
Today could be a very positive day influenced by promotion, profits and money; but there may be also a degree of frustation if your expectations are not fulfilled the way you feel they should. Concentrate in the positive and learn from what you perceive as negative.	Om Ganga mataye nama swaha Om Varuna Devta aye Pahimam 11 times

MONEY	LOVE	CAREER	FAMILY	TRAVEL	WEDDING	MOVE	BUSINESS	HEALTH	Lotto #'s	play 3 #s
Bad	Bad	Bad	Fair	Bad	Bad	Bad	Bad	Bad	16,3,42,22,4,22,3	444

SHOPPING	GAMBLE	SEX	KEYWORD	KEYWORD						
Bad	Bad	is very bad	KARMA	Destruction,Losses,Death,Sickness - cold,Legal matter,Abusive,Karmic debts,God - Karma						

STRESS LEVEL	LUCKY COLORS	JEWELERY	MOONS EFFECT	GRAHA EFFECT	DAILY DEITY
High	Gold/Brown//Green	Saphire/Hessonite	Ivestments	Evil Graha	Agnidev

DAILY PUJA	DAILY PSALMS
Remembrance of family members who died, worship of older people. gifts to grand parents	9, 18, 36 ,45, 54, 63, 81, 108, 126

Wednesday, August 3, 2016 — This is considered a NEUTRAL day for you — Planet: Sun

ADVICE & DETAILS	MANTRA FOR TODAY
You will be enjoying profits and money from your endeavors today, but on the other hand you will have sizable expenses that will give you great pleasure.	Om Namo Bhagawate Mukhtanandaya, 108 times

MONEY	LOVE	CAREER	FAMILY	TRAVEL	WEDDING	MOVE	BUSINESS	HEALTH	Lotto #'s	play 3 #s
Fair	Bad	Good	Bad	Fair	Bad	Fair	Fair	Fair	19,21,59,64,3,18,11	594

SHOPPING	GAMBLE	SEX	KEYWORD	KEYWORD						
Fair	Fair	is fair	MIND	Independence,Loneliness,Meditative,Worry,Dominating,Illness - Cold,On Your Own,Commanding						

STRESS LEVEL	LUCKY COLORS	JEWELERY	MOONS EFFECT	GRAHA EFFECT	DAILY DEITY
High	White/Yellow/	Pearl/Quartz	Arrogance	Status Graha	Saraswaty

DAILY PUJA	DAILY PSALMS
Give Gifts to Priests, Invite holy ones to your home, Feed Swamis and Yogis, Do Shiva Puja.	1, 10, 28 ,37, 46, 55, 73, 100, 118

Thursday, August 4, 2016 — This is considered a POSITIVE day for you — Planet: Moon

ADVICE & DETAILS

This is a very positive day as long as you are willing to serve and cooperate with others. Make sure that every word your lips utter is with purpose, loving and kind. It is a propitious day for marriage and romance.

MANTRA FOR TODAY

Kali Durge Namo Nama Om Durge aye nama swaha 108 times

MONEY	LOVE	CAREER	FAMILY	TRAVEL	WEDDING	MOVE	BUSINESS	HEALTH	Lotto #'s	play 3 #s
Good	Excellent	Good	Good	Excellent	Good	Good	Good	Good	16,70,20,22,67,53,33	360

SHOPPING	GAMBLE	SEX	KEYWORD	KEYWORD						
Good	Good	is good	LOVE	Romance,Popularity,Visitors,Shopping,Food, Drinks,Co-operation,Friendships,Affection						

STRESS LEVEL		LUCKY COLORS	JEWELERY	MOONS EFFECT	GRAHA EFFECT	DAILY DEITY
Low		Red/Yellow/Pink	Topaz/Diamonds	Conservative	Love Graha	Gauri

DAILY PUJA	DAILY PSALMS
Give Gifts to females andnMother, Serve milk Products, Worship Durga forms	2, 11, 29 ,38, 47, 56, 74, 101, 119

Friday, August 5, 2016 — This is considered a POSITIVE day for you — Planet: Mercury

ADVICE & DETAILS

Finances are in your mind today. It is a great day to make money, get profits and get a promotion at your job. You may also have to deal with children or younger adults and their financial needs.

MANTRA FOR TODAY

Om hareem Kleem Hreem Aem Saraswataye namaha 21 times

MONEY	LOVE	CAREER	FAMILY	TRAVEL	WEDDING	MOVE	BUSINESS	HEALTH	Lotto #'s	play 3 #s
Good	Fair	Good	Good	Excellent	Good	Good	Good	Excellent	70,32,36,55,28,30,60	960

SHOPPING	GAMBLE	SEX	KEYWORD	KEYWORD						
Good	Good	is great	SOCIAL	Children,Education,Astrology,Bargains,Social Functions,Childishness,Groups - Parties,Teacher						

STRESS LEVEL		LUCKY COLORS	JEWELERY	MOONS EFFECT	GRAHA EFFECT	DAILY DEITY
Low		Green/Sky Blue/	Diamonds/Silver	Enthusiastic	Social Graha	Vishnu

DAILY PUJA	DAILY PSALMS
Wash the feet of Children, Do Satnarayan Pooja, Read & chant Geeta	3, 12, 30 ,39, 48, 57, 75, 102, 120

Saturday, August 6, 2016 — This is considered a NEGATIVE day for you — Planet: Pluto

ADVICE & DETAILS

Money is coming and/or going out today, but it will be pleasurable. You may be changing locations and enjoying the company of someone known or famous from TV or the entertainment industry.

MANTRA FOR TODAY

Om Jai Viganeshwaraya.. Lambodaraya Namo Namaha 21 times

MONEY	LOVE	CAREER	FAMILY	TRAVEL	WEDDING	MOVE	BUSINESS	HEALTH	Lotto #'s	play 3 #s
Bad	Fair	Bad	Fair	Bad	Good	Bad	Bad	Bad	70,69,47,29,58,26,31	777

SHOPPING	GAMBLE	SEX	KEYWORD	KEYWORD						
Bad	Bad	is tough	CAREER	Career,Hard Work,Co-workers,Low Payment,Job Problems,High Temper,Low Pay,Laziness						

STRESS LEVEL		LUCKY COLORS	JEWELERY	MOONS EFFECT	GRAHA EFFECT	DAILY DEITY
High		Dark Blue/ Purple/	Amethyst/Gold	Emotional	Job Graha	Lingam

DAILY PUJA	DAILY PSALMS
Worship Ganesh, Give gifts to father, and co -workers, Plant gardens, farms	4, 13, 31 ,40, 49, 58, 76, 103, 121

Sunday, August 7, 2016 — This is considered a POSITIVE day for you — Planet: Venus

ADVICE & DETAILS

This is a positive day to invest. To improve your results in this arena make sure you show gratitude to the universe by praying and meditating.

MANTRA FOR TODAY

Om Graam Greem Graum Sa Gurave namah swaha 21 times

MONEY	LOVE	CAREER	FAMILY	TRAVEL	WEDDING	MOVE	BUSINESS	HEALTH	Lotto #'s	play 3 #s
Bad	Excellent	Fair	Good	Excellent	Good	Excellent	Good	Excellent	25,21,62,3,66,17,66	597

SHOPPING	GAMBLE	SEX	KEYWORD	KEYWORD						
Good	Good	is good	CHANGE	Sexuality,Travel,Change,Distant, far,Travel delays,Deception,Excercise,Illicit Affairs						

STRESS LEVEL		LUCKY COLORS	JEWELERY	MOONS EFFECT	GRAHA EFFECT	DAILY DEITY
Fair		Tan/Green/ Beige	Pearl/Silver/quartz	Courageous	Travel Graha	Nataraja

DAILY PUJA	DAILY PSALMS
Artistic gifts, Pray to Krishna, Do good deeds, do Spiritual trips	5, 14, 32 ,41, 50, 59, 77, 104, 122

Monday, August 8, 2016 — This is considered a NEGATIVE day for you — Planet: Mars

ADVICE & DETAILS

It will be difficult, but possible to overcome your sadness today. Your mind will tend to veer towards thoughts of losses, doubts, denial and death; if you cannot control it you will be creating this in your life. Pray, meditate and place your trust in the Higher Power.

MANTRA FOR TODAY

Om Mana Swasti Shanti Kuru kuru Swaha Shivoham Shivoham 27 times

MONEY	LOVE	CAREER	FAMILY	TRAVEL	WEDDING	MOVE	BUSINESS	HEALTH	Lotto #'s	play 3 #s
Bad	Bad	Bad	Bad	Bad	Bad	Bad	Fair	Bad	38,16,12,71,59,8,27	539

SHOPPING	GAMBLE	SEX	KEYWORD	KEYWORD				
Fair	Bad	is frustrating	POWER	Responsibilty,Disagreement,Family,Back Pain,Family Conflicts,Traffic Ticket,Quarrels,Jealousy				

STRESS LEVEL	LUCKY COLORS	JEWELERY	MOONS EFFECT	GRAHA EFFECT	DAILY DEITY
High	Purple/Blue/Rose	Emerald/Saphire	Educational	Family Graha	Mahakali

DAILY PUJA	DAILY PSALMS
Meditate, Control temper, Pray to Hanuman, Chant Hanuman Chalisa	6, 15, 33 ,42, 51, 60, 78, 105, 123

Tuesday, August 9, 2016 — This is considered a NEUTRAL day for you — Planet: Uranus

ADVICE & DETAILS

Finances are in your mind today. It is a great day to make money, get profits and get a promotion at your job. You may also have to deal with children or younger adults and their financial needs.

MANTRA FOR TODAY

Jai Jai Shiva Shambo.(2) ...Mahadeva Shambo (2) 21 times 8

MONEY	LOVE	CAREER	FAMILY	TRAVEL	WEDDING	MOVE	BUSINESS	HEALTH	Lotto #'s	play 3 #s
Good	Good	Fair	Good	Good	Bad	Good	Bad	Fair	49,6,4,73,74,68,63	289

SHOPPING	GAMBLE	SEX	KEYWORD	KEYWORD				
Bad	Fair	is quiet	DIVINE	Spirituality,Religious,Astrology,Inner Conflicts,Religious ,Sleepiness,Advice given,Alcohol - drugs				

STRESS LEVEL	LUCKY COLORS	JEWELERY	MOONS EFFECT	GRAHA EFFECT	DAILY DEITY
Fair	Light Blue/Peach	Tiger's eye/Gold/Silver	Affectionate	God'S Graha	Shesnaag

DAILY PUJA	DAILY PSALMS
Chant Shiva Mantras, Take gifts to Ocean - Ganga Puja, Donate to Temple, Priests, etc.	7, 16, 34 ,43, 52, 61, 79, 106, 124

Wednesday, August 10, 2016 — This is considered a POSITIVE day for you — Planet: Jupiter

ADVICE & DETAILS

Money is coming and/or going out today, but it will be pleasurable. You may be changing locations and enjoying the company of someone known or famous from TV or the entertainment industry.

MANTRA FOR TODAY

Om Hareem Nama Swaha..Shri Maha Laxmi Aye Namah swaha 12 times

MONEY	LOVE	CAREER	FAMILY	TRAVEL	WEDDING	MOVE	BUSINESS	HEALTH	Lotto #'s	play 3 #s
Excellent	Good	Excellent	Good	Good	Excellent	Good	Excellent	Excellent	7,21,54,41,22,73,37	244

SHOPPING	GAMBLE	SEX	KEYWORD	KEYWORD				
Excellent	Excellent	is excellent	MONEY	Business,Major Expense,Money - Profits,Income,Investments,Power,Promotion,Fame - TV				

STRESS LEVEL	LUCKY COLORS	JEWELERY	MOONS EFFECT	GRAHA EFFECT	DAILY DEITY
Low	Yellow/Silver	Diamonds/Gold/Pearls	Secretive	Money Graha	Mahalaxmi

DAILY PUJA	DAILY PSALMS
Decorate Land, Feed the poor, Donate milk /products to all, Feed holy guests,	8, 17, 35 ,44, 53, 62, 80, 107, 125

Thursday, August 11, 2016 — This is considered a NEGATIVE day for you — Planet: Saturn

ADVICE & DETAILS

Today could be a very positive day influenced by promotion, profits and money; but there may be also a degree of frustation if your expectations are not fulfilled the way you feel they should. Concentrate in the positive and learn from what you perceive as negative.

MANTRA FOR TODAY

Om Ganga mataye nama swaha Om Varuna Devta aye Pahimam 11 times

MONEY	LOVE	CAREER	FAMILY	TRAVEL	WEDDING	MOVE	BUSINESS	HEALTH	Lotto #'s	play 3 #s
Bad	Bad	Bad	Fair	Bad	Bad	Bad	Bad	Bad	4,23,74,28,20,41,34	339

SHOPPING	GAMBLE	SEX	KEYWORD	KEYWORD				
Bad	Bad	is very bad	KARMA	Destruction,Losses,Death,Sickness - cold,Legal matter,Abusive,Karmic debts,God - Karma				

STRESS LEVEL	LUCKY COLORS	JEWELERY	MOONS EFFECT	GRAHA EFFECT	DAILY DEITY
High	Gold/Brown//Green	Saphire/Hessonite	Ivestments	Evil Graha	Agnidev

DAILY PUJA	DAILY PSALMS
Remembrance of family members who died, worship of older people. gifts to grand parents	9, 18, 36 ,45, 54, 63, 81, 108, 126

Friday, August 12, 2016 — This is considered a NEUTRAL day for you — Planet: Sun

ADVICE & DETAILS	MANTRA FOR TODAY
You will be enjoying profits and money from your endeavors today, but on the other hand you will have sizable expenses that will give you great pleasure.	Om Namo Bhagawate Mukhtanandaya, 108 times

MONEY	LOVE	CAREER	FAMILY	TRAVEL	WEDDING	MOVE	BUSINESS	HEALTH	Lotto #'s	play 3 #s
Fair	Bad	Good	Bad	Fair	Bad	Fair	Fair	Fair	6,51,20,16,2,28,59	839

SHOPPING	GAMBLE	SEX	KEYWORD	KEYWORD						
Fair	Fair	is fair	MIND	Independence,Loneliness,Meditative,Worry,Dominating,Illness - Cold,On Your Own,Commanding						

STRESS LEVEL	LUCKY COLORS	JEWELERY	MOONS EFFECT	GRAHA EFFECT	DAILY DEITY
High	White/Yellow/	Pearl/Quartz	Arrogance	Status Graha	Saraswaty

DAILY PUJA	DAILY PSALMS
Give Gifts to Priests, Invite holy ones to your home, Feed Swamis and Yogis, Do Shiva Puja.	1, 10, 28 ,37, 46, 55, 73, 100, 118

Saturday, August 13, 2016 — This is considered a POSITIVE day for you — Planet: Moon

ADVICE & DETAILS	MANTRA FOR TODAY
This is a very positive day as long as you are willing to serve and cooperate with others. Make sure that every word your lips utter is with purpose, loving and kind. It is a propitious day for marriage and romance.	Kali Durge Namo Nama Om Durge aye nama swaha 108 times

MONEY	LOVE	CAREER	FAMILY	TRAVEL	WEDDING	MOVE	BUSINESS	HEALTH	Lotto #'s	play 3 #s
Good	Excellent	Good	Good	Excellent	Good	Good	Good	Good	68,71,49,70,56,2,61	947

SHOPPING	GAMBLE	SEX	KEYWORD	KEYWORD						
Good	Good	is good	LOVE	Romance,Popularity,Visitors,Shopping,Food, Drinks,Co-operation,Friendships,Affection						

STRESS LEVEL	LUCKY COLORS	JEWELERY	MOONS EFFECT	GRAHA EFFECT	DAILY DEITY
Low	Red/Yellow/Pink	Topaz/Diamonds	Conservative	Love Graha	Gauri

DAILY PUJA	DAILY PSALMS
Give Gifts to females andnMother, Serve milk Products, Worship Durga forms	2, 11, 29 ,38, 47, 56, 74, 101, 119

Sunday, August 14, 2016 — This is considered a POSITIVE day for you — Planet: Mercury

ADVICE & DETAILS	MANTRA FOR TODAY
Finances are in your mind today. It is a great day to make money, get profits and get a promotion at your job. You may also have to deal with children or younger adults and their financial needs.	Om hareem Kleem Hreem Aem Saraswataye namaha 21 times

MONEY	LOVE	CAREER	FAMILY	TRAVEL	WEDDING	MOVE	BUSINESS	HEALTH	Lotto #'s	play 3 #s
Good	Fair	Good	Good	Excellent	Good	Good	Good	Excellent	70,57,70,31,67,47,34	956

SHOPPING	GAMBLE	SEX	KEYWORD	KEYWORD						
Good	Good	is great	SOCIAL	Children,Education,Astrology,Bargains,Social Functions,Childishness,Groups - Parties,Teacher						

STRESS LEVEL	LUCKY COLORS	JEWELERY	MOONS EFFECT	GRAHA EFFECT	DAILY DEITY
Low	Green/Sky Blue/	Diamonds/Silver	Enthusiastic	Social Graha	Vishnu

DAILY PUJA	DAILY PSALMS
Wash the feet of Children, Do Satnarayan Pooja, Read & chant Geeta	3, 12, 30 ,39, 48, 57, 75, 102, 120

Monday, August 15, 2016 — This is considered a NEGATIVE day for you — Planet: Pluto

ADVICE & DETAILS	MANTRA FOR TODAY
Money is coming and/or going out today, but it will be pleasurable. You may be changing locations and enjoying the company of someone known or famous from TV or the entertainment industry.	Om Jai Viganeshwaraya.. Lambodaraya Namo Namaha 21 times

MONEY	LOVE	CAREER	FAMILY	TRAVEL	WEDDING	MOVE	BUSINESS	HEALTH	Lotto #'s	play 3 #s
Bad	Fair	Bad	Fair	Bad	Good	Bad	Bad	Bad	47,74,26,19,43,52,6	568

SHOPPING	GAMBLE	SEX	KEYWORD	KEYWORD						
Bad	Bad	is tough	CAREER	Career,Hard Work,Co-workers,Low Payment,Job Problems,High Temper,Low Pay,Laziness						

STRESS LEVEL	LUCKY COLORS	JEWELERY	MOONS EFFECT	GRAHA EFFECT	DAILY DEITY
High	Dark Blue/ Purple/	Amethyst/Gold	Emotional	Job Graha	Lingam

DAILY PUJA	DAILY PSALMS
Worship Ganesh, Give gifts to father, and co -workers, Plant gardens, farms	4, 13, 31 ,40, 49, 58, 76, 103, 121

Tuesday, August 16, 2016 — This is considered a POSITIVE day for you — Planet: Venus

ADVICE & DETAILS

This is a positive day to invest. To improve your results in this arena make sure you show gratitude to the universe by praying and meditating.

MANTRA FOR TODAY

Om Graam Greem Graum Sa Gurave namah swaha 21 times

MONEY	LOVE	CAREER	FAMILY	TRAVEL	WEDDING	MOVE	BUSINESS	HEALTH	Lotto #'s	play 3 #s
Bad	Excellent	Fair	Good	Excellent	Good	Excellent	Good	Excellent	32,3,14,32,27,48,4	434

SHOPPING	GAMBLE	SEX	KEYWORD	KEYWORD						
Good	Good	is good	CHANGE	Sexuality,Travel,Change,Distant, far,Travel delays,Deception,Excercise,Illicit Affairs						

STRESS LEVEL	LUCKY COLORS	JEWELERY	MOONS EFFECT	GRAHA EFFECT	DAILY DEITY
Fair	Tan/Green/ Beige	Pearl/Silver/quartz	Courageous	Travel Graha	Nataraja

DAILY PUJA	DAILY PSALMS
Artistic gifts, Pray to Krishna, Do good deeds, do Spiritual trips	5, 14, 32 ,41, 50, 59, 77, 104, 122

Wednesday, August 17, 2016 — This is considered a NEGATIVE day for you — Planet: Mars

ADVICE & DETAILS

It will be difficult, but possible to overcome your sadness today. Your mind will tend to veer towards thoughts of losses, doubts, denial and death; if you cannot control it you will be creating this in your life. Pray, meditate and place your trust in the Higher Power.

MANTRA FOR TODAY

Om Mana Swasti Shanti Kuru kuru Swaha Shivoham Shivoham 27 times

MONEY	LOVE	CAREER	FAMILY	TRAVEL	WEDDING	MOVE	BUSINESS	HEALTH	Lotto #'s	play 3 #s
Bad	Bad	Bad	Bad	Bad	Bad	Bad	Fair	Bad	50,20,51,6,69,20,13	676

SHOPPING	GAMBLE	SEX	KEYWORD	KEYWORD						
Fair	Bad	is frustrating	POWER	Responsibilty,Disagreement,Family,Back Pain,Family Conflicts,Traffic Ticket,Quarrels,Jealousy						

STRESS LEVEL	LUCKY COLORS	JEWELERY	MOONS EFFECT	GRAHA EFFECT	DAILY DEITY
High	Purple/Blue/Rose	Emerald/Saphire	Educational	Family Graha	Mahakali

DAILY PUJA	DAILY PSALMS
Meditate, Control temper, Pray to Hanuman, Chant Hanuman Chalisa	6, 15, 33 ,42, 51, 60, 78, 105, 123

Thursday, August 18, 2016 — This is considered a NEUTRAL day for you — Planet: Uranus

ADVICE & DETAILS

Finances are in your mind today. It is a great day to make money, get profits and get a promotion at your job. You may also have to deal with children or younger adults and their financial needs.

MANTRA FOR TODAY

Jai Jai Shiva Shambo.(2) ...Mahadeva Shambo (2) 21 times 8

MONEY	LOVE	CAREER	FAMILY	TRAVEL	WEDDING	MOVE	BUSINESS	HEALTH	Lotto #'s	play 3 #s
Good	Good	Fair	Good	Good	Bad	Good	Bad	Fair	67,22,16,70,50,20,1	207

SHOPPING	GAMBLE	SEX	KEYWORD	KEYWORD						
Bad	Fair	is quiet	DIVINE	Spirituality,Religious,Astrology,Inner Conflicts,Religious ,Sleepiness,Advice given,Alcohol - drugs						

STRESS LEVEL	LUCKY COLORS	JEWELERY	MOONS EFFECT	GRAHA EFFECT	DAILY DEITY
Fair	Light Blue/Peach	Tiger's eye/Gold/Silver	Affectionate	God'S Graha	Shesnaag

DAILY PUJA	DAILY PSALMS
Chant Shiva Mantras, Take gifts to Ocean - Ganga Puja, Donate to Temple, Priests, etc.	7, 16, 34 ,43, 52, 61, 79, 106, 124

Friday, August 19, 2016 — This is considered a POSITIVE day for you — Planet: Jupiter

ADVICE & DETAILS

Money is coming and/or going out today, but it will be pleasurable. You may be changing locations and enjoying the company of someone known or famous from TV or the entertainment industry.

MANTRA FOR TODAY

Om Hareem Nama Swaha..Shri Maha Laxmi Aye Namah swaha 12 times

MONEY	LOVE	CAREER	FAMILY	TRAVEL	WEDDING	MOVE	BUSINESS	HEALTH	Lotto #'s	play 3 #s
Excellent	Good	Excellent	Good	Good	Excellent	Good	Excellent	Excellent	13,53,57,63,63,65,54	239

SHOPPING	GAMBLE	SEX	KEYWORD	KEYWORD						
Excellent	Excellent	is excellent	MONEY	Business,Major Expense,Money - Profits,Income,Investments,Power,Promotion,Fame - TV						

STRESS LEVEL	LUCKY COLORS	JEWELERY	MOONS EFFECT	GRAHA EFFECT	DAILY DEITY
Low	Yellow/Silver	Diamonds/Gold/Pearls	Secretive	Money Graha	Mahalaxmi

DAILY PUJA	DAILY PSALMS
Decorate Land, Feed the poor, Donate milk /products to all, Feed holy guests,	8, 17, 35 ,44, 53, 62, 80, 107, 125

Saturday, August 20, 2016 — This is considered a NEGATIVE day for you — Planet: Saturn

ADVICE & DETAILS	MANTRA FOR TODAY
Today could be a very positive day influenced by promotion, profits and money; but there may be also a degree of frustation if your expectations are not fulfilled the way you feel they should. Concentrate in the positive and learn from what you perceive as negative.	Om Ganga mataye nama swaha Om Varuna Devta aye Pahimam 11 times

MONEY	LOVE	CAREER	FAMILY	TRAVEL	WEDDING	MOVE	BUSINESS	HEALTH	Lotto #'s	play 3 #s
Bad	Bad	Bad	Fair	Bad	Bad	Bad	Bad	Bad	69,67,52,37,9,3,68	937

SHOPPING	GAMBLE	SEX	KEYWORD	KEYWORD				
Bad	Bad	is very bad	KARMA	Destruction,Losses,Death,Sickness - cold,Legal matter,Abusive,Karmic debts,God - Karma				

STRESS LEVEL	LUCKY COLORS	JEWELERY	MOONS EFFECT	GRAHA EFFECT	DAILY DEITY
High	Gold/Brown//Green	Saphire/Hessonite	Ivestments	Evil Graha	Agnidev

DAILY PUJA	DAILY PSALMS
Remembrance of family members who died, worship of older people. gifts to grand parents	9, 18, 36 ,45, 54, 63, 81, 108, 126

Sunday, August 21, 2016 — This is considered a NEUTRAL day for you — Planet: Sun

ADVICE & DETAILS	MANTRA FOR TODAY
You will be enjoying profits and money from your endeavors today, but on the other hand you will have sizable expenses that will give you great pleasure.	Om Namo Bhagawate Mukhtanandaya, 108 times

MONEY	LOVE	CAREER	FAMILY	TRAVEL	WEDDING	MOVE	BUSINESS	HEALTH	Lotto #'s	play 3 #s
Fair	Bad	Good	Bad	Fair	Bad	Fair	Fair	Fair	49,34,22,19,56,57,50	162

SHOPPING	GAMBLE	SEX	KEYWORD	KEYWORD				
Fair	Fair	is fair	MIND	Independence,Loneliness,Meditative,Worry,Dominating,Illness - Cold,On Your Own,Commanding				

STRESS LEVEL	LUCKY COLORS	JEWELERY	MOONS EFFECT	GRAHA EFFECT	DAILY DEITY
High	White/Yellow/	Pearl/Quartz	Arrogance	Status Graha	Saraswaty

DAILY PUJA	DAILY PSALMS
Give Gifts to Priests, Invite holy ones to your home, Feed Swamis and Yogis, Do Shiva Puja.	1, 10, 28 ,37, 46, 55, 73, 100, 118

Monday, August 22, 2016 — This is considered a POSITIVE day for you — Planet: Moon

ADVICE & DETAILS	MANTRA FOR TODAY
This is a very positive day as long as you are willing to serve and cooperate with others. Make sure that every word your lips utter is with purpose, loving and kind. It is a propitious day for marriage and romance.	Kali Durge Namo Nama Om Durge aye nama swaha 108 times

MONEY	LOVE	CAREER	FAMILY	TRAVEL	WEDDING	MOVE	BUSINESS	HEALTH	Lotto #'s	play 3 #s
Good	Excellent	Good	Good	Excellent	Good	Good	Good	Good	41,2,75,10,64,67,62	303

SHOPPING	GAMBLE	SEX	KEYWORD	KEYWORD				
Good	Good	is good	LOVE	Romance,Popularity,Visitors,Shopping,Food, Drinks,Co-operation,Friendships,Affection				

STRESS LEVEL	LUCKY COLORS	JEWELERY	MOONS EFFECT	GRAHA EFFECT	DAILY DEITY
Low	Red/Yellow/Pink	Topaz/Diamonds	Conservative	Love Graha	Gauri

DAILY PUJA	DAILY PSALMS
Give Gifts to females andnMother, Serve milk Products, Worship Durga forms	2, 11, 29 ,38, 47, 56, 74, 101, 119

Tuesday, August 23, 2016 — This is considered a POSITIVE day for you — Planet: Mercury

ADVICE & DETAILS	MANTRA FOR TODAY
Finances are in your mind today. It is a great day to make money, get profits and get a promotion at your job. You may also have to deal with children or younger adults and their financial needs.	Om hareem Kleem Hreem Aem Saraswataye namaha 21 times

MONEY	LOVE	CAREER	FAMILY	TRAVEL	WEDDING	MOVE	BUSINESS	HEALTH	Lotto #'s	play 3 #s
Good	Fair	Good	Good	Excellent	Good	Good	Good	Excellent	64,27,23,68,3,36,56	772

SHOPPING	GAMBLE	SEX	KEYWORD	KEYWORD				
Good	Good	is great	SOCIAL	Children,Education,Astrology,Bargains,Social Functions,Childishness,Groups - Parties,Teacher				

STRESS LEVEL	LUCKY COLORS	JEWELERY	MOONS EFFECT	GRAHA EFFECT	DAILY DEITY
Low	Green/Sky Blue/	Diamonds/Silver	Enthusiastic	Social Graha	Vishnu

DAILY PUJA	DAILY PSALMS
Wash the feet of Children, Do Satnarayan Pooja, Read & chant Geeta	3, 12, 30 ,39, 48, 57, 75, 102, 120

Wednesday, August 24, 2016 — This is considered a NEGATIVE day for you — Planet: Pluto

ADVICE & DETAILS

Money is coming and/or going out today, but it will be pleasurable. You may be changing locations and enjoying the company of someone known or famous from TV or the entertainment industry.

MANTRA FOR TODAY

Om Jai Viganeshwaraya.. Lambodaraya Namo Namaha 21 times

MONEY	LOVE	CAREER	FAMILY	TRAVEL	WEDDING	MOVE	BUSINESS	HEALTH	Lotto #'s	play 3 #s
Bad	Fair	Bad	Fair	Bad	Good	Bad	Bad	Bad	47,69,68,7,71,59,8	683

SHOPPING	GAMBLE	SEX	KEYWORD	KEYWORD						
Bad	Bad	is tough	CAREER	Career,Hard Work,Co-workers,Low Payment,Job Problems,High Temper,Low Pay,Laziness						

STRESS LEVEL	LUCKY COLORS	JEWELERY	MOONS EFFECT	GRAHA EFFECT	DAILY DEITY
High	Dark Blue/ Purple/	Amethyst/Gold	Emotional	Job Graha	Lingam

DAILY PUJA	DAILY PSALMS
Worship Ganesh, Give gifts to father, and co -workers, Plant gardens, farms	4, 13, 31 ,40, 49, 58, 76, 103, 121

Thursday, August 25, 2016 — This is considered a POSITIVE day for you — Planet: Venus

ADVICE & DETAILS

This is a positive day to invest. To improve your results in this arena make sure you show gratitude to the universe by praying and meditating.

MANTRA FOR TODAY

Om Graam Greem Graum Sa Gurave namah swaha 21 times

MONEY	LOVE	CAREER	FAMILY	TRAVEL	WEDDING	MOVE	BUSINESS	HEALTH	Lotto #'s	play 3 #s
Bad	Excellent	Fair	Good	Excellent	Good	Excellent	Good	Excellent	15,42,59,6,74,17,31	531

SHOPPING	GAMBLE	SEX	KEYWORD	KEYWORD						
Good	Good	is good	CHANGE	Sexuality,Travel,Change,Distant, far,Travel delays,Deception,Excercise,Illicit Affairs						

STRESS LEVEL	LUCKY COLORS	JEWELERY	MOONS EFFECT	GRAHA EFFECT	DAILY DEITY
Fair	Tan/Green/ Beige	Pearl/Silver/quartz	Courageous	Travel Graha	Nataraja

DAILY PUJA	DAILY PSALMS
Artistic gifts, Pray to Krishna, Do good deeds, do Spiritual trips	5, 14, 32 ,41, 50, 59, 77, 104, 122

Friday, August 26, 2016 — This is considered a NEGATIVE day for you — Planet: Mars

ADVICE & DETAILS

It will be difficult, but possible to overcome your sadness today. Your mind will tend to veer towards thoughts of losses, doubts, denial and death; if you cannot control it you will be creating this in your life. Pray, meditate and place your trust in the Higher Power.

MANTRA FOR TODAY

Om Mana Swasti Shanti Kuru kuru Swaha Shivoham Shivoham 27 times

MONEY	LOVE	CAREER	FAMILY	TRAVEL	WEDDING	MOVE	BUSINESS	HEALTH	Lotto #'s	play 3 #s
Bad	Bad	Bad	Bad	Bad	Bad	Bad	Fair	Bad	65,59,58,67,39,55,3	56

SHOPPING	GAMBLE	SEX	KEYWORD	KEYWORD						
Fair	Bad	is frustrating	POWER	Responsibilty,Disagreement,Family,Back Pain,Family Conflicts,Traffic Ticket,Quarrels,Jealousy						

STRESS LEVEL	LUCKY COLORS	JEWELERY	MOONS EFFECT	GRAHA EFFECT	DAILY DEITY
High	Purple/Blue/Rose	Emerald/Saphire	Educational	Family Graha	Mahakali

DAILY PUJA	DAILY PSALMS
Meditate, Control temper, Pray to Hanuman, Chant Hanuman Chalisa	6, 15, 33 ,42, 51, 60, 78, 105, 123

Saturday, August 27, 2016 — This is considered a NEUTRAL day for you — Planet: Uranus

ADVICE & DETAILS

Finances are in your mind today. It is a great day to make money, get profits and get a promotion at your job. You may also have to deal with children or younger adults and their financial needs.

MANTRA FOR TODAY

Jai Jai Shiva Shambo.(2) ...Mahadeva Shambo (2) 21 times 8

MONEY	LOVE	CAREER	FAMILY	TRAVEL	WEDDING	MOVE	BUSINESS	HEALTH	Lotto #'s	play 3 #s
Good	Good	Fair	Good	Good	Bad	Good	Bad	Fair	37,5,24,57,41,9,56	89

SHOPPING	GAMBLE	SEX	KEYWORD	KEYWORD						
Bad	Fair	is quiet	DIVINE	Spirituality,Religious,Astrology,Inner Conflicts,Religious ,Sleepiness,Advice given,Alcohol - drugs						

STRESS LEVEL	LUCKY COLORS	JEWELERY	MOONS EFFECT	GRAHA EFFECT	DAILY DEITY
Fair	Light Blue/Peach	Tiger's eye/Gold/Silver	Affectionate	God'S Graha	Shesnaag

DAILY PUJA	DAILY PSALMS
Chant Shiva Mantras, Take gifts to Ocean - Ganga Puja, Donate to Temple, Priests, etc.	7, 16, 34 ,43, 52, 61, 79, 106, 124

Sunday, August 28, 2016 — This is considered a POSITIVE day for you — Planet: Jupiter

ADVICE & DETAILS	MANTRA FOR TODAY
Money is coming and/or going out today, but it will be pleasurable. You may be changing locations and enjoying the company of someone known or famous from TV or the entertainment industry.	Om Hareem Nama Swaha..Shri Maha Laxmi Aye Namah swaha 12 times

MONEY	LOVE	CAREER	FAMILY	TRAVEL	WEDDING	MOVE	BUSINESS	HEALTH	Lotto #'s	play 3 #s
Excellent	Good	Excellent	Good	Good	Excellent	Good	Excellent	Excellent	27,6,43,35,37,8,59	528

SHOPPING	GAMBLE	SEX	KEYWORD	KEYWORD						
Excellent	Excellent	is excellent	MONEY	Business,Major Expense,Money - Profits,Income,Investments,Power,Promotion,Fame - TV						

STRESS LEVEL	LUCKY COLORS	JEWELERY	MOONS EFFECT	GRAHA EFFECT	DAILY DEITY
Low	Yellow/Silver	Diamonds/Gold/Pearls	Secretive	Money Graha	Mahalaxmi

DAILY PUJA	DAILY PSALMS
Decorate Land, Feed the poor, Donate milk /products to all, Feed holy guests,	8, 17, 35 ,44, 53, 62, 80, 107, 125

Monday, August 29, 2016 — This is considered a NEGATIVE day for you — Planet: Saturn

ADVICE & DETAILS	MANTRA FOR TODAY
Today could be a very positive day influenced by promotion, profits and money; but there may be also a degree of frustation if your expectations are not fulfilled the way you feel they should. Concentrate in the positive and learn from what you perceive as negative.	Om Ganga mataye nama swaha Om Varuna Devta aye Pahimam 11 times

MONEY	LOVE	CAREER	FAMILY	TRAVEL	WEDDING	MOVE	BUSINESS	HEALTH	Lotto #'s	play 3 #s
Bad	Bad	Bad	Fair	Bad	Bad	Bad	Bad	Bad	17,45,64,34,50,54,70	861

SHOPPING	GAMBLE	SEX	KEYWORD	KEYWORD						
Bad	Bad	is very bad	KARMA	Destruction,Losses,Death,Sickness - cold,Legal matter,Abusive,Karmic debts,God - Karma						

STRESS LEVEL	LUCKY COLORS	JEWELERY	MOONS EFFECT	GRAHA EFFECT	DAILY DEITY
High	Gold/Brown//Green	Saphire/Hessonite	Ivestments	Evil Graha	Agnidev

DAILY PUJA	DAILY PSALMS
Remembrance of family members who died, worship of older people. gifts to grand parents	9, 18, 36 ,45, 54, 63, 81, 108, 126

Tuesday, August 30, 2016 — This is considered a NEUTRAL day for you — Planet: Sun

ADVICE & DETAILS	MANTRA FOR TODAY
You will be enjoying profits and money from your endeavors today, but on the other hand you will have sizable expenses that will give you great pleasure.	Om Namo Bhagawate Mukhtanandaya, 108 times

MONEY	LOVE	CAREER	FAMILY	TRAVEL	WEDDING	MOVE	BUSINESS	HEALTH	Lotto #'s	play 3 #s
Fair	Bad	Good	Bad	Fair	Bad	Fair	Fair	Fair	45,67,40,22,6,69,32	644

SHOPPING	GAMBLE	SEX	KEYWORD	KEYWORD						
Fair	Fair	is fair	MIND	Independence,Loneliness,Meditative,Worry,Dominating,Illness - Cold,On Your Own,Commanding						

STRESS LEVEL	LUCKY COLORS	JEWELERY	MOONS EFFECT	GRAHA EFFECT	DAILY DEITY
High	White/Yellow/	Pearl/Quartz	Arrogance	Status Graha	Saraswaty

DAILY PUJA	DAILY PSALMS
Give Gifts to Priests, Invite holy ones to your home, Feed Swamis and Yogis, Do Shiva Puja.	1, 10, 28 ,37, 46, 55, 73, 100, 118

Wednesday, August 31, 2016 — This is considered a POSITIVE day for you — Planet: Moon

ADVICE & DETAILS	MANTRA FOR TODAY
This is a very positive day as long as you are willing to serve and cooperate with others. Make sure that every word your lips utter is with purpose, loving and kind. It is a propitious day for marriage and romance.	Kali Durge Namo Nama Om Durge aye nama swaha 108 times

MONEY	LOVE	CAREER	FAMILY	TRAVEL	WEDDING	MOVE	BUSINESS	HEALTH	Lotto #'s	play 3 #s
Good	Excellent	Good	Good	Excellent	Good	Good	Good	Good	51,8,6,28,52,32,46	389

SHOPPING	GAMBLE	SEX	KEYWORD	KEYWORD						
Good	Good	is good	LOVE	Romance,Popularity,Visitors,Shopping,Food, Drinks,Co-operation,Friendships,Affection						

STRESS LEVEL	LUCKY COLORS	JEWELERY	MOONS EFFECT	GRAHA EFFECT	DAILY DEITY
Low	Red/Yellow/Pink	Topaz/Diamonds	Conservative	Love Graha	Gauri

DAILY PUJA	DAILY PSALMS
Give Gifts to females andnMother, Serve milk Products, Worship Durga forms	2, 11, 29 ,38, 47, 56, 74, 101, 119

Thursday, September 1, 2016 — This is considered a POSITIVE day for you — Planet: Jupiter

ADVICE & DETAILS

Watch out for accidents or tickets, today is a day of moving or trips that if you are not careful could have negative consequences.

MANTRA FOR TODAY

Om Hareem Nama Swaha..Shri Maha Laxmi Aye Namah swaha 12 times

MONEY	LOVE	CAREER	FAMILY	TRAVEL	WEDDING	MOVE	BUSINESS	HEALTH	Lotto #'s	play 3 #s
Excellent	Good	Excellent	Good	Good	Excellent	Good	Excellent	Excellent	32,57,6,50,5,26,61	691

SHOPPING	GAMBLE	SEX	KEYWORD	KEYWORD						
Excellent	Excellent	is excellent	MONEY	Business,Major Expense,Money - Profits,Income,Investments,Power,Promotion,Fame - TV						

STRESS LEVEL	LUCKY COLORS	JEWELERY	MOONS EFFECT	GRAHA EFFECT	DAILY DEITY
Low	Yellow/Silver	Diamonds/Gold/Pearls	Secretive	Money Graha	Mahalaxmi

DAILY PUJA	DAILY PSALMS
Decorate Land, Feed the poor, Donate milk /products to all, Feed holy guests,	8, 17, 35 ,44, 53, 62, 80, 107, 125

Friday, September 2, 2016 — This is considered a NEGATIVE day for you — Planet: Saturn

ADVICE & DETAILS

The law of "action and reaction" or karma will be present in your life today. Stay God-centered while maintaining your full attention to avoid troubles with government, accidents and/or death.

MANTRA FOR TODAY

Om Ganga mataye nama swaha Om Varuna Devta aye Pahimam 11 times

MONEY	LOVE	CAREER	FAMILY	TRAVEL	WEDDING	MOVE	BUSINESS	HEALTH	Lotto #'s	play 3 #s
Bad	Bad	Bad	Fair	Bad	Bad	Bad	Bad	Bad	29,72,36,37,2,27,21	660

SHOPPING	GAMBLE	SEX	KEYWORD	KEYWORD						
Bad	Bad	is very bad	KARMA	Destruction,Losses,Death,Sickness - cold,Legal matter,Abusive,Karmic debts,God - Karma						

STRESS LEVEL	LUCKY COLORS	JEWELERY	MOONS EFFECT	GRAHA EFFECT	DAILY DEITY
High	Gold/Brown//Green	Saphire/Hessonite	Ivestments	Evil Graha	Agnidev

DAILY PUJA	DAILY PSALMS
Remembrance of family members who died, worship of older people. gifts to grand parents	9, 18, 36 ,45, 54, 63, 81, 108, 126

Saturday, September 3, 2016 — This is considered a NEUTRAL day for you — Planet: Sun

ADVICE & DETAILS

This is not a day to begin any new project. Concentrate on finishing anything you have started before. There is the possibility of death or end of someone, a project, a situation, an idea or thought; it may be positive or negative. Watch out for accidents, they may have serious consequences. Stay in a prayerful attitude.

MANTRA FOR TODAY

Om Namo Bhagawate Mukhtanandaya, 108 times

MONEY	LOVE	CAREER	FAMILY	TRAVEL	WEDDING	MOVE	BUSINESS	HEALTH	Lotto #'s	play 3 #s
Fair	Bad	Good	Bad	Fair	Bad	Fair	Fair	Fair	41,11,3,14,11,47,44	605

SHOPPING	GAMBLE	SEX	KEYWORD	KEYWORD						
Fair	Fair	is fair	MIND	Independence,Loneliness,Meditative,Worry,Dominating,Illness - Cold,On Your Own,Commanding						

STRESS LEVEL	LUCKY COLORS	JEWELERY	MOONS EFFECT	GRAHA EFFECT	DAILY DEITY
High	White/Yellow/	Pearl/Quartz	Arrogance	Status Graha	Saraswaty

DAILY PUJA	DAILY PSALMS
Give Gifts to Priests, Invite holy ones to your home, Feed Swamis and Yogis, Do Shiva Puja.	1, 10, 28 ,37, 46, 55, 73, 100, 118

Sunday, September 4, 2016 — This is considered a POSITIVE day for you — Planet: Moon

ADVICE & DETAILS

It is a great day to begin partnerships, associations or friendships with people that are or may become your teachers or have something to offer you.

MANTRA FOR TODAY

Kali Durge Namo Nama Om Durge aye nama swaha 108 times

MONEY	LOVE	CAREER	FAMILY	TRAVEL	WEDDING	MOVE	BUSINESS	HEALTH	Lotto #'s	play 3 #s
Good	Excellent	Good	Good	Excellent	Good	Good	Good	Good	57,49,75,22,23,12,16	232

SHOPPING	GAMBLE	SEX	KEYWORD	KEYWORD						
Good	Good	is good	LOVE	Romance,Popularity,Visitors,Shopping,Food, Drinks,Co-operation,Friendships,Affection						

STRESS LEVEL	LUCKY COLORS	JEWELERY	MOONS EFFECT	GRAHA EFFECT	DAILY DEITY
Low	Red/Yellow/Pink	Topaz/Diamonds	Conservative	Love Graha	Gauri

DAILY PUJA	DAILY PSALMS
Give Gifts to females andnMother, Serve milk Products, Worship Durga forms	2, 11, 29 ,38, 47, 56, 74, 101, 119

Monday, September 5, 2016 — This is considered a POSITIVE day for you — Planet: Mercury

ADVICE & DETAILS

Doubts and denial will plague your mind today. You may have encounters today with people in government agencies; people that are famous or are somewhat related to television. Anything that you perceive as negative that happens today is probably a payment of a karmic debt.

MANTRA FOR TODAY

Om hareem Kleem Hreem Aem Saraswataye namaha 21 times

MONEY	LOVE	CAREER	FAMILY	TRAVEL	WEDDING	MOVE	BUSINESS	HEALTH	Lotto #'s	play 3 #s
Good	Fair	Good	Good	Excellent	Good	Good	Good	Excellent	45,39,70,32,10,26,57	627

SHOPPING	GAMBLE	SEX	KEYWORD	KEYWORD						
Good	Good	is great	SOCIAL	Children,Education,Astrology,Bargains,Social Functions,Childishness,Groups - Parties,Teacher						

STRESS LEVEL		LUCKY COLORS	JEWELERY	MOONS EFFECT	GRAHA EFFECT	DAILY DEITY
Low		Green/Sky Blue/	Diamonds/Silver	Enthusiastic	Social Graha	Vishnu

DAILY PUJA	DAILY PSALMS
Wash the feet of Children, Do Satnarayan Pooja, Read & chant Geeta	3, 12, 30 ,39, 48, 57, 75, 102, 120

Tuesday, September 6, 2016 — This is considered a NEGATIVE day for you — Planet: Pluto

ADVICE & DETAILS

Your doubts may bring losses in the financial or personal arenas, you are advised not to deny facts that are in front of you and that are valuable information; you need to face them. Your day may be influenced by interaction with government agencies.

MANTRA FOR TODAY

Om Jai Viganeshwaraya.. Lambodaraya Namo Namaha 21 times

MONEY	LOVE	CAREER	FAMILY	TRAVEL	WEDDING	MOVE	BUSINESS	HEALTH	Lotto #'s	play 3 #s
Bad	Fair	Bad	Fair	Bad	Good	Bad	Bad	Bad	1,10,16,58,22,11,14	526

SHOPPING	GAMBLE	SEX	KEYWORD	KEYWORD						
Bad	Bad	is tough	CAREER	Career,Hard Work,Co-workers,Low Payment,Job Problems,High Temper,Low Pay,Laziness						

STRESS LEVEL		LUCKY COLORS	JEWELERY	MOONS EFFECT	GRAHA EFFECT	DAILY DEITY
High		Dark Blue/ Purple/	Amethyst/Gold	Emotional	Job Graha	Lingam

DAILY PUJA	DAILY PSALMS
Worship Ganesh, Give gifts to father, and co -workers, Plant gardens, farms	4, 13, 31 ,40, 49, 58, 76, 103, 121

Wednesday, September 7, 2016 — This is considered a POSITIVE day for you — Planet: Venus

ADVICE & DETAILS

This is a day when you may have a big expense, make sure it is the right decision; otherwise you may find out that you wasted your money. Do not make any rushed decisions and do not purchase on impulse. You may be promoted in some manner as long as you are not lazy or inactive.

MANTRA FOR TODAY

Om Graam Greem Graum Sa Gurave namah swaha 21 times

MONEY	LOVE	CAREER	FAMILY	TRAVEL	WEDDING	MOVE	BUSINESS	HEALTH	Lotto #'s	play 3 #s
Bad	Excellent	Fair	Good	Excellent	Good	Excellent	Good	Excellent	11,28,17,2,39,26,10	103

SHOPPING	GAMBLE	SEX	KEYWORD	KEYWORD						
Good	Good	is good	CHANGE	Sexuality,Travel,Change,Distant, far,Travel delays,Deception,Excercise,Illicit Affairs						

STRESS LEVEL		LUCKY COLORS	JEWELERY	MOONS EFFECT	GRAHA EFFECT	DAILY DEITY
Fair		Tan/Green/ Beige	Pearl/Silver/quartz	Courageous	Travel Graha	Nataraja

DAILY PUJA	DAILY PSALMS
Artistic gifts, Pray to Krishna, Do good deeds, do Spiritual trips	5, 14, 32 ,41, 50, 59, 77, 104, 122

Thursday, September 8, 2016 — This is considered a NEGATIVE day for you — Planet: Mars

ADVICE & DETAILS

Karmic debts may make you infamous today. You have influences from the law, doubts and denial and a karmic account that is overdue.

MANTRA FOR TODAY

Om Mana Swasti Shanti Kuru kuru Swaha Shivoham Shivoham 27 times

MONEY	LOVE	CAREER	FAMILY	TRAVEL	WEDDING	MOVE	BUSINESS	HEALTH	Lotto #'s	play 3 #s
Bad	Bad	Bad	Bad	Bad	Bad	Bad	Fair	Bad	52,15,21,33,72,8,37	426

SHOPPING	GAMBLE	SEX	KEYWORD	KEYWORD						
Fair	Bad	is frustrating	POWER	Responsibilty,Disagreement,Family,Back Pain,Family Conflicts,Traffic Ticket,Quarrels,Jealousy						

STRESS LEVEL		LUCKY COLORS	JEWELERY	MOONS EFFECT	GRAHA EFFECT	DAILY DEITY
High		Purple/Blue/Rose	Emerald/Saphire	Educational	Family Graha	Mahakali

DAILY PUJA	DAILY PSALMS
Meditate, Control temper, Pray to Hanuman, Chant Hanuman Chalisa	6, 15, 33 ,42, 51, 60, 78, 105, 123

Friday, September 9, 2016 — This is considered a NEUTRAL day for you — Planet: Uranus

ADVICE & DETAILS

Doubts and denial will plague your mind today. You may have encounters today with people in government agencies; people that are famous or are somewhat related to television. Anything that you perceive as negative that happens today is probably a payment of a karmic debt.

MANTRA FOR TODAY

Jai Jai Shiva Shambo.(2) ...Mahadeva Shambo (2) 21 times 8

MONEY	LOVE	CAREER	FAMILY	TRAVEL	WEDDING	MOVE	BUSINESS	HEALTH	Lotto #'s	play 3 #s
Good	Good	Fair	Good	Good	Bad	Good	Bad	Fair	21,42,72,4,20,75,47	591

SHOPPING	GAMBLE	SEX	KEYWORD	KEYWORD						
Bad	Fair	is quiet	DIVINE	Spirituality,Religious,Astrology,Inner Conflicts,Religious ,Sleepiness,Advice given,Alcohol - drugs						

STRESS LEVEL	LUCKY COLORS	JEWELERY	MOONS EFFECT	GRAHA EFFECT	DAILY DEITY
Fair	Light Blue/Peach	Tiger's eye/Gold/Silver	Affectionate	God'S Graha	Shesnaag

DAILY PUJA
Chant Shiva Mantras, Take gifts to Ocean - Ganga Puja, Donate to Temple, Priests, etc.

DAILY PSALMS
7, 16, 34 ,43, 52, 61, 79, 106, 124

Saturday, September 10, 2016 — This is considered a POSITIVE day for you — Planet: Jupiter

ADVICE & DETAILS

Watch out for accidents or tickets, today is a day of moving or trips that if you are not careful could have negative consequences.

MANTRA FOR TODAY

Om Hareem Nama Swaha..Shri Maha Laxmi Aye Namah swaha 12 times

MONEY	LOVE	CAREER	FAMILY	TRAVEL	WEDDING	MOVE	BUSINESS	HEALTH	Lotto #'s	play 3 #s
Excellent	Good	Excellent	Good	Good	Excellent	Good	Excellent	Excellent	63,65,7,24,29,54,64	801

SHOPPING	GAMBLE	SEX	KEYWORD	KEYWORD						
Excellent	Excellent	is excellent	MONEY	Business,Major Expense,Money - Profits,Income,Investments,Power,Promotion,Fame - TV						

STRESS LEVEL	LUCKY COLORS	JEWELERY	MOONS EFFECT	GRAHA EFFECT	DAILY DEITY
Low	Yellow/Silver	Diamonds/Gold/Pearls	Secretive	Money Graha	Mahalaxmi

DAILY PUJA
Decorate Land, Feed the poor, Donate milk /products to all, Feed holy guests,

DAILY PSALMS
8, 17, 35 ,44, 53, 62, 80, 107, 125

Sunday, September 11, 2016 — This is considered a NEGATIVE day for you — Planet: Saturn

ADVICE & DETAILS

The law of "action and reaction" or karma will be present in your life today. Stay God-centered while maintaining your full attention to avoid troubles with government, accidents and/or death.

MANTRA FOR TODAY

Om Ganga mataye nama swaha Om Varuna Devta aye Pahimam 11 times

MONEY	LOVE	CAREER	FAMILY	TRAVEL	WEDDING	MOVE	BUSINESS	HEALTH	Lotto #'s	play 3 #s
Bad	Bad	Bad	Fair	Bad	Bad	Bad	Bad	Bad	60,25,13,9,6,36,64	988

SHOPPING	GAMBLE	SEX	KEYWORD	KEYWORD						
Bad	Bad	is very bad	KARMA	Destruction,Losses,Death,Sickness - cold,Legal matter,Abusive,Karmic debts,God - Karma						

STRESS LEVEL	LUCKY COLORS	JEWELERY	MOONS EFFECT	GRAHA EFFECT	DAILY DEITY
High	Gold/Brown//Green	Saphire/Hessonite	Ivestments	Evil Graha	Agnidev

DAILY PUJA
Remembrance of family members who died, worship of older people. gifts to grand parents

DAILY PSALMS
9, 18, 36 ,45, 54, 63, 81, 108, 126

Monday, September 12, 2016 — This is considered a NEUTRAL day for you — Planet: Sun

ADVICE & DETAILS

This is not a day to begin any new project. Concentrate on finishing anything you have started before. There is the possibility of death or end of someone, a project, a situation, an idea or thought; it may be positive or negative. Watch out for accidents, they may have serious consequences. Stay in a prayerful attitude.

MANTRA FOR TODAY

Om Namo Bhagawate Mukhtanandaya, 108 times

MONEY	LOVE	CAREER	FAMILY	TRAVEL	WEDDING	MOVE	BUSINESS	HEALTH	Lotto #'s	play 3 #s
Fair	Bad	Good	Bad	Fair	Bad	Fair	Fair	Fair	63,14,72,71,65,13,37	856

SHOPPING	GAMBLE	SEX	KEYWORD	KEYWORD						
Fair	Fair	is fair	MIND	Independence,Loneliness,Meditative,Worry,Dominating,Illness - Cold,On Your Own,Commanding						

STRESS LEVEL	LUCKY COLORS	JEWELERY	MOONS EFFECT	GRAHA EFFECT	DAILY DEITY
High	White/Yellow/	Pearl/Quartz	Arrogance	Status Graha	Saraswaty

DAILY PUJA
Give Gifts to Priests, Invite holy ones to your home, Feed Swamis and Yogis, Do Shiva Puja.

DAILY PSALMS
1, 10, 28 ,37, 46, 55, 73, 100, 118

Tuesday, September 13, 2016 — This is considered a POSITIVE day for you — Planet: Moon

ADVICE & DETAILS

It is a great day to begin partnerships, associations or friendships with people that are or may become your teachers or have something to offer you.

MANTRA FOR TODAY

Kali Durge Namo Nama Om Durge aye nama swaha 108 times

MONEY	LOVE	CAREER	FAMILY	TRAVEL	WEDDING	MOVE	BUSINESS	HEALTH	Lotto #'s	play 3 #s
Good	Excellent	Good	Good	Excellent	Good	Good	Good	Good	8,45,42,52,28,3,13	959

SHOPPING	GAMBLE	SEX	KEYWORD	KEYWORD						
Good	Good	is good	LOVE	Romance,Popularity,Visitors,Shopping,Food, Drinks,Co-operation,Friendships,Affection						

STRESS LEVEL		LUCKY COLORS	JEWELERY	MOONS EFFECT	GRAHA EFFECT	DAILY DEITY
Low		Red/Yellow/Pink	Topaz/Diamonds	Conservative	Love Graha	Gauri

DAILY PUJA	DAILY PSALMS
Give Gifts to females andnMother, Serve milk Products, Worship Durga forms	2, 11, 29 ,38, 47, 56, 74, 101, 119

Wednesday, September 14, 2016 — This is considered a POSITIVE day for you — Planet: Mercury

ADVICE & DETAILS

Doubts and denial will plague your mind today. You may have encounters today with people in government agencies; people that are famous or are somewhat related to television. Anything that you perceive as negative that happens today is probably a payment of a karmic debt.

MANTRA FOR TODAY

Om hareem Kleem Hreem Aem Saraswataye namaha 21 times

MONEY	LOVE	CAREER	FAMILY	TRAVEL	WEDDING	MOVE	BUSINESS	HEALTH	Lotto #'s	play 3 #s
Good	Fair	Good	Good	Excellent	Good	Good	Good	Excellent	24,6,66,49,74,22,67	194

SHOPPING	GAMBLE	SEX	KEYWORD	KEYWORD						
Good	Good	is great	SOCIAL	Children,Education,Astrology,Bargains,Social Functions,Childishness,Groups - Parties,Teacher						

STRESS LEVEL		LUCKY COLORS	JEWELERY	MOONS EFFECT	GRAHA EFFECT	DAILY DEITY
Low		Green/Sky Blue/	Diamonds/Silver	Enthusiastic	Social Graha	Vishnu

DAILY PUJA	DAILY PSALMS
Wash the feet of Children, Do Satnarayan Pooja, Read & chant Geeta	3, 12, 30 ,39, 48, 57, 75, 102, 120

Thursday, September 15, 2016 — This is considered a NEGATIVE day for you — Planet: Pluto

ADVICE & DETAILS

Your doubts may bring losses in the financial or personal arenas, you are advised not to deny facts that are in front of you and that are valuable information; you need to face them. Your day may be influenced by interaction with government agencies.

MANTRA FOR TODAY

Om Jai Viganeshwaraya.. Lambodaraya Namo Namaha 21 times

MONEY	LOVE	CAREER	FAMILY	TRAVEL	WEDDING	MOVE	BUSINESS	HEALTH	Lotto #'s	play 3 #s
Bad	Fair	Bad	Fair	Bad	Good	Bad	Bad	Bad	61,73,60,46,24,9,6	146

SHOPPING	GAMBLE	SEX	KEYWORD	KEYWORD						
Bad	Bad	is tough	CAREER	Career,Hard Work,Co-workers,Low Payment,Job Problems,High Temper,Low Pay,Laziness						

STRESS LEVEL		LUCKY COLORS	JEWELERY	MOONS EFFECT	GRAHA EFFECT	DAILY DEITY
High		Dark Blue/ Purple/	Amethyst/Gold	Emotional	Job Graha	Lingam

DAILY PUJA	DAILY PSALMS
Worship Ganesh, Give gifts to father, and co -workers, Plant gardens, farms	4, 13, 31 ,40, 49, 58, 76, 103, 121

Friday, September 16, 2016 — This is considered a POSITIVE day for you — Planet: Venus

ADVICE & DETAILS

This is a day when you may have a big expense, make sure it is the right decision; otherwise you may find out that you wasted your money. Do not make any rushed decisions and do not purchase on impulse. You may be promoted in some manner as long as you are not lazy or inactive.

MANTRA FOR TODAY

Om Graam Greem Graum Sa Gurave namah swaha 21 times

MONEY	LOVE	CAREER	FAMILY	TRAVEL	WEDDING	MOVE	BUSINESS	HEALTH	Lotto #'s	play 3 #s
Bad	Excellent	Fair	Good	Excellent	Good	Excellent	Good	Excellent	7,15,39,41,59,57,46	246

SHOPPING	GAMBLE	SEX	KEYWORD	KEYWORD						
Good	Good	is good	CHANGE	Sexuality,Travel,Change,Distant, far,Travel delays,Deception,Excercise,Illicit Affairs						

STRESS LEVEL		LUCKY COLORS	JEWELERY	MOONS EFFECT	GRAHA EFFECT	DAILY DEITY
Fair		Tan/Green/ Beige	Pearl/Silver/quartz	Courageous	Travel Graha	Nataraja

DAILY PUJA	DAILY PSALMS
Artistic gifts, Pray to Krishna, Do good deeds, do Spiritual trips	5, 14, 32 ,41, 50, 59, 77, 104, 122

Saturday, September 17, 2016 — This is considered a NEGATIVE day for you — Planet: Mars

ADVICE & DETAILS

Karmic debts may make you infamous today. You have influences from the law, doubts and denial and a karmic account that is overdue.

MANTRA FOR TODAY

Om Mana Swasti Shanti Kuru kuru Swaha Shivoham Shivoham 27 times

MONEY	LOVE	CAREER	FAMILY	TRAVEL	WEDDING	MOVE	BUSINESS	HEALTH	Lotto #'s	play 3 #s
Bad	Bad	Bad	Bad	Bad	Bad	Bad	Fair	Bad	68,47,41,71,16,40,66	982

SHOPPING	GAMBLE	SEX	KEYWORD	KEYWORD						
Fair	Bad	is frustrating	POWER	Responsibilty,Disagreement,Family,Back Pain,Family Conflicts,Traffic Ticket,Quarrels,Jealousy						

STRESS LEVEL	LUCKY COLORS	JEWELERY	MOONS EFFECT	GRAHA EFFECT	DAILY DEITY
High	Purple/Blue/Rose	Emerald/Saphire	Educational	Family Graha	Mahakali

DAILY PUJA
Meditate, Control temper, Pray to Hanuman, Chant Hanuman Chalisa

DAILY PSALMS
6, 15, 33 ,42, 51, 60, 78, 105, 123

Sunday, September 18, 2016 — This is considered a NEUTRAL day for you — Planet: Uranus

ADVICE & DETAILS

Doubts and denial will plague your mind today. You may have encounters today with people in government agencies; people that are famous or are somewhat related to television. Anything that you perceive as negative that happens today is probably a payment of a karmic debt.

MANTRA FOR TODAY

Jai Jai Shiva Shambo.(2) ...Mahadeva Shambo (2) 21 times 8

MONEY	LOVE	CAREER	FAMILY	TRAVEL	WEDDING	MOVE	BUSINESS	HEALTH	Lotto #'s	play 3 #s
Good	Good	Fair	Good	Good	Bad	Good	Bad	Fair	65,52,55,33,68,74,68	934

SHOPPING	GAMBLE	SEX	KEYWORD	KEYWORD						
Bad	Fair	is quiet	DIVINE	Spirituality,Religious,Astrology,Inner Conflicts,Religious ,Sleepiness,Advice given,Alcohol - drugs						

STRESS LEVEL	LUCKY COLORS	JEWELERY	MOONS EFFECT	GRAHA EFFECT	DAILY DEITY
Fair	Light Blue/Peach	Tiger's eye/Gold/Silver	Affectionate	God'S Graha	Shesnaag

DAILY PUJA
Chant Shiva Mantras, Take gifts to Ocean - Ganga Puja, Donate to Temple, Priests, etc.

DAILY PSALMS
7, 16, 34 ,43, 52, 61, 79, 106, 124

Monday, September 19, 2016 — This is considered a POSITIVE day for you — Planet: Jupiter

ADVICE & DETAILS

Watch out for accidents or tickets, today is a day of moving or trips that if you are not careful could have negative consequences.

MANTRA FOR TODAY

Om Hareem Nama Swaha..Shri Maha Laxmi Aye Namah swaha 12 times

MONEY	LOVE	CAREER	FAMILY	TRAVEL	WEDDING	MOVE	BUSINESS	HEALTH	Lotto #'s	play 3 #s
Excellent	Good	Excellent	Good	Good	Excellent	Good	Excellent	Excellent	50,27,51,39,64,50,9	537

SHOPPING	GAMBLE	SEX	KEYWORD	KEYWORD						
Excellent	Excellent	is excellent	MONEY	Business,Major Expense,Money - Profits,Income,Investments,Power,Promotion,Fame - TV						

STRESS LEVEL	LUCKY COLORS	JEWELERY	MOONS EFFECT	GRAHA EFFECT	DAILY DEITY
Low	Yellow/Silver	Diamonds/Gold/Pearls	Secretive	Money Graha	Mahalaxmi

DAILY PUJA
Decorate Land, Feed the poor, Donate milk /products to all, Feed holy guests,

DAILY PSALMS
8, 17, 35 ,44, 53, 62, 80, 107, 125

Tuesday, September 20, 2016 — This is considered a NEGATIVE day for you — Planet: Saturn

ADVICE & DETAILS

The law of "action and reaction" or karma will be present in your life today. Stay God-centered while maintaining your full attention to avoid troubles with government, accidents and/or death.

MANTRA FOR TODAY

Om Ganga mataye nama swaha Om Varuna Devta aye Pahimam 11 times

MONEY	LOVE	CAREER	FAMILY	TRAVEL	WEDDING	MOVE	BUSINESS	HEALTH	Lotto #'s	play 3 #s
Bad	Bad	Bad	Fair	Bad	Bad	Bad	Bad	Bad	57,42,2,33,30,42,63	216

SHOPPING	GAMBLE	SEX	KEYWORD	KEYWORD						
Bad	Bad	is very bad	KARMA	Destruction,Losses,Death,Sickness - cold,Legal matter,Abusive,Karmic debts,God - Karma						

STRESS LEVEL	LUCKY COLORS	JEWELERY	MOONS EFFECT	GRAHA EFFECT	DAILY DEITY
High	Gold/Brown//Green	Saphire/Hessonite	Ivestments	Evil Graha	Agnidev

DAILY PUJA
Remembrance of family members who died, worship of older people. gifts to grand parents

DAILY PSALMS
9, 18, 36 ,45, 54, 63, 81, 108, 126

Wednesday, September 21, 2016 — This is considered a NEUTRAL day for you — Planet: Sun

ADVICE & DETAILS

This is not a day to begin any new project. Concentrate on finishing anything you have started before. There is the possibility of death or end of someone, a project, a situation, an idea or thought; it may be positive or negative. Watch out for accidents, they may have serious consequences. Stay in a prayerful attitude.

MANTRA FOR TODAY

Om Namo Bhagawate Mukhtanandaya, 108 times

MONEY	LOVE	CAREER	FAMILY	TRAVEL	WEDDING	MOVE	BUSINESS	HEALTH	Lotto #'s	play 3 #s
Fair	Bad	Good	Bad	Fair	Bad	Fair	Fair	Fair	19,19,45,2,69,47,67	412

SHOPPING	GAMBLE	SEX	KEYWORD	KEYWORD
Fair	Fair	is fair	MIND	Independence,Loneliness,Meditative,Worry,Dominating,Illness - Cold,On Your Own,Commanding

STRESS LEVEL	LUCKY COLORS	JEWELERY	MOONS EFFECT	GRAHA EFFECT	DAILY DEITY
High	White/Yellow/	Pearl/Quartz	Arrogance	Status Graha	Saraswaty

DAILY PUJA
Give Gifts to Priests, Invite holy ones to your home, Feed Swamis and Yogis, Do Shiva Puja.

DAILY PSALMS
1, 10, 28 ,37, 46, 55, 73, 100, 118

Thursday, September 22, 2016 — This is considered a POSITIVE day for you — Planet: Moon

ADVICE & DETAILS

It is a great day to begin partnerships, associations or friendships with people that are or may become your teachers or have something to offer you.

MANTRA FOR TODAY

Kali Durge Namo Nama Om Durge aye nama swaha 108 times

MONEY	LOVE	CAREER	FAMILY	TRAVEL	WEDDING	MOVE	BUSINESS	HEALTH	Lotto #'s	play 3 #s
Good	Excellent	Good	Good	Excellent	Good	Good	Good	Good	70,1,66,48,52,11,32	975

SHOPPING	GAMBLE	SEX	KEYWORD	KEYWORD
Good	Good	is good	LOVE	Romance,Popularity,Visitors,Shopping,Food, Drinks,Co-operation,Friendships,Affection

STRESS LEVEL	LUCKY COLORS	JEWELERY	MOONS EFFECT	GRAHA EFFECT	DAILY DEITY
Low	Red/Yellow/Pink	Topaz/Diamonds	Conservative	Love Graha	Gauri

DAILY PUJA
Give Gifts to females andnMother, Serve milk Products, Worship Durga forms

DAILY PSALMS
2, 11, 29 ,38, 47, 56, 74, 101, 119

Friday, September 23, 2016 — This is considered a POSITIVE day for you — Planet: Mercury

ADVICE & DETAILS

Doubts and denial will plague your mind today. You may have encounters today with people in government agencies; people that are famous or are somewhat related to television. Anything that you perceive as negative that happens today is probably a payment of a karmic debt.

MANTRA FOR TODAY

Om hareem Kleem Hreem Aem Saraswataye namaha 21 times

MONEY	LOVE	CAREER	FAMILY	TRAVEL	WEDDING	MOVE	BUSINESS	HEALTH	Lotto #'s	play 3 #s
Good	Fair	Good	Good	Excellent	Good	Good	Good	Excellent	68,45,5,50,59,42,46	159

SHOPPING	GAMBLE	SEX	KEYWORD	KEYWORD
Good	Good	is great	SOCIAL	Children,Education,Astrology,Bargains,Social Functions,Childishness,Groups - Parties,Teacher

STRESS LEVEL	LUCKY COLORS	JEWELERY	MOONS EFFECT	GRAHA EFFECT	DAILY DEITY
Low	Green/Sky Blue/	Diamonds/Silver	Enthusiastic	Social Graha	Vishnu

DAILY PUJA
Wash the feet of Children, Do Satnarayan Pooja, Read & chant Geeta

DAILY PSALMS
3, 12, 30 ,39, 48, 57, 75, 102, 120

Saturday, September 24, 2016 — This is considered a NEGATIVE day for you — Planet: Pluto

ADVICE & DETAILS

Your doubts may bring losses in the financial or personal arenas, you are advised not to deny facts that are in front of you and that are valuable information; you need to face them. Your day may be influenced by interaction with government agencies.

MANTRA FOR TODAY

Om Jai Viganeshwaraya.. Lambodaraya Namo Namaha 21 times

MONEY	LOVE	CAREER	FAMILY	TRAVEL	WEDDING	MOVE	BUSINESS	HEALTH	Lotto #'s	play 3 #s
Bad	Fair	Bad	Fair	Bad	Good	Bad	Bad	Bad	75,29,65,50,45,60,44	577

SHOPPING	GAMBLE	SEX	KEYWORD	KEYWORD
Bad	Bad	is tough	CAREER	Career,Hard Work,Co-workers,Low Payment,Job Problems,High Temper,Low Pay,Laziness

STRESS LEVEL	LUCKY COLORS	JEWELERY	MOONS EFFECT	GRAHA EFFECT	DAILY DEITY
High	Dark Blue/ Purple/	Amethyst/Gold	Emotional	Job Graha	Lingam

DAILY PUJA
Worship Ganesh, Give gifts to father, and co -workers, Plant gardens, farms

DAILY PSALMS
4, 13, 31 ,40, 49, 58, 76, 103, 121

Sunday, September 25, 2016 — This is considered a POSITIVE day for you — Planet: Venus

ADVICE & DETAILS

This is a day when you may have a big expense, make sure it is the right decision; otherwise you may find out that you wasted your money. Do not make any rushed decisions and do not purchase on impulse. You may be promoted in some manner as long as you are not lazy or inactive.

MONEY	LOVE	CAREER	FAMILY	TRAVEL	WEDDING	MOVE	BUSINESS	HEALTH	Lotto #'s	play 3 #s
Bad	Excellent	Fair	Good	Excellent	Good	Excellent	Good	Excellent	34,1,32,3,72,30,14	649

SHOPPING	GAMBLE	SEX	KEYWORD	KEYWORD						
Good	Good	is good	CHANGE	Sexuality,Travel,Change,Distant, far,Travel delays,Deception,Excercise,Illicit Affairs						

STRESS LEVEL	LUCKY COLORS	JEWELERY	MOONS EFFECT	GRAHA EFFECT	DAILY DEITY
Fair	Tan/Green/ Beige	Pearl/Silver/quartz	Courageous	Travel Graha	Nataraja

DAILY PUJA	DAILY PSALMS
Artistic gifts, Pray to Krishna, Do good deeds, do Spiritual trips	5, 14, 32 ,41, 50, 59, 77, 104, 122

Monday, September 26, 2016 — This is considered a NEGATIVE day for you — Planet: Mars

ADVICE & DETAILS

Karmic debts may make you infamous today. You have influences from the law, doubts and denial and a karmic account that is overdue.

MONEY	LOVE	CAREER	FAMILY	TRAVEL	WEDDING	MOVE	BUSINESS	HEALTH	Lotto #'s	play 3 #s
Bad	Bad	Bad	Bad	Bad	Bad	Bad	Fair	Bad	28,24,61,51,49,32,3	746

SHOPPING	GAMBLE	SEX	KEYWORD	KEYWORD						
Fair	Bad	is frustrating	POWER	Responsibilty,Disagreement,Family,Back Pain,Family Conflicts,Traffic Ticket,Quarrels,Jealousy						

STRESS LEVEL	LUCKY COLORS	JEWELERY	MOONS EFFECT	GRAHA EFFECT	DAILY DEITY
High	Purple/Blue/Rose	Emerald/Saphire	Educational	Family Graha	Mahakali

DAILY PUJA	DAILY PSALMS
Meditate, Control temper, Pray to Hanuman, Chant Hanuman Chalisa	6, 15, 33 ,42, 51, 60, 78, 105, 123

Tuesday, September 27, 2016 — This is considered a NEUTRAL day for you — Planet: Uranus

ADVICE & DETAILS

Doubts and denial will plague your mind today. You may have encounters today with people in government agencies; people that are famous or are somewhat related to television. Anything that you perceive as negative that happens today is probably a payment of a karmic debt.

MONEY	LOVE	CAREER	FAMILY	TRAVEL	WEDDING	MOVE	BUSINESS	HEALTH	Lotto #'s	play 3 #s
Good	Good	Fair	Good	Good	Bad	Good	Bad	Fair	51,3,63,13,1,38,30	746

SHOPPING	GAMBLE	SEX	KEYWORD	KEYWORD						
Bad	Fair	is quiet	DIVINE	Spirituality,Religious,Astrology,Inner Conflicts,Religious ,Sleepiness,Advice given,Alcohol - drugs						

STRESS LEVEL	LUCKY COLORS	JEWELERY	MOONS EFFECT	GRAHA EFFECT	DAILY DEITY
Fair	Light Blue/Peach	Tiger's eye/Gold/Silver	Affectionate	God'S Graha	Shesnaag

DAILY PUJA	DAILY PSALMS
Chant Shiva Mantras, Take gifts to Ocean - Ganga Puja, Donate to Temple, Priests, etc.	7, 16, 34 ,43, 52, 61, 79, 106, 124

Wednesday, September 28, 2016 — This is considered a POSITIVE day for you — Planet: Jupiter

ADVICE & DETAILS

Watch out for accidents or tickets, today is a day of moving or trips that if you are not careful could have negative consequences.

MONEY	LOVE	CAREER	FAMILY	TRAVEL	WEDDING	MOVE	BUSINESS	HEALTH	Lotto #'s	play 3 #s
Excellent	Good	Excellent	Good	Good	Excellent	Good	Excellent	Excellent	52,69,28,14,14,62,22	303

SHOPPING	GAMBLE	SEX	KEYWORD	KEYWORD						
Excellent	Excellent	is excellent	MONEY	Business,Major Expense,Money - Profits,Income,Investments,Power,Promotion,Fame - TV						

STRESS LEVEL	LUCKY COLORS	JEWELERY	MOONS EFFECT	GRAHA EFFECT	DAILY DEITY
Low	Yellow/Silver	Diamonds/Gold/Pearls	Secretive	Money Graha	Mahalaxmi

DAILY PUJA	DAILY PSALMS
Decorate Land, Feed the poor, Donate milk /products to all, Feed holy guests,	8, 17, 35 ,44, 53, 62, 80, 107, 125

Thursday, September 29, 2016 — This is considered a NEGATIVE day for you — Planet: Saturn

ADVICE & DETAILS

The law of "action and reaction" or karma will be present in your life today. Stay God-centered while maintaining your full attention to avoid troubles with government, accidents and/or death.

MANTRA FOR TODAY

Om Ganga mataye nama swaha
Om Varuna Devta aye Pahimam 11 times

MONEY	LOVE	CAREER	FAMILY	TRAVEL	WEDDING	MOVE	BUSINESS	HEALTH	Lotto #'s	play 3 #s
Bad	Bad	Bad	Fair	Bad	Bad	Bad	Bad	Bad	72,62,44,17,60,20,2	683

SHOPPING	GAMBLE	SEX	KEYWORD	KEYWORD						
Bad	Bad	is very bad	KARMA	Destruction,Losses,Death,Sickness - cold,Legal matter,Abusive,Karmic debts,God - Karma						

STRESS LEVEL	LUCKY COLORS	JEWELERY	MOONS EFFECT	GRAHA EFFECT	DAILY DEITY
High	Gold/Brown//Green	Saphire/Hessonite	Ivestments	Evil Graha	Agnidev

DAILY PUJA
Remembrance of family members who died, worship of older people. gifts to grand parents

DAILY PSALMS
9, 18, 36 ,45, 54, 63, 81, 108, 126

Friday, September 30, 2016 — This is considered a NEUTRAL day for you — Planet: Sun

ADVICE & DETAILS

This is not a day to begin any new project. Concentrate on finishing anything you have started before. There is the possibility of death or end of someone, a project, a situation, an idea or thought; it may be positive or negative. Watch out for accidents, they may have serious consequences. Stay in a prayerful attitude.

MANTRA FOR TODAY

Om Namo Bhagawate Mukhtanandaya, 108 times

MONEY	LOVE	CAREER	FAMILY	TRAVEL	WEDDING	MOVE	BUSINESS	HEALTH	Lotto #'s	play 3 #s
Fair	Bad	Good	Bad	Fair	Bad	Fair	Fair	Fair	46,35,59,30,67,27,23	279

SHOPPING	GAMBLE	SEX	KEYWORD	KEYWORD						
Fair	Fair	is fair	MIND	Independence,Loneliness,Meditative,Worry,Dominating,Illness - Cold,On Your Own,Commanding						

STRESS LEVEL	LUCKY COLORS	JEWELERY	MOONS EFFECT	GRAHA EFFECT	DAILY DEITY
High	White/Yellow/	Pearl/Quartz	Arrogance	Status Graha	Saraswaty

DAILY PUJA
Give Gifts to Priests, Invite holy ones to your home, Feed Swamis and Yogis, Do Shiva Puja.

DAILY PSALMS
1, 10, 28 ,37, 46, 55, 73, 100, 118

Saturday, October 1, 2016 — This is considered a POSITIVE day for you — Planet: Jupiter

ADVICE & DETAILS

If you can, take short trips and enjoy high pleasure. There will be lots of moving today.

MANTRA FOR TODAY

Om Hareem Nama Swaha..Shri Maha Laxmi Aye Namah swaha 12 times

MONEY	LOVE	CAREER	FAMILY	TRAVEL	WEDDING	MOVE	BUSINESS	HEALTH	Lotto #'s	play 3 #s
Excellent	Good	Excellent	Good	Good	Excellent	Good	Excellent	Excellent	66,31,19,54,49,32,12	748

SHOPPING	GAMBLE	SEX	KEYWORD	KEYWORD						
Excellent	Excellent	is excellent	MONEY	Business,Major Expense,Money - Profits,Income,Investments,Power,Promotion,Fame - TV						

STRESS LEVEL	LUCKY COLORS	JEWELERY	MOONS EFFECT	GRAHA EFFECT	DAILY DEITY
Low	Yellow/Silver	Diamonds/Gold/Pearls	Secretive	Money Graha	Mahalaxmi

DAILY PUJA
Decorate Land, Feed the poor, Donate milk /products to all, Feed holy guests,

DAILY PSALMS
8, 17, 35 ,44, 53, 62, 80, 107, 125

Sunday, October 2, 2016 — This is considered a NEGATIVE day for you — Planet: Saturn

ADVICE & DETAILS

Connect with the God within today so you can avoid the loneliness that can result from being boastful and criticizing others. Look at yourself first instead of trying to fix others.

MANTRA FOR TODAY

Om Ganga mataye nama swaha
Om Varuna Devta aye Pahimam 11 times

MONEY	LOVE	CAREER	FAMILY	TRAVEL	WEDDING	MOVE	BUSINESS	HEALTH	Lotto #'s	play 3 #s
Bad	Bad	Bad	Fair	Bad	Bad	Bad	Bad	Bad	49,62,41,33,51,16,72	543

SHOPPING	GAMBLE	SEX	KEYWORD	KEYWORD						
Bad	Bad	is very bad	KARMA	Destruction,Losses,Death,Sickness - cold,Legal matter,Abusive,Karmic debts,God - Karma						

STRESS LEVEL	LUCKY COLORS	JEWELERY	MOONS EFFECT	GRAHA EFFECT	DAILY DEITY
High	Gold/Brown//Green	Saphire/Hessonite	Ivestments	Evil Graha	Agnidev

DAILY PUJA
Remembrance of family members who died, worship of older people. gifts to grand parents

DAILY PSALMS
9, 18, 36 ,45, 54, 63, 81, 108, 126

Monday, October 3, 2016 — This is considered a NEUTRAL day for you — Planet: Sun

ADVICE & DETAILS	MANTRA FOR TODAY
Today, you may be home alone, you may feel a bit confined, but at the same time you will have a sense of independence and the realization of your capabilities. This day may be influenced by dealings with the government, courts or legal institutions.	Om Namo Bhagawate Mukhtanandaya, 108 times

MONEY	LOVE	CAREER	FAMILY	TRAVEL	WEDDING	MOVE	BUSINESS	HEALTH	Lotto #'s	play 3 #s
Fair	Bad	Good	Bad	Fair	Bad	Fair	Fair	Fair	2,39,27,42,72,18,9	511

SHOPPING	GAMBLE	SEX	KEYWORD	KEYWORD						
Fair	Fair	is fair	MIND	Independence,Loneliness,Meditative,Worry,Dominating,Illness - Cold,On Your Own,Commanding						

STRESS LEVEL		LUCKY COLORS	JEWELERY	MOONS EFFECT	GRAHA EFFECT	DAILY DEITY
High		White/Yellow/	Pearl/Quartz	Arrogance	Status Graha	Saraswaty

DAILY PUJA	DAILY PSALMS
Give Gifts to Priests, Invite holy ones to your home, Feed Swamis and Yogis, Do Shiva Puja.	1, 10, 28 ,37, 46, 55, 73, 100, 118

Tuesday, October 4, 2016 — This is considered a POSITIVE day for you — Planet: Moon

ADVICE & DETAILS	MANTRA FOR TODAY
There will be opportunity for romantic dates or encounters. You will make money today and get profits. There is a good chance of promotion.	Kali Durge Namo Nama Om Durge aye nama swaha 108 times

MONEY	LOVE	CAREER	FAMILY	TRAVEL	WEDDING	MOVE	BUSINESS	HEALTH	Lotto #'s	play 3 #s
Good	Excellent	Good	Good	Excellent	Good	Good	Good	Good	41,58,33,5,34,71,49	702

SHOPPING	GAMBLE	SEX	KEYWORD	KEYWORD						
Good	Good	is good	LOVE	Romance,Popularity,Visitors,Shopping,Food, Drinks,Co-operation,Friendships,Affection						

STRESS LEVEL		LUCKY COLORS	JEWELERY	MOONS EFFECT	GRAHA EFFECT	DAILY DEITY
Low		Red/Yellow/Pink	Topaz/Diamonds	Conservative	Love Graha	Gauri

DAILY PUJA	DAILY PSALMS
Give Gifts to females andnMother, Serve milk Products, Worship Durga forms	2, 11, 29 ,38, 47, 56, 74, 101, 119

Wednesday, October 5, 2016 — This is considered a POSITIVE day for you — Planet: Mercury

ADVICE & DETAILS	MANTRA FOR TODAY
This is slow and lazy day, but for your karma you are advised to work and to be industrious. Your accomplishments today will be important for your personal growth.	Om hareem Kleem Hreem Aem Saraswataye namaha 21 times

MONEY	LOVE	CAREER	FAMILY	TRAVEL	WEDDING	MOVE	BUSINESS	HEALTH	Lotto #'s	play 3 #s
Good	Fair	Good	Good	Excellent	Good	Good	Good	Excellent	69,9,45,15,34,71,36	231

SHOPPING	GAMBLE	SEX	KEYWORD	KEYWORD						
Good	Good	is great	SOCIAL	Children,Education,Astrology,Bargains,Social Functions,Childishness,Groups - Parties,Teacher						

STRESS LEVEL		LUCKY COLORS	JEWELERY	MOONS EFFECT	GRAHA EFFECT	DAILY DEITY
Low		Green/Sky Blue/	Diamonds/Silver	Enthusiastic	Social Graha	Vishnu

DAILY PUJA	DAILY PSALMS
Wash the feet of Children, Do Satnarayan Pooja, Read & chant Geeta	3, 12, 30 ,39, 48, 57, 75, 102, 120

Thursday, October 6, 2016 — This is considered a NEGATIVE day for you — Planet: Pluto

ADVICE & DETAILS	MANTRA FOR TODAY
If you can, take short trips and enjoy high pleasure. There will be lots of moving today.	Om Jai Viganeshwaraya.. Lambodaraya Namo Namaha 21 times

MONEY	LOVE	CAREER	FAMILY	TRAVEL	WEDDING	MOVE	BUSINESS	HEALTH	Lotto #'s	play 3 #s
Bad	Fair	Bad	Fair	Bad	Good	Bad	Bad	Bad	75,26,60,28,17,41,60	171

SHOPPING	GAMBLE	SEX	KEYWORD	KEYWORD						
Bad	Bad	is tough	CAREER	Career,Hard Work,Co-workers,Low Payment,Job Problems,High Temper,Low Pay,Laziness						

STRESS LEVEL		LUCKY COLORS	JEWELERY	MOONS EFFECT	GRAHA EFFECT	DAILY DEITY
High		Dark Blue/ Purple/	Amethyst/Gold	Emotional	Job Graha	Lingam

DAILY PUJA	DAILY PSALMS
Worship Ganesh, Give gifts to father, and co -workers, Plant gardens, farms	4, 13, 31 ,40, 49, 58, 76, 103, 121

Friday, October 7, 2016 — This is considered a POSITIVE day for you — Planet: Venus

ADVICE & DETAILS

Today is a positive day to spend with others. You will be surrounded by partners, friends, associates and teachers. The exchange is beneficial, even if it is not what you expect.

MANTRA FOR TODAY

Om Graam Greem Graum Sa Gurave namah swaha 21 times

MONEY	LOVE	CAREER	FAMILY	TRAVEL	WEDDING	MOVE	BUSINESS	HEALTH	Lotto #'s	play 3 #s
Bad	Excellent	Fair	Good	Excellent	Good	Excellent	Good	Excellent	43,42,2,18,22,61,27	641

SHOPPING	GAMBLE	SEX	KEYWORD	KEYWORD
Good	Good	is good	CHANGE	Sexuality,Travel,Change,Distant, far,Travel delays,Deception,Excercise,Illicit Affairs

STRESS LEVEL	LUCKY COLORS	JEWELERY	MOONS EFFECT	GRAHA EFFECT	DAILY DEITY
Fair	Tan/Green/ Beige	Pearl/Silver/quartz	Courageous	Travel Graha	Nataraja

DAILY PUJA: Artistic gifts, Pray to Krishna, Do good deeds, do Spiritual trips

DAILY PSALMS: 5, 14, 32 ,41, 50, 59, 77, 104, 122

Saturday, October 8, 2016 — This is considered a NEGATIVE day for you — Planet: Mars

ADVICE & DETAILS

You will feel in command of everything today, be careful not to be too bossy and to be careful with your expression. It is a good day for creative endeavors such as publishing or writing. You will have an opportunity to work or be in groups or to be invited to parties.

MANTRA FOR TODAY

Om Mana Swasti Shanti Kuru kuru Swaha Shivoham Shivoham 27 times

MONEY	LOVE	CAREER	FAMILY	TRAVEL	WEDDING	MOVE	BUSINESS	HEALTH	Lotto #'s	play 3 #s
Bad	Bad	Bad	Bad	Bad	Bad	Bad	Fair	Bad	66,34,40,64,72,59,61	432

SHOPPING	GAMBLE	SEX	KEYWORD	KEYWORD
Fair	Bad	is frustrating	POWER	Responsibilty,Disagreement,Family,Back Pain,Family Conflicts,Traffic Ticket,Quarrels,Jealousy

STRESS LEVEL	LUCKY COLORS	JEWELERY	MOONS EFFECT	GRAHA EFFECT	DAILY DEITY
High	Purple/Blue/Rose	Emerald/Saphire	Educational	Family Graha	Mahakali

DAILY PUJA: Meditate, Control temper, Pray to Hanuman, Chant Hanuman Chalisa

DAILY PSALMS: 6, 15, 33 ,42, 51, 60, 78, 105, 123

Sunday, October 9, 2016 — This is considered a NEUTRAL day for you — Planet: Uranus

ADVICE & DETAILS

This is a day for expressing yourself in oral, visual or written form. Talk to others possibly in a group or at a gathering, paint or write a poem, book or article. This is also a day that if you are negative the use of alcohol or drugs will create danger for you, try to avoid it.

MANTRA FOR TODAY

Jai Jai Shiva Shambo.(2) ...Mahadeva Shambo (2) 21 times 8

MONEY	LOVE	CAREER	FAMILY	TRAVEL	WEDDING	MOVE	BUSINESS	HEALTH	Lotto #'s	play 3 #s
Good	Good	Fair	Good	Good	Bad	Good	Bad	Fair	30,55,15,3,53,62,15	953

SHOPPING	GAMBLE	SEX	KEYWORD	KEYWORD
Bad	Fair	is quiet	DIVINE	Spirituality,Religious,Astrology,Inner Conflicts,Religious ,Sleepiness,Advice given,Alcohol - drugs

STRESS LEVEL	LUCKY COLORS	JEWELERY	MOONS EFFECT	GRAHA EFFECT	DAILY DEITY
Fair	Light Blue/Peach	Tiger's eye/Gold/Silver	Affectionate	God'S Graha	Shesnaag

DAILY PUJA: Chant Shiva Mantras, Take gifts to Ocean - Ganga Puja, Donate to Temple, Priests, etc.

DAILY PSALMS: 7, 16, 34 ,43, 52, 61, 79, 106, 124

Monday, October 10, 2016 — This is considered a POSITIVE day for you — Planet: Jupiter

ADVICE & DETAILS

If you can, take short trips and enjoy high pleasure. There will be lots of moving today.

MANTRA FOR TODAY

Om Hareem Nama Swaha..Shri Maha Laxmi Aye Namah swaha 12 times

MONEY	LOVE	CAREER	FAMILY	TRAVEL	WEDDING	MOVE	BUSINESS	HEALTH	Lotto #'s	play 3 #s
Excellent	Good	Excellent	Good	Good	Excellent	Good	Excellent	Excellent	41,70,8,66,18,35,20	53

SHOPPING	GAMBLE	SEX	KEYWORD	KEYWORD
Excellent	Excellent	is excellent	MONEY	Business,Major Expense,Money - Profits,Income,Investments,Power,Promotion,Fame - TV

STRESS LEVEL	LUCKY COLORS	JEWELERY	MOONS EFFECT	GRAHA EFFECT	DAILY DEITY
Low	Yellow/Silver	Diamonds/Gold/Pearls	Secretive	Money Graha	Mahalaxmi

DAILY PUJA: Decorate Land, Feed the poor, Donate milk /products to all, Feed holy guests,

DAILY PSALMS: 8, 17, 35 ,44, 53, 62, 80, 107, 125

Tuesday, October 11, 2016 — This is considered a NEGATIVE day for you — Planet: Saturn

ADVICE & DETAILS

Connect with the God within today so you can avoid the loneliness that can result from being boastful and criticizing others. Look at yourself first instead of trying to fix others.

MANTRA FOR TODAY

Om Ganga mataye nama swaha
Om Varuna Devta aye Pahimam 11 times

MONEY	LOVE	CAREER	FAMILY	TRAVEL	WEDDING	MOVE	BUSINESS	HEALTH	Lotto #'s	play 3 #s
Bad	Bad	Bad	Fair	Bad	Bad	Bad	Bad	Bad	13,32,28,74,42,24,30	170

SHOPPING	GAMBLE	SEX	KEYWORD	KEYWORD						
Bad	Bad	is very bad	KARMA	Destruction,Losses,Death,Sickness - cold,Legal matter,Abusive,Karmic debts,God - Karma						

STRESS LEVEL	LUCKY COLORS	JEWELERY	MOONS EFFECT	GRAHA EFFECT	DAILY DEITY
High	Gold/Brown//Green	Saphire/Hessonite	Ivestments	Evil Graha	Agnidev

DAILY PUJA
Remembrance of family members who died, worship of older people. gifts to grand parents

DAILY PSALMS
9, 18, 36 ,45, 54, 63, 81, 108, 126

Wednesday, October 12, 2016 — This is considered a NEUTRAL day for you — Planet: Sun

ADVICE & DETAILS

Today, you may be home alone, you may feel a bit confined, but at the same time you will have a sense of independence and the realization of your capabilities. This day may be influenced by dealings with the government, courts or legal institutions.

MANTRA FOR TODAY

Om Namo Bhagawate Mukhtanandaya, 108 times

MONEY	LOVE	CAREER	FAMILY	TRAVEL	WEDDING	MOVE	BUSINESS	HEALTH	Lotto #'s	play 3 #s
Fair	Bad	Good	Bad	Fair	Bad	Fair	Fair	Fair	71,75,48,47,2,4,50	616

SHOPPING	GAMBLE	SEX	KEYWORD	KEYWORD						
Fair	Fair	is fair	MIND	Independence,Loneliness,Meditative,Worry,Dominating,Illness - Cold,On Your Own,Commanding						

STRESS LEVEL	LUCKY COLORS	JEWELERY	MOONS EFFECT	GRAHA EFFECT	DAILY DEITY
High	White/Yellow/	Pearl/Quartz	Arrogance	Status Graha	Saraswaty

DAILY PUJA
Give Gifts to Priests, Invite holy ones to your home, Feed Swamis and Yogis, Do Shiva Puja.

DAILY PSALMS
1, 10, 28 ,37, 46, 55, 73, 100, 118

Thursday, October 13, 2016 — This is considered a POSITIVE day for you — Planet: Moon

ADVICE & DETAILS

There will be opportunity for romantic dates or encounters. You will make money today and get profits. There is a good chance of promotion.

MANTRA FOR TODAY

Kali Durge Namo Nama Om Durge aye nama swaha 108 times

MONEY	LOVE	CAREER	FAMILY	TRAVEL	WEDDING	MOVE	BUSINESS	HEALTH	Lotto #'s	play 3 #s
Good	Excellent	Good	Good	Excellent	Good	Good	Good	Good	55,43,59,12,31,59,41	464

SHOPPING	GAMBLE	SEX	KEYWORD	KEYWORD						
Good	Good	is good	LOVE	Romance,Popularity,Visitors,Shopping,Food, Drinks,Co-operation,Friendships,Affection						

STRESS LEVEL	LUCKY COLORS	JEWELERY	MOONS EFFECT	GRAHA EFFECT	DAILY DEITY
Low	Red/Yellow/Pink	Topaz/Diamonds	Conservative	Love Graha	Gauri

DAILY PUJA
Give Gifts to females andnMother, Serve milk Products, Worship Durga forms

DAILY PSALMS
2, 11, 29 ,38, 47, 56, 74, 101, 119

Friday, October 14, 2016 — This is considered a POSITIVE day for you — Planet: Mercury

ADVICE & DETAILS

This is slow and lazy day, but for your karma you are advised to work and to be industrious. Your accomplishments today will be important for your personal growth.

MANTRA FOR TODAY

Om hareem Kleem Hreem Aem Saraswataye namaha 21 times

MONEY	LOVE	CAREER	FAMILY	TRAVEL	WEDDING	MOVE	BUSINESS	HEALTH	Lotto #'s	play 3 #s
Good	Fair	Good	Good	Excellent	Good	Good	Good	Excellent	2,16,21,4,18,48,28	427

SHOPPING	GAMBLE	SEX	KEYWORD	KEYWORD						
Good	Good	is great	SOCIAL	Children,Education,Astrology,Bargains,Social Functions,Childishness,Groups - Parties,Teacher						

STRESS LEVEL	LUCKY COLORS	JEWELERY	MOONS EFFECT	GRAHA EFFECT	DAILY DEITY
Low	Green/Sky Blue/	Diamonds/Silver	Enthusiastic	Social Graha	Vishnu

DAILY PUJA
Wash the feet of Children, Do Satnarayan Pooja, Read & chant Geeta

DAILY PSALMS
3, 12, 30 ,39, 48, 57, 75, 102, 120

Saturday, October 15, 2016 — This is considered a NEGATIVE day for you — Planet: Pluto

ADVICE & DETAILS	MANTRA FOR TODAY
If you can, take short trips and enjoy high pleasure. There will be lots of moving today.	Om Jai Viganeshwaraya.. Lambodaraya Namo Namaha 21 times

MONEY	LOVE	CAREER	FAMILY	TRAVEL	WEDDING	MOVE	BUSINESS	HEALTH	Lotto #'s	play 3 #s
Bad	Fair	Bad	Fair	Bad	Good	Bad	Bad	Bad	31,9,25,16,70,3,8	787

SHOPPING	GAMBLE	SEX	KEYWORD	KEYWORD						
Bad	Bad	is tough	CAREER	Career,Hard Work,Co-workers,Low Payment,Job Problems,High Temper,Low Pay,Laziness						

STRESS LEVEL		LUCKY COLORS	JEWELERY	MOONS EFFECT	GRAHA EFFECT	DAILY DEITY
High		Dark Blue/ Purple/	Amethyst/Gold	Emotional	Job Graha	Lingam

DAILY PUJA	DAILY PSALMS
Worship Ganesh, Give gifts to father, and co-workers, Plant gardens, farms	4, 13, 31 ,40, 49, 58, 76, 103, 121

Sunday, October 16, 2016 — This is considered a POSITIVE day for you — Planet: Venus

ADVICE & DETAILS	MANTRA FOR TODAY
Today is a positive day to spend with others. You will be surrounded by partners, friends, associates and teachers. The exchange is beneficial, even if it is not what you expect.	Om Graam Greem Graum Sa Gurave namah swaha 21 times

MONEY	LOVE	CAREER	FAMILY	TRAVEL	WEDDING	MOVE	BUSINESS	HEALTH	Lotto #'s	play 3 #s
Bad	Excellent	Fair	Good	Excellent	Good	Excellent	Good	Excellent	53,43,60,7,16,58,55	27

SHOPPING	GAMBLE	SEX	KEYWORD	KEYWORD						
Good	Good	is good	CHANGE	Sexuality,Travel,Change,Distant, far,Travel delays,Deception,Excercise,Illicit Affairs						

STRESS LEVEL		LUCKY COLORS	JEWELERY	MOONS EFFECT	GRAHA EFFECT	DAILY DEITY
Fair		Tan/Green/ Beige	Pearl/Silver/quartz	Courageous	Travel Graha	Nataraja

DAILY PUJA	DAILY PSALMS
Artistic gifts, Pray to Krishna, Do good deeds, do Spiritual trips	5, 14, 32 ,41, 50, 59, 77, 104, 122

Monday, October 17, 2016 — This is considered a NEGATIVE day for you — Planet: Mars

ADVICE & DETAILS	MANTRA FOR TODAY
You will feel in command of everything today, be careful not to be too bossy and to be careful with your expression. It is a good day for creative endeavors such as publishing or writing. You will have an opportunity to work or be in groups or to be invited to parties.	Om Mana Swasti Shanti Kuru kuru Swaha Shivoham Shivoham 27 times

MONEY	LOVE	CAREER	FAMILY	TRAVEL	WEDDING	MOVE	BUSINESS	HEALTH	Lotto #'s	play 3 #s
Bad	Bad	Bad	Bad	Bad	Bad	Bad	Fair	Bad	30,60,45,13,18,64,54	433

SHOPPING	GAMBLE	SEX	KEYWORD	KEYWORD						
Fair	Bad	is frustrating	POWER	Responsibilty,Disagreement,Family,Back Pain,Family Conflicts,Traffic Ticket,Quarrels,Jealousy						

STRESS LEVEL		LUCKY COLORS	JEWELERY	MOONS EFFECT	GRAHA EFFECT	DAILY DEITY
High		Purple/Blue/Rose	Emerald/Saphire	Educational	Family Graha	Mahakali

DAILY PUJA	DAILY PSALMS
Meditate, Control temper, Pray to Hanuman, Chant Hanuman Chalisa	6, 15, 33 ,42, 51, 60, 78, 105, 123

Tuesday, October 18, 2016 — This is considered a NEUTRAL day for you — Planet: Uranus

ADVICE & DETAILS	MANTRA FOR TODAY
This is a day for expressing yourself in oral, visual or written form. Talk to others possibly in a group or at a gathering, paint or write a poem, book or article. This is also a day that if you are negative the use of alcohol or drugs will create danger for you, try to avoid it.	Jai Jai Shiva Shambo.(2) ...Mahadeva Shambo (2) 21 times 8

MONEY	LOVE	CAREER	FAMILY	TRAVEL	WEDDING	MOVE	BUSINESS	HEALTH	Lotto #'s	play 3 #s
Good	Good	Fair	Good	Good	Bad	Good	Bad	Fair	75,58,2,64,1,6,17	728

SHOPPING	GAMBLE	SEX	KEYWORD	KEYWORD						
Bad	Fair	is quiet	DIVINE	Spirituality,Religious,Astrology,Inner Conflicts,Religious ,Sleepiness,Advice given,Alcohol - drugs						

STRESS LEVEL		LUCKY COLORS	JEWELERY	MOONS EFFECT	GRAHA EFFECT	DAILY DEITY
Fair		Light Blue/Peach	Tiger's eye/Gold/Silver	Affectionate	God'S Graha	Shesnaag

DAILY PUJA	DAILY PSALMS
Chant Shiva Mantras, Take gifts to Ocean - Ganga Puja, Donate to Temple, Priests, etc.	7, 16, 34 ,43, 52, 61, 79, 106, 124

Wednesday, October 19, 2016 | This is considered a POSITIVE day for you | Planet: Jupiter

ADVICE & DETAILS	MANTRA FOR TODAY
If you can, take short trips and enjoy high pleasure. There will be lots of moving today.	Om Hareem Nama Swaha..Shri Maha Laxmi Aye Namah swaha 12 times

MONEY	LOVE	CAREER	FAMILY	TRAVEL	WEDDING	MOVE	BUSINESS	HEALTH	Lotto #'s	play 3 #s
Excellent	Good	Excellent	Good	Good	Excellent	Good	Excellent	Excellent	8,61,51,2,37,73,10	477

SHOPPING	GAMBLE	SEX	KEYWORD	KEYWORD						
Excellent	Excellent	is excellent	MONEY	Business,Major Expense,Money - Profits,Income,Investments,Power,Promotion,Fame - TV						

STRESS LEVEL	LUCKY COLORS	JEWELERY	MOONS EFFECT	GRAHA EFFECT	DAILY DEITY
Low	Yellow/Silver	Diamonds/Gold/Pearls	Secretive	Money Graha	Mahalaxmi

DAILY PUJA	DAILY PSALMS
Decorate Land, Feed the poor, Donate milk /products to all, Feed holy guests,	8, 17, 35 ,44, 53, 62, 80, 107, 125

Thursday, October 20, 2016 | This is considered a NEGATIVE day for you | Planet: Saturn

ADVICE & DETAILS	MANTRA FOR TODAY
Connect with the God within today so you can avoid the loneliness that can result from being boastful and criticizing others. Look at yourself first instead of trying to fix others.	Om Ganga mataye nama swaha Om Varuna Devta aye Pahimam 11 times

MONEY	LOVE	CAREER	FAMILY	TRAVEL	WEDDING	MOVE	BUSINESS	HEALTH	Lotto #'s	play 3 #s
Bad	Bad	Bad	Fair	Bad	Bad	Bad	Bad	Bad	37,12,10,61,33,71,54	449

SHOPPING	GAMBLE	SEX	KEYWORD	KEYWORD						
Bad	Bad	is very bad	KARMA	Destruction,Losses,Death,Sickness - cold,Legal matter,Abusive,Karmic debts,God - Karma						

STRESS LEVEL	LUCKY COLORS	JEWELERY	MOONS EFFECT	GRAHA EFFECT	DAILY DEITY
High	Gold/Brown//Green	Saphire/Hessonite	Ivestments	Evil Graha	Agnidev

DAILY PUJA	DAILY PSALMS
Remembrance of family members who died, worship of older people. gifts to grand parents	9, 18, 36 ,45, 54, 63, 81, 108, 126

Friday, October 21, 2016 | This is considered a NEUTRAL day for you | Planet: Sun

ADVICE & DETAILS	MANTRA FOR TODAY
Today, you may be home alone, you may feel a bit confined, but at the same time you will have a sense of independence and the realization of your capabilities. This day may be influenced by dealings with the government, courts or legal institutions.	Om Namo Bhagawate Mukhtanandaya, 108 times

MONEY	LOVE	CAREER	FAMILY	TRAVEL	WEDDING	MOVE	BUSINESS	HEALTH	Lotto #'s	play 3 #s
Fair	Bad	Good	Bad	Fair	Bad	Fair	Fair	Fair	9,59,44,10,28,35,44	581

SHOPPING	GAMBLE	SEX	KEYWORD	KEYWORD						
Fair	Fair	is fair	MIND	Independence,Loneliness,Meditative,Worry,Dominating,Illness - Cold,On Your Own,Commanding						

STRESS LEVEL	LUCKY COLORS	JEWELERY	MOONS EFFECT	GRAHA EFFECT	DAILY DEITY
High	White/Yellow/	Pearl/Quartz	Arrogance	Status Graha	Saraswaty

DAILY PUJA	DAILY PSALMS
Give Gifts to Priests, Invite holy ones to your home, Feed Swamis and Yogis, Do Shiva Puja.	1, 10, 28 ,37, 46, 55, 73, 100, 118

Saturday, October 22, 2016 | This is considered a POSITIVE day for you | Planet: Moon

ADVICE & DETAILS	MANTRA FOR TODAY
There will be opportunity for romantic dates or encounters. You will make money today and get profits. There is a good chance of promotion.	Kali Durge Namo Nama Om Durge aye nama swaha 108 times

MONEY	LOVE	CAREER	FAMILY	TRAVEL	WEDDING	MOVE	BUSINESS	HEALTH	Lotto #'s	play 3 #s
Good	Excellent	Good	Good	Excellent	Good	Good	Good	Good	41,8,3,67,62,44,58	477

SHOPPING	GAMBLE	SEX	KEYWORD	KEYWORD						
Good	Good	is good	LOVE	Romance,Popularity,Visitors,Shopping,Food, Drinks,Co-operation,Friendships,Affection						

STRESS LEVEL	LUCKY COLORS	JEWELERY	MOONS EFFECT	GRAHA EFFECT	DAILY DEITY
Low	Red/Yellow/Pink	Topaz/Diamonds	Conservative	Love Graha	Gauri

DAILY PUJA	DAILY PSALMS
Give Gifts to females andnMother, Serve milk Products, Worship Durga forms	2, 11, 29 ,38, 47, 56, 74, 101, 119

Sunday, October 23, 2016 — This is considered a POSITIVE day for you — Planet: Mercury

ADVICE & DETAILS

This is slow and lazy day, but for your karma you are advised to work and to be industrious. Your accomplishments today will be important for your personal growth.

MANTRA FOR TODAY

Om hareem Kleem Hreem Aem Saraswataye namaha 21 times

MONEY	LOVE	CAREER	FAMILY	TRAVEL	WEDDING	MOVE	BUSINESS	HEALTH	Lotto #'s	play 3 #s
Good	Fair	Good	Good	Excellent	Good	Good	Good	Excellent	29,60,48,49,3,58,44	758

SHOPPING	GAMBLE	SEX	KEYWORD	KEYWORD				
Good	Good	is great	SOCIAL	Children,Education,Astrology,Bargains,Social Functions,Childishness,Groups - Parties,Teacher				

STRESS LEVEL	LUCKY COLORS	JEWELERY	MOONS EFFECT	GRAHA EFFECT	DAILY DEITY
Low	Green/Sky Blue/	Diamonds/Silver	Enthusiastic	Social Graha	Vishnu

DAILY PUJA
Wash the feet of Children, Do Satnarayan Pooja, Read & chant Geeta

DAILY PSALMS
3, 12, 30 ,39, 48, 57, 75, 102, 120

Monday, October 24, 2016 — This is considered a NEGATIVE day for you — Planet: Pluto

ADVICE & DETAILS

If you can, take short trips and enjoy high pleasure. There will be lots of moving today.

MANTRA FOR TODAY

Om Jai Viganeshwaraya.. Lambodaraya Namo Namaha 21 times

MONEY	LOVE	CAREER	FAMILY	TRAVEL	WEDDING	MOVE	BUSINESS	HEALTH	Lotto #'s	play 3 #s
Bad	Fair	Bad	Fair	Bad	Good	Bad	Bad	Bad	38,53,21,18,45,49,12	823

SHOPPING	GAMBLE	SEX	KEYWORD	KEYWORD				
Bad	Bad	is tough	CAREER	Career,Hard Work,Co-workers,Low Payment,Job Problems,High Temper,Low Pay,Laziness				

STRESS LEVEL	LUCKY COLORS	JEWELERY	MOONS EFFECT	GRAHA EFFECT	DAILY DEITY
High	Dark Blue/ Purple/	Amethyst/Gold	Emotional	Job Graha	Lingam

DAILY PUJA
Worship Ganesh, Give gifts to father, and co -workers, Plant gardens, farms

DAILY PSALMS
4, 13, 31 ,40, 49, 58, 76, 103, 121

Tuesday, October 25, 2016 — This is considered a POSITIVE day for you — Planet: Venus

ADVICE & DETAILS

Today is a positive day to spend with others. You will be surrounded by partners, friends, associates and teachers. The exchange is beneficial, even if it is not what you expect.

MANTRA FOR TODAY

Om Graam Greem Graum Sa Gurave namah swaha 21 times

MONEY	LOVE	CAREER	FAMILY	TRAVEL	WEDDING	MOVE	BUSINESS	HEALTH	Lotto #'s	play 3 #s
Bad	Excellent	Fair	Good	Excellent	Good	Excellent	Good	Excellent	48,6,21,19,27,52,74	361

SHOPPING	GAMBLE	SEX	KEYWORD	KEYWORD				
Good	Good	is good	CHANGE	Sexuality,Travel,Change,Distant, far,Travel delays,Deception,Excercise,Illicit Affairs				

STRESS LEVEL	LUCKY COLORS	JEWELERY	MOONS EFFECT	GRAHA EFFECT	DAILY DEITY
Fair	Tan/Green/ Beige	Pearl/Silver/quartz	Courageous	Travel Graha	Nataraja

DAILY PUJA
Artistic gifts, Pray to Krishna, Do good deeds, do Spiritual trips

DAILY PSALMS
5, 14, 32 ,41, 50, 59, 77, 104, 122

Wednesday, October 26, 2016 — This is considered a NEGATIVE day for you — Planet: Mars

ADVICE & DETAILS

You will feel in command of everything today, be careful not to be too bossy and to be careful with your expression. It is a good day for creative endeavors such as publishing or writing. You will have an opportunity to work or be in groups or to be invited to parties.

MANTRA FOR TODAY

Om Mana Swasti Shanti Kuru kuru Swaha Shivoham Shivoham 27 times

MONEY	LOVE	CAREER	FAMILY	TRAVEL	WEDDING	MOVE	BUSINESS	HEALTH	Lotto #'s	play 3 #s
Bad	Bad	Bad	Bad	Bad	Bad	Bad	Fair	Bad	64,16,38,71,61,20,31	881

SHOPPING	GAMBLE	SEX	KEYWORD	KEYWORD				
Fair	Bad	is frustrating	POWER	Responsibilty,Disagreement,Family,Back Pain,Family Conflicts,Traffic Ticket,Quarrels,Jealousy				

STRESS LEVEL	LUCKY COLORS	JEWELERY	MOONS EFFECT	GRAHA EFFECT	DAILY DEITY
High	Purple/Blue/Rose	Emerald/Saphire	Educational	Family Graha	Mahakali

DAILY PUJA
Meditate, Control temper, Pray to Hanuman, Chant Hanuman Chalisa

DAILY PSALMS
6, 15, 33 ,42, 51, 60, 78, 105, 123

Thursday, October 27, 2016 — This is considered a NEUTRAL day for you — Planet: Uranus

ADVICE & DETAILS	MANTRA FOR TODAY
This is a day for expressing yourself in oral, visual or written form. Talk to others possibly in a group or at a gathering, paint or write a poem, book or article. This is also a day that if you are negative the use of alcohol or drugs will create danger for you, try to avoid it.	Jai Jai Shiva Shambo.(2) ...Mahadeva Shambo (2) 21 times 8

MONEY	LOVE	CAREER	FAMILY	TRAVEL	WEDDING	MOVE	BUSINESS	HEALTH	Lotto #'s	play 3 #s
Good	Good	Fair	Good	Good	Bad	Good	Bad	Fair	26,17,48,59,60,67,14	224

SHOPPING	GAMBLE	SEX	KEYWORD	KEYWORD						
Bad	Fair	is quiet	DIVINE	Spirituality,Religious,Astrology,Inner Conflicts,Religious ,Sleepiness,Advice given,Alcohol - drugs						

STRESS LEVEL	LUCKY COLORS	JEWELERY	MOONS EFFECT	GRAHA EFFECT	DAILY DEITY
Fair	Light Blue/Peach	Tiger's eye/Gold/Silver	Affectionate	God'S Graha	Shesnaag

DAILY PUJA: Chant Shiva Mantras, Take gifts to Ocean - Ganga Puja, Donate to Temple, Priests, etc.

DAILY PSALMS: 7, 16, 34 ,43, 52, 61, 79, 106, 124

Friday, October 28, 2016 — This is considered a POSITIVE day for you — Planet: Jupiter

ADVICE & DETAILS	MANTRA FOR TODAY
If you can, take short trips and enjoy high pleasure. There will be lots of moving today.	Om Hareem Nama Swaha..Shri Maha Laxmi Aye Namah swaha 12 times

MONEY	LOVE	CAREER	FAMILY	TRAVEL	WEDDING	MOVE	BUSINESS	HEALTH	Lotto #'s	play 3 #s
Excellent	Good	Excellent	Good	Good	Excellent	Good	Excellent	Excellent	61,57,60,2,62,58,23	511

SHOPPING	GAMBLE	SEX	KEYWORD	KEYWORD						
Excellent	Excellent	is excellent	MONEY	Business,Major Expense,Money - Profits,Income,Investments,Power,Promotion,Fame - TV						

STRESS LEVEL	LUCKY COLORS	JEWELERY	MOONS EFFECT	GRAHA EFFECT	DAILY DEITY
Low	Yellow/Silver	Diamonds/Gold/Pearls	Secretive	Money Graha	Mahalaxmi

DAILY PUJA: Decorate Land, Feed the poor, Donate milk /products to all, Feed holy guests,

DAILY PSALMS: 8, 17, 35 ,44, 53, 62, 80, 107, 125

Saturday, October 29, 2016 — This is considered a NEGATIVE day for you — Planet: Saturn

ADVICE & DETAILS	MANTRA FOR TODAY
Connect with the God within today so you can avoid the loneliness that can result from being boastful and criticizing others. Look at yourself first instead of trying to fix others.	Om Ganga mataye nama swaha Om Varuna Devta aye Pahimam 11 times

MONEY	LOVE	CAREER	FAMILY	TRAVEL	WEDDING	MOVE	BUSINESS	HEALTH	Lotto #'s	play 3 #s
Bad	Bad	Bad	Fair	Bad	Bad	Bad	Bad	Bad	64,48,72,72,54,72,73	920

SHOPPING	GAMBLE	SEX	KEYWORD	KEYWORD						
Bad	Bad	is very bad	KARMA	Destruction,Losses,Death,Sickness - cold,Legal matter,Abusive,Karmic debts,God - Karma						

STRESS LEVEL	LUCKY COLORS	JEWELERY	MOONS EFFECT	GRAHA EFFECT	DAILY DEITY
High	Gold/Brown//Green	Saphire/Hessonite	Ivestments	Evil Graha	Agnidev

DAILY PUJA: Remembrance of family members who died, worship of older people. gifts to grand parents

DAILY PSALMS: 9, 18, 36 ,45, 54, 63, 81, 108, 126

Sunday, October 30, 2016 — This is considered a NEUTRAL day for you — Planet: Sun

ADVICE & DETAILS	MANTRA FOR TODAY
Today, you may be home alone, you may feel a bit confined, but at the same time you will have a sense of independence and the realization of your capabilities. This day may be influenced by dealings with the government, courts or legal institutions.	Om Namo Bhagawate Mukhtanandaya, 108 times

MONEY	LOVE	CAREER	FAMILY	TRAVEL	WEDDING	MOVE	BUSINESS	HEALTH	Lotto #'s	play 3 #s
Fair	Bad	Good	Bad	Fair	Bad	Fair	Fair	Fair	35,73,59,50,20,32,15	750

SHOPPING	GAMBLE	SEX	KEYWORD	KEYWORD						
Fair	Fair	is fair	MIND	Independence,Loneliness,Meditative,Worry,Dominating,Illness - Cold,On Your Own,Commanding						

STRESS LEVEL	LUCKY COLORS	JEWELERY	MOONS EFFECT	GRAHA EFFECT	DAILY DEITY
High	White/Yellow/	Pearl/Quartz	Arrogance	Status Graha	Saraswaty

DAILY PUJA: Give Gifts to Priests, Invite holy ones to your home, Feed Swamis and Yogis, Do Shiva Puja.

DAILY PSALMS: 1, 10, 28 ,37, 46, 55, 73, 100, 118

Monday, October 31, 2016 — This is considered a POSITIVE day for you — Planet: Moon

ADVICE & DETAILS

There will be opportunity for romantic dates or encounters. You will make money today and get profits. There is a good chance of promotion.

MANTRA FOR TODAY

Kali Durge Namo Nama Om Durge aye nama swaha 108 times

MONEY	LOVE	CAREER	FAMILY	TRAVEL	WEDDING	MOVE	BUSINESS	HEALTH	Lotto #'s	play 3 #s
Good	Excellent	Good	Good	Excellent	Good	Good	Good	Good	6,67,21,72,37,72,36	969

SHOPPING	GAMBLE	SEX	KEYWORD	KEYWORD
Good	Good	is good	LOVE	Romance,Popularity,Visitors,Shopping,Food, Drinks,Co-operation,Friendships,Affection

STRESS LEVEL	LUCKY COLORS	JEWELERY	MOONS EFFECT	GRAHA EFFECT	DAILY DEITY
Low	Red/Yellow/Pink	Topaz/Diamonds	Conservative	Love Graha	Gauri

DAILY PUJA	DAILY PSALMS
Give Gifts to females andnMother, Serve milk Products, Worship Durga forms	2, 11, 29 ,38, 47, 56, 74, 101, 119

Tuesday, November 1, 2016 — This is considered a POSITIVE day for you — Planet: Jupiter

ADVICE & DETAILS

You will probably be taking short trips today or you will be moving. You will feel like moving and exercising and you should do it! There will be opportunity for illicit affairs, stay aware of how this affects you and others around you.

MANTRA FOR TODAY

Om Hareem Nama Swaha..Shri Maha Laxmi Aye Namah swaha 12 times

MONEY	LOVE	CAREER	FAMILY	TRAVEL	WEDDING	MOVE	BUSINESS	HEALTH	Lotto #'s	play 3 #s
Excellent	Good	Excellent	Good	Good	Excellent	Good	Excellent	Excellent	53,45,27,69,24,29,42	738

SHOPPING	GAMBLE	SEX	KEYWORD	KEYWORD
Excellent	Excellent	is excellent	MONEY	Business,Major Expense,Money - Profits,Income,Investments,Power,Promotion,Fame - TV

STRESS LEVEL	LUCKY COLORS	JEWELERY	MOONS EFFECT	GRAHA EFFECT	DAILY DEITY
Low	Yellow/Silver	Diamonds/Gold/Pearls	Secretive	Money Graha	Mahalaxmi

DAILY PUJA	DAILY PSALMS
Decorate Land, Feed the poor, Donate milk /products to all, Feed holy guests,	8, 17, 35 ,44, 53, 62, 80, 107, 125

Wednesday, November 2, 2016 — This is considered a NEGATIVE day for you — Planet: Saturn

ADVICE & DETAILS

Try to remember that when you criticize others, you are seeing in others what you think you are missing, be kind and concentrate on the positive characteristics of others not in what you perceive are negatives. The influence of this day will make you introspective and thoughts about your spiritual self will arise. Remember that loves heals all, try to have loving, healing thoughts as much as possible. Rest today if you can.

MANTRA FOR TODAY

Om Ganga mataye nama swaha Om Varuna Devta aye Pahimam 11 times

MONEY	LOVE	CAREER	FAMILY	TRAVEL	WEDDING	MOVE	BUSINESS	HEALTH	Lotto #'s	play 3 #s
Bad	Bad	Bad	Fair	Bad	Bad	Bad	Bad	Bad	55,1,20,36,8,53,70	991

SHOPPING	GAMBLE	SEX	KEYWORD	KEYWORD
Bad	Bad	is very bad	KARMA	Destruction,Losses,Death,Sickness - cold,Legal matter,Abusive,Karmic debts,God - Karma

STRESS LEVEL	LUCKY COLORS	JEWELERY	MOONS EFFECT	GRAHA EFFECT	DAILY DEITY
High	Gold/Brown//Green	Saphire/Hessonite	Ivestments	Evil Graha	Agnidev

DAILY PUJA	DAILY PSALMS
Remembrance of family members who died, worship of older people. gifts to grand parents	9, 18, 36 ,45, 54, 63, 81, 108, 126

Thursday, November 3, 2016 — This is considered a NEUTRAL day for you — Planet: Sun

ADVICE & DETAILS

The only obstacle to this very positive day is your speech. If you are careful and kind with your words expect money, romance and positive outlook for partnerships in any area.

MANTRA FOR TODAY

Om Namo Bhagawate Mukhtanandaya, 108 times

MONEY	LOVE	CAREER	FAMILY	TRAVEL	WEDDING	MOVE	BUSINESS	HEALTH	Lotto #'s	play 3 #s
Fair	Bad	Good	Bad	Fair	Bad	Fair	Fair	Fair	8,26,48,18,19,62,25	687

SHOPPING	GAMBLE	SEX	KEYWORD	KEYWORD
Fair	Fair	is fair	MIND	Independence,Loneliness,Meditative,Worry,Dominating,Illness - Cold,On Your Own,Commanding

STRESS LEVEL	LUCKY COLORS	JEWELERY	MOONS EFFECT	GRAHA EFFECT	DAILY DEITY
High	White/Yellow/	Pearl/Quartz	Arrogance	Status Graha	Saraswaty

DAILY PUJA	DAILY PSALMS
Give Gifts to Priests, Invite holy ones to your home, Feed Swamis and Yogis, Do Shiva Puja.	1, 10, 28 ,37, 46, 55, 73, 100, 118

Friday, November 4, 2016 — This is considered a POSITIVE day for you — Planet: Moon

ADVICE & DETAILS	MANTRA FOR TODAY
Every word your lips utter today have great power and they must be used with love and positive intention to avoid conflict. You will have the opportunity to serve and cooperate with others today, use it. Listen to music or express your feelings through music to get blessings today.	Kali Durge Namo Nama Om Durge aye nama swaha 108 times

MONEY	LOVE	CAREER	FAMILY	TRAVEL	WEDDING	MOVE	BUSINESS	HEALTH	Lotto #'s	play 3 #s
Good	Excellent	Good	Good	Excellent	Good	Good	Good	Good	59,21,33,21,72,25,15	821

SHOPPING	GAMBLE	SEX	KEYWORD	KEYWORD						
Good	Good	is good	LOVE	Romance,Popularity,Visitors,Shopping,Food, Drinks,Co-operation,Friendships,Affection						

STRESS LEVEL	LUCKY COLORS	JEWELERY	MOONS EFFECT	GRAHA EFFECT	DAILY DEITY
Low	Red/Yellow/Pink	Topaz/Diamonds	Conservative	Love Graha	Gauri

DAILY PUJA	DAILY PSALMS
Give Gifts to females andnMother, Serve milk Products, Worship Durga forms	2, 11, 29 ,38, 47, 56, 74, 101, 119

Saturday, November 5, 2016 — This is considered a POSITIVE day for you — Planet: Mercury

ADVICE & DETAILS	MANTRA FOR TODAY
You may spend your day at home alone watching TV or may instead opt for luxurious and pleasurable activities that may bring you around fame or famous people. You will be influenced by money, so you will worry about it, make it or spend it.	Om hareem Kleem Hreem Aem Saraswataye namaha 21 times

MONEY	LOVE	CAREER	FAMILY	TRAVEL	WEDDING	MOVE	BUSINESS	HEALTH	Lotto #'s	play 3 #s
Good	Fair	Good	Good	Excellent	Good	Good	Good	Excellent	30,50,35,60,14,70,64	820

SHOPPING	GAMBLE	SEX	KEYWORD	KEYWORD						
Good	Good	is great	SOCIAL	Children,Education,Astrology,Bargains,Social Functions,Childishness,Groups - Parties,Teacher						

STRESS LEVEL	LUCKY COLORS	JEWELERY	MOONS EFFECT	GRAHA EFFECT	DAILY DEITY
Low	Green/Sky Blue/	Diamonds/Silver	Enthusiastic	Social Graha	Vishnu

DAILY PUJA	DAILY PSALMS
Wash the feet of Children, Do Satnarayan Pooja, Read & chant Geeta	3, 12, 30 ,39, 48, 57, 75, 102, 120

Sunday, November 6, 2016 — This is considered a NEGATIVE day for you — Planet: Pluto

ADVICE & DETAILS	MANTRA FOR TODAY
This will be a positive day if you can control your tongue and do not criticize anyone, particularly your loved ones and especially your partner. The influences are love and marriage. This is the opportunity to create a special surprise meal for your partner and share it with love in a romantic setting with soothing music as background.	Om Jai Viganeshwaraya.. Lambodaraya Namo Namaha 21 times

MONEY	LOVE	CAREER	FAMILY	TRAVEL	WEDDING	MOVE	BUSINESS	HEALTH	Lotto #'s	play 3 #s
Bad	Fair	Bad	Fair	Bad	Good	Bad	Bad	Bad	59,41,65,68,18,58,43	950

SHOPPING	GAMBLE	SEX	KEYWORD	KEYWORD						
Bad	Bad	is tough	CAREER	Career,Hard Work,Co-workers,Low Payment,Job Problems,High Temper,Low Pay,Laziness						

STRESS LEVEL	LUCKY COLORS	JEWELERY	MOONS EFFECT	GRAHA EFFECT	DAILY DEITY
High	Dark Blue/ Purple/	Amethyst/Gold	Emotional	Job Graha	Lingam

DAILY PUJA	DAILY PSALMS
Worship Ganesh, Give gifts to father, and co -workers, Plant gardens, farms	4, 13, 31 ,40, 49, 58, 76, 103, 121

Monday, November 7, 2016 — This is considered a POSITIVE day for you — Planet: Venus

ADVICE & DETAILS	MANTRA FOR TODAY
Show your affection, cooperate with others and listen to music today; these activities will help you with the paymente of some karmic debts that may become overdue this day.	Om Graam Greem Graum Sa Gurave namah swaha 21 times

MONEY	LOVE	CAREER	FAMILY	TRAVEL	WEDDING	MOVE	BUSINESS	HEALTH	Lotto #'s	play 3 #s
Bad	Excellent	Fair	Good	Excellent	Good	Excellent	Good	Excellent	2,3,32,43,54,1,56	590

SHOPPING	GAMBLE	SEX	KEYWORD	KEYWORD						
Good	Good	is good	CHANGE	Sexuality,Travel,Change,Distant, far,Travel delays,Deception,Excercise,Illicit Affairs						

STRESS LEVEL	LUCKY COLORS	JEWELERY	MOONS EFFECT	GRAHA EFFECT	DAILY DEITY
Fair	Tan/Green/ Beige	Pearl/Silver/quartz	Courageous	Travel Graha	Nataraja

DAILY PUJA	DAILY PSALMS
Artistic gifts, Pray to Krishna, Do good deeds, do Spiritual trips	5, 14, 32 ,41, 50, 59, 77, 104, 122

Tuesday, November 8, 2016 — This is considered a NEGATIVE day for you — Planet: Mars

ADVICE & DETAILS

You must watch out for misleading statements from others. There will be many changes today. Your sexual energy will be high. You will be thinking a great deal today about very deep and profound subjects.

MANTRA FOR TODAY

Om Mana Swasti Shanti Kuru kuru Swaha Shivoham Shivoham 27 times

MONEY	LOVE	CAREER	FAMILY	TRAVEL	WEDDING	MOVE	BUSINESS	HEALTH	Lotto #'s	play 3 #s
Bad	Bad	Bad	Bad	Bad	Bad	Bad	Fair	Bad	37,29,65,52,1,7,71	391

SHOPPING	GAMBLE	SEX	KEYWORD	KEYWORD				
Fair	Bad	is frustrating	POWER	Responsibilty,Disagreement,Family,Back Pain,Family Conflicts,Traffic Ticket,Quarrels,Jealousy				

STRESS LEVEL	LUCKY COLORS	JEWELERY	MOONS EFFECT	GRAHA EFFECT	DAILY DEITY
High	Purple/Blue/Rose	Emerald/Saphire	Educational	Family Graha	Mahakali

DAILY PUJA	DAILY PSALMS
Meditate, Control temper, Pray to Hanuman, Chant Hanuman Chalisa	6, 15, 33 ,42, 51, 60, 78, 105, 123

Wednesday, November 9, 2016 — This is considered a NEUTRAL day for you — Planet: Uranus

ADVICE & DETAILS

You will feel like watching television and would probably prefer the company of children today. You may be acting somewhat immaturely today so be careful of choices and words that may have long term consequences. Today will be a good day for creativity related to writing and publishing.

MANTRA FOR TODAY

Jai Jai Shiva Shambo.(2) ...Mahadeva Shambo (2) 21 times 8

MONEY	LOVE	CAREER	FAMILY	TRAVEL	WEDDING	MOVE	BUSINESS	HEALTH	Lotto #'s	play 3 #s
Good	Good	Fair	Good	Good	Bad	Good	Bad	Fair	19,42,24,15,36,33,65	991

SHOPPING	GAMBLE	SEX	KEYWORD	KEYWORD				
Bad	Fair	is quiet	DIVINE	Spirituality,Religious,Astrology,Inner Conflicts,Religious ,Sleepiness,Advice given,Alcohol - drugs				

STRESS LEVEL	LUCKY COLORS	JEWELERY	MOONS EFFECT	GRAHA EFFECT	DAILY DEITY
Fair	Light Blue/Peach	Tiger's eye/Gold/Silver	Affectionate	God'S Graha	Shesnaag

DAILY PUJA	DAILY PSALMS
Chant Shiva Mantras, Take gifts to Ocean - Ganga Puja, Donate to Temple, Priests, etc.	7, 16, 34 ,43, 52, 61, 79, 106, 124

Thursday, November 10, 2016 — This is considered a POSITIVE day for you — Planet: Jupiter

ADVICE & DETAILS

You will probably be taking short trips today or you will be moving. You will feel like moving and exercising and you should do it! There will be opportunity for illicit affairs, stay aware of how this affects you and others around you.

MANTRA FOR TODAY

Om Hareem Nama Swaha..Shri Maha Laxmi Aye Namah swaha 12 times

MONEY	LOVE	CAREER	FAMILY	TRAVEL	WEDDING	MOVE	BUSINESS	HEALTH	Lotto #'s	play 3 #s
Excellent	Good	Excellent	Good	Good	Excellent	Good	Excellent	Excellent	67,60,30,54,51,61,61	932

SHOPPING	GAMBLE	SEX	KEYWORD	KEYWORD				
Excellent	Excellent	is excellent	MONEY	Business,Major Expense,Money - Profits,Income,Investments,Power,Promotion,Fame - TV				

STRESS LEVEL	LUCKY COLORS	JEWELERY	MOONS EFFECT	GRAHA EFFECT	DAILY DEITY
Low	Yellow/Silver	Diamonds/Gold/Pearls	Secretive	Money Graha	Mahalaxmi

DAILY PUJA	DAILY PSALMS
Decorate Land, Feed the poor, Donate milk /products to all, Feed holy guests,	8, 17, 35 ,44, 53, 62, 80, 107, 125

Friday, November 11, 2016 — This is considered a NEGATIVE day for you — Planet: Saturn

ADVICE & DETAILS

Try to remember that when you criticize others, you are seeing in others what you think you are missing, be kind and concentrate on the positive characteristics of others not in what you perceive are negatives. The influence of this day will make you introspective and thoughts about your spiritual self will arise. Remember that loves heals all, try to have loving, healing thoughts as much as possible. Rest today if you can.

MANTRA FOR TODAY

Om Ganga mataye nama swaha Om Varuna Devta aye Pahimam 11 times

MONEY	LOVE	CAREER	FAMILY	TRAVEL	WEDDING	MOVE	BUSINESS	HEALTH	Lotto #'s	play 3 #s
Bad	Bad	Bad	Fair	Bad	Bad	Bad	Bad	Bad	24,41,7,58,46,73,17	143

SHOPPING	GAMBLE	SEX	KEYWORD	KEYWORD				
Bad	Bad	is very bad	KARMA	Destruction,Losses,Death,Sickness - cold,Legal matter,Abusive,Karmic debts,God - Karma				

STRESS LEVEL	LUCKY COLORS	JEWELERY	MOONS EFFECT	GRAHA EFFECT	DAILY DEITY
High	Gold/Brown//Green	Saphire/Hessonite	Ivestments	Evil Graha	Agnidev

DAILY PUJA	DAILY PSALMS
Remembrance of family members who died, worship of older people. gifts to grand parents	9, 18, 36 ,45, 54, 63, 81, 108, 126

Saturday, November 12, 2016 — This is considered a NEUTRAL day for you — Planet: Sun

ADVICE & DETAILS

The only obstacle to this very positive day is your speech. If you are careful and kind with your words expect money, romance and positive outlook for partnerships in any area.

MANTRA FOR TODAY

Om Namo Bhagawate Mukhtanandaya, 108 times

MONEY	LOVE	CAREER	FAMILY	TRAVEL	WEDDING	MOVE	BUSINESS	HEALTH	Lotto #'s	play 3 #s
Fair	Bad	Good	Bad	Fair	Bad	Fair	Fair	Fair	11,3,30,6,20,14,17	48

SHOPPING	GAMBLE	SEX	KEYWORD	KEYWORD						
Fair	Fair	is fair	MIND	Independence,Loneliness,Meditative,Worry,Dominating,Illness - Cold,On Your Own,Commanding						

STRESS LEVEL	LUCKY COLORS	JEWELERY	MOONS EFFECT	GRAHA EFFECT	DAILY DEITY
High	White/Yellow/	Pearl/Quartz	Arrogance	Status Graha	Saraswaty

DAILY PUJA	DAILY PSALMS
Give Gifts to Priests, Invite holy ones to your home, Feed Swamis and Yogis, Do Shiva Puja.	1, 10, 28 ,37, 46, 55, 73, 100, 118

Sunday, November 13, 2016 — This is considered a POSITIVE day for you — Planet: Moon

ADVICE & DETAILS

Every word your lips utter today have great power and they must be used with love and positive intention to avoid conflict. You will have the opportunity to serve and cooperate with others today, use it. Listen to music or express your feelings through music to get blessings today.

MANTRA FOR TODAY

Kali Durge Namo Nama Om Durge aye nama swaha 108 times

MONEY	LOVE	CAREER	FAMILY	TRAVEL	WEDDING	MOVE	BUSINESS	HEALTH	Lotto #'s	play 3 #s
Good	Excellent	Good	Good	Excellent	Good	Good	Good	Good	19,2,58,24,18,15,29	94

SHOPPING	GAMBLE	SEX	KEYWORD	KEYWORD						
Good	Good	is good	LOVE	Romance,Popularity,Visitors,Shopping,Food, Drinks,Co-operation,Friendships,Affection						

STRESS LEVEL	LUCKY COLORS	JEWELERY	MOONS EFFECT	GRAHA EFFECT	DAILY DEITY
Low	Red/Yellow/Pink	Topaz/Diamonds	Conservative	Love Graha	Gauri

DAILY PUJA	DAILY PSALMS
Give Gifts to females andnMother, Serve milk Products, Worship Durga forms	2, 11, 29 ,38, 47, 56, 74, 101, 119

Monday, November 14, 2016 — This is considered a POSITIVE day for you — Planet: Mercury

ADVICE & DETAILS

You may spend your day at home alone watching TV or may instead opt for luxurious and pleasurable activities that may bring you around fame or famous people. You will be influenced by money, so you will worry about it, make it or spend it.

MANTRA FOR TODAY

Om hareem Kleem Hreem Aem Saraswataye namaha 21 times

MONEY	LOVE	CAREER	FAMILY	TRAVEL	WEDDING	MOVE	BUSINESS	HEALTH	Lotto #'s	play 3 #s
Good	Fair	Good	Good	Excellent	Good	Good	Good	Excellent	6,36,63,33,30,34,32	541

SHOPPING	GAMBLE	SEX	KEYWORD	KEYWORD						
Good	Good	is great	SOCIAL	Children,Education,Astrology,Bargains,Social Functions,Childishness,Groups - Parties,Teacher						

STRESS LEVEL	LUCKY COLORS	JEWELERY	MOONS EFFECT	GRAHA EFFECT	DAILY DEITY
Low	Green/Sky Blue/	Diamonds/Silver	Enthusiastic	Social Graha	Vishnu

DAILY PUJA	DAILY PSALMS
Wash the feet of Children, Do Satnarayan Pooja, Read & chant Geeta	3, 12, 30 ,39, 48, 57, 75, 102, 120

Tuesday, November 15, 2016 — This is considered a NEGATIVE day for you — Planet: Pluto

ADVICE & DETAILS

This will be a positive day if you can control your tongue and do not criticize anyone, particularly your loved ones and especially your partner. The influences are love and marriage. This is the opportunity to create a special surprise meal for your partner and share it with love in a romantic setting with soothing music as background.

MANTRA FOR TODAY

Om Jai Viganeshwaraya.. Lambodaraya Namo Namaha 21 times

MONEY	LOVE	CAREER	FAMILY	TRAVEL	WEDDING	MOVE	BUSINESS	HEALTH	Lotto #'s	play 3 #s
Bad	Fair	Bad	Fair	Bad	Good	Bad	Bad	Bad	7,68,49,8,16,9,1	364

SHOPPING	GAMBLE	SEX	KEYWORD	KEYWORD						
Bad	Bad	is tough	CAREER	Career,Hard Work,Co-workers,Low Payment,Job Problems,High Temper,Low Pay,Laziness						

STRESS LEVEL	LUCKY COLORS	JEWELERY	MOONS EFFECT	GRAHA EFFECT	DAILY DEITY
High	Dark Blue/ Purple/	Amethyst/Gold	Emotional	Job Graha	Lingam

DAILY PUJA	DAILY PSALMS
Worship Ganesh, Give gifts to father, and co -workers, Plant gardens, farms	4, 13, 31 ,40, 49, 58, 76, 103, 121

Wednesday, November 16, 2016 | This is considered a POSITIVE day for you | Planet: Venus

ADVICE & DETAILS	MANTRA FOR TODAY
Show your affection, cooperate with others and listen to music today; these activities will help you with the paymente of some karmic debts that may become overdue this day.	Om Graam Greem Graum Sa Gurave namah swaha 21 times

MONEY	LOVE	CAREER	FAMILY	TRAVEL	WEDDING	MOVE	BUSINESS	HEALTH	Lotto #'s	play 3 #s
Bad	Excellent	Fair	Good	Excellent	Good	Excellent	Good	Excellent	74,20,63,10,9,32,44	724

SHOPPING	GAMBLE	SEX	KEYWORD	KEYWORD					
Good	Good	is good	CHANGE	Sexuality,Travel,Change,Distant, far,Travel delays,Deception,Excercise,Illicit Affairs					

STRESS LEVEL	LUCKY COLORS	JEWELERY	MOONS EFFECT	GRAHA EFFECT	DAILY DEITY
Fair	Tan/Green/ Beige	Pearl/Silver/quartz	Courageous	Travel Graha	Nataraja

DAILY PUJA	DAILY PSALMS
Artistic gifts, Pray to Krishna, Do good deeds, do Spiritual trips	5, 14, 32 ,41, 50, 59, 77, 104, 122

Thursday, November 17, 2016 | This is considered a NEGATIVE day for you | Planet: Mars

ADVICE & DETAILS	MANTRA FOR TODAY
You must watch out for misleading statements from others. There will be many changes today. Your sexual energy will be high. You will be thinking a great deal today about very deep and profound subjects.	Om Mana Swasti Shanti Kuru kuru Swaha Shivoham Shivoham 27 times

MONEY	LOVE	CAREER	FAMILY	TRAVEL	WEDDING	MOVE	BUSINESS	HEALTH	Lotto #'s	play 3 #s
Bad	Bad	Bad	Bad	Bad	Bad	Bad	Fair	Bad	54,15,71,25,38,64,54	669

SHOPPING	GAMBLE	SEX	KEYWORD	KEYWORD					
Fair	Bad	is frustrating	POWER	Responsibilty,Disagreement,Family, Back Pain,Family Conflicts,Traffic Ticket,Quarrels,Jealousy					

STRESS LEVEL	LUCKY COLORS	JEWELERY	MOONS EFFECT	GRAHA EFFECT	DAILY DEITY
High	Purple/Blue/Rose	Emerald/Saphire	Educational	Family Graha	Mahakali

DAILY PUJA	DAILY PSALMS
Meditate, Control temper, Pray to Hanuman, Chant Hanuman Chalisa	6, 15, 33 ,42, 51, 60, 78, 105, 123

Friday, November 18, 2016 | This is considered a NEUTRAL day for you | Planet: Uranus

ADVICE & DETAILS	MANTRA FOR TODAY
You will feel like watching television and would probably prefer the company of children today. You may be acting somewhat immaturely today so be careful of choices and words that may have long term consequences. Today will be a good day for creativity related to writing and publishing.	Jai Jai Shiva Shambo.(2) ...Mahadeva Shambo (2) 21 times 8

MONEY	LOVE	CAREER	FAMILY	TRAVEL	WEDDING	MOVE	BUSINESS	HEALTH	Lotto #'s	play 3 #s
Good	Good	Fair	Good	Good	Bad	Good	Bad	Fair	74,50,14,6,1,5,32	509

SHOPPING	GAMBLE	SEX	KEYWORD	KEYWORD					
Bad	Fair	is quiet	DIVINE	Spirituality,Religious,Astrology,Inner Conflicts,Religious ,Sleepiness,Advice given,Alcohol - drugs					

STRESS LEVEL	LUCKY COLORS	JEWELERY	MOONS EFFECT	GRAHA EFFECT	DAILY DEITY
Fair	Light Blue/Peach	Tiger's eye/Gold/Silver	Affectionate	God'S Graha	Shesnaag

DAILY PUJA	DAILY PSALMS
Chant Shiva Mantras, Take gifts to Ocean - Ganga Puja, Donate to Temple, Priests, etc.	7, 16, 34 ,43, 52, 61, 79, 106, 124

Saturday, November 19, 2016 | This is considered a POSITIVE day for you | Planet: Jupiter

ADVICE & DETAILS	MANTRA FOR TODAY
You will probably be taking short trips today or you will be moving. You will feel like moving and exercising and you should do it! There will be opportunity for illicit affairs, stay aware of how this affects you and others around you.	Om Hareem Nama Swaha..Shri Maha Laxmi Aye Namah swaha 12 times

MONEY	LOVE	CAREER	FAMILY	TRAVEL	WEDDING	MOVE	BUSINESS	HEALTH	Lotto #'s	play 3 #s
Excellent	Good	Excellent	Good	Good	Excellent	Good	Excellent	Excellent	54,11,53,55,65,75,23	796

SHOPPING	GAMBLE	SEX	KEYWORD	KEYWORD					
Excellent	Excellent	is excellent	MONEY	Business,Major Expense,Money - Profits,Income,Investments,Power,Promotion,Fame - TV					

STRESS LEVEL	LUCKY COLORS	JEWELERY	MOONS EFFECT	GRAHA EFFECT	DAILY DEITY
Low	Yellow/Silver	Diamonds/Gold/Pearls	Secretive	Money Graha	Mahalaxmi

DAILY PUJA	DAILY PSALMS
Decorate Land, Feed the poor, Donate milk /products to all, Feed holy guests,	8, 17, 35 ,44, 53, 62, 80, 107, 125

Sunday, November 20, 2016 — This is considered a NEGATIVE day for you — Planet: Saturn

ADVICE & DETAILS	MANTRA FOR TODAY
Try to remember that when you criticize others, you are seeing in others what you think you are missing, be kind and concentrate on the positive characteristics of others not in what you perceive are negatives. The influence of this day will make you introspective and thoughts about your spiritual self will arise. Remember that loves heals all, try to have loving, healing thoughts as much as possible. Rest today if you can.	Om Ganga mataye nama swaha Om Varuna Devta aye Pahimam 11 times

MONEY	LOVE	CAREER	FAMILY	TRAVEL	WEDDING	MOVE	BUSINESS	HEALTH	Lotto #'s	play 3 #s
Bad	Bad	Bad	Fair	Bad	Bad	Bad	Bad	Bad	72,73,14,12,74,70,73	50

SHOPPING	GAMBLE	SEX	KEYWORD	KEYWORD						
Bad	Bad	is very bad	KARMA	Destruction,Losses,Death,Sickness - cold,Legal matter,Abusive,Karmic debts,God - Karma						

STRESS LEVEL	LUCKY COLORS	JEWELERY	MOONS EFFECT	GRAHA EFFECT	DAILY DEITY
High	Gold/Brown//Green	Saphire/Hessonite	Ivestments	Evil Graha	Agnidev

DAILY PUJA	DAILY PSALMS
Remembrance of family members who died, worship of older people. gifts to grand parents	9, 18, 36 ,45, 54, 63, 81, 108, 126

Monday, November 21, 2016 — This is considered a NEUTRAL day for you — Planet: Sun

ADVICE & DETAILS	MANTRA FOR TODAY
The only obstacle to this very positive day is your speech. If you are careful and kind with your words expect money, romance and positive outlook for partnerships in any area.	Om Namo Bhagawate Mukhtanandaya, 108 times

MONEY	LOVE	CAREER	FAMILY	TRAVEL	WEDDING	MOVE	BUSINESS	HEALTH	Lotto #'s	play 3 #s
Fair	Bad	Good	Bad	Fair	Bad	Fair	Fair	Fair	8,40,52,6,12,7,15	902

SHOPPING	GAMBLE	SEX	KEYWORD	KEYWORD						
Fair	Fair	is fair	MIND	Independence,Loneliness,Meditative,Worry,Dominating,Illness - Cold,On Your Own,Commanding						

STRESS LEVEL	LUCKY COLORS	JEWELERY	MOONS EFFECT	GRAHA EFFECT	DAILY DEITY
High	White/Yellow/	Pearl/Quartz	Arrogance	Status Graha	Saraswaty

DAILY PUJA	DAILY PSALMS
Give Gifts to Priests, Invite holy ones to your home, Feed Swamis and Yogis, Do Shiva Puja.	1, 10, 28 ,37, 46, 55, 73, 100, 118

Tuesday, November 22, 2016 — This is considered a POSITIVE day for you — Planet: Moon

ADVICE & DETAILS	MANTRA FOR TODAY
Every word your lips utter today have great power and they must be used with love and positive intention to avoid conflict. You will have the opportunity to serve and cooperate with others today, use it. Listen to music or express your feelings through music to get blessings today.	Kali Durge Namo Nama Om Durge aye nama swaha 108 times

MONEY	LOVE	CAREER	FAMILY	TRAVEL	WEDDING	MOVE	BUSINESS	HEALTH	Lotto #'s	play 3 #s
Good	Excellent	Good	Good	Excellent	Good	Good	Good	Good	41,14,20,52,3,39,56	403

SHOPPING	GAMBLE	SEX	KEYWORD	KEYWORD						
Good	Good	is good	LOVE	Romance,Popularity,Visitors,Shopping,Food, Drinks,Co-operation,Friendships,Affection						

STRESS LEVEL	LUCKY COLORS	JEWELERY	MOONS EFFECT	GRAHA EFFECT	DAILY DEITY
Low	Red/Yellow/Pink	Topaz/Diamonds	Conservative	Love Graha	Gauri

DAILY PUJA	DAILY PSALMS
Give Gifts to females andnMother, Serve milk Products, Worship Durga forms	2, 11, 29 ,38, 47, 56, 74, 101, 119

Wednesday, November 23, 2016 — This is considered a POSITIVE day for you — Planet: Mercury

ADVICE & DETAILS	MANTRA FOR TODAY
You may spend your day at home alone watching TV or may instead opt for luxurious and pleasurable activities that may bring you around fame or famous people. You will be influenced by money, so you will worry about it, make it or spend it.	Om hareem Kleem Hreem Aem Saraswataye namaha 21 times

MONEY	LOVE	CAREER	FAMILY	TRAVEL	WEDDING	MOVE	BUSINESS	HEALTH	Lotto #'s	play 3 #s
Good	Fair	Good	Good	Excellent	Good	Good	Good	Excellent	72,21,51,8,54,1,64	260

SHOPPING	GAMBLE	SEX	KEYWORD	KEYWORD						
Good	Good	is great	SOCIAL	Children,Education,Astrology,Bargains,Social Functions,Childishness,Groups - Parties,Teacher						

STRESS LEVEL	LUCKY COLORS	JEWELERY	MOONS EFFECT	GRAHA EFFECT	DAILY DEITY
Low	Green/Sky Blue/	Diamonds/Silver	Enthusiastic	Social Graha	Vishnu

DAILY PUJA	DAILY PSALMS
Wash the feet of Children, Do Satnarayan Pooja, Read & chant Geeta	3, 12, 30 ,39, 48, 57, 75, 102, 120

Thursday, November 24, 2016 — This is considered a NEGATIVE day for you — Planet: Pluto

ADVICE & DETAILS

This will be a positive day if you can control your tongue and do not criticize anyone, particularly your loved ones and especially your partner. The influences are love and marriage. This is the opportunity to create a special surprise meal for your partner and share it with love in a romantic setting with soothing music as background.

MANTRA FOR TODAY

Om Jai Viganeshwaraya.. Lambodaraya Namo Namaha 21 times

MONEY	LOVE	CAREER	FAMILY	TRAVEL	WEDDING	MOVE	BUSINESS	HEALTH	Lotto #'s	play 3 #s
Bad	Fair	Bad	Fair	Bad	Good	Bad	Bad	Bad	69,17,43,15,59,59,75	239

SHOPPING	GAMBLE	SEX	KEYWORD	KEYWORD				
Bad	Bad	is tough	CAREER	Career,Hard Work,Co-workers,Low Payment,Job Problems,High Temper,Low Pay,Laziness				

STRESS LEVEL	LUCKY COLORS	JEWELERY	MOONS EFFECT	GRAHA EFFECT	DAILY DEITY
High	Dark Blue/ Purple/	Amethyst/Gold	Emotional	Job Graha	Lingam

DAILY PUJA
Worship Ganesh, Give gifts to father, and co -workers, Plant gardens, farms

DAILY PSALMS
4, 13, 31 ,40, 49, 58, 76, 103, 121

Friday, November 25, 2016 — This is considered a POSITIVE day for you — Planet: Venus

ADVICE & DETAILS

Show your affection, cooperate with others and listen to music today; these activities will help you with the paymente of some karmic debts that may become overdue this day.

MANTRA FOR TODAY

Om Graam Greem Graum Sa Gurave namah swaha 21 times

MONEY	LOVE	CAREER	FAMILY	TRAVEL	WEDDING	MOVE	BUSINESS	HEALTH	Lotto #'s	play 3 #s
Bad	Excellent	Fair	Good	Excellent	Good	Excellent	Good	Excellent	40,12,66,63,58,50,52	324

SHOPPING	GAMBLE	SEX	KEYWORD	KEYWORD				
Good	Good	is good	CHANGE	Sexuality,Travel,Change,Distant, far,Travel delays,Deception,Excercise,Illicit Affairs				

STRESS LEVEL	LUCKY COLORS	JEWELERY	MOONS EFFECT	GRAHA EFFECT	DAILY DEITY
Fair	Tan/Green/ Beige	Pearl/Silver/quartz	Courageous	Travel Graha	Nataraja

DAILY PUJA
Artistic gifts, Pray to Krishna, Do good deeds, do Spiritual trips

DAILY PSALMS
5, 14, 32 ,41, 50, 59, 77, 104, 122

Saturday, November 26, 2016 — This is considered a NEGATIVE day for you — Planet: Mars

ADVICE & DETAILS

You must watch out for misleading statements from others. There will be many changes today. Your sexual energy will be high. You will be thinking a great deal today about very deep and profound subjects.

MANTRA FOR TODAY

Om Mana Swasti Shanti Kuru kuru Swaha Shivoham Shivoham 27 times

MONEY	LOVE	CAREER	FAMILY	TRAVEL	WEDDING	MOVE	BUSINESS	HEALTH	Lotto #'s	play 3 #s
Bad	Bad	Bad	Bad	Bad	Bad	Bad	Fair	Bad	26,39,34,74,33,22,55	680

SHOPPING	GAMBLE	SEX	KEYWORD	KEYWORD				
Fair	Bad	is frustrating	POWER	Responsibilty,Disagreement,Family, Back Pain,Family Conflicts,Traffic Ticket,Quarrels,Jealousy				

STRESS LEVEL	LUCKY COLORS	JEWELERY	MOONS EFFECT	GRAHA EFFECT	DAILY DEITY
High	Purple/Blue/Rose	Emerald/Saphire	Educational	Family Graha	Mahakali

DAILY PUJA
Meditate, Control temper, Pray to Hanuman, Chant Hanuman Chalisa

DAILY PSALMS
6, 15, 33 ,42, 51, 60, 78, 105, 123

Sunday, November 27, 2016 — This is considered a NEUTRAL day for you — Planet: Uranus

ADVICE & DETAILS

You will feel like watching television and would probably prefer the company of children today. You may be acting somewhat immaturely today so be careful of choices and words that may have long term consequences. Today will be a good day for creativity related to writing and publishing.

MANTRA FOR TODAY

Jai Jai Shiva Shambo.(2) ...Mahadeva Shambo (2) 21 times 8

MONEY	LOVE	CAREER	FAMILY	TRAVEL	WEDDING	MOVE	BUSINESS	HEALTH	Lotto #'s	play 3 #s
Good	Good	Fair	Good	Good	Bad	Good	Bad	Fair	70,46,34,51,17,70,11	778

SHOPPING	GAMBLE	SEX	KEYWORD	KEYWORD				
Bad	Fair	is quiet	DIVINE	Spirituality,Religious,Astrology,Inner Conflicts,Religious ,Sleepiness,Advice given,Alcohol - drugs				

STRESS LEVEL	LUCKY COLORS	JEWELERY	MOONS EFFECT	GRAHA EFFECT	DAILY DEITY
Fair	Light Blue/Peach	Tiger's eye/Gold/Silver	Affectionate	God'S Graha	Shesnaag

DAILY PUJA
Chant Shiva Mantras, Take gifts to Ocean - Ganga Puja, Donate to Temple, Priests, etc.

DAILY PSALMS
7, 16, 34 ,43, 52, 61, 79, 106, 124

Monday, November 28, 2016 — This is considered a POSITIVE day for you — Planet: Jupiter

ADVICE & DETAILS

You will probably be taking short trips today or you will be moving. You will feel like moving and exercising and you should do it! There will be opportunity for illicit affairs, stay aware of how this affects you and others around you.

MANTRA FOR TODAY

Om Hareem Nama Swaha..Shri Maha Laxmi Aye Namah swaha 12 times

MONEY	LOVE	CAREER	FAMILY	TRAVEL	WEDDING	MOVE	BUSINESS	HEALTH	Lotto #'s	play 3 #s
Excellent	Good	Excellent	Good	Good	Excellent	Good	Excellent	Excellent	74,35,24,34,35,10,24	473

SHOPPING	GAMBLE	SEX	KEYWORD	KEYWORD				
Excellent	Excellent	is excellent	MONEY	Business,Major Expense,Money - Profits,Income,Investments,Power,Promotion,Fame - TV				

STRESS LEVEL	LUCKY COLORS	JEWELERY	MOONS EFFECT	GRAHA EFFECT	DAILY DEITY
Low	Yellow/Silver	Diamonds/Gold/Pearls	Secretive	Money Graha	Mahalaxmi

DAILY PUJA	DAILY PSALMS
Decorate Land, Feed the poor, Donate milk /products to all, Feed holy guests,	8, 17, 35 ,44, 53, 62, 80, 107, 125

Tuesday, November 29, 2016 — This is considered a NEGATIVE day for you — Planet: Saturn

ADVICE & DETAILS

Try to remember that when you criticize others, you are seeing in others what you think you are missing, be kind and concentrate on the positive characteristics of others not in what you perceive are negatives. The influence of this day will make you introspective and thoughts about your spiritual self will arise. Remember that loves heals all, try to have loving, healing thoughts as much as possible. Rest today if you can.

MANTRA FOR TODAY

Om Ganga mataye nama swaha Om Varuna Devta aye Pahimam 11 times

MONEY	LOVE	CAREER	FAMILY	TRAVEL	WEDDING	MOVE	BUSINESS	HEALTH	Lotto #'s	play 3 #s
Bad	Bad	Bad	Fair	Bad	Bad	Bad	Bad	Bad	69,9,61,33,35,59,25	242

SHOPPING	GAMBLE	SEX	KEYWORD	KEYWORD				
Bad	Bad	is very bad	KARMA	Destruction,Losses,Death,Sickness - cold,Legal matter,Abusive,Karmic debts,God - Karma				

STRESS LEVEL	LUCKY COLORS	JEWELERY	MOONS EFFECT	GRAHA EFFECT	DAILY DEITY
High	Gold/Brown//Green	Saphire/Hessonite	Ivestments	Evil Graha	Agnidev

DAILY PUJA	DAILY PSALMS
Remembrance of family members who died, worship of older people. gifts to grand parents	9, 18, 36 ,45, 54, 63, 81, 108, 126

Wednesday, November 30, 2016 — This is considered a NEUTRAL day for you — Planet: Sun

ADVICE & DETAILS

The only obstacle to this very positive day is your speech. If you are careful and kind with your words expect money, romance and positive outlook for partnerships in any area.

MANTRA FOR TODAY

Om Namo Bhagawate Mukhtanandaya, 108 times

MONEY	LOVE	CAREER	FAMILY	TRAVEL	WEDDING	MOVE	BUSINESS	HEALTH	Lotto #'s	play 3 #s
Fair	Bad	Good	Bad	Fair	Bad	Fair	Fair	Fair	28,34,7,19,57,34,28	71

SHOPPING	GAMBLE	SEX	KEYWORD	KEYWORD				
Fair	Fair	is fair	MIND	Independence,Loneliness,Meditative,Worry,Dominating,Illness - Cold,On Your Own,Commanding				

STRESS LEVEL	LUCKY COLORS	JEWELERY	MOONS EFFECT	GRAHA EFFECT	DAILY DEITY
High	White/Yellow/	Pearl/Quartz	Arrogance	Status Graha	Saraswaty

DAILY PUJA	DAILY PSALMS
Give Gifts to Priests, Invite holy ones to your home, Feed Swamis and Yogis, Do Shiva Puja.	1, 10, 28 ,37, 46, 55, 73, 100, 118

Thursday, December 1, 2016 — This is considered a POSITIVE day for you — Planet: Jupiter

ADVICE & DETAILS

The power of your expression today is great. Use this power to communicate with others, to write and publish or to entertain others when in groups or parties. There is the influence of someone that is jealous of you, be aware of it and try to be modest.

MANTRA FOR TODAY

Om Hareem Nama Swaha..Shri Maha Laxmi Aye Namah swaha 12 times

MONEY	LOVE	CAREER	FAMILY	TRAVEL	WEDDING	MOVE	BUSINESS	HEALTH	Lotto #'s	play 3 #s
Excellent	Good	Excellent	Good	Good	Excellent	Good	Excellent	Excellent	48,59,72,55,34,56,63	899

SHOPPING	GAMBLE	SEX	KEYWORD	KEYWORD				
Excellent	Excellent	is excellent	MONEY	Business,Major Expense,Money - Profits,Income,Investments,Power,Promotion,Fame - TV				

STRESS LEVEL	LUCKY COLORS	JEWELERY	MOONS EFFECT	GRAHA EFFECT	DAILY DEITY
Low	Yellow/Silver	Diamonds/Gold/Pearls	Secretive	Money Graha	Mahalaxmi

DAILY PUJA	DAILY PSALMS
Decorate Land, Feed the poor, Donate milk /products to all, Feed holy guests,	8, 17, 35 ,44, 53, 62, 80, 107, 125

Friday, December 2, 2016 — This is considered a NEGATIVE day for you — Planet: Saturn

ADVICE & DETAILS

Although this will be a day open for you to socialize with others, you must avoid extremes and parties with alcohol and drugs. Your enemies will take advantage of you today when they see you in your weakest state. Try to rest, you will be sleepy.

MANTRA FOR TODAY

Om Ganga mataye nama swaha
Om Varuna Devta aye Pahimam 11 times

MONEY	LOVE	CAREER	FAMILY	TRAVEL	WEDDING	MOVE	BUSINESS	HEALTH	Lotto #'s	play 3 #s
Bad	Bad	Bad	Fair	Bad	Bad	Bad	Bad	Bad	58,67,64,41,33,38,1	480

SHOPPING	GAMBLE	SEX	KEYWORD	KEYWORD				
Bad	Bad	is very bad	KARMA	Destruction,Losses,Death,Sickness - cold,Legal matter,Abusive,Karmic debts,God - Karma				

STRESS LEVEL	LUCKY COLORS	JEWELERY	MOONS EFFECT	GRAHA EFFECT	DAILY DEITY
High	Gold/Brown//Green	Saphire/Hessonite	Ivestments	Evil Graha	Agnidev

DAILY PUJA
Remembrance of family members who died, worship of older people. gifts to grand parents

DAILY PSALMS
9, 18, 36 ,45, 54, 63, 81, 108, 126

Saturday, December 3, 2016 — This is considered a NEUTRAL day for you — Planet: Sun

ADVICE & DETAILS

There may be sickness of children or you may be getting sick. There will be losses and sadness.

MANTRA FOR TODAY

Om Namo Bhagawate Mukhtanandaya, 108 times

MONEY	LOVE	CAREER	FAMILY	TRAVEL	WEDDING	MOVE	BUSINESS	HEALTH	Lotto #'s	play 3 #s
Fair	Bad	Good	Bad	Fair	Bad	Fair	Fair	Fair	30,12,50,26,64,24,56	439

SHOPPING	GAMBLE	SEX	KEYWORD	KEYWORD				
Fair	Fair	is fair	MIND	Independence,Loneliness,Meditative,Worry,Dominating,Illness - Cold,On Your Own,Commanding				

STRESS LEVEL	LUCKY COLORS	JEWELERY	MOONS EFFECT	GRAHA EFFECT	DAILY DEITY
High	White/Yellow/	Pearl/Quartz	Arrogance	Status Graha	Saraswaty

DAILY PUJA
Give Gifts to Priests, Invite holy ones to your home, Feed Swamis and Yogis, Do Shiva Puja.

DAILY PSALMS
1, 10, 28 ,37, 46, 55, 73, 100, 118

Sunday, December 4, 2016 — This is considered a POSITIVE day for you — Planet: Moon

ADVICE & DETAILS

Express your thoughts, opinions or information to partners and/or children. Day is influenced by children and ability to acquire information by reading or other means.

MANTRA FOR TODAY

Kali Durge Namo Nama Om Durge aye nama swaha 108 times

MONEY	LOVE	CAREER	FAMILY	TRAVEL	WEDDING	MOVE	BUSINESS	HEALTH	Lotto #'s	play 3 #s
Good	Excellent	Good	Good	Excellent	Good	Good	Good	Good	69,71,73,25,23,54,72	316

SHOPPING	GAMBLE	SEX	KEYWORD	KEYWORD				
Good	Good	is good	LOVE	Romance,Popularity,Visitors,Shopping,Food, Drinks,Co-operation,Friendships,Affection				

STRESS LEVEL	LUCKY COLORS	JEWELERY	MOONS EFFECT	GRAHA EFFECT	DAILY DEITY
Low	Red/Yellow/Pink	Topaz/Diamonds	Conservative	Love Graha	Gauri

DAILY PUJA
Give Gifts to females andnMother, Serve milk Products, Worship Durga forms

DAILY PSALMS
2, 11, 29 ,38, 47, 56, 74, 101, 119

Monday, December 5, 2016 — This is considered a POSITIVE day for you — Planet: Mercury

ADVICE & DETAILS

Reading will benefit you today. You will have to hone your communication skills and speak clearly and listen carefully, especially when dealing with Real Estate and teachers of any type.

MANTRA FOR TODAY

Om hareem Kleem Hreem Aem Saraswataye namaha 21 times

MONEY	LOVE	CAREER	FAMILY	TRAVEL	WEDDING	MOVE	BUSINESS	HEALTH	Lotto #'s	play 3 #s
Good	Fair	Good	Good	Excellent	Good	Good	Good	Excellent	66,14,54,31,27,13,9	392

SHOPPING	GAMBLE	SEX	KEYWORD	KEYWORD				
Good	Good	is great	SOCIAL	Children,Education,Astrology,Bargains,Social Functions,Childishness,Groups - Parties,Teacher				

STRESS LEVEL	LUCKY COLORS	JEWELERY	MOONS EFFECT	GRAHA EFFECT	DAILY DEITY
Low	Green/Sky Blue/	Diamonds/Silver	Enthusiastic	Social Graha	Vishnu

DAILY PUJA
Wash the feet of Children, Do Satnarayan Pooja, Read & chant Geeta

DAILY PSALMS
3, 12, 30 ,39, 48, 57, 75, 102, 120

Tuesday, December 6, 2016 | This is considered a NEGATIVE day for you | Planet: Pluto

ADVICE & DETAILS	MANTRA FOR TODAY
Overcome laziness and low pay today and improve your karma by being industrious, hard working and controlling your high temper.	Om Jai Viganeshwaraya.. Lambodaraya Namo Namaha 21 times

MONEY	LOVE	CAREER	FAMILY	TRAVEL	WEDDING	MOVE	BUSINESS	HEALTH	Lotto #'s	play 3 #s
Bad	Fair	Bad	Fair	Bad	Good	Bad	Bad	Bad	4,40,5,60,68,45,74	996

SHOPPING	GAMBLE	SEX	KEYWORD	KEYWORD						
Bad	Bad	is tough	CAREER	Career,Hard Work,Co-workers,Low Payment,Job Problems,High Temper,Low Pay,Laziness						

STRESS LEVEL	LUCKY COLORS	JEWELERY	MOONS EFFECT	GRAHA EFFECT	DAILY DEITY
High	Dark Blue/ Purple/	Amethyst/Gold	Emotional	Job Graha	Lingam

DAILY PUJA	DAILY PSALMS
Worship Ganesh, Give gifts to father, and co -workers, Plant gardens, farms	4, 13, 31 ,40, 49, 58, 76, 103, 121

Wednesday, December 7, 2016 | This is considered a POSITIVE day for you | Planet: Venus

ADVICE & DETAILS	MANTRA FOR TODAY
Although this will be a day open for you to socialize with others, you must avoid extremes and parties with alcohol and drugs. Your enemies will take advantage of you today when they see you in your weakest state. Try to rest, you will be sleepy.	Om Graam Greem Graum Sa Gurave namah swaha 21 times

MONEY	LOVE	CAREER	FAMILY	TRAVEL	WEDDING	MOVE	BUSINESS	HEALTH	Lotto #'s	play 3 #s
Bad	Excellent	Fair	Good	Excellent	Good	Excellent	Good	Excellent	46,53,48,12,12,18,22	439

SHOPPING	GAMBLE	SEX	KEYWORD	KEYWORD						
Good	Good	is good	CHANGE	Sexuality,Travel,Change,Distant, far,Travel delays,Deception,Excercise,Illicit Affairs						

STRESS LEVEL	LUCKY COLORS	JEWELERY	MOONS EFFECT	GRAHA EFFECT	DAILY DEITY
Fair	Tan/Green/ Beige	Pearl/Silver/quartz	Courageous	Travel Graha	Nataraja

DAILY PUJA	DAILY PSALMS
Artistic gifts, Pray to Krishna, Do good deeds, do Spiritual trips	5, 14, 32 ,41, 50, 59, 77, 104, 122

Thursday, December 8, 2016 | This is considered a NEGATIVE day for you | Planet: Mars

ADVICE & DETAILS	MANTRA FOR TODAY
Children will be prevalent today. This day is marked with a great deal of creativity ideal for areas related to the left side of the brain such as writing, painting, handcrafts, baking, cooking or needlework.	Om Mana Swasti Shanti Kuru kuru Swaha Shivoham Shivoham 27 times

MONEY	LOVE	CAREER	FAMILY	TRAVEL	WEDDING	MOVE	BUSINESS	HEALTH	Lotto #'s	play 3 #s
Bad	Bad	Bad	Bad	Bad	Bad	Bad	Fair	Bad	50,37,6,29,74,44,13	415

SHOPPING	GAMBLE	SEX	KEYWORD	KEYWORD						
Fair	Bad	is frustrating	POWER	Responsibilty,Disagreement,Family,Back Pain,Family Conflicts,Traffic Ticket,Quarrels,Jealousy						

STRESS LEVEL	LUCKY COLORS	JEWELERY	MOONS EFFECT	GRAHA EFFECT	DAILY DEITY
High	Purple/Blue/Rose	Emerald/Saphire	Educational	Family Graha	Mahakali

DAILY PUJA	DAILY PSALMS
Meditate, Control temper, Pray to Hanuman, Chant Hanuman Chalisa	6, 15, 33 ,42, 51, 60, 78, 105, 123

Friday, December 9, 2016 | This is considered a NEUTRAL day for you | Planet: Uranus

ADVICE & DETAILS	MANTRA FOR TODAY
The thought of watching TV is very appealing today. Spending time with children will benefit your creativity, but you must refrain from allowing immaturity to control your actions today.	Jai Jai Shiva Shambo.(2) ...Mahadeva Shambo (2) 21 times 8

MONEY	LOVE	CAREER	FAMILY	TRAVEL	WEDDING	MOVE	BUSINESS	HEALTH	Lotto #'s	play 3 #s
Good	Good	Fair	Good	Good	Bad	Good	Bad	Fair	25,32,46,26,74,22,14	564

SHOPPING	GAMBLE	SEX	KEYWORD	KEYWORD						
Bad	Fair	is quiet	DIVINE	Spirituality,Religious,Astrology,Inner Conflicts,Religious ,Sleepiness,Advice given,Alcohol - drugs						

STRESS LEVEL	LUCKY COLORS	JEWELERY	MOONS EFFECT	GRAHA EFFECT	DAILY DEITY
Fair	Light Blue/Peach	Tiger's eye/Gold/Silver	Affectionate	God'S Graha	Shesnaag

DAILY PUJA	DAILY PSALMS
Chant Shiva Mantras, Take gifts to Ocean - Ganga Puja, Donate to Temple, Priests, etc.	7, 16, 34 ,43, 52, 61, 79, 106, 124

Saturday, December 10, 2016 — This is considered a POSITIVE day for you — Planet: Jupiter

ADVICE & DETAILS

The power of your expression today is great. Use this power to communicate with others, to write and publish or to entertain others when in groups or parties. There is the influence of someone that is jealous of you, be aware of it and try to be modest.

MANTRA FOR TODAY

Om Hareem Nama Swaha..Shri Maha Laxmi Aye Namah swaha 12 times

MONEY	LOVE	CAREER	FAMILY	TRAVEL	WEDDING	MOVE	BUSINESS	HEALTH	Lotto #'s	play 3 #s
Excellent	Good	Excellent	Good	Good	Excellent	Good	Excellent	Excellent	36,25,19,38,61,11,11	263

SHOPPING	GAMBLE	SEX	KEYWORD	KEYWORD				
Excellent	Excellent	is excellent	MONEY	Business,Major Expense,Money - Profits,Income,Investments,Power,Promotion,Fame - TV				

STRESS LEVEL	LUCKY COLORS	JEWELERY	MOONS EFFECT	GRAHA EFFECT	DAILY DEITY
Low	Yellow/Silver	Diamonds/Gold/Pearls	Secretive	Money Graha	Mahalaxmi

DAILY PUJA
Decorate Land, Feed the poor, Donate milk /products to all, Feed holy guests,

DAILY PSALMS
8, 17, 35 ,44, 53, 62, 80, 107, 125

Sunday, December 11, 2016 — This is considered a NEGATIVE day for you — Planet: Saturn

ADVICE & DETAILS

Although this will be a day open for you to socialize with others, you must avoid extremes and parties with alcohol and drugs. Your enemies will take advantage of you today when they see you in your weakest state. Try to rest, you will be sleepy.

MANTRA FOR TODAY

Om Ganga mataye nama swaha Om Varuna Devta aye Pahimam 11 times

MONEY	LOVE	CAREER	FAMILY	TRAVEL	WEDDING	MOVE	BUSINESS	HEALTH	Lotto #'s	play 3 #s
Bad	Bad	Bad	Fair	Bad	Bad	Bad	Bad	Bad	3,31,28,36,11,22,73	589

SHOPPING	GAMBLE	SEX	KEYWORD	KEYWORD				
Bad	Bad	is very bad	KARMA	Destruction,Losses,Death,Sickness - cold,Legal matter,Abusive,Karmic debts,God - Karma				

STRESS LEVEL	LUCKY COLORS	JEWELERY	MOONS EFFECT	GRAHA EFFECT	DAILY DEITY
High	Gold/Brown//Green	Saphire/Hessonite	Ivestments	Evil Graha	Agnidev

DAILY PUJA
Remembrance of family members who died, worship of older people. gifts to grand parents

DAILY PSALMS
9, 18, 36 ,45, 54, 63, 81, 108, 126

Monday, December 12, 2016 — This is considered a NEUTRAL day for you — Planet: Sun

ADVICE & DETAILS

There may be sickness of children or you may be getting sick. There will be losses and sadness.

MANTRA FOR TODAY

Om Namo Bhagawate Mukhtanandaya, 108 times

MONEY	LOVE	CAREER	FAMILY	TRAVEL	WEDDING	MOVE	BUSINESS	HEALTH	Lotto #'s	play 3 #s
Fair	Bad	Good	Bad	Fair	Bad	Fair	Fair	Fair	8,41,32,6,59,57,6	686

SHOPPING	GAMBLE	SEX	KEYWORD	KEYWORD				
Fair	Fair	is fair	MIND	Independence,Loneliness,Meditative,Worry,Dominating,Illness - Cold,On Your Own,Commanding				

STRESS LEVEL	LUCKY COLORS	JEWELERY	MOONS EFFECT	GRAHA EFFECT	DAILY DEITY
High	White/Yellow/	Pearl/Quartz	Arrogance	Status Graha	Saraswaty

DAILY PUJA
Give Gifts to Priests, Invite holy ones to your home, Feed Swamis and Yogis, Do Shiva Puja.

DAILY PSALMS
1, 10, 28 ,37, 46, 55, 73, 100, 118

Tuesday, December 13, 2016 — This is considered a POSITIVE day for you — Planet: Moon

ADVICE & DETAILS

Express your thoughts, opinions or information to partners and/or children. Day is influenced by children and ability to acquire information by reading or other means.

MANTRA FOR TODAY

Kali Durge Namo Nama Om Durge aye nama swaha 108 times

MONEY	LOVE	CAREER	FAMILY	TRAVEL	WEDDING	MOVE	BUSINESS	HEALTH	Lotto #'s	play 3 #s
Good	Excellent	Good	Good	Excellent	Good	Good	Good	Good	50,15,66,65,38,61,59	523

SHOPPING	GAMBLE	SEX	KEYWORD	KEYWORD				
Good	Good	is good	LOVE	Romance,Popularity,Visitors,Shopping,Food, Drinks,Co-operation,Friendships,Affection				

STRESS LEVEL	LUCKY COLORS	JEWELERY	MOONS EFFECT	GRAHA EFFECT	DAILY DEITY
Low	Red/Yellow/Pink	Topaz/Diamonds	Conservative	Love Graha	Gauri

DAILY PUJA
Give Gifts to females andnMother, Serve milk Products, Worship Durga forms

DAILY PSALMS
2, 11, 29 ,38, 47, 56, 74, 101, 119

Wednesday, December 14, 2016 — This is considered a POSITIVE day for you — Planet: Mercury

ADVICE & DETAILS

Reading will benefit you today. You will have to hone your communication skills and speak clearly and listen carefully, especially when dealing with Real Estate and teachers of any type.

MANTRA FOR TODAY

Om hareem Kleem Hreem Aem Saraswataye namaha 21 times

MONEY	LOVE	CAREER	FAMILY	TRAVEL	WEDDING	MOVE	BUSINESS	HEALTH	Lotto #'s	play 3 #s
Good	Fair	Good	Good	Excellent	Good	Good	Good	Excellent	63,73,74,67,74,73,47	983

SHOPPING	GAMBLE	SEX	KEYWORD	KEYWORD						
Good	Good	is great	SOCIAL	Children,Education,Astrology,Bargains,Social Functions,Childishness,Groups - Parties,Teacher						

STRESS LEVEL		LUCKY COLORS	JEWELERY	MOONS EFFECT	GRAHA EFFECT	DAILY DEITY
Low		Green/Sky Blue/	Diamonds/Silver	Enthusiastic	Social Graha	Vishnu

DAILY PUJA
Wash the feet of Children, Do Satnarayan Pooja, Read & chant Geeta

DAILY PSALMS
3, 12, 30 ,39, 48, 57, 75, 102, 120

Thursday, December 15, 2016 — This is considered a NEGATIVE day for you — Planet: Pluto

ADVICE & DETAILS

Overcome laziness and low pay today and improve your karma by being industrious, hard working and controlling your high temper.

MANTRA FOR TODAY

Om Jai Viganeshwaraya.. Lambodaraya Namo Namaha 21 times

MONEY	LOVE	CAREER	FAMILY	TRAVEL	WEDDING	MOVE	BUSINESS	HEALTH	Lotto #'s	play 3 #s
Bad	Fair	Bad	Fair	Bad	Good	Bad	Bad	Bad	48,61,18,50,20,48,32	463

SHOPPING	GAMBLE	SEX	KEYWORD	KEYWORD						
Bad	Bad	is tough	CAREER	Career,Hard Work,Co-workers,Low Payment,Job Problems,High Temper,Low Pay,Laziness						

STRESS LEVEL		LUCKY COLORS	JEWELERY	MOONS EFFECT	GRAHA EFFECT	DAILY DEITY
High		Dark Blue/ Purple/	Amethyst/Gold	Emotional	Job Graha	Lingam

DAILY PUJA
Worship Ganesh, Give gifts to father, and co -workers, Plant gardens, farms

DAILY PSALMS
4, 13, 31 ,40, 49, 58, 76, 103, 121

Friday, December 16, 2016 — This is considered a POSITIVE day for you — Planet: Venus

ADVICE & DETAILS

Although this will be a day open for you to socialize with others, you must avoid extremes and parties with alcohol and drugs. Your enemies will take advantage of you today when they see you in your weakest state. Try to rest, you will be sleepy.

MANTRA FOR TODAY

Om Graam Greem Graum Sa Gurave namah swaha 21 times

MONEY	LOVE	CAREER	FAMILY	TRAVEL	WEDDING	MOVE	BUSINESS	HEALTH	Lotto #'s	play 3 #s
Bad	Excellent	Fair	Good	Excellent	Good	Excellent	Good	Excellent	14,66,55,63,57,75,17	123

SHOPPING	GAMBLE	SEX	KEYWORD	KEYWORD						
Good	Good	is good	CHANGE	Sexuality,Travel,Change,Distant, far,Travel delays,Deception,Excercise,Illicit Affairs						

STRESS LEVEL		LUCKY COLORS	JEWELERY	MOONS EFFECT	GRAHA EFFECT	DAILY DEITY
Fair		Tan/Green/ Beige	Pearl/Silver/quartz	Courageous	Travel Graha	Nataraja

DAILY PUJA
Artistic gifts, Pray to Krishna, Do good deeds, do Spiritual trips

DAILY PSALMS
5, 14, 32 ,41, 50, 59, 77, 104, 122

Saturday, December 17, 2016 — This is considered a NEGATIVE day for you — Planet: Mars

ADVICE & DETAILS

Children will be prevalent today. This day is marked with a great deal of creativity ideal for areas related to the left side of the brain such as writing, painting, handcrafts, baking, cooking or needlework.

MANTRA FOR TODAY

Om Mana Swasti Shanti Kuru kuru Swaha Shivoham Shivoham 27 times

MONEY	LOVE	CAREER	FAMILY	TRAVEL	WEDDING	MOVE	BUSINESS	HEALTH	Lotto #'s	play 3 #s
Bad	Bad	Bad	Bad	Bad	Bad	Bad	Fair	Bad	34,16,17,69,23,31,41	12

SHOPPING	GAMBLE	SEX	KEYWORD	KEYWORD						
Fair	Bad	is frustrating	POWER	Responsibilty,Disagreement,Family,Back Pain,Family Conflicts,Traffic Ticket,Quarrels,Jealousy						

STRESS LEVEL		LUCKY COLORS	JEWELERY	MOONS EFFECT	GRAHA EFFECT	DAILY DEITY
High		Purple/Blue/Rose	Emerald/Saphire	Educational	Family Graha	Mahakali

DAILY PUJA
Meditate, Control temper, Pray to Hanuman, Chant Hanuman Chalisa

DAILY PSALMS
6, 15, 33 ,42, 51, 60, 78, 105, 123

Sunday, December 18, 2016 — This is considered a NEUTRAL day for you — Planet: Uranus

ADVICE & DETAILS

The thought of watching TV is very appealing today. Spending time with children will benefit your creativity, but you must refrain from allowing immaturity to control your actions today.

MANTRA FOR TODAY

Jai Jai Shiva Shambo.(2) ...Mahadeva Shambo (2) 21 times 8

MONEY	LOVE	CAREER	FAMILY	TRAVEL	WEDDING	MOVE	BUSINESS	HEALTH	Lotto #'s	play 3 #'s
Good	Good	Fair	Good	Good	Bad	Good	Bad	Fair	7,30,64,31,57,60,30	207

SHOPPING	GAMBLE	SEX	KEYWORD	KEYWORD						
Bad	Fair	is quiet	DIVINE	Spirituality,Religious,Astrology,Inner Conflicts,Religious ,Sleepiness,Advice given,Alcohol - drugs						

STRESS LEVEL	LUCKY COLORS	JEWELERY	MOONS EFFECT	GRAHA EFFECT	DAILY DEITY
Fair	Light Blue/Peach	Tiger's eye/Gold/Silver	Affectionate	God'S Graha	Shesnaag

DAILY PUJA	DAILY PSALMS
Chant Shiva Mantras, Take gifts to Ocean - Ganga Puja, Donate to Temple, Priests, etc.	7, 16, 34 ,43, 52, 61, 79, 106, 124

Monday, December 19, 2016 — This is considered a POSITIVE day for you — Planet: Jupiter

ADVICE & DETAILS

The power of your expression today is great. Use this power to communicate with others, to write and publish or to entertain others when in groups or parties. There is the influence of someone that is jealous of you, be aware of it and try to be modest.

MANTRA FOR TODAY

Om Hareem Nama Swaha..Shri Maha Laxmi Aye Namah swaha 12 times

MONEY	LOVE	CAREER	FAMILY	TRAVEL	WEDDING	MOVE	BUSINESS	HEALTH	Lotto #'s	play 3 #'s
Excellent	Good	Excellent	Good	Good	Excellent	Good	Excellent	Excellent	5,20,32,57,67,66,61	974

SHOPPING	GAMBLE	SEX	KEYWORD	KEYWORD						
Excellent	Excellent	is excellent	MONEY	Business,Major Expense,Money - Profits,Income,Investments,Power,Promotion,Fame - TV						

STRESS LEVEL	LUCKY COLORS	JEWELERY	MOONS EFFECT	GRAHA EFFECT	DAILY DEITY
Low	Yellow/Silver	Diamonds/Gold/Pearls	Secretive	Money Graha	Mahalaxmi

DAILY PUJA	DAILY PSALMS
Decorate Land, Feed the poor, Donate milk /products to all, Feed holy guests,	8, 17, 35 ,44, 53, 62, 80, 107, 125

Tuesday, December 20, 2016 — This is considered a NEGATIVE day for you — Planet: Saturn

ADVICE & DETAILS

Although this will be a day open for you to socialize with others, you must avoid extremes and parties with alcohol and drugs. Your enemies will take advantage of you today when they see you in your weakest state. Try to rest, you will be sleepy.

MANTRA FOR TODAY

Om Ganga mataye nama swaha Om Varuna Devta aye Pahimam 11 times

MONEY	LOVE	CAREER	FAMILY	TRAVEL	WEDDING	MOVE	BUSINESS	HEALTH	Lotto #'s	play 3 #'s
Bad	Bad	Bad	Fair	Bad	Bad	Bad	Bad	Bad	12,35,59,1,62,18,48	302

SHOPPING	GAMBLE	SEX	KEYWORD	KEYWORD						
Bad	Bad	is very bad	KARMA	Destruction,Losses,Death,Sickness - cold,Legal matter,Abusive,Karmic debts,God - Karma						

STRESS LEVEL	LUCKY COLORS	JEWELERY	MOONS EFFECT	GRAHA EFFECT	DAILY DEITY
High	Gold/Brown//Green	Saphire/Hessonite	Ivestments	Evil Graha	Agnidev

DAILY PUJA	DAILY PSALMS
Remembrance of family members who died, worship of older people. gifts to grand parents	9, 18, 36 ,45, 54, 63, 81, 108, 126

Wednesday, December 21, 2016 — This is considered a NEUTRAL day for you — Planet: Sun

ADVICE & DETAILS

There may be sickness of children or you may be getting sick. There will be losses and sadness.

MANTRA FOR TODAY

Om Namo Bhagawate Mukhtanandaya, 108 times

MONEY	LOVE	CAREER	FAMILY	TRAVEL	WEDDING	MOVE	BUSINESS	HEALTH	Lotto #'s	play 3 #'s
Fair	Bad	Good	Bad	Fair	Bad	Fair	Fair	Fair	45,48,39,57,69,35,26	832

SHOPPING	GAMBLE	SEX	KEYWORD	KEYWORD						
Fair	Fair	is fair	MIND	Independence,Loneliness,Meditative,Worry,Dominating,Illness - Cold,On Your Own,Commanding						

STRESS LEVEL	LUCKY COLORS	JEWELERY	MOONS EFFECT	GRAHA EFFECT	DAILY DEITY
High	White/Yellow/	Pearl/Quartz	Arrogance	Status Graha	Saraswaty

DAILY PUJA	DAILY PSALMS
Give Gifts to Priests, Invite holy ones to your home, Feed Swamis and Yogis, Do Shiva Puja.	1, 10, 28 ,37, 46, 55, 73, 100, 118

Thursday, December 22, 2016 — This is considered a POSITIVE day for you — Planet: Moon

ADVICE & DETAILS

Express your thoughts, opinions or information to partners and/or children. Day is influenced by children and ability to acquire information by reading or other means.

MANTRA FOR TODAY

Kali Durge Namo Nama Om Durge aye nama swaha 108 times

MONEY	LOVE	CAREER	FAMILY	TRAVEL	WEDDING	MOVE	BUSINESS	HEALTH	Lotto #'s	play 3 #s
Good	Excellent	Good	Good	Excellent	Good	Good	Good	Good	1,56,72,48,30,57,43	369

SHOPPING	GAMBLE	SEX	KEYWORD	KEYWORD						
Good	Good	is good	LOVE	Romance,Popularity,Visitors,Shopping,Food, Drinks,Co-operation,Friendships,Affection						

STRESS LEVEL	LUCKY COLORS	JEWELERY	MOONS EFFECT	GRAHA EFFECT	DAILY DEITY
Low	Red/Yellow/Pink	Topaz/Diamonds	Conservative	Love Graha	Gauri

DAILY PUJA	DAILY PSALMS
Give Gifts to females andnMother, Serve milk Products, Worship Durga forms	2, 11, 29 ,38, 47, 56, 74, 101, 119

Friday, December 23, 2016 — This is considered a POSITIVE day for you — Planet: Mercury

ADVICE & DETAILS

Reading will benefit you today. You will have to hone your communication skills and speak clearly and listen carefully, especially when dealing with Real Estate and teachers of any type.

MANTRA FOR TODAY

Om hareem Kleem Hreem Aem Saraswataye namaha 21 times

MONEY	LOVE	CAREER	FAMILY	TRAVEL	WEDDING	MOVE	BUSINESS	HEALTH	Lotto #'s	play 3 #s
Good	Fair	Good	Good	Excellent	Good	Good	Good	Excellent	69,52,41,37,6,44,56	605

SHOPPING	GAMBLE	SEX	KEYWORD	KEYWORD						
Good	Good	is great	SOCIAL	Children,Education,Astrology,Bargains,Social Functions,Childishness,Groups - Parties,Teacher						

STRESS LEVEL	LUCKY COLORS	JEWELERY	MOONS EFFECT	GRAHA EFFECT	DAILY DEITY
Low	Green/Sky Blue/	Diamonds/Silver	Enthusiastic	Social Graha	Vishnu

DAILY PUJA	DAILY PSALMS
Wash the feet of Children, Do Satnarayan Pooja, Read & chant Geeta	3, 12, 30 ,39, 48, 57, 75, 102, 120

Saturday, December 24, 2016 — This is considered a NEGATIVE day for you — Planet: Pluto

ADVICE & DETAILS

Overcome laziness and low pay today and improve your karma by being industrious, hard working and controlling your high temper.

MANTRA FOR TODAY

Om Jai Viganeshwaraya.. Lambodaraya Namo Namaha 21 times

MONEY	LOVE	CAREER	FAMILY	TRAVEL	WEDDING	MOVE	BUSINESS	HEALTH	Lotto #'s	play 3 #s
Bad	Fair	Bad	Fair	Bad	Good	Bad	Bad	Bad	54,35,73,25,50,60,30	657

SHOPPING	GAMBLE	SEX	KEYWORD	KEYWORD						
Bad	Bad	is tough	CAREER	Career,Hard Work,Co-workers,Low Payment,Job Problems,High Temper,Low Pay,Laziness						

STRESS LEVEL	LUCKY COLORS	JEWELERY	MOONS EFFECT	GRAHA EFFECT	DAILY DEITY
High	Dark Blue/ Purple/	Amethyst/Gold	Emotional	Job Graha	Lingam

DAILY PUJA	DAILY PSALMS
Worship Ganesh, Give gifts to father, and co -workers, Plant gardens, farms	4, 13, 31 ,40, 49, 58, 76, 103, 121

Sunday, December 25, 2016 — This is considered a POSITIVE day for you — Planet: Venus

ADVICE & DETAILS

Although this will be a day open for you to socialize with others, you must avoid extremes and parties with alcohol and drugs. Your enemies will take advantage of you today when they see you in your weakest state. Try to rest, you will be sleepy.

MANTRA FOR TODAY

Om Graam Greem Graum Sa Gurave namah swaha 21 times

MONEY	LOVE	CAREER	FAMILY	TRAVEL	WEDDING	MOVE	BUSINESS	HEALTH	Lotto #'s	play 3 #s
Bad	Excellent	Fair	Good	Excellent	Good	Excellent	Good	Excellent	36,17,55,69,61,28,3	383

SHOPPING	GAMBLE	SEX	KEYWORD	KEYWORD						
Good	Good	is good	CHANGE	Sexuality,Travel,Change,Distant, far,Travel delays,Deception,Excercise,Illicit Affairs						

STRESS LEVEL	LUCKY COLORS	JEWELERY	MOONS EFFECT	GRAHA EFFECT	DAILY DEITY
Fair	Tan/Green/ Beige	Pearl/Silver/quartz	Courageous	Travel Graha	Nataraja

DAILY PUJA	DAILY PSALMS
Artistic gifts, Pray to Krishna, Do good deeds, do Spiritual trips	5, 14, 32 ,41, 50, 59, 77, 104, 122

Monday, December 26, 2016 — This is considered a NEGATIVE day for you — Planet: Mars

ADVICE & DETAILS

Children will be prevalent today. This day is marked with a great deal of creativity ideal for areas related to the left side of the brain such as writing, painting, handcrafts, baking, cooking or needlework.

MANTRA FOR TODAY

Om Mana Swasti Shanti Kuru kuru Swaha Shivoham Shivoham 27 times

MONEY	LOVE	CAREER	FAMILY	TRAVEL	WEDDING	MOVE	BUSINESS	HEALTH	Lotto #'s	play 3 #s
Bad	Bad	Bad	Bad	Bad	Bad	Bad	Fair	Bad	58,41,8,64,61,75,59	825

SHOPPING	GAMBLE	SEX	KEYWORD	KEYWORD						
Fair	Bad	is frustrating	POWER	Responsibilty,Disagreement,Family,Back Pain,Family Conflicts,Traffic Ticket,Quarrels,Jealousy						

STRESS LEVEL	LUCKY COLORS	JEWELERY	MOONS EFFECT	GRAHA EFFECT	DAILY DEITY
High	Purple/Blue/Rose	Emerald/Saphire	Educational	Family Graha	Mahakali

DAILY PUJA
Meditate, Control temper, Pray to Hanuman, Chant Hanuman Chalisa

DAILY PSALMS
6, 15, 33 ,42, 51, 60, 78, 105, 123

Tuesday, December 27, 2016 — This is considered a NEUTRAL day for you — Planet: Uranus

ADVICE & DETAILS

The thought of watching TV is very appealing today. Spending time with children will benefit your creativity, but you must refrain from allowing immaturity to control your actions today.

MANTRA FOR TODAY

Jai Jai Shiva Shambo.(2) ...Mahadeva Shambo (2) 21 times 8

MONEY	LOVE	CAREER	FAMILY	TRAVEL	WEDDING	MOVE	BUSINESS	HEALTH	Lotto #'s	play 3 #s
Good	Good	Fair	Good	Good	Bad	Good	Bad	Fair	64,9,28,58,24,67,60	29

SHOPPING	GAMBLE	SEX	KEYWORD	KEYWORD						
Bad	Fair	is quiet	DIVINE	Spirituality,Religious,Astrology,Inner Conflicts,Religious ,Sleepiness,Advice given,Alcohol - drugs						

STRESS LEVEL	LUCKY COLORS	JEWELERY	MOONS EFFECT	GRAHA EFFECT	DAILY DEITY
Fair	Light Blue/Peach	Tiger's eye/Gold/Silver	Affectionate	God'S Graha	Shesnaag

DAILY PUJA
Chant Shiva Mantras, Take gifts to Ocean - Ganga Puja, Donate to Temple, Priests, etc.

DAILY PSALMS
7, 16, 34 ,43, 52, 61, 79, 106, 124

Wednesday, December 28, 2016 — This is considered a POSITIVE day for you — Planet: Jupiter

ADVICE & DETAILS

The power of your expression today is great. Use this power to communicate with others, to write and publish or to entertain others when in groups or parties. There is the influence of someone that is jealous of you, be aware of it and try to be modest.

MANTRA FOR TODAY

Om Hareem Nama Swaha..Shri Maha Laxmi Aye Namah swaha 12 times

MONEY	LOVE	CAREER	FAMILY	TRAVEL	WEDDING	MOVE	BUSINESS	HEALTH	Lotto #'s	play 3 #s
Excellent	Good	Excellent	Good	Good	Excellent	Good	Excellent	Excellent	58,52,32,28,23,28,22	548

SHOPPING	GAMBLE	SEX	KEYWORD	KEYWORD						
Excellent	Excellent	is excellent	MONEY	Business,Major Expense,Money - Profits,Income,Investments,Power,Promotion,Fame - TV						

STRESS LEVEL	LUCKY COLORS	JEWELERY	MOONS EFFECT	GRAHA EFFECT	DAILY DEITY
Low	Yellow/Silver	Diamonds/Gold/Pearls	Secretive	Money Graha	Mahalaxmi

DAILY PUJA
Decorate Land, Feed the poor, Donate milk /products to all, Feed holy guests,

DAILY PSALMS
8, 17, 35 ,44, 53, 62, 80, 107, 125

Thursday, December 29, 2016 — This is considered a NEGATIVE day for you — Planet: Saturn

ADVICE & DETAILS

Although this will be a day open for you to socialize with others, you must avoid extremes and parties with alcohol and drugs. Your enemies will take advantage of you today when they see you in your weakest state. Try to rest, you will be sleepy.

MANTRA FOR TODAY

Om Ganga mataye nama swaha Om Varuna Devta aye Pahimam 11 times

MONEY	LOVE	CAREER	FAMILY	TRAVEL	WEDDING	MOVE	BUSINESS	HEALTH	Lotto #'s	play 3 #s
Bad	Bad	Bad	Fair	Bad	Bad	Bad	Bad	Bad	52,69,9,33,24,5,40	809

SHOPPING	GAMBLE	SEX	KEYWORD	KEYWORD						
Bad	Bad	is very bad	KARMA	Destruction,Losses,Death,Sickness - cold,Legal matter,Abusive,Karmic debts,God - Karma						

STRESS LEVEL	LUCKY COLORS	JEWELERY	MOONS EFFECT	GRAHA EFFECT	DAILY DEITY
High	Gold/Brown//Green	Saphire/Hessonite	Ivestments	Evil Graha	Agnidev

DAILY PUJA
Remembrance of family members who died, worship of older people. gifts to grand parents

DAILY PSALMS
9, 18, 36 ,45, 54, 63, 81, 108, 126

Friday, December 30, 2016	This is considered a NEUTRAL day for you							Planet: Sun			

ADVICE & DETAILS	MANTRA FOR TODAY
There may be sickness of children or you may be getting sick. There will be losses and sadness.	Om Namo Bhagawate Mukhtanandaya, 108 times

MONEY	LOVE	CAREER	FAMILY	TRAVEL	WEDDING	MOVE	BUSINESS	HEALTH	Lotto #'s		play 3 #s
Fair	Bad	Good	Bad	Fair	Bad	Fair	Fair	Fair	35,22,54,65,59,51,69		544

SHOPPING	GAMBLE	SEX	KEYWORD	KEYWORD			
Fair	Fair	is fair	MIND	Independence,Loneliness,Meditative,Worry,Dominating,Illness - Cold,On Your Own,Commanding			

STRESS LEVEL	LUCKY COLORS	JEWELERY	MOONS EFFECT	GRAHA EFFECT	DAILY DEITY
High	White/Yellow/	Pearl/Quartz	Arrogance	Status Graha	Saraswaty

DAILY PUJA	DAILY PSALMS
Give Gifts to Priests, Invite holy ones to your home, Feed Swamis and Yogis, Do Shiva Puja.	1, 10, 28 ,37, 46, 55, 73, 100, 118

Saturday, December 31, 2016	This is considered a POSITIVE day for you							Planet: Moon			

ADVICE & DETAILS	MANTRA FOR TODAY
Express your thoughts, opinions or information to partners and/or children. Day is influenced by children and ability to acquire information by reading or other means.	Kali Durge Namo Nama Om Durge aye nama swaha 108 times

MONEY	LOVE	CAREER	FAMILY	TRAVEL	WEDDING	MOVE	BUSINESS	HEALTH	Lotto #'s		play 3 #s
Good	Excellent	Good	Good	Excellent	Good	Good	Good	Good	67,46,21,18,3,14,15		412

SHOPPING	GAMBLE	SEX	KEYWORD	KEYWORD			
Good	Good	is good	LOVE	Romance,Popularity,Visitors,Shopping,Food, Drinks,Co-operation,Friendships,Affection			

STRESS LEVEL	LUCKY COLORS	JEWELERY	MOONS EFFECT	GRAHA EFFECT	DAILY DEITY
Low	Red/Yellow/Pink	Topaz/Diamonds	Conservative	Love Graha	Gauri

DAILY PUJA	DAILY PSALMS
Give Gifts to females andnMother, Serve milk Products, Worship Durga forms	2, 11, 29 ,38, 47, 56, 74, 101, 119

Swami Ram's Product Line has been especially designed by him for your well-being and to help you control all types of health and spiritual issues.

This life-changing kit is designed to help relieve asthma, as well as the related Gastro-Esophageal Reflux Disease (GERD), which has been shown to worsen asthma symptoms. The combination of herbs in this kit, designed by Swami Ram™, has been used in Ayurvedic medicine for thousands of years, and has been carefully selected and put together into an easy to use powder and teas to accommodate to the modern lifestyle. *

* These statements have not been evaluated by the FDA

Swami Ram's Rejuvenating Bath is a product that can naturally promote tranquility, well-being, balance chakra energy and help reduce stress. It is a scientifically proven method to drive away negative energy that causes headaches, back pain, stomach and chest pain. The results are amazing. Your aches and pains will disappear, you will sleep better and the quality of your life will dramatically improve. This is a pure Ayurvedic mixture of herbal plant elements that has been especially prepared to help you feel well.

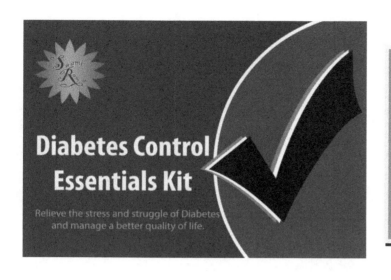

Diabetes Control Essentials Kit

Relieve the stress and struggle of Diabetes and manage a better quality of life.

Swami Ram's Diabetes Kit™ is a Life Changing product. It is designed to prevent diabetes before it appears in the cases of pre-diabetic patients and alleviate diabetes in patients with pancreatic diabetes Type 1 and Type 2.*

*These statements have not been evaluated by the FDA

A Vedic Ritual or Sacrifice performed by Hindus. It is mentioned in the Vedas as a way to bring healing, purification and protection to the Universe and the performer. This kit with complete instructions written by Swami Ram is available at Heendu Learning Center.

Fire Ritual Kit
Agni Hotra

Healing & Purification for
Universal & Individual Wellbeing

Hair Rejuvenation kit

Stops falling hair, prevents hair loss and enriches hair growth.

Revitalize your thinning hair and strengthen it NATURALLY! Swami Ram's Hair Rejuvenation Kit contains an Herbal Shampoo, which removes impurities while adding shine to EVERY STRAND and a specially formulated Hair Crème mixture that contains a unique blend of 10 essential nutrient oils proven to aid hair GROWTH and THICKNESS while preventing further hair loss.

Avoid wasting time and money on treatments and medications filled with chemicals that cause harmful side effects! Swami Ram has designed this kit that contains capsules with certified organic and natural herbs proven to help overall health & control different illnesses and conditions.*

*These statements have not been evaluated by the FDA.

Health Maintenance Essentials Kit

For renewal of Mind & Body: Helps regulate digestion & maintain normal blood pressure, good bone health, proper circulation & Chakra energy.

Home Energy Cleansing Kit

Purifies Home/Business To Drive Away Negative Energies & Invite Divine Forces

1 Day

Swami Ram's Home Energy Cleansing™ is a Life Changing product that can naturally promote tranquility and well-being in your home. It is a scientifically proven method to drive away negative energy that causes headaches, back pain, stomach and chest pain. The results are amazing. Your aches and pains will disappear, you will sleep better and the quality of your life will dramatically improve.

Mantras are words of power spoken in Sanskrit; An ancient Hindu language based on the scientific laws of sound and vibration. Meditating and chanting these sounds creates a vibration through the universe bringing love, health, wealth, prosperity, knowledge, positivity and the ever presence of the supreme God to reign in your life.

Meditation Mantra Kit

Swami Ram

Includes 10 Mantra CDs with Corresponding Cards & Instructions

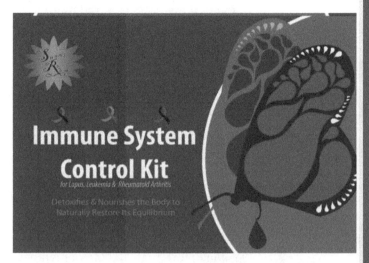

Immune System Control Kit
for Lupus, Leukemia & Rheumatoid Arthritis

Detoxifies & Nourishes the Body to
Naturally Restore Its Equilibrium

This kit was developed to help those afflicted with autoimmune diseases like Lupus, Leukemia, and Rheumatoid Arthritis. It is designed to lower the inner toxins and help relieve the chronic and systematic inflammation. Targeting the different weaknesses each individual may have in their body and system, this all natural assortment of remedies will aid the control and maintenance of living these unbearable diseases. The contents of this kit were specifically assembled to detoxify and nourish the immune system to balance itself back to its natural state of equilibrium. *

*These statements have not been evaluated by the FDA.

Swami Ram has especially designed this oil mixture to make you healthier. The curative qualities of this oil mixture are amazing. They have been used in Ayurvedic Medicine for thousands of years and have been known to rejuvenate the digestive system, remove chronic stomach problems, chronic diseases and improve circulation. It has also been known to help healing leukemia and lupus. It restores skin cells and when a mother-to-be drinks it, it protects the unborn child. It removes blockages to progress that appear when the health and energy of the individual is not optimal. It also improves sexual energy.*

*These statements have not been evaluated by the FDA.

Ayurvedic Oil Healing Kit

Improves Body Circulation, Removes Pains, Aches, Blockages & Enhances Sexual Energy

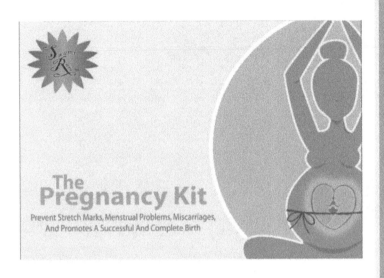

The
Pregnancy Kit
Prevent Stretch Marks, Menstrual Problems, Miscarriages,
And Promotes A Successful And Complete Birth

When a baby is developing in the womb, the emotions of the mother are absorbed by the baby as it develops. It can be love or anger that decides the type of child that will be born. If born out of love the world will rejoice and if out of anger it will be distressed. The products in this package help the mother develop a beautiful inner environment for the child so that when the child is born it brings prosperity and happiness to the couple. Swami Ram's™ method has been very effective in helping more than 10,000 women have safer and complete pregnancies.

*These statements have not been evaluated by the FDA.

This kit contains a unique mix of natural oils and herbs that aids men with any reproductive problems or sterility. It detoxifies the body, removes impotence, back pains and body aches; helps maintaining everyday health of the prostate and indigestion issues. Enhance your quality of life in various aspects with just one easy to use package specially designed by Swami Ram™.*

*

Virility Essentials Kit
Promotes Male Circulatory
Health & Sexual Enhancement

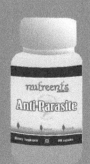